WORKS ISSUED BY
THE HAKLUYT SOCIETY

JERUSALEM PILGRIMAGE 1099–1185

SECOND SERIES
NO. 167

HAKLUYT SOCIETY

JERUSALEM PILGRIMAGE 1099–1185

JOHN WILKINSON
with
JOYCE HILL
and
W. F. RYAN

THE HAKLUYT SOCIETY
LONDON
1988

ISBN 0 904180 21 2

ISSN 0072–9396

Printed in Great Britain at
the University Press, Cambridge

Published by the Hakluyt Society
c/o The Map Library
British Library
London WC1B 3DG

CONTENTS

MAPS AND PLANS

PREFACE

Nearly a century has gone by since the first publication of most of the texts below in an English translation. They were published by the Palestine Pilgrims' Text Society under the general editorship of General Sir Charles Wilson, who from his intimate knowledge of the Middle East wrote excellent notes on each text. The great disadvantage of these translations was that they were each published as separate pamphlets, which meant that they were not viewed as a whole, and there was a great deal of useless repetition.

I was therefore delighted to receive the Hakluyt Society's agreement to republish a translation of the texts. And I was also very happy to have as allies the other scholars whose work this volume contains, Doctor Joyce Hill, who is the translator for the Icelandic texts, and Doctor William Ryan who has done a new translation from the Russian original of the Abbot Daniel's *Pilgrimage*, for in fact the earlier translation by Charles Wilson was from a French translation. To these two I am doubly grateful, both for their translations and for the notes they have provided. Unless I have mentioned otherwise, all notes to do with the Icelandic texts are by Hill and the Russian text by Ryan, wherever they happen to be found in this volume. I thank the President and Fellows of Harvard College for their permission to reprint Hill's translation of the extract of Nikulás' itinerary.

I am also most grateful to another author who died in 1933, Guy Le Strange. I have slightly altered his translation of Muhammad al Idrisi's text, mainly by omitting his explanatory passages, but I am proud to include this translation, and to pay a tribute to Le Strange himself, and the great contribution he has made to British studies of the Near East. I also express my gratitude to the Palestine Exploration Fund, who have given me permission to reprint the translation.

I am thankful too to the following people who have helped me in various different ways. First and foremost to my wife Alix, who has been patient in exploring various hypotheses I have tried on her. Then to Dr M. Angold, Dr Peter Edbury, Dr A. M. Gravgaard, Professor A. Kahzdan, Dr B. Z. Kedar, Dr Denys Pringle, Professor Jonathan Riley-Smith, Miss Shefaly Rovik and Brother Gilbert Sinden, SSM.

My greatest gratitude also to the British School of Archaeology in Jerusalem, under the roof of whose School I started to write this book, to The Ecumenical Institute, Tantur, and to Dumbarton Oaks, of which I was a Fellow when it was finished.

JOHN WILKINSON
Nativity of St Mary, at Tantur

ABBREVIATIONS

AOL = *Archives de l'Orient Latin* (Société de l'Orient Latin), Paris 1881–4

Augustinovič = A. Augustinovič, *Gierico e Dintorni*, Jerusalem 1951

Boeren = P. C. Boeren, *Rorgo Fretellus de Nazareth et sa Description de la Terre Sainte: Histoire et Edition du Texte*, Amsterdam 1980

Btu = Benjamin of Tudela

Dan = Daniel

De Sandoli = S. De Sandoli, *Itinera Hierosolymitana Crucesignatorum*, vols 1 and 2, Jerusalem 1978, 1980

e = J. Wilkinson, *Egeria's Travels*, Warminster and Jerusalem 1981

Gbe = Belard of Ascoli

Gds = Guide before *Work on Geography*

Gej = Guide in *Gesta Francorum Expugnantium Jerusalem*

Gge = Guide perhaps by a German author

Gic = Icelandic Pilgrim

Gid = Muhammad al Idrisi

Got = Ottobonian Guide

Gqu = *Qualiter*

1Gu = *First Guide*

2Gu = *Second Guide*

7Gu = *Seventh Guide*

Halkin = F. Halkin, *Bibliotheca Hagiographica Graeca*, Brussels 1957

Hill = J. Hill, 'From Rome to Jerusalem: An Icelandic Itinerary of the Mid-Twelfth Century', *Harvard Theological Review*, 76:2 (1983) 175–203

j = J. Wilkinson, *Jerusalem Pilgrims before the Crusades*, Warminster 1977

James = M. R. James, *The Apocryphal New Testament*, Oxford 1924

JN	= L. H. Vincent and F. M. Abel, *Jérusalem, Recherches de topographie, d'archéologie et d'histoire*, Paris 1912–26
Jph	= John Phocas
Jwü	= John of Würzburg
MGH	= *Monumenta Germaniae Historica*, ed. G. Pertz, T. Mommsen and others, Hanover 1826 ff
Nik	= Nikulás
Ovadiah	= A. Ovadiah, *Corpus of the Byzantine Churches in the Holy Land, (Theophania 22)*, Bonn 1970
Pde	= Peter the Deacon
PEFQS, PEQ	= *Palestine Exploration [Fund] Quarterly [Statement]*, London 1868 ff
PG, PL	= *Patrologia Graeca, Patrologia Latina*, ed. J. P. Migne
PPTS	= *Palestine Pilgrims' Text Society* (listed as separate pamphlets) collected edition in 13 Vols, London 1896–7
Prawer	= J. Prawer, *The Latin Kingdom of Jerusalem*, London 1972
PUM	= G. Le Strange, *Palestine under the Muslims*, London 1890
RB	= *Revue Biblique*, Paris 1892 ff
RHC	= *Recueil des Histoires des Croisades, Historiens Occidentaux*, 5 vols (Académie des Inscriptions et Belles Lettres), Paris 1844–95
RSV	= Revised Standard Version
Runciman	= S. Runciman, *A History of the Crusades*, 3 vols, London 1952–4
Sae	= Saewulf
Sig	= Sigurðr
Thc	= Theoderic
Tobler, *Desc.*	= T. Tobler, *Descriptiones Terrae Sanctae ex saeculo VIII, IX, XII et XV*, Leipzig 1874
Tobler, *Theod.*	= T. Tobler, *Theoderici Libellus*, Paris 1865
V	= Venevitinov; see p. 351
V-A	= H. Vincent and F.-M. Abel, *Jérusalem Nouvelle*, Paris 1914–26
W	= C. W. Wilson; see p. 351
Wge	= *Work on Geography*

ZDPV	= Zeitschrift der Deutschen Palästina-Vereins, Leipzig 1878 ff

1. INTRODUCTION

A STAGE IN PILGRIMAGE

Christian pilgrimage began in the second century, but there are no connected accounts of it till 333, when a visitor from Bordeaux wrote his itinerary. Yet already he mentions many holy places which were still objects of pilgrimage to the Latin Kingdom pilgrims eight centuries later. Thus Jerusalem pilgrimage after 1099 serves as a sample of a special stage in a continuous process. It is a particularly clear sample, for there are as many extant texts from the years between 1099 and 1187 as from the whole of the previous period.

The Holy Places were assumed to be the same as the ones which had been visited long ago, and to a great extent this was true. But the Crusader movement, with its armies which conquered Jerusalem, and Latin Kingdom pilgrimage, which was inseparable from the Latin occupation of the Holy Land, were bound to bring alterations. The aim of the present book is therefore to make the changes more precise, and in doing so to clarify the later history of pilgrimage. The task of this introduction will therefore be first to consider the texts themselves. Secondly there will be an examination of existing pilgrimage to each site, and the changes made by Latin Kingdom pilgrims.

In a collection of texts such as this the spelling of place-names is bound to be different. Biblical names are not recorded, but when they are names applied in the Latin Kingdom they are noted with their different spellings in the Index.

2. INTRODUCTION TO THE TEXTS

THE TEXTS

The pilgrimage texts translated here were written between 1099 and 1185. The majority were simply for practical use. For those who could come to the Holy Land they served simply as Guides, and for those who could not they served as a means of making a spiritual pilgrimage. But three of these guides seem to have been written outside the Latin Kingdom, for they contain such opening sentences as these:

> Any one who may wish to go to Jerusalem, the Holy City, should continue to travel eastwards . . .[1]

Such a Guide was an advertisement, perhaps distributed or displayed by the churches or the shipping agents.

Most of the others are accounts of their travels written by the pilgrims. But the two categories are not always distinct. For example some documents which have the appearance of being Guides have a paragraph at the end which announces their authorship, such as:

> And I, Brother Belardus of Ascoli, have seen all this and examined it, and I myself have written it down in order to be of use to others.[2]

Quite often it is very hard to tell what places were actually visited by the pilgrims. In their anxiety to produce as full as possible an account of their stay in the Holy Land they quoted long passages from other books, and this tendency increased in the Crusader period, when a pilgrim could not go very far without being within range of the enemy.

[1] See p. 90 below. [2] See p. 230 below.

Included among these translations is a much longer guide to the Holy Land. Since the original manuscript (which we have entitled *The Work on Geography*) has been lost, the modern reader has to look for versions of it in a number of other works written in the Latin Kingdom which have borrowed from it. This book is over ten thousand words in length. It seems to be a general description of the holy places in the Latin Kingdom, but contains several which are beyond its boundaries. The information which this book gives is sometimes up to date, but it is at other times about four hundred years old, since it quotes the names of the Levantine provinces as if they were still in the Roman empire.

This desire to quote earlier works may be seen in two ways. In the Latin Kingdom a pilgrim on his travels was doing something which was of great importance to him. In fact he was entering into an experience which was of great antiquity, and earlier books by those who were in his view authorities, might provide some of the information which he required. The advantage for the author was that the authorities were likely to tell the truth. But the disadvantage to his readers was and is that what a pilgrim quotes as his personal observations, is not always the case: one of the first pilgrims, Saewulf states, for example, that the top of Mt Tabor was 'covered with grass and flowers':[3] this whole phrase was in fact taken from an authority, in this case the Venerable Bede.

[3] See p. 111.

THREE GUIDES OF 1101–1104

THE FIRST GUIDE (1Gu)
QUALITER (Gqu)
THE OTTOBONIAN GUIDE (Got)

For the first of these guides I have chosen the title *First Guide* since in the Latin text it is cited as by 'Anonymous Writer 1'. Several guides have titles of the same kind, but the numbers are not necessarily in chronological order. This guide was attached to the first record of the Crusaders' invasion of the Holy Land, *Gesta Francorum et aliorum Hierosolymitanorum*,[1] which was completed perhaps in 1101, but at any rate before 1104. Since it contains the Temple it must be after 1099, when the building was captured and turned into a Christian holy place. But since the guide forms part of every manuscript of the *Gesta*, it seems to have been one which was added right from the start. The latest edition of this Guide was written in some foreign country west of the Holy Land, probably in France, since it contains quotations from the Pilgrim of Bordeaux's *Itinerary*, which would very likely be available there.[2] None of the other writers on pilgrimage in the Latin Kingdom quotes directly from the Bordeaux pilgrim.

The *Itinerary* was nearly eight centuries old when it was incorporated in the *First Guide*, and it contained some inaccuracies which may have worried its readers in the Latin Kingdom. An example is the pilgrim's reference to 'Isaiah's Tomb', which was its name in 333. But this monument, known today as the 'Tomb of Zechariah', was in Crusader times part of the tomb of St James. Some other authors of guide-books accepted the *First Guide*'s comment as authoritative, but they seem to have copied out the information about 'Isaiah's Tomb' without knowing where it was.[3]

[1] Ed. R. Hill, *Gesta Francorum* (Oxford, 1962), p. xl.
[2] See Runciman, Vol. 1, 330.
[3] Bordeaux Pilgrim, *Itin.* 595.3: *Guide 7*, sec. 10.

GUIDE I	GUIDE 'QUALITER'	GUIDE IN OTT. IA. 169
Invitation	Invitation	
Mount of Joy	Mount of Joy	
Tower of David	Tower of David	Tower of David
Temple (B)		
Mount Sion (B)		
Praetorium (B)		
Holy Sepulchre (B★)	Holy Sepulchre	Holy Sepulchre
St Mary Latin	St Mary Latin	
	Finding the Cross	Finding the Cross
	Beautiful Gate	↓
Temple of the Lord	Temple of the Lord	Temple of the Lord
		Beautiful Gate
Temple of Solomon	Temple of Solomon	Temple of Solomon
		Church of St Anne
Sheep Pool	Sheep Pool	Sheep Pool
Mount of Olives	↓	↓
Valley of Jehoshaphat	Valley of Jehoshaphat	Valley of Jehoshaphat
Tomb of Isaiah (B)		
	Mount of Olives	Mount of Olives
Bethany (B)	Bethany	Bethany
Jericho (B)		
	Quarantana	↓
Jordan (B)	Jordan	↓
Mount of Elijah (B)		
Days to Mount Sinai		
Galilee		
Mount Sion, Siloam	↓	Mount Sion, Siloam
Road to Samaria (B)		
Bethlehem	Bethlehem	Bethlehem
Hebron		
	Mount Sion, Siloam	
	Stoning of St Stephen	
		Quarantana
		Jordan
	I am a witness	

The second guide comes to us linked to the *History* of Archbishop Baudry of Dol. It is called *Qualiter* from the first word of the paragraph linking it to the History. This is a guide-book which has been signed by a pilgrim. It does not cover Sinai, Galilee, or Samaria, which have brief mentions in the *First Guide*, but it is an early one, as can be seen from the second column in the table on the previous page. The headings there correspond well with the *First Guide*, and about half of them are in harmony with the quotations from the pilgrim of Bordeaux (the passages marked *B*). Perhaps *Qualiter* was a guide in circulation at the same time as the original version of the *First Guide*, that is to say between 1099 and 1103. The order of places mentioned in *Qualiter* may have been affected by the individual pilgrim's itinerary.

The third early guide-book is *The Ottobonian Guide*,[1] which covers only Jerusalem. It handles much the same places as *Qualiter*, but, like Saewulf, it mentions the Church of Saint Anne. What is more it follows a logical order in mentioning the holy places, and this both makes it the latest of the three, and fits well with its presentation as a simple guide-book.

These three guides therefore can be dated to the period 1099–1103. Within this period they consist of an earlier stage, represented by the *First Guide* and *Qualiter*, when the church of St Anne is not mentioned, and a later one when it is possible to speak of this church, represented by the *Ottobonian Guide* and by Saewulf.

SAEWULF 1101–1103 (Sae)

Saewulf's travel account begins with the voyage to the Holy Land from Apulia, and ends on his way to visit Constantinople. But his Anglo-Saxon or German name shows that he is from further north. It is quite probable that he was from Britain, since his work relies on a British saint, Bede, and the one manuscript which we possess of it was in the library of Matthew Parker, the sixteenth-century Archbishop of Canterbury.

Saewulf's journey lasted ten or eleven months, starting in July and returning at Pentecost. He returned after March 1102, when

[1] So called because in the Vatican Library it is part of the collection of manuscripts preserved in *Codex Ottobonianus latinus* 169.

the Franks had captured Tartus, and before they captured Acre in 1104. Since the capture of Acre was in May and Pentecost was in June in 1104 his return must have been earlier, and we can thus date his pilgrimage either in 1101–1102 or in 1102–1103.[1]

The original passages by Saewulf are strikingly well-told, for example his account of the shipwreck at Joppa, or his complaints about the buildings wrecked by the pagans. He retails the general view about the contents of the Temple, to judge by Manuscript L of Fulcher's *History*.[2] He relies on authorities, and particularly on Bede. But he shows occasional doubts about what local residents told him.[3]

We have followed the normal modern English spelling of the name 'Saewulf'. In the English of the time however it would have been spelt 'Sæwulf'.

GUIDE PERHAPS BY A GERMAN AUTHOR 1102–1106 (Gge)

This is a very brief guide, dealing with sites in Jerusalem and Bethany. Its author may have been in Germany, since in section 4 he is able to compare the Church at the Holy Sepulchre with Charlemagne's round church at Aix, and the guide is preserved in a manuscript in Trier Cathedral. This guide seems to be written between 1102 and 1106. The Chapel of the Invention of the Cross (sec. 4) had not yet been built, so it was written before Daniel (1106–8) (see his chapter 15). It may be the same period as Saewulf, since there is a church built at St Peter's Tears (sec. 3 and Saewulf 21).

This Guide takes no account of the order of the earlier ones, and the description of the Temple is left to the very end. The commemorations of the Temple are not standard, and its interest lies in displaying what it shows of the reactions of one individual pilgrim.

[1] See M. d'Avezac, *Relation des Voyages de Saewulf*, Paris 1839, 8–10.

[2] Fulcher of Chartres, *Historia Hierosolymitana* I.28, ms. L.

[3] See section 9. He believes what local people tell him in sections 9, 12, 13, 18, 26 and 33.

FULCHER OF CHARTRES

During the Latin Kingdom the first full prose description of the city of Jerusalem may well be by Fulcher, the historian who lived in the city. His is certainly the first account of a visit to Petra, and shows that Fulcher was a good observer.[1] Fulcher was chaplain to King Baldwin the First.

His *Historia Hierosolymitana* is hard to date. It seems that the earliest examples of it were issued in about 1106 by two independent scribes, one who wrote Manuscript L, and the other the author of *Gesta Francorum Iherusalem expugnantium*. Manuscript L of Fulcher's work was known to Guibert of Nogent in a work published in 1108.[2] Fulcher's own work can be seen in two editions, one published in 1118 after the death of Baldwin the First, and the other in 1127.

Between 15 November and 21 December 1100 Fulcher went with Baldwin on a military expedition down to the Dead Sea, and then on to Petra. There he saw the Valley of Moses or Wadi Musa, and the place where Moses struck the rock to produce water for the children of Israel,[3] and once inside Petra he saw the monastery of Moses on top of Mount Hor. But none of the other pilgrims between 1099 and 1187 followed him.

As regards pilgrimage Fulcher, in his descriptions of Jerusalem, says nothing of special importance, apart from his account of the Temple area. Under the previous Muslim rule this area of the city was unknown to Christians, until they invaded Jerusalem. But in 1099 they suddenly had complete control of it, and it seems that they took a long time to understand it. Manuscript L, which does not represent Fulcher's own opinion,[4] says that the Hebrews said that various relics were in the Temple of the Lord, including the Ark of the Covenant, and this position was popularly held for a

[1] See the translation by H. S. Fink, *Fulcher of Chartres: A History of the Expedition to Jerusalem, 1095–1127* (Knoxville 1969), Book 2, chapters 4 and 5, pp. 143–7.

[2] See Fink, *op. cit.* 22, note 12.

[3] Num. 20.11.

[4] Comparison between Ms. L (italic note at foot of *RHC. Occ.* 3, p. 356) with Fulcher's own opinion in *Hist. H.* 1.26 on the same page seems to reveal that by 1106 Fulcher felt that the ark was not in the Temple. That this was his early view receives confirmation in *Gesta Francorum Iherusalem expugnantium* 32 (*ibid.* 3, p. 510).

long time. In 1118 Fulcher still complains about the ugliness and inconvenience of the bare rock which occupied the centre of the Temple, but this seems to be an oversight on Fulcher's part. In 1117 it had been paved over, and in his second edition he says that for nearly fifteen years after the crusaders' arrival the rock had remained visible; it was then given a new floor and made into a choir with an altar.[1]

ABBOT DANIEL 1106–8 (Dan)

The account of Abbot Daniel's pilgrimage to the Holy Land, probably in the years 1106–8 and written down immediately after that time, is the first such account in Old Russian literature and certainly the best, both as a literary monument and as an historical source. It was copied many times (Seeman[2] lists 148 complete or fragmentary manuscript texts, including reworkings, from the fifteenth to the twentieth century) not only for its literary or religious merit, but, to judge from the number of synopses and reworkings, also as a practical guidebook for pilgrims. It covers the whole country, and the monasteries.

Although it can scarcely be supposed that Daniel wrote his account without a Byzantine genre model in mind, his story is nevertheless very much a personal account, which is rather uncommon both for Slavonic and western medieval writing. For example Daniel compares the Jordan with a river near his home, the Snov', he measures things himself, he introduces his own feelings and actions into the story, and if his descriptions of architectural monuments are notably less successful than his descriptions of the countryside, rarely going beyond the adjectives 'big', 'beautiful', 'wonderful' and 'indescribable', they do at least convey the author's sense of awe at what he had seen. And it is clear that with a few obvious exceptions, he did see what he described – as he insists several times: I went there on my own sinful feet and saw with my own sinful eyes. His claims to veracity are sincere: where popular tradition is manifestly false he says so (although we

[1] See Fink, *op. cit*, 1.26.9, p. 118.
[2] Klaus-Dieter Seeman, *Abt Daniil: Wallfahrtsbericht* (Slavische Propyläen, 36), Munich, 1970.

must allow him a reasonable measure of medieval gullibility and a general disregard for any distinction between canonical and apocryphal sources). Where his information comes from an informant he usually says as much, although we must assume that the source of much of his information was the unnamed monk from the monastery or Laura of St Saba who acted as his guide and presumably retailed the standard tourist patter of the period.

Daniel tantalisingly fails to maintain this personal approach in one crucial respect: he does not tell us where he comes from. Linguistic evidence points to one of the southern principalities, and the river Snov' may narrow this down to Chernigov, a little to the north of Kiev. Daniel tells us only that he is an abbot 'of the Russian land', i.e. anywhere from the Black to the White Sea. He is not travelling alone but has an entourage. The names which he gives for some of his companions are names of laymen, and this together with the list of Russian princes for whom Daniel prays, and the evident favour shown him by King Baldwin, has suggested to some scholars that Daniel's journey was perhaps as much a diplomatic mission as a pilgrimage. This possibility is strengthened by the fact that the forty-two Greek words found in the text, and Daniel's explanation of some of them, seem to suggest that Daniel knew Greek, which was probably not an accomplishment of most Russian clerics in the twelfth century.

Daniel's opening remarks about the advantage of reading an account of a pilgrimage, if one cannot oneself make the journey, are comparable to similar remarks by pilgrims, both from east and west.[1]

SIGURÐR 1100 (Sig)

This extract comes from an Icelandic work, *Magnússona saga*, written by Snorri Sturluson, and can be dated *c.* 1220–36. It contains the travels of King Sigurðr to Sicily, the Holy Land and Constantinople. Only the travels to the Holy Land are translated in this book. Sigurðr took part with King Baldwin in the siege of Sidon in December 1110, and afterwards returned to rule in Norway. In spite of the fact that the travels are in effect a story

[1] See Jph 1.6, Jwü, prol. 109, and Thc, prol. 9.

of adventure, they contain two elements which concern pilgrimage. In Chapter 10 Sigurðr bathes in the River Jordan, 'The bold and generous chieftain bathed in the waters of Jórðán (that was a deed worthy of praise)', which was a dramatic experience he shared with Abbot Daniel. Secondly, in Chapter 11, a feast is described at which King Baldwin gives a splinter of the Holy Cross to Sigurðr on condition that he swears an oath to promote Christianity with all his power in his own country.

TWO MORE EARLY GUIDES (Gfe and Gds)

These two texts are guides to Jerusalem, and the first contains passing references to Galilee. Both are in good Latin, but they do not add more holy places to those visited by the three early guides and Saewulf, and for this reason their origin is likely to be early.

One guide (Gfe) forms chapters 31–3 of the *Gesta Francorum Jherusalem expugnantium*. The main book has been dated to before 1109 because in it Tripoli is still ruled by Saracens.[1] But there is some confusion in the dates of the sources, since the guide which forms part of the text of the book mentions the Bishopric of Bethlehem which was formed in 1109. Hence the Guide's description of Jerusalem must therefore be in 1109 or later. This guide also forms the main source of a thirteenth-century description of the Holy Land.[2]

De Situ (Gds) seems to have been written before 1114, at which date the rock in the centre of the Temple of the Lord was paved over, and might very well be a guide-book of the time of Saewulf. This is the guide which comes in front of the *Descriptio* (see below, p. 179), though it may have well have been copied down from an unrelated manuscript.

[1] See *G.F.J.E.* chapters 68 and 71.
[2] Guide in the *Chronicon Universale Anonymi Laudunensis*, ed. A. Cartellieri and W. Stechele, Leipzig 1909, 41–6.

OTHER TEXTS 1114–19

Latin authors still continued to think that the Temple of the Lord had been built by Christians. Abbot Daniel had been told the truth by the Greeks, that it had been built by a Muslim, But perhaps the main cause that Latin Christians maintained a false view was that it was still the opinion of the Prior of the monastery who was in charge of Christian services in the Temple. This was Acard of Arrouaise, who had been appointed soon after 1099, and still maintained his view shortly before 1114. In that year he wrote a poem to King Baldwin which ended with a request that the Temple be repaired. This poem is largely a résumé of the history of the Temple in the Bible, but in lines 479 to 487 Acard says that he does not know which Christian built it. It might have been Empress Helena, or Justinian, or Heraclius. This view is also held by Albert of Aix in his *Historia Hierosolymitana* (VI.24).

Several historical authors mention the ceremony of the Holy Fire, which was held in the Holy Sepulchre on Easter Eve and Ekkehard of Aura, writing in about 1115 (*Hierosolymita* 32) gives an eyewitness account of the service.

THE WORK ON GEOGRAPHY 1128–37 (Wge)

This work seems to be the one of the main sources of two other writings, one the *Descriptio*, which was finished between 1131 and 1143, during the reign of King Fulk, and the other a letter written by Fretellus to Bishop Henri Sdyck in 1137. I have called the latter work *Patri H*. Some of the later manuscripts, based on Fretellus' work, but after his death,[1] about 1157, make additions which are the same as passages in the *Descriptio*,[2] and it is therefore likely that they were drawing on some third book for source material.

[1] See Boeren, p. xi, note 14.

[2] Fretellus' manuscripts of 1162–73 (D : Douai, *Bib. mun.* 882 and D², the interpolations) and of 1181–4 (Vat : Vatican, *Bib. Apost. cod. Reg. lat.* 712) coincide with the *Descriptio*, as shown by Boeren's notes on pp. 9–11, 13, 15, 17, 20–1, 23, 29–30, 32–4, 37–44.

There is a work called *On the Distances between Places* which has been ascribed to Saint Jerome,[1] and a book with the same title was at the end of the twelfth century in the library of the church in Nazareth,[2] of which Fretellus was Archdeacon. Indeed this title has been preserved in a version of Fretellus,[3] no doubt from this book. Generally speaking the book is a collection of the main cities in the area, the places in their neighbourhood, and the distances between them. But it has the *Liber locorum* by Jerome as one of its main sources; and since Jerome's original exists, a reader can tell where both the *Descriptio* and Fretellus make errors in quoting it, and the mistakes of one twelfth-century author do not arise out of the mistakes of the other.

The style of the *Descriptio* is less accomplished than that of the letter of Fretellus, but where Fretellus adds material it provides almost no factual information but is rather of a spiritual nature. The one exception to this is Fretellus' frequent quotations from Jerome's *de Interpretationibus Nominum*, which was also one of the books in the library at Nazareth.[4] It is thus possible to reconstruct the main points of *The Work on Geography*. There are some descriptions of areas beyond the Latin Kingdom, like Damascus and Arabia, as would be expected from a work based on Jerome, but the *Work* seems to be mainly a book about holy places in the Latin Kingdom, since the manuscripts written after Fretellus' death include the kingdom's boundaries.[5]

In the translation of the *Work* which is printed below the order of the *Descriptio* has been followed, but additional material from the manuscripts written after Fretellus' death has also been included in the paragraphs which have a side-line. The order of the source is not known for certain, since it varies in the *Descriptio* and the works of Fretellus, but its contents are clear. They are as follows:

1. Description of Hebron and the Dead Sea.
2. Description of Arabia, mainly composed of a long paraphrase of Jerome's *Letter* 78, and ending with the Roman capital, Bostra.

[1] See Boeren, p. xiii.
[2] See J. S. Beddie, 'Some notices of books in the East in the period of the Crusades', *Speculum* 8 (1933) 240–2.
[3] Eugesippus in his version of Fretellus' *Fratri R.*, *PL* 133.991–1004.
[4] See Boeren, p. xiii.
[5] See Wge 226.

3. Damascus, Jordan.
4. Galilee, Samaria, and (omitting Jerusalem), Bethlehem.
5. Section A on Jerusalem, with a passage describing places mentioned on the order of Christ's Passion.
6. Surroundings of Jerusalem.
7. Jericho.
8. Journey up the coast road to the north, as far as the northern boundary of the Latin Kingdom, the River Albana.
9. Section B on Jerusalem.

This therefore seems to be a guide to the Latin Kingdom produced by some twelfth-century scholar. It may have gone through several versions, since the ending is with the epitaph of Duke Godfrey, which argues for an early date. The addition of *De Situ*, which as we have seen was written before 1114, may form another suggestion that there was an earlier version of the work. The latest dated material common to the *Descriptio* and Fretellus, *Patri H.*, is the death of Patriarch Warmund, so the version used by both these authors was after 1128.

One of the main sources of the 'Work on Geography' was the *Liber locorum* by Saint Jerome, and entries from this are very frequent. Another source deals with the translation of relics, and this seems to be known in the eleventh century, and accounts for most of the references to the empire of Charlemagne. Perhaps the most difficult part to date is the descriptions of cities. The areas round the cities are described in terms of the provinces of the Roman empire, namely Syria, Phoenicia, Palestine, Arabia and Egypt. Such passages may therefore date to long before the time of the Latin Kingdom.

A particularly difficult name for a province is 'Idumaea'. In the period of the New Testament Idumaea was an area whose capital was Hebron, and therefore to the south of Jerusalem, but in the *Work on Geography* it seems to cover roughly the same area as the Roman province of Arabia. Indeed Bostra, the capital of the province of Arabia, is said to have been once the capital of Idumaea (sec.44). It thus seems likely that 'Idumaea' is a name for the traditional enemy of Israel, namely Edom. If the crusaders felt themselves in religious terms to be akin to the Kingdom of David, then they would naturally have Edom as their enemy. Fretellus seems to give an indication of this when, in the prologue to *Patri H.*, he says,

> Look at Sion itself, which is an allegory for Paradise, and how *the mighty men from Israel*, that is to say *the new Maccabees, rise from the bed of the true Solomon*, and drive out from thence the Idumaeans and Amalech.

The quotation in this passage is from St Bernard's *Book to the Soldiers of the Temple*,[1] and it is therefore very likely that the word was in regular use.

One important change from the pilgrimage pattern of the Christians who had been present before the Latin Kingdom is the inclusion in the *Work on Geography* of places listed in the order in which they would be visited during the week before Easter. This order is mentioned in sections 155–170, and also the Holy Fire ceremony on Easter Eve. Fretellus mentions this period at greater length (chapters 60–6). At the beginning he mentions the Day of Palms or Palm Sunday and at the end the 'Fiftieth Day', or Pentecost, putting the events in the order of their celebration during the period round Easter. This was evidently an alternative way of describing the Holy Places. Whether it had results in private pilgrimages apart from Holy Week it is not possible to tell.

The *Work on Geography* was used again and again as a source, first of all by Fretellus in another work which we shall call by part of its opening words *Fratri R.*[2] This was another letter speaking about pilgrimage in much the same way as *Patri H.*, his earlier one. *Fratri R.*, was both copied as whole work, and extracts were also made from it by the German pilgrims John of Würzburg and Theodoric. The family tree is reproduced on the following page.

[1] J. Leclercq, C. H. Talbot and H. M. Rochais, eds (Rome 1957) 3, 213.
[2] Boeren 53–63 and Migne, *PL* 155. 1037–54.

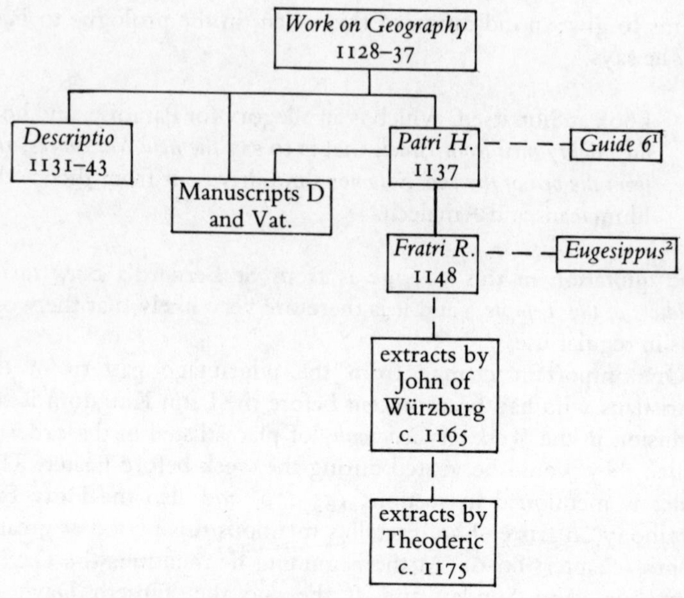

INVENTION OF THE PATRIARCHS 1136

In 1119 a discovery was made of the relics of the Patriarchs in their grave in Hebron. In 1136 this is described by one of the Canons of Hebron, and he gives an interesting description of the monument.

Pilgrims between 1099 and 1187 visited relics, but none of their writings show that (apart from King Baldwin's gift to Sigurðr) they collected any, and relics, important though they were to the history of the Latin Kingdom, will therefore not be described in this book. But original discoveries of saints' bodies, as they believed them to be, were an important part of the Crusaders' psychology, and increased their awareness that they had possession of the Holy Land. One of the first such discoveries in the area of the Latin Kingdom was said to be of St George's body at Lydda,[3] and there is also a Jewish story about a Latin attempt to visit David's Tomb in Jerusalem.[4]

[1] *Guide 6*, also known as Pseudo-Bede, and beginning *Sumamus initium*, is edited by A. Neumann, in *Tübinger Theologische Quartalschrift* (1868) 7, 398ff. See also Boeren, *op. cit.* 4.

[2] Eugesippus, *De distanciis locorum*, Migne, *PL* 133.991–1004. See also Boeren, *op. cit.* 87.

[3] John Phocas, *Descr.* 29.4–6.

[4] Benjamin of Tudela, *Itin.* p. 24f.

PETER THE DEACON 1137 (Pde)

In 1137 the Librarian of Monte Cassino, Peter the Deacon, addressed a work to his Abbot, who was about to go on pilgrimage. In his prologue he said that he had 'collected the material from all the books'. His main book was the work of Bede on the holy places, and he gives several valuable quotations from a fourth-century pilgrim, Egeria. But among the quotations some are clearly from a twelfth-century Guide or description of the Holy Land, of which extracts are given below.[1]

NIKULÁS OF ÞVERÁ about 1140 (Nik)

Embedded in a fourteenth-century encyclopaedic miscellany, MS AM 194, is an independent text, said to have been by a certain Abbot Nikulás, which describes a journey from Iceland to Rome and on to Jerusalem. The journey from Rome to Jerusalem is translated below. Nineteenth-century scholars identified Nikulás with Nikulás Sæmundarson, who died as Abbot of the Icelandic Benedictine monastery of Þingeyrar in 1158, but it is now accepted that the reference is to Nikulás Bergsson, who became abbot of the other Benedictine monastery of Þverá in 1155, and who died in 1159 or 1160.[2] The fact that he is said to have been 'blessed with a good memory' may perhaps suggest that he had made his pilgrimage long before. Another pilgrim, St Willibald, made a pilgrimage fifty years before his biography was written down by a nun, and she too took down the words from his dictation. It is thus impossible to tell when the pilgrimage took place.

Like Saewulf (9) or Daniel (10) he calls the building containing the Holy Sepulchre a 'Church'. But he implies that the centre of the world

[1] In a previous work of mine, J. Wilkinson, *Egeria's Travels*, London 1971, I made a different selection. The main points where I now differ from the previous selection are that the twelfth-century pieces are (I) up to 'Jehoshaphat' and 'holy Stephen' to the end; (M2) 'eleven sons of Jacob' to the end; whole of (P1); (P3) from 'Mount Hermon' to end; and all of (P4).

[2] For these and other details I rely on two articles for which I am most grateful: Joyce Hill, 'From Rome to Jerusalem: an Icelandic Itinerary of the mid-twelfth century', *Harvard Theological Review*, 76 (1983) 175–203, and B. Z. Kedar and Chr. Westergard-Nielsen, 'Icelanders in the crusader kingdom of Jerusalem: a twelfth-century account', *Mediaeval Scandinavia* 11 (1978–79), 193–211.

was outside, in a position where the sun 'shines directly down from the sky on the Feast of St John' (85). The Holy Sepulchre was made into one church and consecrated on 15 July 1149, and it must be before that date. But the dateable material before that is the capture of Acre in 1104. The reference to the Hospital as 'the most magnificent in the world' (94) may tend to make it late in the period before 1149, and I have therefore suggested about 1140.

The list of stages by which Nikulás travelled from Iceland to Jerusalem is even more interesting than his rather summary account of the holy places. The part of the account translated here, brief as it is, is a description of Jerusalem, and the road to Nazareth and the coastal cities to the north.

HUGH OF ST VICTOR before 1141

Whether or not Hugh of St Victor was responsible for the copying of the work named *De locis circa Jerusalem*, it is no more than a paraphrase of Bede's work *De locis Sanctis*, written in 702–3. But it has an addition of considerable interest at the end. This is a story first told in the eleventh century by 'Master Franco of Liège' and it is almost an exact copy of the original.[1] As will be seen on page 75 below, this story is of considerable importance, since it describes King Solomon putting the wood of the Cross into the Sheep Pool near the east gate of Jerusalem. The story was to change the topography of Jerusalem.

AN ICELANDIC PILGRIM about 1150 (Gic)

Another Icelandic pilgrim quoted in *Alfrædi islensk* gives a detailed account of his pilgrimage in Jerusalem. He seems to describe the Holy Sepulchre as one church, with several allusions to its former condition, and this suggests that he was writing not very long after it was rebuilt as one church in 1149.[1] This guide has a different order from that of Abbot Nikulás, and a great deal more detail.[2]

[1] See A. Wilmart, *RB* (1927) 230f.

[2] Gic is clearly the basis for the description of the Emperor Kirialax's visit to the Holy Land in *Kirialax saga*, ed. Kr. Kålund, *Kirialax saga*, Copenhagen 1917. For comment and translation see Kedar and Westergård-Nielsen, *op. cit.*, 197, n.15.

AL IDRISI 1154 (Gid)

Al Idrisi was a Muslim Arab who lived at the court of the Norman King, Roger II, in Sicily. At the King's request he wrote a work on geography, and his description of Jerusalem is evidently a version of a guide to the place by some Christian writing in Arabic.

BELARD OF ASCOLI about 1155 (Gbe)

Since Belard describes himself as a 'Brother' it is likely that he was a monk. Despite the fact that his manuscript is repetitive (perhaps due to careless copying) and written in poor Latin, it gives us yet another individual approach to the Holy Places. Belard may have been told about a description of the places by a guide, or he may have read it, and some of his phrases seem to be borrowed from some earlier source.[1] But such literary parallels seem to lead to no conclusions about his sources.

The earliest person to comment on this work[2] thought it must be before 1120. But it is certainly after 1141, since it mentions a church at Emmaus, and clearly also some time after about 1142, when the choir was begun at the Holy Sepulchre. Since Belard does not speak of the alteration as new, this Guide might have been written in 1155, but it might equally be at any stage between 1142 and 1187.

In addition to his description of Jerusalem Belard writes about Hebron, Shechem, Nazareth and Galilee, and briefly mentions Emmaus and the northern coastal cities.

SEVENTH GUIDE about 1160 (7Gu)

The *Seventh Guide* is partly based on the *First Guide* and the end of it

[1] For instance his statement that Samaria is 'the name of a city and a nation' (3) compares with Fretellus, *Fratri R.* 42, and his statement on the Jor and the Dan (3) compares with Fretellus 31.

[2] W. A. Neumann, *AOL* 1, 225–9.

is very like the *Second Guide*. In its turn this *Seventh Guide* formed the basis of two more guides written after 1187.[1]

It was written before the new church at Gethsemane was built, and therefore before the visit of John of Würzburg, and it has only a 'small church' at the Pater Noster.

The text covers Jerusalem, Hebron and Emmaus and the road to Shechem and Nazareth.

THEOTONIUS' PILGRIMAGE

Saint Theotonius visited Jerusalem twice, not long after 1100, and then returned to Portugal. There he founded the monastery of the Holy Cross near Coimbra. One of his disciples wrote his life not long after 1160 but the author's account of the pilgrimage is modelled so closely on St Jerome's account in *Letter 108* of the pilgrimage of St Paula that it conveys no true information about pilgrimage in the twelfth century.

BENJAMIN OF TUDELA (Btu) and IBN JUBAIR

Benjamin of Tudela visited the Holy land in the course of a longer journey from 1166–71 and wrote an itinerary. Apart from the details it gives about the topography of the Holy Land it is of little relevance to the history of Christian pilgrimage. But for the wider history of the Latin Kingdom it is of great importance, since it reveals a great deal about the life of the Jewish population.

Similarly Ibn Jubair, who travelled across Galilee and wrote an itinerary in 1181 mentioning Muslim holy places, has not been translated in this collection.

[1] Namely the *Ninth Guide* (Si quis de Joppe . . . Jacobus filius Zebedaei), edited by W. A. Neumann, *Tübinger Theologische Quartalschrift* (1874) 534–9, and the *Fifth Guide*, soon after 1198 (Ego ivi de Accon . . . honore B. Virginis), edited by W. A. Neumann, *Österreichische Viertelschrift für Katholische Theologie* (1866) 221–57.

SECOND GUIDE about 1170 (2Gu)

This guide is an account of an individual's approach to pilgrimage, and it reflects the interest which the Templars took in the site of the Probatica pool.

It seems to be at about the same time as the visit of John of Würzburg. But its Latin is poor and the writer of the manuscript was careless. It is a short guide, and this may be why there is no church mentioned at Akeldama. But it covers a lot of ground: Jerusalem, Hebron, Emmaus, and the road to Shechem and Nazareth. There is a very brief description of Galilee.

JOHN OF WÜRZBURG about 1170 (Jwü)

John was a priest of Würzburg and he wrote his account of his visit to the Holy Land for a colleague called Dietrich. He wrote the work in good Latin and showed good powers of observation, especially of the way the monuments were decorated. He disliked the Franks because they were conceited and despised the Germans. He is very informative about his visits to Jerusalem and Nazareth, but seems to have visited very few other places. When he wishes to describe places he has not visited he quotes extensively from the *Work on Geography*, and these passages have not been included in the translation below.

Since Theoderic's quotations from the *Work on Geography* are the same as those of John of Würzburg he must have depended on John's book, and the book was therefore written before Theoderic's. The name 'Theoderic' is cognate with 'Dietrich', so perhaps John's book was addressed to him. The earliest date when John's book was written depends on the rebuilding of the church at Gethsemane (p. 253). Since we do not know the date when the church was rebuilt we have given a conjectural date of about 1170.

THEODERIC 1169–74 (Thc)

Theoderic was a monk, and seems to have come from Germany, since he was familiar with the Church at Aix, and reported the death in the Holy Land of a man from Cologne. If 'Theodoric' means the same person as 'Dietrich', he may well have been the person to whom John's book was dedicated. He was an even better observer and writer than John of Würzburg and displayed none of John of Würzbürg's racist tendencies, though the general pattern of his book is not so good as John's.

For the places he had not visited he depended on John of Würzburg, and had apparently no direct knowledge of the *Work on Geography*. Again, his paraphrases from John are not translated below. He used other books, among them a Martyrology and the works of Josephus.

He was impressed by the castle of Belvoir (his p. 44), and since this cannot have been built until 1168, when the Hospitallers were granted the land, he cannot have been there until 1169, at the earliest. At the time Nur ed Din was the 'enemy', and he died on the 15 May 1174.

He was particularly interested in the constitution of the religious communities he visited and the different communities who owned the holy places.

One of the striking things about this guide is the attention it pays to the finding of the Cross and its relation to Solomon. Evidently he was influenced by some version of the story of 'Master Franco'.

He does not appear to have visited Hebron and his description of Galilee is borrowed from elsewhere. But apart from these sites, he was present in all the other places he described in the Holy Land and the coastal cities to the north.

JOHN PHOCAS 1185 (Jph)

John Phocas' powers of descriptive writing and the devotion with which he made his pilgrimage are quite different from the Latin pilgrims who preceded him. This pilgrimage consisted in visiting holy men as much as Holy Places. He wrote both about monastic saints, and living holy men, or 'Old Men', as he called respected monks.

He was born in Crete. Then he became a soldier, and showed familiarity with places as far apart as Lake Ochrid and Adalia in the southern part of Turkey. He served the Emperor, and was very proud of the decorations which the Emperor had put up, particularly in Bethlehem. He does not seem to have visited Hebron, but otherwise he visited all the Holy Places, and the coastal cities to the north.

A marginal note in the original manuscript states that 'John, son of Phocas' visited the Holy Places in 1185.

3. HISTORY OF PILGRIMAGE

ABBASID AND LATIN KINGDOM PILGRIMAGE

In this section the aim is to compare pilgrimage in Abbasid times with its development under the rule of the Latin Kingdom, up to the year 1187. By 'Abbasid times' we shall also include the eleventh century, when Abbasid power was weak, and the city of Jerusalem and some other parts of Palestine were in fact ruled by the Fatimid Caliphs of Egypt.

First of all the Holy City must be considered. Just before 1099 the walls of Jerusalem stretched round about the same area as they do today (see Figure 1). They excluded the Pool of Siloam, and the steep hilly area to the south of the city (on the figure to the right) and the city was confined to the less hilly area within the walls. Round three sides Jerusalem was defended by valleys, and their names will follow. But the names are important. For the same names had been used in pilgrim accounts of Jerusalem in the Byzantine and Abbasid periods, and reference to the sources (pages 346–350) shows that Jerusalem had not changed very much on the arrival of the Crusaders. All the names that will be used in this description go back to a period long before the invasion of Jerusalem by the Crusaders in 1099.

The Valley on the east of Jerusalem, which divided it from the Mount of Olives,[1] had long been called by a biblical name deriving from the prophet Joel,[2] the Valley of Jehoshaphat. Half a mile to the north of Jerusalem this valley began. It ran east, then southwards past the city. After four miles it turned east to reach the Dead Sea. It was joined by another valley, the 'Valley of

[1] Matt 21.1.
[2] Joel 3.2,12.

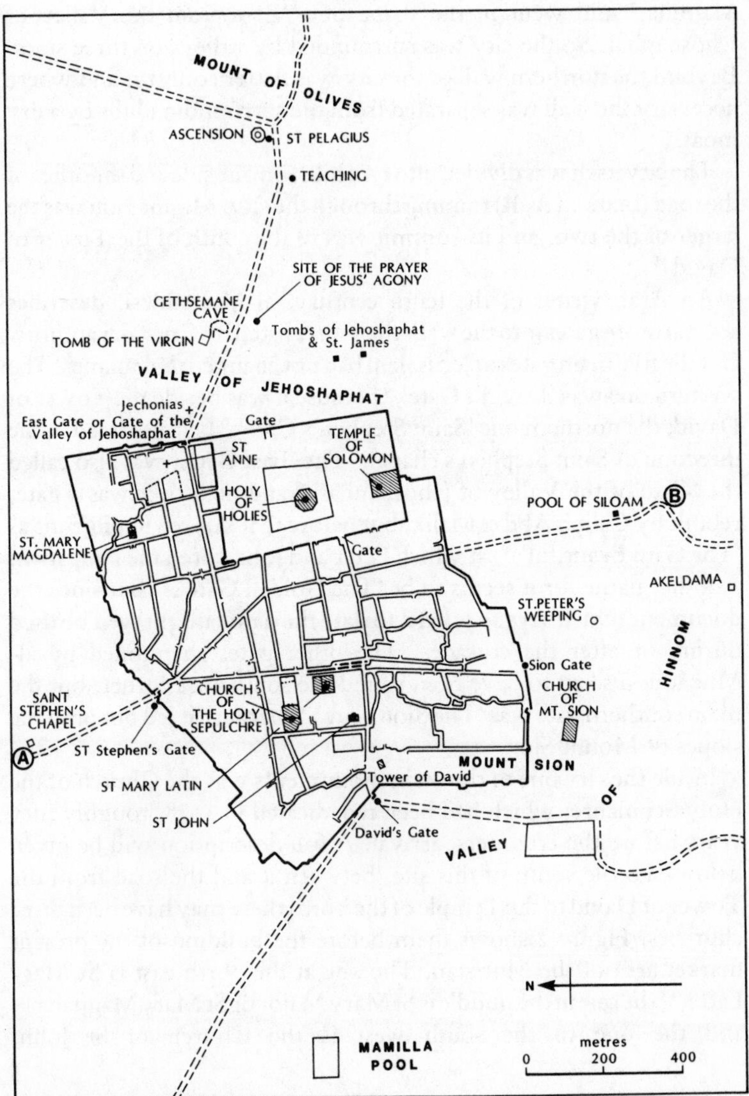

Fig. 1. General Plan of Jerusalem

Hinnom',[1] or 'Gehenna'[2] which started just to the west of the Pool of Mamilla,[3] and went in the shape of a 'Z' to join the Valley of Jehoshaphat. So the city was surrounded by valleys on three sides. Beyond the northern wall of the city was flatter country, and where necessary the wall was separated from the surrounding hills by a dry moat.

The city itself was divided into two hills, on one side and the other of the road (marked A–B) running through the city. Mount Sion was the larger of the two, and its summit was to the south of the Tower of David.[4]

An Arab writer of the tenth century, al-Muqaddesi, describes several more gates into the walls than were listed by Crusader authors. But the five main gates of Jerusalem had not changed their names. The western one was 'David's Gate',[5] because it was beside the Tower of David; the northern one 'Saint Stephen's Gate',[6] because it led in the direction of Saint Stephen's chapel.[7] The 'East Gate'[8] was also called the 'Gate of the Valley of Jehoshaphat',[9] and next to it was a gate, rebuilt by Caliph Abd el Malik, but before that known to pilgrims as 'The Gate Beautiful',[10] at which Peter and John cured the lame man. Another name for it seems to be 'The Golden Gate',[11] but since the document which says so is hard to date the name might well be used during or after the crusades. The other gates mentioned by al-Muqaddesi seem to have been round the south-east corner, but the main southern gate was 'The Sion Gate',[12] because it led out onto the slopes of Mount Sion.

Inside the city one of the main monuments was the Church of the Holy Sepulchre, which had been rededicated in 1048, roughly fifty years before the crusaders' arrival. A full description will be given below. To the south of this site, between it and the road from the Tower of David to the Temple of the Lord, there may have been three churches. Figure 2 shows them before the building of the present market area of the Muristan. The one at the north east is St Mary Latin,[13] the one in the middle is St Mary Major or St Mary Magdalene, and the one to the south west is the Church of St John,

[1] Josh. 18.16.
[2] Matt 5.22.
[3] Strategius 9.6.
[4] Piacenza 21, j.88.
[5] Adomnan 1,1,3, j.95.
[6] Theodosius 28, j.70.
[7] *Passion of Forty Martyrs* 2 (p. 302).
[8] Bordeaux 594.5, e.59.
[9] Bordeaux 594.6, e.59.
[10] Piacenza 17, j.83.
[11] Pseudo-Bede 507: see p. 31, n.1.
[12] El Muqaddesi 167, *PUM*.213.
[13] Bernard 10, j.142.

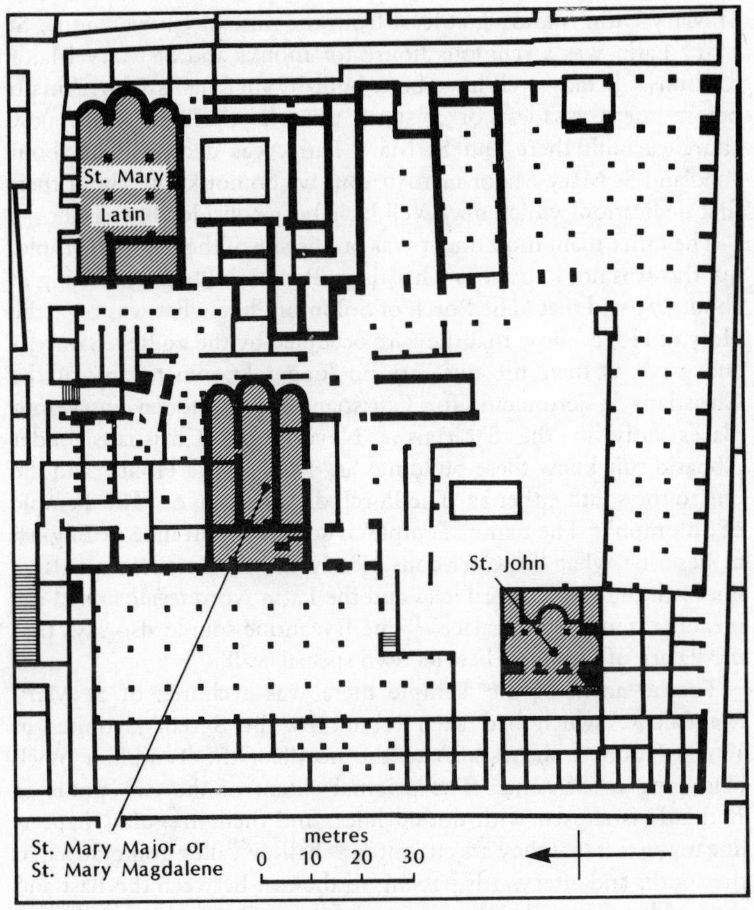

Fig. 2. Plan of Muristan

whose appearance suggests that it was built in the fifth century. Documents exist which say all the three churches were built before the Crusades.[1] Archaeologically St John's certainly did, and St Mary Latin is known at least from the time of Charlemagne. St Mary Latin was a religious house for monks and St Mary Major for nuns.[2] It may well have been built by merchants from Amalfi before the Crusades, or a short time later. There were new churches built there and St Mary Latin was dedicated in about 1060 and St Mary Major in 1080. But we do not know about their first dedication, which may well have been considerably earlier.

The other main monument was on the site of the Jewish Temple, but this was not known to Christians. Patriarch Photius, writing in about 875 said that 'The Porch of Solomon, like what was once the Holy of Holies, now that they are occupied by the godless Saracens and serve as their mosque, are no longer known to any of the Christians in Jerusalem, for Christians are forbidden entry into places holy to the Saracens'.[3] Nevertheless Christians under Abbasid rule knew these buildings as 'The Holy of Holies' and the one to the south either as 'The Porch of Solomon' or 'The Temple of Solomon'.[4] The name 'Temple' is somewhat strange in English to describe what the Christians clearly saw as Solomon's palace, but both the Greek word *naos* and the Latin word *templum* had the meaning 'temple' or 'palace'.[5] The Byzantine source also says that the Palace of Solomon has 'its own special wall'.

To the north of the Temple there was a church of St Mary Magdalene, which had been rebuilt by the Syrian Jacobites in 1092.[6] Figure 1 shows also to the north of the Temple a block belonging to St Anne. The original extent of the two pools of Bethesda is shown with dotted lines, and their irregular shape is due to the fact that they are cut out in a shallow valley going down to the south, and afterwards passing to the east between the East and the Golden Gates. The lower part of this valley had been filled in

[1] See J. Riley-Smith, *The Knights of St John in Jerusalem and Cyprus*, London 1967, 32–7.

[2] See Riley-Smith 36 for a quotation from *Vetus Chronicon Amalphitarum*, ed. F. Ughelli and N. Coleti, in *Italia Sacra*, VII, 198.

[3] Photius, *Q.107* (p. 328), j.123.

[4] Epiphanius M. 2.18, j.117.

[5] See Septuagint Psalm 45.15, Dan 4.29 and Vulgate Psalm 45.15 and Nah 2.6.

[6] See M. De Vogüé, *Les Eglises de la Terre Sainte*, Paris 1860, 291–6, and E. Cerulli, *Etiopi in Palestina*, Vol. 1, Rome 1943, 10–19.

Herodian times. Figure 3 shows a diagram of the buildings remaining today at St Anne's. The commemoration at Saint Anne's had been double. It recalled the Sheep Pool where Jesus had cured the paralysed man (John 5) and it also recalled the upbringing of the Blessed Virgin Mary according to the legendary version in *The Book* (or *Protevangelium*) *of James*, chapters 5 and 6. Of the buildings shown in Figure 3, the right-hand one was rebuilt in about 1140 to house the new Abbey of Nuns. It was then known as the House or the Tomb of St Anne,[1] since it was over a cave. The left-hand church is at present the older of the two, and is over a walled-off part of the smaller pool. But there was an earlier building occupying the site of the right-hand church, and the date of the one on the left is hard to determine. The earliest of the documents translated below both seem to speak of it as the Church of the Sheep Pool,[2] and it might therefore have been built before the Crusades.

On Mount Sion there was a hospice for the Monks of St Saba which was near the Tower of David at a point not certainly known.[3] Outside the walls was the church of Sion, to which we shall return below. Suffice it to say here that this was the earliest known place of Christian worship,[4] and it had been rebuilt in 965.[5] Half way down the hill to the east there was the place of Saint Peter's weeping after he had denied Christ,[6] and down at the bottom was the Pool of Siloam.[7] On the right of this, at the bottom of the Valley of Hinnom, was the field called Akeldama, bought with the thirty pieces of silver returned to the Priests by Judas, and used for the burial of strangers.[8] There was a church there in the ninth century.[9]

In Abbasid times to leave the East Gate of Jerusalem was to start one of three journeys. The longest one was to Jericho, twelve miles away. There was one to Bethany, two miles there and back, and there was the shortest one, up to the top of the Mount of Olives

[1] House of Joachim and Anna, Dan 16, Jph 14.29: Tomb of St Anne Thc 64.
[2] 1Gu 2, Gqu 6.
[3] Cyril of Scythopolis, *Saba* (Schwartz 116.5).
[4] Cyril Jer. *Cat.* 16.4.
[5] Yahya 3,7 in JN 245.
[6] Epiphanius M. 3,16, j.117, and *Commemoratorium* 3, j.137.
[7] Is 8.6, John 9.7, Bordeaux 592, e.157. Church last mentioned by Piacenza 24, j.84.
[8] Eusebius, *On.* 38.20.
[9] Epiphanius M. 8,6, j.120.

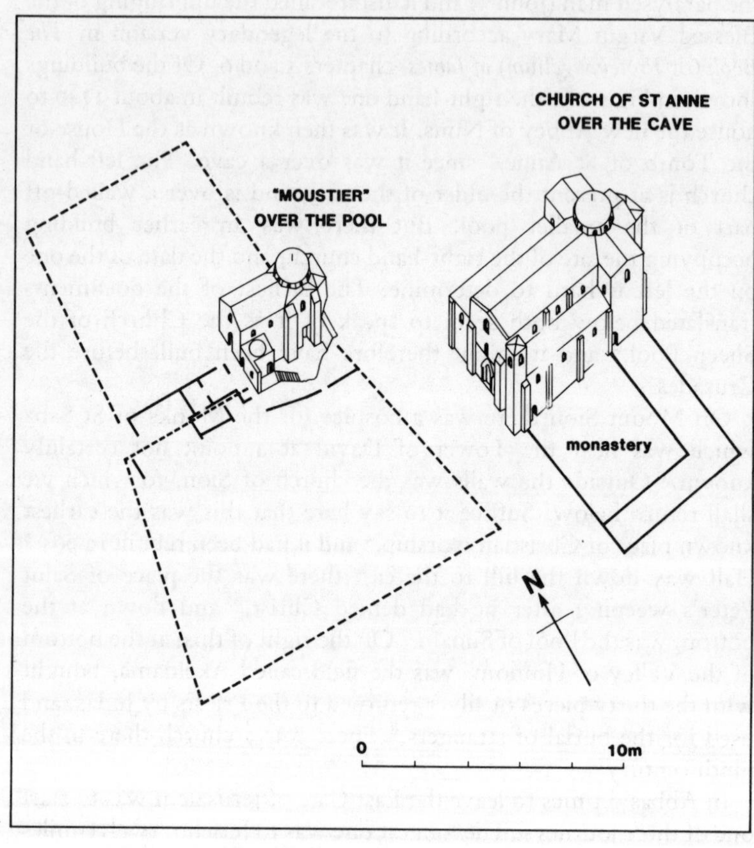

Fig. 3. Diagram of St Anne's

half a mile away. On leaving the East Gate the first monument at which one arrived was a shrine, which marked the place where a Jew named 'Jephonias' in the sources from the Abbasid period had wished to insult the body of the Blessed Virgin Mary as it was being taken to the Tomb.[1] The Tomb of the Virgin was in the bottom of the valley, just across the bed of the Brook Kidron.[2] This had in the ninth century been a monastery,[3] and it was in the 'hamlet' or 'village' of Gethsemane, following the Latin Bible's text.[4] It is not known whether there was a real village there. Next to the Virgin's Tomb was a cave where the disciples are said to have gone to sleep while the prayer of Jesus' Agony took place.[5] This site was marked with a rock a stone's throw away. Jesus then came back to the cave for his arrest.[6]

From Gethsemane could be seen one of the tombs further to the south in the Kidron Valley. They were called by several names, but the ones which persisted till the time of the Crusades were the Tomb of Jehoshaphat, for the one which was visible and nearer, and the Tomb of St James for the further one.[7] Near these tombs there were hermits.[8]

Near the top of the Mount of Olives there were two churches. One of them had been largely ruined in 614 by the Persians, and it was the Church of Christ's Teaching,[9] which Christian authors of the Abbasid period held to be his teaching after the resurrection.[10] But one such pilgrim, Bernard the Monk, was taken there and shown a stone, to which, as he reports, the woman taken in adultery was brought to see Jesus writing on the ground.[11] At any rate, probably from before the Crusades, the Lord's Prayer is the proper subject of Christ's teaching in this church.[12]

At the summit of the Mount of Olives was the cell of St

[1] *Breviarius* 7, j.61.
[2] *Commemoratorium* 10, j.137.
[3] Matt 26.36.
[4] Theodosius 10, j.66.
[5] Eusebius, *On.* 74,16. There was a church there till about 725, Hugeburc 21, j.131, but it was destroyed by the earthquake of A.D. 746.
[6] Bernard 13, j.144.
[7] Jehoshaphat, Adomnan 1.13, j.199. James, Theodosius 9, j.166. See also j.160.
[8] *Commemoratorium* 26, j.137.
[9] Eusebius, *Dem.* 6.18.23.
[10] Epiphanius M. X.20, j.120.
[11] Bernard 14, j.144.
[12] See Daniel 24.

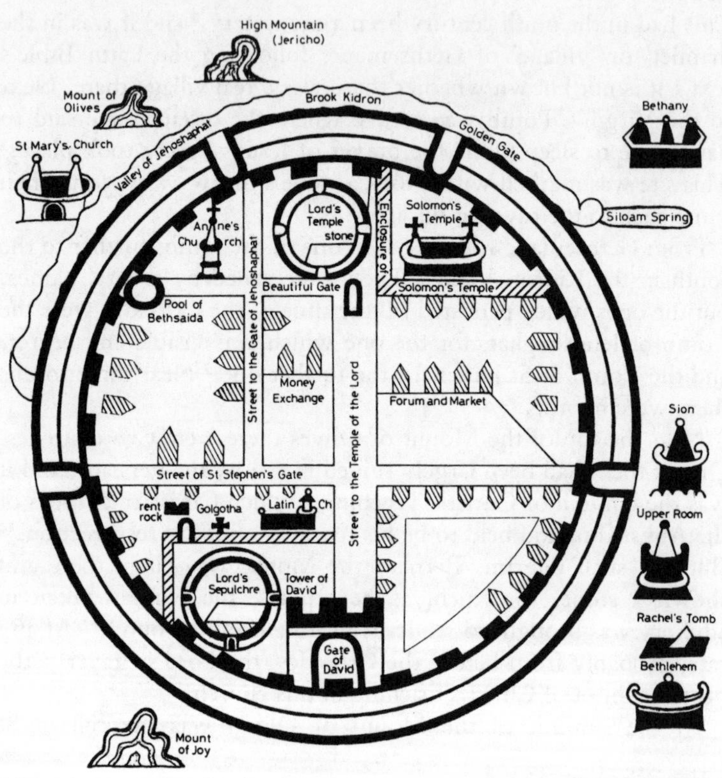

Fig. 4. A plan of Jerusalem copied in the thirteenth or fourteenth century, from Paris (Bib. Nat. Cod. lat. No. 8865 fol. 133).

Pelagius, who lived there as a hermit and until death concealed the fact that she was really a woman.[1] On the Summit of the Mount of Olives was a circular space of rock surrounded by a portico, which commemorated the Ascension of Christ.[2]

There are a good many copies of round maps of Jerusalem,[3] which were made early in the crusader period, and of which we reproduce as Figure 4 the one in Paris. Apart from the Mount of Joy, for which we have no evidence before Crusader times, this map seems to be near the head of it tradition (since all the sites in the city are in roughly the right position). The main horizontal lower street is not divided into three, and the old Church of the Holy Sepulchre is shown. The wall round the Temple of Solomon is shown, but this existed long before the organisation of the Templars. I believe that the relative positions of the Pool of Bethsaida and the Church of Saint Anne, do not give us any reliable information about their true position. The map clearly originates from before 1114, the date when the stone was covered over in the Temple.

CHURCH OF THE HOLY SEPULCHRE

Two phases of work in our period are discernible in the Church of the Holy Sepulchre. The first is the restoration of Emperor Constantine Monomachus, which was dedicated in 1048, of which we know only through the early documents of the Latin Kingdom. The second is the gradual alteration of this building culminating in the addition of a new choir. The completed building was dedicated on 15 July 1149. Two excellent architectural studies have been made of the church, a short one by Father Charles Coüasnon O.P. and a fuller one by Father Virgilio Corbo O.F.M.[4]

[1] Piacenza 16, j.83.

[2] Jerome, *C.Zeph.* 1.15f, Paulinus of Nola, *Letter* 31.4, see j.166b.

[3] The original selection was made by R. Röhricht, *ZDPV* 1890–2, and his plans and some extra ones are reproduced by De Sandoli in Vols 1 and 2 as pages between his sections.

[4] C. Coüasnon, *The Church of the Holy Sepulchre in Jerusalem* (British Academy Schweich Lecture, London 1974) and V. C. Corbo, *Il Santo Sepolcro di Gerusalemme* (Studium Biblicum Franciscanum, Coll.Major, 29) 3 vols, Jerusalem 1981–2.

Not until the nineteenth century was any doubt cast on the authenticity of the site of the Tomb, and then on thoroughly inadequate grounds.[1] Starting in about 160 A.D. pilgrims had objected to the fact that the tomb was inside the city, which was an intolerable position; the Bible said otherwise,[2] and it was contrary to the customs of ancient cities. Inhabitants told the pilgrims that the wall had been extended beyond the tomb after Jesus had been buried, which was historically true. Thus perhaps the site of the Church of the Holy Sepulchre may not be where Jesus was buried, but it probably was.

In 1009 a mad Fatimid Caliph called Hakim had destroyed the Holy Sepulchre itself and a large church known as Constantine's Basilica. This church overlapped the chapels H,G and F shown in Figure 5, and stretched east a long way, down to the bottom of the page. The Tomb of Christ itself was replaced by a replica, standing on the same site as the old one, and Daniel gives a good description of it,[3] even though it may have changed since 1099. The building (called 'The Resurrection' or 'Anastasis'), which had been part of the building of Constantine's period,[4] was given a new roof, which was conical in shape with a hole at the top.[5] According to Daniel[6] it had twelve round columns, but at present it has fourteen. It gave a general impression of being like Charlemagne's church at Aachen (or Aix-la-Chapelle).[7] It had an apse on the east[8] and four gates leading into the court.[9]

The court outside was completely rebuilt within its original north and south walls by Monomachus, and it had a new series of three chapels (which have not been excavated) at the centre on the east. From left to right the first two (H,G) commemorated where Christ was crowned and dressed in the purple robe, where he was stripped of his garments and where his clothes were shared out.[10] The third (F) is where he was bound to a column and scourged.[11] Then came some steps, going down to a place where the Wood of the Cross was said to have been discovered by Empress Helena,[12] and the last chapel in the corner (D) was Christ's Prison.[13] Daniel

[1] C. Gordon, *PEFQS* (1885) 79f.

[2] Melito of Sardis, *On Pascha* ed. S. G. Hall, 1979, pp. 72, 94.

[3] Dan. 10.

[4] 1Gu 2.

[5] Gqu 4.

[6] Dan 10.

[7] Gge 4.

[8] Dan 10.

[9] Gds 3.

[10] See Gqu 4, Got 2, Sae 10.

[11] Gqu 4, Dan 13.

[12] Gqu 4, Got 2.

[13] Epiphanius M. 1,14 j.117, 1Gu 3.

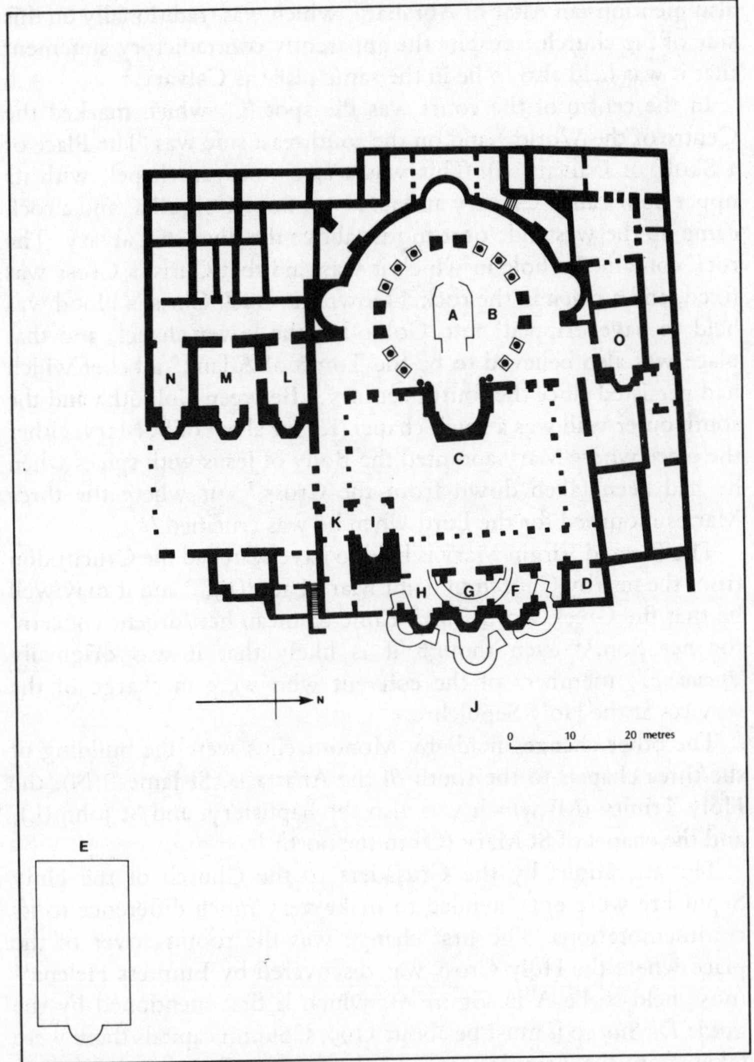

Fig. 5. Rebuilding of the Holy Sepulchre by Monomachus.

also mentions an Altar of Abraham, which was traditionally on this side of the church,[1] despite the apparently contradictory statement that it was held also to be in the same place as Calvary.[2]

In the centre of the court was the spot (C) which marked the Centre of the World,[3] and on the south-east side was 'The Place of a Skull' or Calvary (I). This was a two-storeyed chapel, with its upper floor called Calvary and its lower floor Golgotha, and a rock came up the west side of it to just above the floor of Calvary. The rock contained a hole in which it was said that Christ's Cross was fixed, and a crack in the rock.[4] Down the crack Christ's blood was held to have dripped[5] into Golgotha, the lower chapel, and that place was also believed to be the Tomb of Adam,[6] a belief which had persisted since the fourth century.[7] Between Golgotha and the south outer wall was a small chapel (K)[8] or altar[9] of St Mary: either the place where Mary anointed the Body of Jesus with spices when he had been taken down from the Cross,[10] or where the three Maries mourned for the Lord when he was crucified.[11]

The Blessed Virgin Mary is held to have watched the Crucifixion from the nearby Church of Saint Mary Latin (E),[12] and it may well be that the Greek word *spoudē* came to mean her 'urgent concern' for her Son,[13] even though it is likely that it was originally '*spoudaioi*', members of the convent who were in charge of the services at the Holy Sepulchre.

The other changes made by Monomachus were the building of the three chapels to the south of the Anastasis, St James' (N), the Holy Trinity (M) which was also the baptistery, and St John (L), and the chapel of St Mary (O) to the north.[14]

The alterations by the Crusaders to the Church of the Holy Sepulchre were not intended to make very much difference to its commemorations. The first change was the roofing over of the place where the Holy Cross was discovered by Empress Helena[15] (now held to be A in Figure 6), which is first mentioned by the guide *De Situ* so it must be about 1109. Column capitals there were taken from the Temple area, and the four in Chapel A are exactly

[1] Dan 13, in agreement with the ancient plans by Adomnan: see j.197.
[2] 1Gu 2.
[3] 1Gu 2, Sae 10.
[4] Got 2.
[5] Nik 87.
[6] 1Gu 2.
[7] Epiphanius of Salamis, *Haer.*4,6,5.
[8] Sae 11.
[9] Gds 3.
[10] Jn 19.39 (?) and Sae 11.
[11] Wge 162.
[12] 1Gu 2, Sae 13.
[13] Dan 13.
[14] Sae 12.
[15] Gds 03, Jwü 151f.

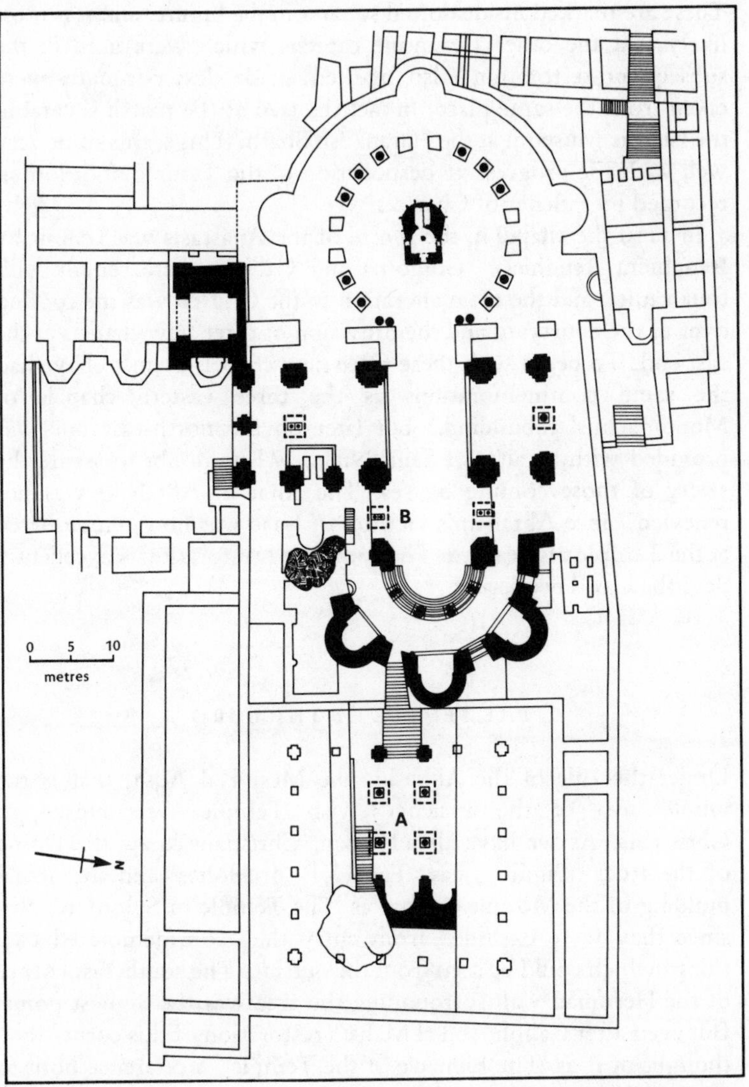

Fig. 6. The completed Latin Kingdom rebuilding of the Holy Sepulchre.

the same size as the ones in Al Aksa, or the Temple of Solomon. These are marked inside dotted squares in the Figure, and it is most likely that the other Byzantine capitals which were used in the subsequent restoration (also marked inside dotted squares)were taken from the same place. In fact the two at (B) match several in the Islamic Museum at the Haram esh Sharif. This seems to fit very well with the progressive despoliation of the Temple of Solomon recorded by Fulcher of Chartres.

In 1119 the chapel in the centre of the Anastasis was rebuilt by Renghiera Renghieri.[1] Golgotha and Calvary were rebuilt with four vaults, and the main alteration to the Church was the roofing over of the courtyard and the provision of three new chapels at the east end. To begin with these three new chapels seem to have had the same commemorations as the three eastern chapels of Monomachus' rebuilding,[2] but later on the north-east one was provided with an altar of Saint Nicholas,[3] no doubt to assure the safety of those coming by sea. The Altar of Abraham was not renewed, since Abraham's sacrifice of Isaac was now remembered at the Temple of the Lord. The completed restoration is excellently described by Theoderic.[4]

THE TEMPLE OF THE LORD

Under the rule of the Abbasids the Mesjid al Aqsa, that is the whole area of the ancient Jewish Temple, was closed to Christians. As we have already seen, Christians knew the Dome of the Rock (Figure 7) as 'The Holy of Holies' and the actual building of the Mosque al Aqsa as 'The Temple of Solomon'. But since they were excluded from entry they commemorated two things which could be seen from the outside. The south-east corner of the Herodian wall surrounding the area was the highest point. But even after Caliph Abd al Malik's restoration of this corner they thought of it as 'The Pinnacle of the Temple', a reference both to

[1] See Corbo, *Sepolcro*, vol. 1, p. 199, referring to G. Mariti, *Istoria dello stato presente della città di Gerusalemme*, Tom. 1, Livorno 1790, 142.
[2] See Gic 38, 41.
[3] Thc 24.
[4] Thc 11–33.

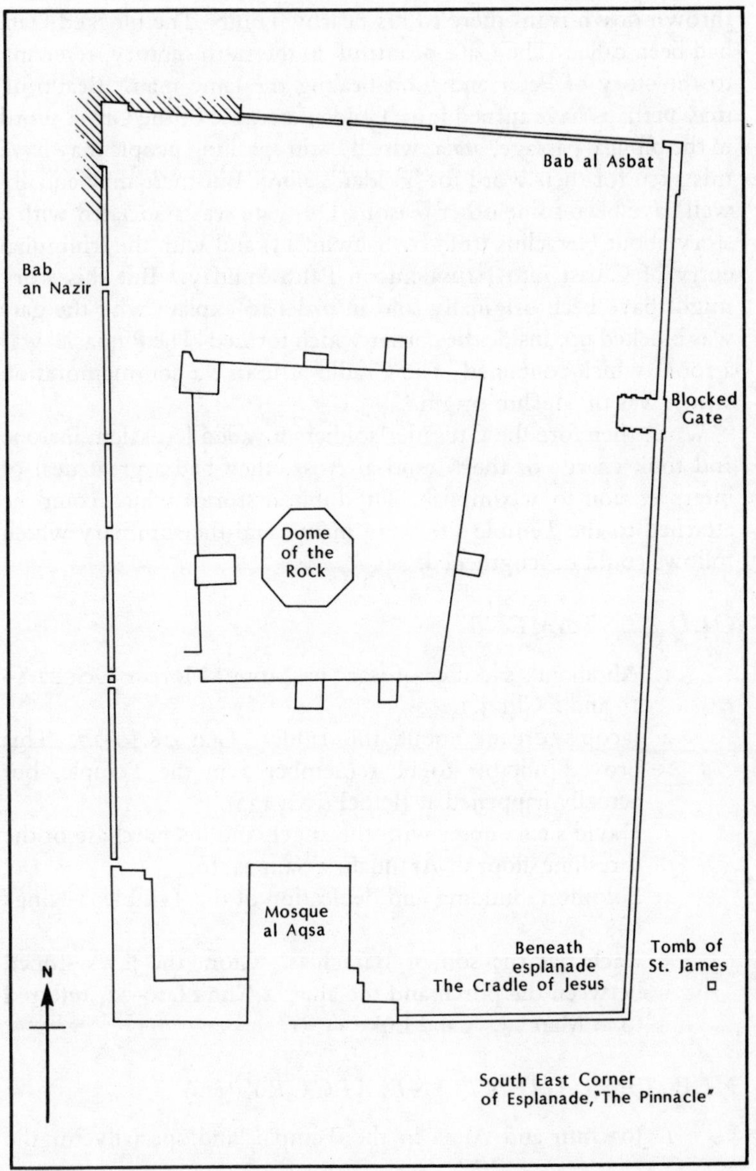

Fig. 7. The Masjid al Aqsa under Abbasid rule.

Christ's temptation[1] and to the death of St James,[2] who had been thrown down from there to his nearby Tomb. The blocked Gate had been called 'The Gate Beautiful' in the sixth century, referring to the story of Peter and John healing the lame man. 'Beautiful' may perhaps have turned into 'Golden' because of the Greek word in the biblical passage, *oraia*, which Latin speaking people may have mistaken for their word for 'golden', *aurea*. But there may equally well have been some other reason. This gate was associated with a story about Heraclius (told by Saewulf 15) and with the triumphal entry of Christ into Jerusalem on Palm Sunday.[4] But this story might have been originally told in order to explain why the gate was blocked up. Inside the corner which formed 'The Pinnacle' was a room which contained 'The Cradle of Jesus', a commemoration which was of Muslim origin.[5]

When therefore the Crusader soldiers invaded Jerusalem in 1099 and took charge of the Mesjid al Aqsa, they had a great deal of interpretation to accomplish. The biblical stories which could be attached to the Temple site were many, and the summary which follows could be lengthened.

OLD TESTAMENT

1. Abraham's sacrifice of Isaac on Mount Moriah: Gen 22.1–19 and 2 Chr 3.1.
2. Jacob's dream about the ladder: Gen 28.10–17. This proved suitable to be remembered in the Temple, but actually happened at Bethel (Jwu 122).
3. David's encounter with the angel, and his purchase of the threshing-floor of Araunah: 2 Sam 24.16.
4. Solomon' building and dedication of the Temple: 1 Kings 6–8.
5. Zacharias the son of Barachias, whom the Jews stoned between the porch and the altar: 2 Chr 24.20–22, referred to in Matt 23.35 and Luke 11.51.

NEW TESTAMENT AND APOCRYPHA

1. Joachim and Anna in the Temple, and specially for the

[1] Matt 4.5. [2] Gregory of Tours, *Miracles* 1.27.
[3] Acts 3.2. [4] Mark 11.11, Hrabanus Maurus, *Homilies* 70.
[5] Ibn Abd Rabbih, 3.367, Muqaddesi 170f, *PUM* 166.

Presentation of the Blessed Virgin Mary: *Book* (or *Protevangelium*) *of James* 7.

2. The Angel Gabriel's announcement to Zacharias that he would have a son, John the Baptist: Luke 1.5–23.
3. The Presentation of Christ in the Temple and the prophecy of Simeon: Luke 2.22–35.
4. Christ sitting among the doctors: Luke 2.46.
5. Jesus driving the money-changers out of the Temple: Matt 21.12, John 2.14–16.
6. Jesus forgiving the adulterous woman: John 8.2–11.
7. Peter and John healing a lame man at the Gate Beautiful: Acts 3.1–10.

Pilgrims in Crusader times approached the Temple down the street now called the 'Street of the Chain', and entered by going across a bridge to 'The Gate of the Chain' (Figure 8). Some pilgrims still treated the Blocked Gate on the other side of the enclosure as the Gate Beautiful,[1] but the majority of pilgrims thought that it was the gate by which they entered the enclosure.[2] There was a pool on the way through the outer court,[3] but there are so many cisterns and pools in the Haram esh Sharif today that it is hard to know to which one they referred. Then they went up the steps to the west of the Dome of the Rock and, when they reached the top, saw in front of them an altar turned into a sundial, which may have been on the site of al Qubbat al Miraj or al Qubbat an Nebi. Perhaps the Qubbat al Miraj was the site of the altar, and the Qubbat an Nebi was where Zacharias the son of Berechiah was killed,[5] but an alternative site for the altar may have been the mosaic picture of the Roman column.[6]

The Dome of the Rock, or the Templum Domini, was a confusing building to the Crusaders. Some of them thought that the building had been built by a Byzantine Emperor, among them the first Prior of the religious community attached to the Temple.[7] Some did not know.[8] But from 1106 onwards some Latins and, we

[1] Got 3.
[2] For instance Gqu 5.
[3] Thc 35.
[4] Wge 142, Gid 33, 7Gu 101.
[5] Thc 37.
[6] 7Gu 102, Thc 39.
[7] Acard of Arrouaise, *Tractatus super Templo Domini, A.O.L.* 1,579, lines 481f, 486, and Thc 44,46.
[8] Jwü 123, Albert of Aix, *Hist. Hierosol.* 6.24.

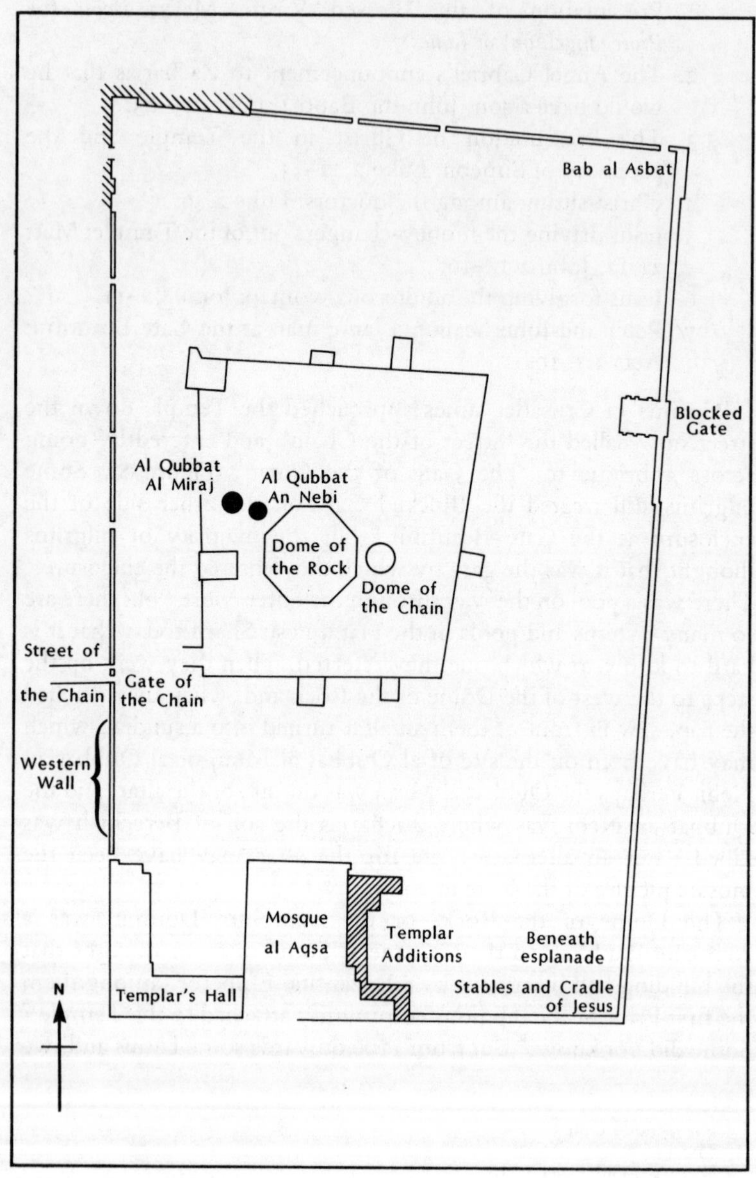

Fig. 8. The Temple of the Lord.

may suppose, all Greeks realised that it had been built by 'pagans' or Muslims.[1] The confusion between pagans and Muslims was real enough. Some people who wrote early on in the Latin Kingdom thought that before 1099 the Muslims in the Dome of the Rock worshipped an idol of the Prophet Muhammad.[2]

The Dome of the Rock is well described by several pilgrims,[3] but its likeness to the Temple was questioned. By the Greeks the Dome was known as 'The Holy of Holies',[4] and most people thought that the ancient Holy of Holies had been at or somewhere near the site, on the Rock in the middle,[5] or in the cave underneath.[6] Al Idrisi thought that it was the Dome of the Chain to the east.[7] The Rock was covered and surrounded by walls in 1115,[8] but the existence of it was obvious to those who went down to the cave. By 1170 a Cross had been put on top of the Dome, which caused great annoyance to Muslims.[9]

Other biblical memories were common. The stone pillow of Jacob was shown in the Dome of the Rock.[10] Various liturgical objects suitable to Solomon's erection of the Temple were said by early pilgrims to be hidden in the building.[11] And one of the cisterns to the north of the Dome was associated with Ezekiel's prophecy about water coming forth from the Temple.[12]

The chief gospel event which was celebrated in the Templum Domini was the Presentation of Christ,[13] but there was a subsidiary place just inside the old Pinnacle of the Temple, the Mosque of Mary which contained the Cradle of Jesus.[14] This seems to be a Muslim site taken over by Christians, for no Christian could have gone there before 1099. The Angel Gabriel announced that Zachariah would have a son in the cave below the Dome of the Rock,[15] and this was also the place where Christ forgave the adulteress. Hence it became known as the place where pilgrims came for Confession.[16] A footprint of Christ was shown on the

[1] Dan 17, Fulcher, *Hist.* 1,26 (ms.L).
[2] Fulcher, *Hist.* 1.28 (ms.L) and Raoul of Caen, *Gesta Tancredi*, 129. See also X. Muratova, in *Crusader Art in the Twelfth Century*, ed. J. Folda (*BAR International Series No. 152*), Oxford 1982, pp. 47–69.
[3] Dan 17, Jwu 125, Thc 38.
[4] Dan 17m Jph 20.22.
[5] 7Gu 102.
[6] Sae 14, Dan 17, Pde C3.
[7] Gid 33.
[8] Pde C3.
[9] Jwü 126.
[10] Gqu 5, Dan 17.
[11] Gqu 5, Got 3, and 7Gu 102.
[12] Ezek 47.1 and Jwu 125.
[13] Sae 15, Gds 2.
[14] Nasir-i-Khosrau 33, *PMU*.166.
[15] Got 3.
[16] Sae 15, Gge 4.

Rock, connected with one or another of his visits to the Temple,[1] and the Lamp which hung in the middle of the Dome[2] is later said to be filled with the Blood of Christ.[3] Another New Testament memory which involved a change of location, was the martyrdom of St James, eventually celebrated at the Dome of the Chain,[4] and John of Würzburg reports both the old and the new positions for the Pinnacle of the Temple.[5] Another seemingly biblical memory is that of Christ turning water into wine in a marble urn in the Temple.[6]

Many of the Latin Kingdom pilgrims give the above references, which are in one sense a series of biblical events creating a sacred history of the Temple. But the key notion which summed up the meaning of the place was that it was the site of the 'Tabernacle', a theological and not a literal notion. *Qualiter* 5 is shown the Rock in the Temple of the Lord as 'the Temple not made with hands', which would fit very well the phrase in Mark 14.58 where Jesus Christ says he is to build such a Temple. Solomon's Temple was a prophecy for the Christian reality, the church, and people in the crusader period still used the word 'temple' in Greek or Latin to mean a church.[7] Like that ancient Temple, the church was a place where God hears prayer, and was itself a foretaste of heaven. Hence the site of Solomon's Temple becomes a place for remembering the Christian church. So John of Würzburg and Theoderic give a list of inscriptions from the Dome of the Rock which are almost all of them taken from services to do with the Christian dedication of a church.[8]

Inside the Dome of the Rock an altar was dedicated to St Nicholas,[9] no doubt for the same reason that it had been in the Holy Sepulchre, for safety at sea. It has a date on it which may be 1161 or 1162.

The northern part of the upper platform containing the Dome of the Rock was occupied by the Canons of the Temple of the Lord, and as an archaeological reminder of this the two north-west arched entrances which lead down to the Lower Court have crusader capitals on their columns, which is no doubt a sign that the upper court had to be cleared by the Muslims on the return of the Haram

[1] See Sae 15, Pde C3, and Jwü 121.
[2] Gqu 5.
[3] Pde C3.
[4] 7Gu 102.
[5] Jwü 120 (as Gge 1) and Jwü 123.
[6] Gqu 5, Pde C3.
[7] For instance Jph 12.12, Gge 4, Pde C1, Gic 42).
[8] Jwü 127, Thc 38.
[9] Thc 40. For the date see P. Thomsen, *ZDPV* (1921) 38, note 71.

esh Sharif to their care. The other entrances[1] all have Byzantine capitals. The Canons must also have had the rest of the area to the north in the lower court.

The south part of the area, behind the wall which is shown in Figure 4, became the property of the Templars, who were founded in 1118. The chief building this contained was the Mosque al Aqsa[2] (Figure 8), but the Templars also went underground to the Umayyad vaults holding up the platform, which they had as their stable[3]. They built defences outside the south wall of the Haram esh Sharif,[4] and one of the many new buildings they erected,[5] still most impressive in size, is the hall to the west of the Mosque al Aqsa (N).

The Canons of the Temple controlled the northern part of the Haram esh Sharif from a time very soon after 1099, but the other holy places were under no general authority except that of the King. When King Baldwin was dead in 1118, Fulcher of Chartres wrote as follows.

> 'It is now a matter for serious regret that the fabric of the roof [of the Temple of Solomon] needs repairing, ever since it passed into the hands of King Baldwin and our people. This is due to our lack of resources. Indeed if any lead fell down, or was taken down from the roof by his orders, he was even selling it to the merchants'.[6]

In his second revision, published in 1128, he wrote,

> 'Because of our lack of resources we were not able even to maintain this building in the condition in which we found it. For this reason it is mostly destroyed'.[7]

This sad tale would be in harmony with the stealing of the capitals for the Holy Sepulchre.

Jews went outside the Haram to the Western Wall,[8] but some Saracens came in to pray in the time of John of Würzburg. They prayed at the Qubbat al Miraj.[9]

[1] Jwü 128f, Thc 36.
[2] Dan 18.
[3] Thc 48–50.
[4] Btu 23, Jwü 130, Thc 36.
[5] Gid. 33, Jwü 129, Thc 46.
[6] Fulcher, *Hist.* 1.26, revision of 1118.
[7] *Ibid.* revision of 1124.27.
[8] Btu 23.
[9] Jwü 123.

MOUNT SION IN ABBASID TIMES

Though it has already been briefly described, Mount Sion is the next place to be considered. Since it lay off the general route, which often enough was to go to the Holy Sepulchre and then to the Temple of the Lord, Mount Sion seems to have been fitted in to any place which was convenient in the pilgrimage.

To reach Mount Sion from the Tower of David a visitor had to go outside the walls, until the Church of Mount Sion had been fortified,[1] or failing that through the Sion Gate, which meant a journey two hundred and fifty yards east to the gate, and then back up the hill to the Church.

The Tower of David is well analysed by John Phocas[2] as being originally the work of Herod, but pilgrims still went up it and remembered where David wrote the Psalter.[3] Near it was the Hospice of St Saba, and a little further up the street to the south a chapel belonging to St Menas, which was never mentioned by pilgrims.[4] Near the Sion Gate were the Prison of St Peter and the House of Judas,[5] if we are to rely on the account of Daniel, who may well have been shown sites traditional in pilgrimage before 1099.

Outside Sion Gate to the right there were three holy sites: the one on the south was the Church of Mount Sion, rebuilt in 965 by a learned Jacobite Christian called Ali Suwar,[6] and the one on the left was a Chapel, the Praetorium.[7] Between these was a chapel called was the Pavement (*lithostrōton*),[8] which by its name suggests that it was where Pilate judged Christ. Before 614 this commemoration had been in a different place near the Temple.

Sion Church was held to be the first church in the world, 'The Mother of all the Churches' in the words of a fourth-century prayer,[9] and hence it had had a wealth of commemorations. Christians thought of it basically as the house and the upper room[10] to which the Apostles retreated after the Resurrection, and where

[1] Gid 34, Thc 55.
[2] Jph 26.1.
[3] Piacenza 21, j.83 and Dan 14.
[4] Cyril Sc., *Euthymius*, Schwartz 49.3.
[5] Dan 14.
[6] Yahya 3,7, *JN* 245.
[7] *Commemoratorium* 4, j.137.
[8] Epiphanius M. II.21, j.117.
[9] F. E. Brightman, *Liturgies Eastern and Western*, Vol. 1, Oxford 1896, 54, line 27.
[10] Acts 1.13.

they experienced the descent of the Holy Spirit at Pentecost.[1] Hence it was also regarded as the house in which the risen Jesus appeared twice to his apostles,[2] and to have been the upper room of the Last Supper,[3] and where Christ washed the feet of his disciples.[4] The belief that it was the house of the Apostles led to the belief that it was the property of St John the Evangelist (or 'Theologian'). After Jesus had committed the Blessed Virgin Mary into his care she lived and died there.[5]

In fact a plan, made in about 680, of the church before the rebuilding exists in a copy made a few years later.[6] Figure 9 is a diagram of this plan, with an axis at right angles to the original, to make it easier to compare with Figure 10. Figure 10 is a perspective diagram of the arrangement of the Church of Sion after 965. The levels are not at all clear, and the position of Mary's death is not certain. But the general positions are as the crusader pilgrims describe them. The only real change seems to be that the Descent of the Holy Spirit has moved from the west end of the church to the east end, and that there are fewer signs of the trial of Jesus in the church itself, although there was a column near the choir which simple people had the practice of walking round.[7] There is no sign that this column had anything to do with the column of scourging which appears on the seventh-century plan.

In fact the seventh-century plan seems to be a mixture of the trial by Pilate (the top chapel, which was corrected to form part of the main church by some reader), and the scourging, represented by the pillar. This turned out to be a temporary arrangement, as by 808 the new Praetorium on Mount Sion had been built, and before the Crusades there was also a place on Mount Sion (if not yet a chapel) of the Pavement. Mount Sion thus became devoted to Pilate's trial and scourging of Jesus Christ.

Below Mount Sion Church there was another, dedicated to the Tears of St Peter after he had denied Christ,[8] and under this church there was a cave where he hid. In crusader times the same name was

[1] Acts 12.1–13, Cyril, *Cat.* 16.4.
[2] John 20, 19,26, Egeria, *Travels* 39, e.140.
[3] Luke 22.12, Hippolytus of Thebes, *Texts* 1.5 (Diekamp 30).
[4] John 13.2–5, Sophronius, *Anacr.* 20.62, j.91.
[5] Hippolytus of Thebes, *Texts* 1.4 (Diekamp 6).
[6] Adomnan 1,18,1, j.100, and see j.195, Plate 3.
[7] Thc 56.
[8] *Commemoratorium* 3, j.137, Sae 21.

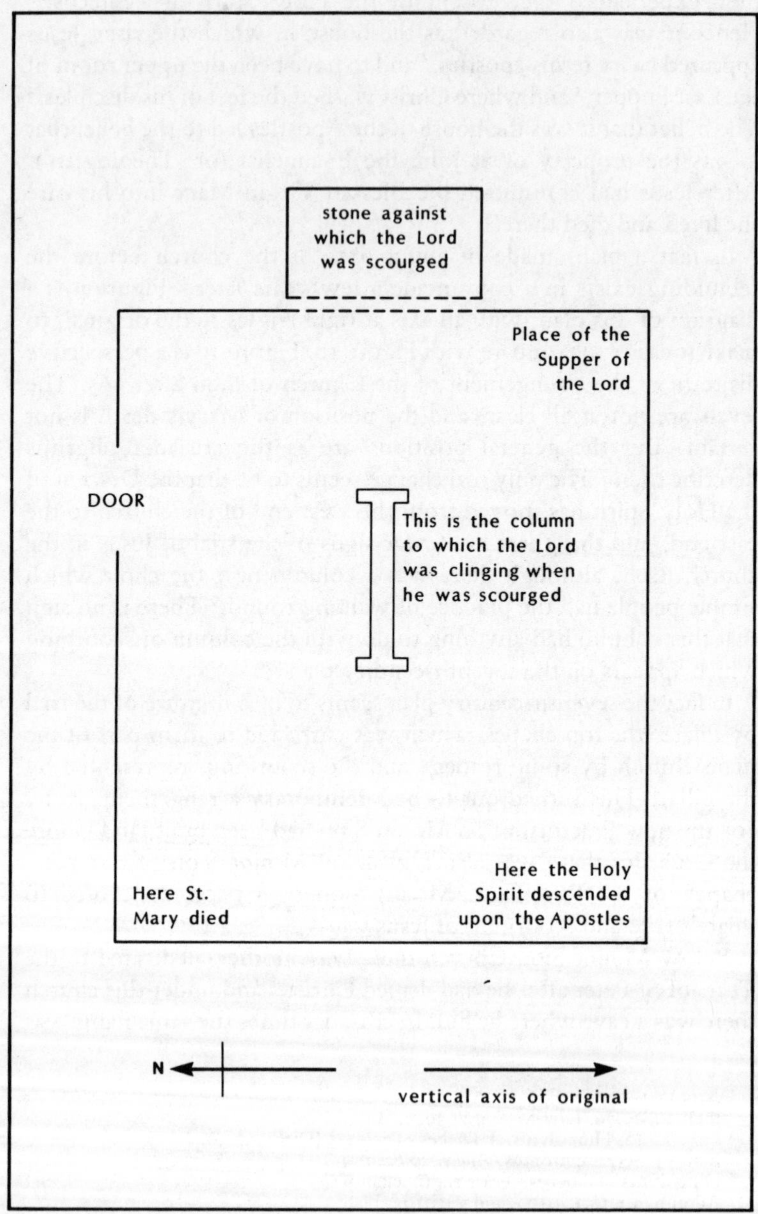

Fig. 9. Seventh-century plan of the Church on Mount Sion.

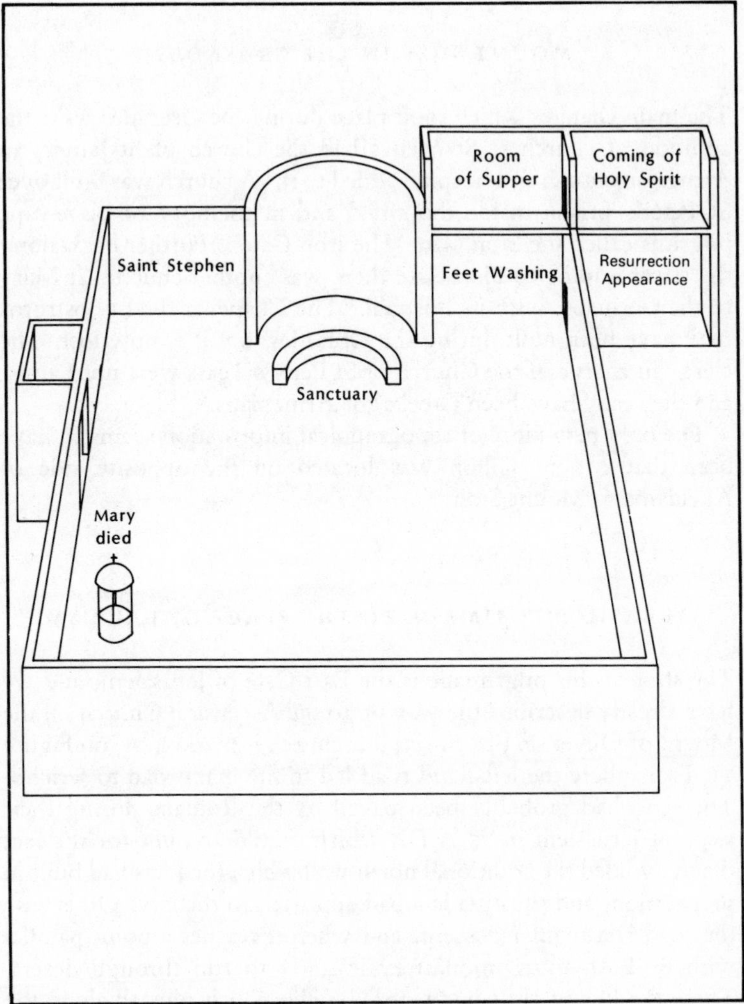

Fig. 10. Mount Sion Church, built in 965.

used for the chapel of the Resurrection appearance on the south of the east end of Sion Church and for the cave of St Peter. This may be further evidence that the muddle arising out of the Persian invasion had not yet been cleared up.

MOUNT SION IN THE CRUSADES

The main changes which took place during the Crusades were the addition of churches. St Menas had the church of St James, an Armenian church and hospital added to it.[1] A church was built over St Peter's prison inside the city,[2] and in memory of his escape pilgrims called the Sion Gate 'The Iron Gate'.[3] Further back along the street leading to Sion Gate there was another church, St Mary of the Germans, with its hospital.[4] The Chapel at the Lithostrotos may have been built during the Crusades, but it is now lost. The clergy in charge of the Church of St Peter's Tears were not Latins, and they may have been Greeks[5] or Armenians.[6]

The only new piece of topographical information seems to have been that Mount Gihon was located on the opposite side of Akeldama to Mount Sion.[7]

ABBASID PILGRIMAGE TO THE PLACE OF BAPTISM

The start of this pilgrimage is the East Gate of Jerusalem, and we have already described the way up to the Ascension Church on the Mount of Olives on pp. 29–33: this church is marked 'A' on Figure 11. From there the left-hand road led to the main road to Jericho. The road had probably been paved by the Romans during their siege of Jerusalem in 70 A.D., which would account for the fact that it avoided the additional north wall which the Jews had built in preparation, and thus made a bad approach to the city. Otherwise the road is a regular descent, and when it reaches a point parallel with St Euthymius' monastery it starts to run through desert. There is a line of cliffs just before Jericho which runs all along the valley, and while Jericho is watered by some springs, it is in fact an

[1] Jwü 160.
[2] Dan 15, Jwü 161, and see N. Avigad, *Discovering Jerusalem*, Nashville, Tennessee, 1983, 249f.
[3] Jwü 163.
[4] Jwü 161, A. Sharon, *Planning Jerusalem*, Jerusalem 1973, 182.
[5] Jwü 140.
[6] Thc 63.
[7] Jwü 158.

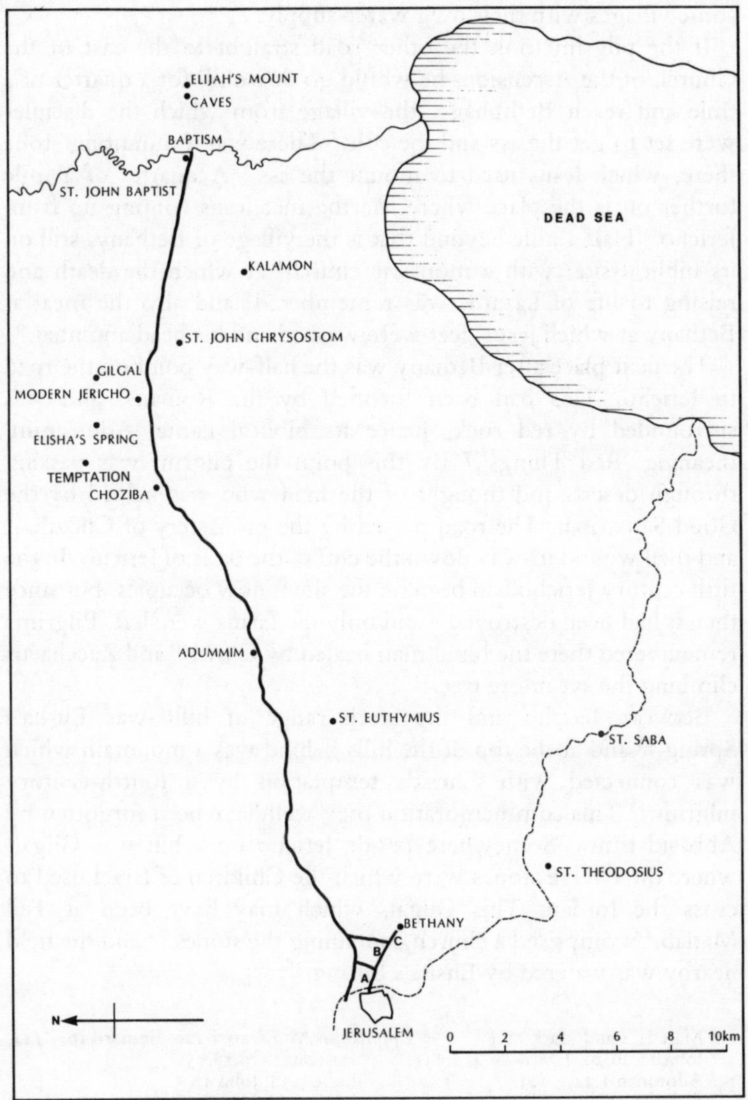

Fig. 11. Road from Jerusalem to Place of Baptism.

oasis in the plain of the Jordan River, which is all desert, apart from some villages with their own water-supply.

If the pilgrim took the other road straight to the east of the Church of the Ascension, he would go downhill for a quarter of a mile and reach Bethphage, the village from which the disciples were set to get the ass and the colt.[1] There was a mounting stone there, which Jesus used to mount the ass.[2] A quarter of a mile further on is the place where Martha met Jesus coming up from Jericho.[3] Half a mile beyond that is the village of Bethany, still on its biblical site, with a monastic church[4] at which the death and raising to life of Lazarus was remembered[5] and also the meal at Bethany at which Jesus' feet were washed and his head anointed.[6]

The next place after Bethany was the half-way point on the road to Jericho. This had been fortified by the Romans, and was surrounded by red rock, hence its biblical name 'Adummim' meaning 'Red Things'.[7] By this point the pilgrim was passing through desert, and thought of the man who was helped by the Good Samaritan. The road passed by the monastery of Choziba,[8] and then wound its way down the cliff to the oasis of Jericho. In the fifth century Jericho had been on the site it now occupies, but since then it had been destroyed,[9] and only the farms were left. Pilgrims remembered there the blind man healed by Christ[10] and Zacchaeus climbing the sycamore tree.[11]

Between Jericho and the steep range of hills was Elisha's Spring,[12] and at the top of the hills behind was a mountain which was connected with Christ's temptation by a fourth-century pilgrim.[13] This commemoration may well have been forgotten by Abbasid times. Somewhere beside Jericho on a hill was Gilgal, where the twelve stones were which the Children of Israel used to cross the Jordan. This Gilgal, which may have been at Tell Matlab,[14] comprised a church containing the stones,[15] and the field nearby was watered by Elisha's Spring.[16]

[1] Matt 21.1 and Mark 11.1 [2] Epiphanius M. IX.10, j.120, Bernard 16, j.144.
[3] John 11 20,29, Egeria 29.4, e.131. [4] Eusebius, *On.*58.15.
[5] Adomnan 1.24, j.101. [6] Luke 7.38, John 12.3.
[7] A different source of the name is given in Jerome, *Letter* 108, 12,3, j.51.
[8] Cyril Scyth. *Saba* (Schwartz 134).
[9] Piacenza 11 and Adomnan 2,13,4, j.81,106.
[10] Matt 10.46. [11] Luke 19.2.
[12] 2 Kgs 2.19–22, Epiphanius M.IX,16, j.121. [13] see Valerius, *Letter* 26, e.177.
[14] A. Augustinović, *Gierico e Dintorni*, Jerusalem 1951, 145ff.
[15] Josh 4.19, 5.3,10, Hugeburc 17, j.129. [16] Theodosius 18, j.69.

From this point the road to the Place of Baptism soon reverted to desert. There had been many monasteries and hermitages down by the Jordan, and there was a monastery of St John the Baptist[1] at the top of the steep slope which led down to the river bed. The road went down to the river, and to the Place of Baptism, where there was a column.[2] The Place of Baptism was also associated with the crossing of the Jordan by Elijah and Elisha,[3] and beyond the river near the Wadi Kharrar were the cave where Elijah stayed[4] and the mountain from which he arose in his fiery chariot.[5] This mountain may also have been called 'Hermoniim'.[6] There was also a cave where St John the Baptist is said to have lived.[7]

The view from Jericho included Mount Nebo, to the north of the end of the Dead Sea.[8] The Place of Baptism was famous for the ceremony at the Feast of Epiphany when Christians went down and bathed there.[9]

CRUSADER PILGRIMAGE TO THE PLACE OF BAPTISM

The way from the East Gate of Jerusalem to Bethany was rebuilt by the Latin Kingdom with new churches. The Tomb of the Virgin was still ruined in 1106, but in 1112 work had already begun to restore it.[10] Later the new church is described.[11] A place for the stoning of St Stephen seems to have been pointed out in the Valley of Jehoshaphat,[12] and this was an alternative to other places. By the time the *Second Guide* was written there was a new church built over the site of Christ's prayer of Agony in Gethsemane.[13] Up the Mount of Olives the first Church was still connected with the Teaching of Christ, but nearly all crusader pilgrims specially connected it with his teaching of the Lord's Prayer, and the stone on which it was written was shown[14] in the church.[15] There was a

[1] Epiphanius M. XI,17, j. 121.
[2] Mark 1.9–11, Theodosius 20, j.69.
[3] 2 Kgs 2.8,14, Jerome, *Letter* 108, 12,5, j.51.
[4] See under the word 'Cherith', j.154a.
[5] 2 Kgs 2.1–11, Bordeaux 598.1, e.161.
[6] Theodosius 20, j.59, and see 163a.
[7] Epiphanius M. XII,1, j.121.
[8] Egeria 12, e.106.
[9] Piacenza 11, j.82.
[10] See the Letter of Patriarch Arnulf of Rohes, in N.-F. Delaborde, *Chartes de la Terre Sainte provenant de l'Abbaye de N.-D. de Josaphat*, Paris 1880, 21f.
[11] Gid 14, Jwü 163, Thc 57.
[12] Gge 1, Wge 172, Pde I.
[13] 2Gu 124.
[14] Gej 15, Thc 68; 2Gu 125.
[15] Dan 23f, Gid 34.

new church of the Ascension, still with its footprint,[1] a new church of Pelagia,[2] and a new monastery on the site of Melania's Foundation, which was built by Emperor Manuel Porphyrogenitus.[3] The view from the Mount of Olives is pointed out.[4]

Bethphage is at first described as 'ruined',[5] and Daniel, whether by design or mistake, says that the pillar which is there was where Martha met Jesus,[6] though other pilgrims point out site 'C' on Figure 11.[7] John of Würzburg is the first to mention the new church there. Bethany now has a 'double church',[8] perhaps a public one for the raising of St Lazarus and another one of St Mary and St Martha for nuns,[9] which must have been built after 1143, when the convent was founded.

Six crusader pilgrims came through Bethany to the Place of Baptism and eight, choosing the slightly shorter journey, did not. The Jordan was the boundary between 'Judaea', in the political sense of the Latin Kingdom, and 'Arabia', the country of the hostile Saracens, and was thus a front line of defence. This and previous hardships had led to the diminution of the number of monasteries there, and Daniel and John Phocas visit only three;[11] they also seem to have transferred Hermoniim to the Judaean side of the river.[12] But they continued to bathe in the River Jordan.[13] As a result of pilgrims having to spend the night there a special camp, Abraham's Garden, was designed for their use, and became well defended.[14]

New emphasis was placed on the High Mountain,[15] the Mount of Christ's Temptation, or the Quarantana.[16] The monastery there was Latin, and a Latin saint was commemorated there,[17] and neither of the two people with loyalty to the Greeks visited it. Details of Christ being tempted there varied from one reporter to another.[18] And by 1170 the place was fortified.

1 Thc 66; Gic 52.
2 Wge 168.
3 Jph 15.14.
4 See Dan 25.
5 Sae 23.
6 Dan 19.
7 Gbe 6, 7Gu 105.
8 Gds 7.
9 Thc 68.
10 Sae 24.
11 Dan 34, 37, Jph 22.1, 23.2, 24.5.
12 Dan 28, Jph 23.1.
13 Sig 14.
14 Sae 24, Thc 74.
15 Matt 4.8.
16 Gej 18, Gqu 8, Got 7; see 'Gabaon' in Dan 36.
17 Piligrinus, Thc 71.
18 See Wge 201.

When Daniel reports on the Shunammite woman's house 'not far from Gilgal'[1] he may have been making a mistake. But the two accounts are set together in the Bible.[2]

The pilgrimage to the Jordan included a great deal of desert travelling. Hence there may be some reference to an earlier pilgrimage to the desert, and the references to the distance to Mount Sinai[3] may have been part of a guide to this pilgrimage. Soldiers went there, but Mount Sinai was not a place included in crusader pilgrimage.

ABBASID PILGRIMAGE TO HEBRON

It was a good day's journey from Jerusalem to Hebron, and if the pilgrim stopped long at Bethlehem it was longer than a day. In Jerusalem, once out of the Gate by the Tower of David the left-hand road went down the Valley of Hinnom, and up the other side to the south. After three miles there was a monastery of the Blessed Virgin Mary, once called the Old Kathisma, at which there was a well.[4] The country beyond was called Rama.[5] A mile beyond that at Rachel's Tomb[6] there was a fork in the road; the east road went to Bethlehem and the one going on to the south was the main road to Hebron. Bethlehem was surrounded by a wall, identical with, or perhaps built on the same foundations, as the one Emperor Justinian had built.[7] They went in and visited the Church, built by the same Emperor, and went down to the cave of Christ's birth[8] and the Manger.[9] There they also saw the well over which the star stopped when the Magi came,[10] and this may have been the well from which David desired water.[11] Near this cave were the tombs of St Jerome[12] and of St Paula,[13] and part of the remains of the Holy Innocents.[14]

[1] 2Gu 124, Thc 69–71.
[2] 2 Kgs 4.8–37, 38.
[3] 1Gu 3, Sae 25, [7Gu 106], Jph 25.5.
[4] See *Book* (or *Protevangelium*) *of James* 17.2, Piacenza 28, j.85. Holy Qur'an s.19.
[5] Piacenza 28, j.85.
[6] Jerome, *Letter* 108.10.1, j.49.
[7] Eutychius of Alexandria, *PG* 111,1070, Procopius, *Buildings* 5,9,12, j.77.
[8] Justin, *Trypho* 78.
[9] Origen, *C.Celsum* 151.
[10] Gregory of Tours, *Miracles* 1,1, *PL* 71, 707.
[11] Epiphanius M. iv,8, j.117.
[12] Piacenza 29, j.85.
[13] Jerome, *Letter* 108, 29, 3.
[14] Bethlehem, *Armen.Lec.*55, e.272, and west of Jerusalem, Epiphanius M., 4.19, j.119.

Outside the church was the Bath of Christ.[1] In Bethlehem was the House of David's father Jesse,[2] and east of Bethlehem were the Shepherd's Fields.[3]

On the way from Bethlehem to Hebron they passed the Well of the Oath.[4] This is a translation of the biblical 'Beer-sheba', but it was over twenty-five miles north of the biblical site. In the sixth century the name was applied to Bir al Daraj, a copious spring which, though it was ten miles away, supplied Jerusalem by an aqueduct. To the left a road led to Tekoa,[5] and nearby was the field from which the prophet Habakkuk was sent with food to Daniel in the lion's den in Babylon.[6] Nearby was the cave and monastery of St Chariton.[7]

Along the main road was the Spring at which the Apostle Philip baptized the eunuch, perhaps last mentioned in about 780 by Hugeburc,[8] and not recognized by the crusader pilgrims. Two miles before Hebron on the right was the Valley of Eshcol (or 'the Bunch of Grapes'),[9] and after that on the right-hand side was Mamre, the place of the terebinth or oak tree under which Abraham entertained the three persons known in Christian interpretation as the Trinity.[10]

Hebron was famous for the Tombs of the Patriarchs[11] and of Joseph.[12] Hebron was also called by another name, Kiriath Arba or 'The City of the Four'. Christian and Jewish interpreters knew that three of the four were Abraham, Isaac and Jacob, and Patriarchs. But in ancient versions of the Bible Joshua 14.15 has words which can be interpreted 'Adam, the greatest, was buried among the Anakim', and the fourth was held to be Adam.[13] In Hebron stood the House of Abraham, a Muslim hostel known as such in 985.[14]

To the east of Hebron was the village of Caphar Barucha, to which Abraham led the three persons to send them on their journey,[15] and to the south was the Tomb of Lot.[16] Both places had

[1] Adomnan 2,3, j.104.
[2] Epiphanius M. IV,11, j.117.
[3] *Armen. Lec.* 1, e.262.
[4] Piacenza 32, j.85.
[5] Jerome, *Letter* 108,12.1, j.50.
[6] *Bel and the Dragon* 33–9 and Piacenza 32, j.85.
[7] Epiphanius M. IV.15, j.119.
[8] Piacenze 32, j.85, Hugeburc 24, j.131.
[9] W. el Kaf: Jerome, *Letter* 108,11,2, j.50.
[10] Bordeaux 599, e.162.
[11] Bordeaux 599, e.163.
[12] Piacenza 30, j.85. The building was a result of Caliph el Mahdi's restoration in 918, Nasir-i-Khosrau 53f, *PUM* 314.
[13] Jerome, *Q.H.Gen.* 23.2.
[14] Muqaddesi 172, *PUM* 310.
[15] Jerome, *Letter* 108,11,5, j.50.
[16] Suyuti (1470 A.D.) *Ithāf al Akhissa* 295, *PUM* 469.

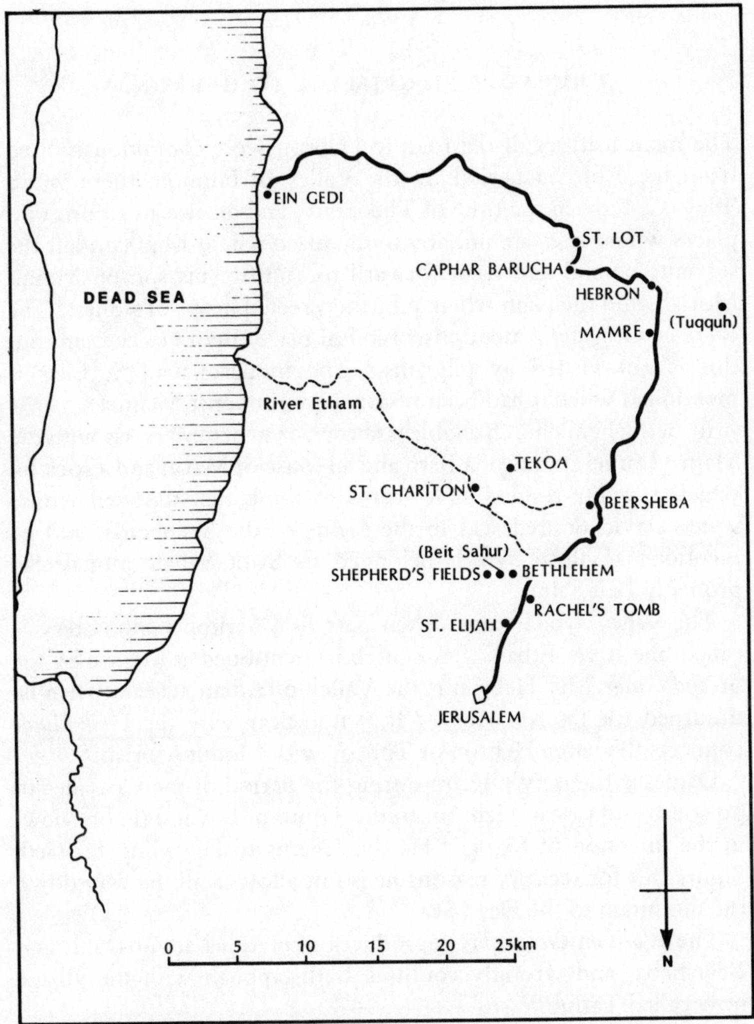

Fig. 12. Road from Jerusalem to Hebron.

a good view of the Dead Sea, and of Zoara or Sigor, which was on the opposite side of the sea, down at the southern end.[1]

CRUSADER PILGRIMAGE TO HEBRON

The main features of the road to Hebron were continuously used from the Abbasid period. In the Valley of Hinnom there was a 'New Cistern' in the time of Theoderic, and he also mentions two places whose sites are unknown: the place where Abraham left the servants behind and went forward to sacrifice his son on Mount Moriah, and the plain where pilgrims erected heaps of stones.[2] The *Work on Geography* mentions a biblical place, Beth Haccherem, but this is not visited by pilgrims.[3] The monastery of St Elias is mentioned when it had been restored by Emperor Manuel.[4]

In Bethlehem church a table is shown at which Mary sat with the Magi.[5] Daniel speaks of a Bath and a House of Mary, and a rock by which a stylite resided.[6] He seems to think that the well whose water David desired was in the Fields of the Shepherds, and he mentions a village which belonged to Saint Saba's monastery, probably Beit Sahur.[7]

The valley which runs down past St Chariton's monastery is called 'the River Etham'.[8] A church is mentioned at Mamre by the *Second Guide*.[9] By Hebron is the Valley of Adam's Tears when he mourned for his son Abel.[10] It is not clear why the *First Guide* connects the name Hebron or Thocor with Mount Moriah.[11]

Daniel is the only pilgrim during the period of the Crusades to go south and east of Hebron, to the Tomb of Lot and (in his view) in the direction of Sigor.[12] He thus seems to be calling En Gedi Sigor. But for security reasons he is not allowed all the way down the mountain to the Dead Sea.

The *Work on Geography* reproduces quotations about Dabir and Beersheba, and wrongly confuses Beth-tappuah with the village now called Taffuh.[13]

1 Piacenza 34, j.85: see *RB* (1932) 256.
2 Thc 77.
3 Wge 26.
4 7Gu 105, Jph 27.3.
5 Got 6.
6 Dan 48f.
7 Dan 50.
8 Dan 51.
9 2Gu 126.
10 Wge 14.
11 1Gu 7.
12 Dan 56.
13 Wge 21, 23, 24.

THE ABBASID ROAD TO NAZARETH AND ACRE

The road to Nazareth starts at St Stephen's Gate, and St Stephen's church[1] is half a kilometre away on the left. The road rises to the top of the hill, and then goes down across the beginning of the Kidron Valley. Up the other side is the mountain probably called Scopus,[2] and it was one of the points from which the Temple area was visible. On the right the road went by a hill, the biblical name of which was Gibeah of Saul,[3] where King Saul had his palace (see Figure 13), and to the left was a small mountain which commemorated things to do with the Prophet Samuel. It was named either Ramathaim-Zophim[4] where he was born, Mizpah[5] where he judged, or Rama (Ramatha)[6] where he was buried.

In the Abbasid period no other holy places are mentioned by pilgrims for another forty kilometres, even though the road passed very close to Sailun. This in fact was the biblical Shiloh, a holy place for earlier Christian pilgrims, but in the Latin Kingdom neglected, perhaps because it was not on the main road or visible from it. Thus the next places the pilgrims of the Latin Kingdom visited were Jacob's Well and Joseph's Tomb[7] in Sychar,[8] or as some preferred to say, Shechem. This was biblically correct, for Jacob's Well is at the southern edge of an ancient hill which contains the remains of Shechem. But many pilgrims seemed to think that the city Neapolis, a mile away to the west, was called Shechem.[9] Since Neapolis was also the centre of the Samaritan community, it was sometimes mistakenly held to be the biblical city of Samaria.[10] To the south of the city stood Mount Gerizim and to the north Mount Ebal.[11]

The next holy place was at Sebaste, the true site of biblical Samaria.[12] There was a tomb where the ashes of St John the Baptist

[1] *Passion of Forty Martyrs* 2.302.
[2] Josephus, *War* 2.528, which is the same as 'Sapheim' [Lookout], *Ant.* 9.329.
[3] Jerome, *Letter* 108.8,2, j.47f.
[4] Theodosius 6, j.65.
[5] Theodosius 4, j.65.
[6] *Georgian Kanonarion* 1159.
[7] Egeria (P)R, e.193.
[8] Adomnan 2,21,1, j.108.
[9] Jerome, *Letter* 108,13,3, j.51, *Commemoratorium* 49, j.138.
[10] Theodosius 2, j.63.
[11] Epiphanius of Salamis, *Gems* (ed. Blake and de Vis, pp. 184–93), and Bordeaux 587.3, e.154.
[12] Egeria (P)R, e.193.

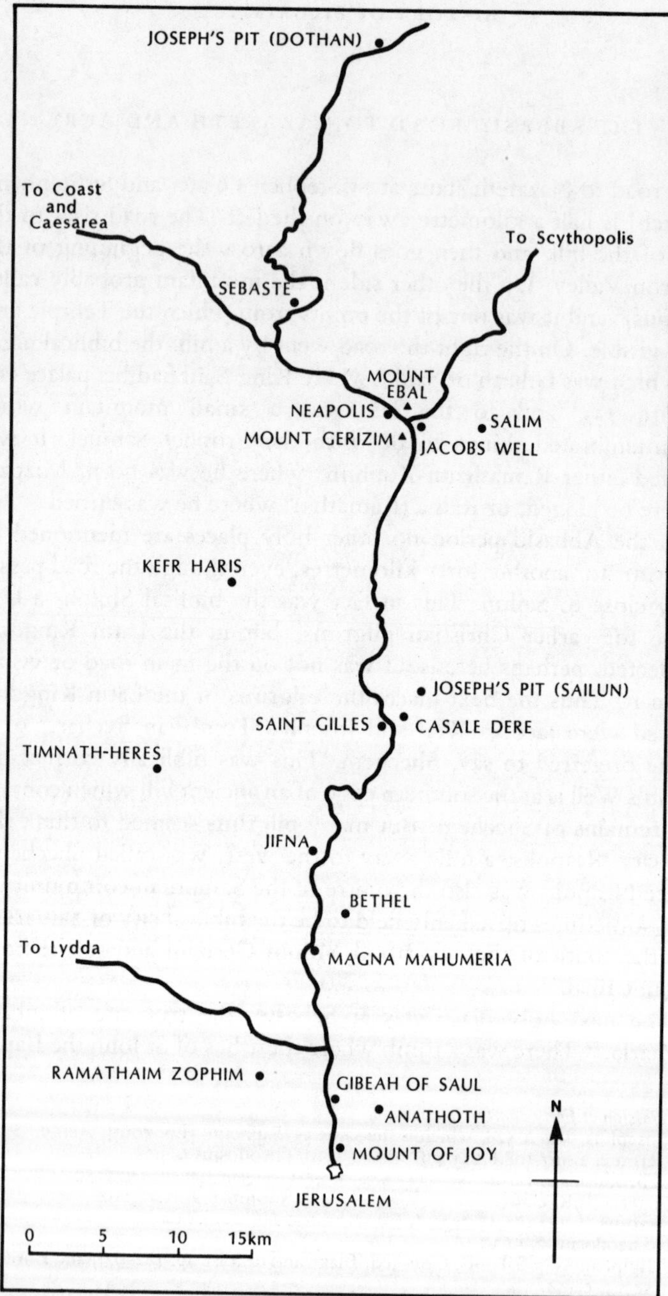

Fig. 13. Road from Jerusalem to Sebaste.

were shown,[1] and the remains of the Prophets Elisha and Obadiah. In the sixth century a tradition grew up that John the Baptist had been beheaded in Samaria, and his prison was shown there.[2]

The way into the Great Plain,[3] or the Plain of Megiddo,[4] was by a town now called Jenin. Coming into the Plain one saw to the north Mount Tabor, where Christ was transfigured. When they climbed up it the pilgrims saw three churches,[5] and they then admired the view,[6] which included the villages of Nain and Endor, and the small nearby hill called Mount Hermon. On the way down they visited the Cave of Melchizedek, where Abraham offered him bread and wine.[7] They then went to Nazareth, a village among some hills, and on the way up they saw the Fall,[8] a precipice over which the Jews threatened to throw Jesus. In Nazareth were two churches, one of the Annunciation[9] and the other above a spring[10] and pilgrims were also shown the Synagogue.[11]

Beyond Nazareth was Cana,[12] and to the west Sepphoris, where, according to its inhabitants, the Blessed Virgin Mary had lived as a child.[13] From this place it was a day's journey to Acre.

THE CRUSADER ROAD FROM JERUSALEM TO ACRE

During the Latin Kingdom this road became 'The Upper Road' leading from Acre, the chief port, to Jerusalem.[14] But it had all long been used by pilgrims, even though very few of them before this period went to Acre as their main port. The main additions made to this road come through the writer of the *Work on Geography* looking up his books and, at least sometimes, going to the places.

The first change that was made was rather a change of language

[1] Philostorgius, *Eccl. Hist.* 7.4, *Commemoratorium* 48, j.138.
[2] John Malalas, *Chron.* 10 and 48.
[3] Jerome, *L.loc.* 109.12, and *Letter* 108,13.5, j.51.
[4] Jerome, ibid.8,1, j.47, and *Comm. Zech.* 12.11.
[5] Piacenza 6, j.81.
[6] Ibid.
[7] Epiphanius M. X,16, j.120.
[8] *Commemoratorium* 42, j.138.
[9] Piacenza 5, j.79, Hugeburc 13, j.128.
[10] Adomnan 2,26,1–4, j.109.
[11] Piacenza 5, j.79.
[12] Jerome *L.loc.* 117.7, Piacenza 4, j.79.
[13] Piacenza 4, j.79.
[14] Thc 106.

than of site, since Scopus was renamed the Mount of Joy.[1] When the pilgrim first arrived there, which he would normally do whether he chose the 'Upper Road' or the alternative, 'The Coast Road', he was in sight of Jerusalem, and he put on his cross.[2]

The *Work on Geography* surrounds this part of the road with quotations, about Anathoth,[3] a muddled quotation about Gibeah of Saul, which is mixed up with Gibeah of Phineas,[4] and another muddle, between the Latin Kingdom pilgrims in general, with 'Gibeon'. Biblical Gibeon was el Jib, a mile to the north of the mountain of Samuel, but the Crusaders seem to have adopted the Jewish idea that it was at el Bireh, four miles to the north, which was called by the Latin Kingdom Magna Mahumeria[5] (see Figure 13).

Daniel came this way with the King and his troops, and may therefore have wandered somewhat from the road. He mentions el Bireh by the name it had in Arabic, translating it as 'The Well of the Holy Mother of God'; this is where the Holy Family stopped on their way back to Nazareth and found Jesus missing.[6] Daniel confused Jifna with Mount Gilboa,[7] and he mentions David's Well and Cave, not known today. He adopts a Muslim commemoration for Sailun (the biblical Shiloh) and places Joseph's Pit there.[8] He also calls Sailun 'Shechem'. About thirty years later Nikulás mentions a village called 'Casal',[9] and he may well mean Casale Dere.

The *Work on Geography* mentions as a point of history and not of pilgrimage the village of Saint-Gilles.[10] The author pointed out the Tomb of Joshua both at the Samaritan site of Kafr Haris,[11] which showed that he or his source depended not only on books but also on personal research, and he later mentions the Jewish location of this place.[12] His entry about the 'Terebinth' is not at all clear.[13]

Jacob's Well is mentioned, but the only person who mentions the Tomb of Joseph is the Jewish traveller, Benjamin of Tudela.[14] The

[1] Gqu 3.
[2] Thc 92.
[3] Wge 78.
[4] Wge 181f.
[5] Wge 188. see Btu 21.
[6] Luke 2.45, Dan 71.
[7] Dan 71.
[8] Dan 71.
[9] Nik 81.
[10] Wge 115.
[11] Wge 114.
[12] Wge 203.
[13] Wge 113.
[14] Btu 20.

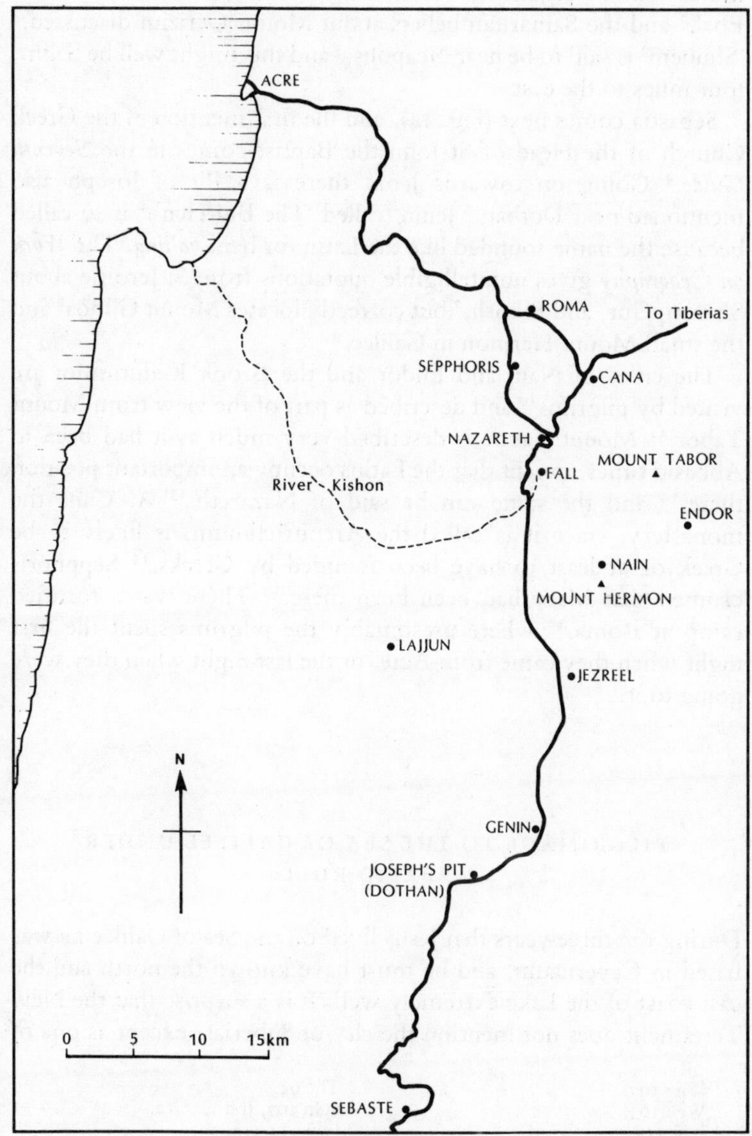

Fig. 14. Road from Sebaste to Acre.

fourth century arguments are resumed about Mounts Gerizim and Ebal,[1] and the Samaritan beliefs about Mount Gerizim discussed.[2] 'Shunem' is said to be near Neapolis,[3] and this might well be Salim, four miles to the east.

Sebastia comes next (Fig. 14), and the first mention of the Greek Church of the Head of St John the Baptist comes in the *Seventh Guide*.[4] Going on towards Jenin there is a Pit of Joseph also mentioned near Dothan.[5] Jenin (called 'The Big Hen')[6] is so called because the name sounded like the Latin for hen, *gallina*. The *Work on Geography* gives unintelligible quotations from St Jerome about Sharon, Gur, and Elkosh,[7] but correctly locates Mount Gilboa[8] and the small Mount Hermon in Galilee.[9]

The cities of Nain and Endor and the Brook Kedummim are visited by pilgrims[10] and described as part of the view from Mount Tabor.[11] Mount Tabor is described very much as it had been in Abbasid times, except that the Latins occupy an important position there,[12] and the same can be said of Nazareth.[13] At Cana the monastery, since it is called the Architriclinium, is likely to be Greek or at least to have been founded by Greeks.[14] Sepphoris claimed that Mary had been born there.[15] There was a fortified camp at Roma,[16] where presumably the pilgrims spent the first night when they came from Acre, or the last night when they were going to it.

PILGRIMAGE TO THE SEA OF GALILEE UNDER ABBASID RULE

During the three years that Jesus lived on the Sea of Galilee he was based in Capernaum, and he must have known the north and the east coast of the Lake extremely well. It is a surprise that the New Testament does not mention the city of Tiberias, except as one of

[1] Wge 107f.
[2] Thc 94.
[3] Wge 103.
[4] 7Gu 107, Jph 12.2,12.
[5] Jwü 114.
[6] Jwü 114,113.
[7] Wge 95f.
[8] Wge 90,94, Gbe 3.
[9] Wge 87, Pde P3.
[10] Jwü 113, Thc 98.
[11] Wge 89.
[12] Jph 11.1.
[13] Thc 104f.
[14] Sae 29.
[15] Jwü 111.
[16] Thc 106.

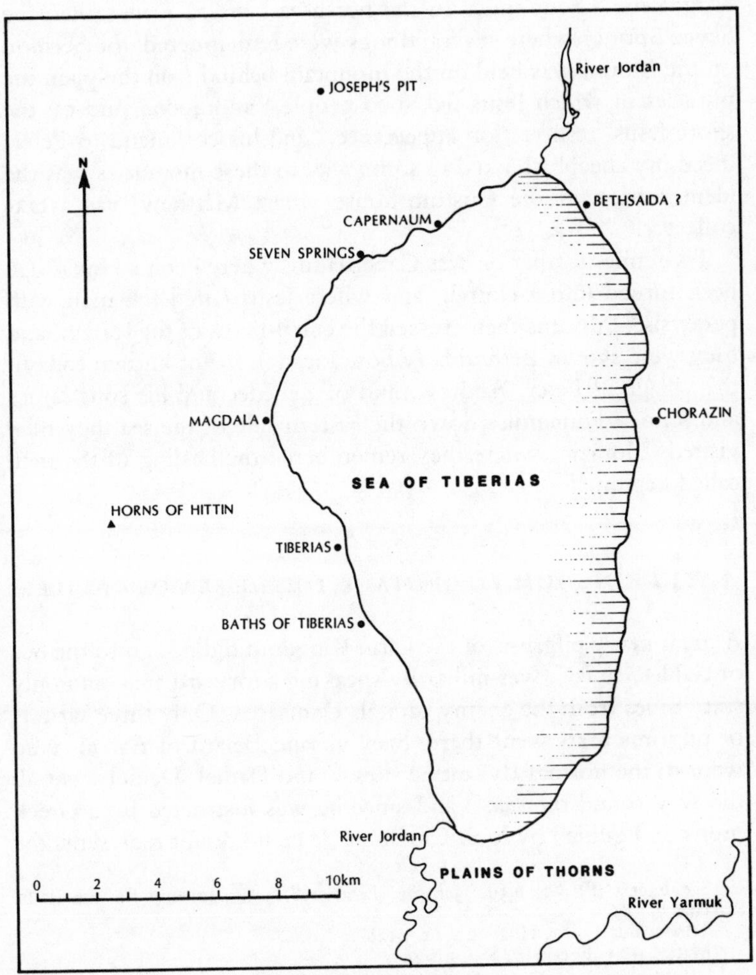

Fig. 15. Sea of Tiberias.

the names for the Sea.[1] The Holy Places started to the north of the city. Magdala was the first place, the home of Saint Mary Magdalene.[2] Four miles to the north-east was a place called the Seven Springs where several things were remembered: the Sermon on the Mount was held on the mountain behind,[3] on the plain the miracles in which Jesus fed 5000 people,[4] and 4000,[5] and on the shore Jesus' resurrection appearance,[6] and his command to Peter, 'Feed my sheep!'[7] Linked in some way to these memories was the identification of the Custom-house where Matthew was a tax-collector.[8]

Two miles further on was Capernaum, where Peter's House had been turned into a church, and where Jesus cured the man with paralysis.[9] Pilgrims then crossed the entry-point of the Jordan, and they were shown Bethsaida (whose location is not known today), the village of Peter, Andrew, and of Zebedee and his sons James and John.[10] Four miles down the eastern side of the sea they then visited Chorazin, where they remembered the healing of the man called Legion.[11]

LATIN KINGDOM PILGRIMAGE TO THE SEA OF GALILEE

A great many pilgrims of the Latin Kingdom did not go to the Sea of Galilee, since it was militarily speaking a forward area, and only sixty miles from the enemy capital, Damascus. Only three writers of pilgrims texts went there, Saewulf and Belard of Ascoli, who went to the normal Byzantine sites,[12] and Daniel. Daniel went all the way round the sea,[13] and since he was instructed by a Greek monk and guided by local Christians,[14] he no doubt represents the

[1] See Egeria (P) V2, e.194, Jerome, *Letter* 108,13,5, j.52, and for the Baths Piacenza 7, j.81.
[2] Theodosius 2, j.63, Hugeburc 14, j.128.
[3] Matt 5.1–11, Egeria (P) V3f, e.200.
[4] Jerome, *Letter* 108,13,5, j.52, Theodosius 2, j.65.
[5] *Life of Constantine* 7, j.203.
[6] John 21.1–14, Egeria (P) V2f, e.196.
[7] John 21.15–19.
[8] Egeria (P) V3, e.200.
[9] Egeria (P) V2, e.194.
[10] Theodosius 2, j.63.
[11] Hugeburc 14, j.128.
[12] Sae 29f, Gbe 5.
[13] Dan 82–4.
[14] Dan 77,85.

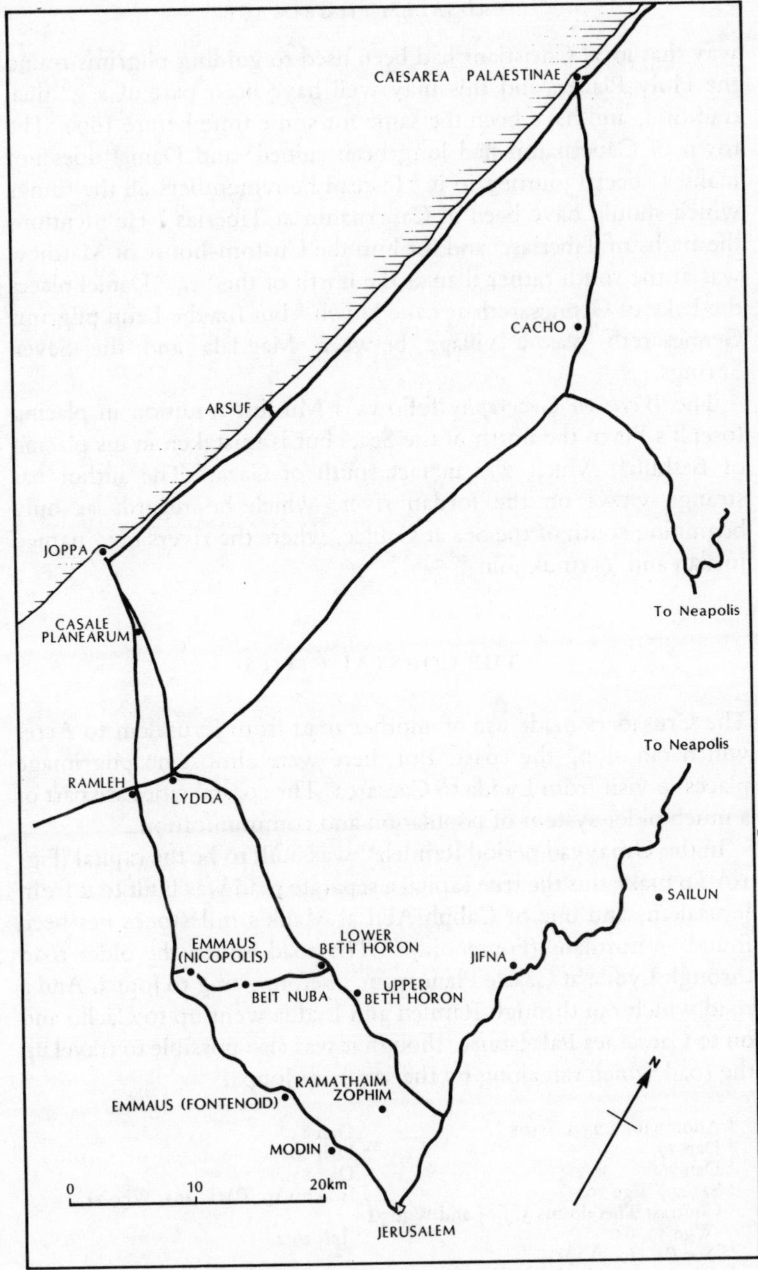

Fig. 16. Road from Jerusalem to Joppa and Caesarea.

way that local Christians had been used to guiding pilgrims round the Holy Places, and this may well have been part of a gradual tradition, and have been the same for some time before 1099. The town of Capernaum had long been ruined[1] and Daniel does not make a special journey to it.[2] Instead he remembers all the things which should have been in Capernaum at Tiberias.[3] He mentions the Baths of Tiberias,[4] and for him the Custom-house of Matthew was at the south rather than at the north of the Sea.[5] Daniel places the Lake of Gennesareth at Lake Huleh,[6] but for the Latin pilgrims Gennesareth was a village between Magdala and the Seven Springs.[7]

The *Work on Geography* follows a Muslim tradition in placing Joseph's Pit to the north of the Sea,[8] but is mistaken in his placing of Bethulia, which was in fact south of Gaza.[9] The author has strange views on the Jordan river, which he regards as only beginning south of the Sea at Galilee, where the rivers now named Jordan and Yarmuk join.[10]

THE COASTAL CITIES

The Crusaders made use of another road from Jerusalem to Acre, which ran along the coast. But there were almost no pilgrimage places to visit from Lydda to Caesarea. The coastal cities are part of a much older system of population and communication.

In the Umayyad period Ramleh[11] was built to be the capital (Fig. 16) To make this the true capital a separate road was built to it from Jerusalem, and one of Caliph Abd al Malik's milestones has been found at Emmaus (Fontenoid).[12] The road joined the older road through Lydda at Casale Planearum[13] before going to Joppa. And a road which ran through Ramleh and Lydda went up to Cacho and on to Caesaraea Palaestinae, though it was also possible to travel up the road which ran along by the sea from Joppa.

[1] Adomnan, 2,25,2, j.108.
[2] Dan 83.
[3] Dan 79.
[4] Dan 79.
[5] Dan 76f.
[6] Dan 83.
[7] Sae 29, Wge 70.
[8] Istakhri 59, *PMU* 465, Wge 74.
[9] Contrast Theodosius 3, j.65 and Wge 74.
[10] Wge 59, 65.
[11] Jph 29.2.
[12] See *RB* (1907) 291.
[13] Wge 206 reads *Casale Balnearum*, which seems to be a mistake for the true name.

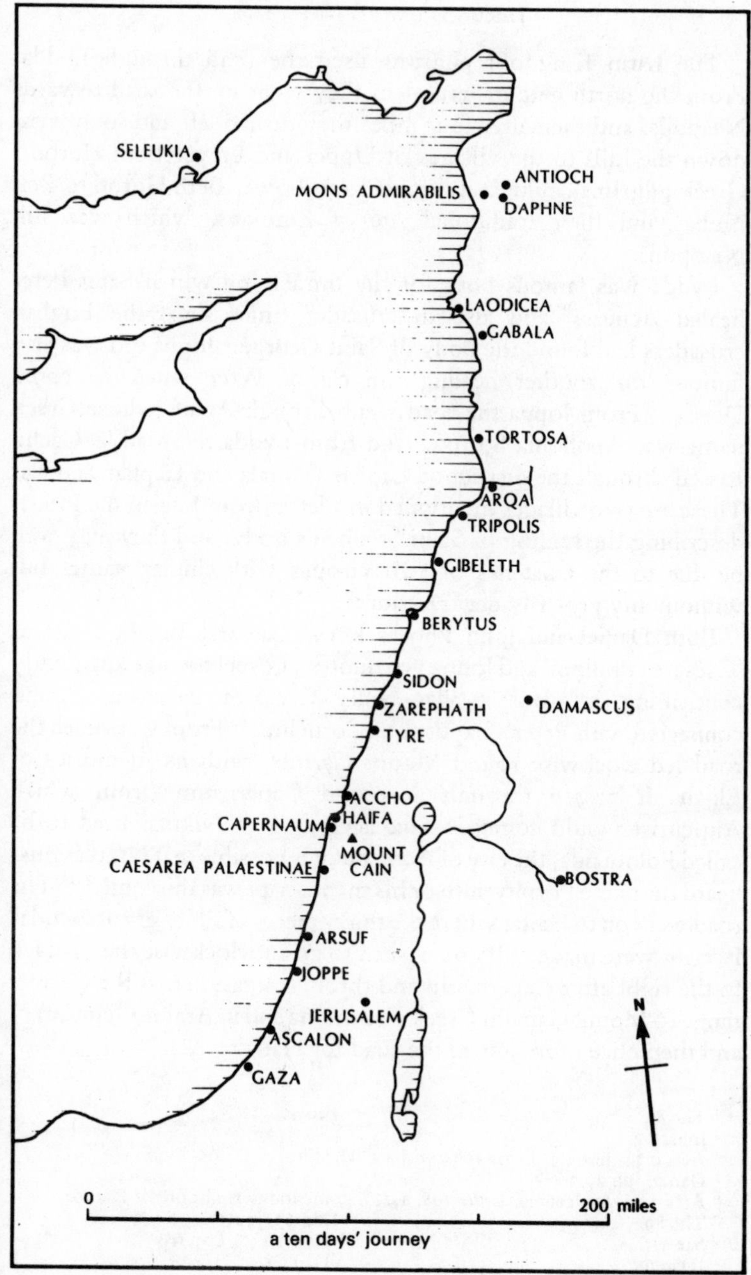

Fig. 17. The Coastal Cities.

The Latin Kingdom pilgrims used the road through Lydda. From the north gate of Jerusalem they went up the road towards Neapolis, and then after four miles they turned left and soon went down the hills to the villages of Upper and Lower Beth Horon.[1] Greek pilgrims could easily travel from Lower Beth Horon to Beit Nuba[2] and their traditional site of Emmaus, which was still Nicopolis.[3]

Lydda was famous both for the miracle by which Saint Peter healed Aeneas,[4] and also in crusader times since the English crusaders had found the body of Saint George.[5] Joppa too was also famous for another healing miracle of Peter when he cured Dorcas.[6] From Joppa the road went through Arsuf, whose Greek name was Apollonia Sozusa. And from Lydda the road to Cacho passed through the district of Caphar Gamala and Caphar Semala. These are two villages mentioned in a letter from Lucian the Priest, describing the finding of Saint Stephen's body, and they may well be due to the existence of two villages with similar names but without any pre-crusader tradition.[7]

Both Daniel and John Phocas knew Caesarea on the coast as 'Caesarea Philippi' and John even quotes a gospel passage apparently confirming it.[8] But it was really Caesarea Palaestinae,[9] and connected with Peter's baptism of Cornelius.[10] From Caesaraea the road led clockwise round Mount Carmel, with its memories of Elijah. It passed through a second Capernaum (from which Antichrist would come).[11] This according to Nikulás used to be called Polomaida, the city of Acre, but it is possible that Nikulás misheard the name Porphyrium or his manuscript was miscopied.[13] The road went on to Haifa, where the thirty pieces of silver given to Judas Iscariot were made.[14] If one wished to go anticlockwise the road led to the right after Capernaum and through a pass across the Carmel range to Mount Cain (in Greek Kammōna and in Arabic Qeimūn),[15] and then once more joined the road for Haifa to Acre.

[1] Thc 87.
[2] Btu 27.
[3] Jph.29.2.
[4] Acts 9.32, Jerome, *Letter* 108,1,2, j.47, Theodosius 4, j.65.
[5] Dan 7, Jph 29.2–6.
[6] Acts 9.36–43. Jerome, *Letter* 108, 1,2, j.47 mentions Andromeda. Dan.64.
[7] Thc 89.
[8] Dan 65, Jph 30.1–3.
[9] Sae 31f.
[10] Acts 10.48, Dan 65.
[11] Dan 66.
[12] Dan 66.
[13] See Wge 214, Nik 61.
[14] Thc 89.
[15] Eusebius, *On.* 116.21.

Beginning with Caesarea, the *Work on Geography* describes cities from sources which are wholly or partly pre-crusader.[1] The description of Acre is a good example, the first half of which is new, and perhaps the second old.[2] Acre was the end of what the pilgrims of the Latin Kingdom called 'The Coast Road', and most of them went no further to the north, but boarded ship.[3] Since this was the main Christian port it was overcrowded during the pilgrimage season, and not a healthy place, since its drains were not large enough to cope with the sewage (Fig. 17).[4]

By land the next place to the north was Tyre,[5] connected with King Hiram, the friend of Solomon, and with a stone on which Jesus had sat.[6] The next place was Zarephath, connected with Elisha.[7] And then came Sidon,[8] which, like Tyre, had its stone where Jesus stood and taught.[9] There were three more cities, Berytus, with its portrait of Christ by Nicodemus,[10] Gibeleth[11] and Tripoli[12] before one came to the River Albana,[13] which marked the frontier of the Latin Kingdom after the summer of 1109. Beyond the frontier, on the way to Antioch, were Tortosa,[14] Jabala,[15] and Laodicea.[16] In New Testament times Peter had been leader of the church in Antioch,[17] and in 1185 it is well described by John Phocas.[18]

•

GREEK AND LATIN PILGRIMAGE TO EMMAUS

There was considerable doubt about the position of Emmaus in the eleventh century. The Bishop of Euchaïta, John, who lived in about 1050 and had been to Jerusalem as a pilgrim, speaks of 'The men who copied down the Gospels not being infallible'. As an example he cites the distance of Emmaus from Jerusalem: 'On the "village

[1] Perhaps an old description [o.d.], Wge 210–12.
[2] New description [n.d.] in first half of Wge 217, and perhaps o.d. in the second.
[3] Jph 9.1.
[4] Jph 9.2.
[5] O.d. in Wge 218, first paragraph of 220. In 221 the first and third paragraphs may be old.
[6] Wge 220.
[7] O.d. Wge 22.
[8] O.d. Wge 219,224, n.d. Jph 6.1–3.
[9] Jph.6.3.
[10] Wge 225, Jph 5.1.
[11] Wge 226, Jph 5.1.
[12] Jph 3.2–5.
[13] Wge 226.
[14] Jph 3.1.
[15] Jph 3.1.
[16] Jph 3.1.
[17] Nik 68.
[18] Jph 2.

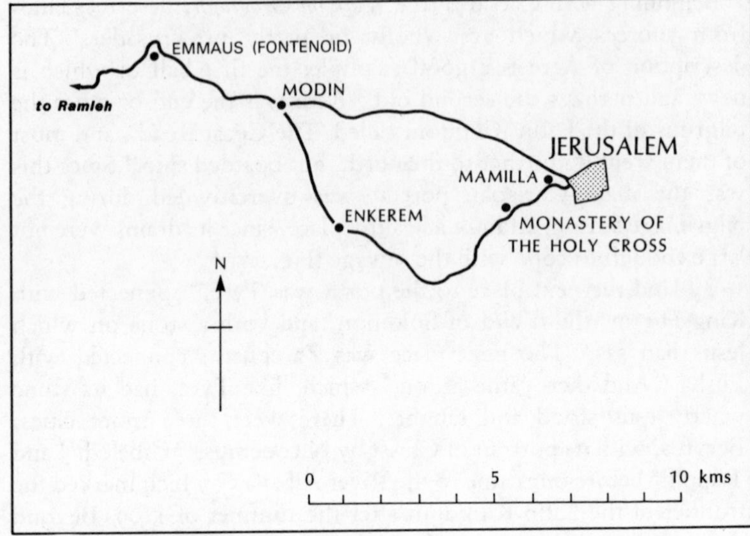

Fig. 18. The Latin pilgrimage from Jerusalem to Emmaus.

sixty stades distant" some make the number much greater, while others reduce it to thirty'.[1]

The Greeks held a tradition that Emmaus was Nicopolis (see Fig. 16), and the Palestinian manuscripts of the New Testament give one hundred and sixty stades as its distance from Jerusalem. So pilgrims in the Greek tradition, Daniel and John Phocas,[2] thought that Nicopolis was Emmaus.

Daniel was on his way down to Joppa. He starts from the Gate of David and sees a place (at present unknown) where David killed Goliath.[3] He goes to the Pool of Mamilla and the cave with bodies of Christian martyrs.[4] Then he goes over the hill to the west where there was a Georgian monastery[5] where the tree which produced the wood of the Holy Cross grew.[6] He goes west to Ain Karim,

[1] Euchaïta was 100 miles south of Sinope on the Black Sea. John Euchaïta, *Ep.* 117 (ed. J. Bollig and P. Lagarde, 63).

[2] See Jph 29.2.

[3] Dan 57.

[4] Bernard 19, j.144, see also Epiphanius M. IV.18, j.119.

[5] Syrians are in charge in Thc.86.

[6] Dan 58.

where there was the House of Zacharias,[1] and the cave where Elizabeth hid with John the Baptist during the slaughter of the Innocents.[2] Rama is the next place reported by Daniel, but the place and its name are hard to fit into this journey.[3] Then at length he reaches Emmaus-Nicopolis,[4] having gone at least sixteen miles.

The Latins, perhaps profiting by researches made before 1099, fixed on another location for Emmaus, at Qiriat al Inab, the modern Abu Ghosh. Like Emmaus-Nikopolis, famous for its spring,[5] this too had a spring, which the French called Fontenoid. One of the advantages of this Latin location for Emmaus is that the pilgrimage there and back from Jerusalem is about twenty miles. There are certainly some steep hills on the way, but it could well be done in one day, even though it is very hilly.[6]

The first account of the places concerned is in the *Work on Geography*,[7] and when Theoderic makes this pilgrimage he adds another site, Modin, to his list of places. This was not the biblical site, down near Lydda,[8] but a site to the west of Jerusalem from which both the Mediterranean and the Dead Sea could be seen. This must be Qastal, with its Latin Kingdom name '*Belveer*'. The village nearby is called Motsa, which might well have sounded like 'Modin' to Christians in the twelfth century.

THE WAY OF THE CROSS AND THE TEMPLARS

Pope Urban's original sermon at the Council of Clermont is not fully known. But at least in some versions of it he refers to pilgrimage to Jerusalem, and quotes Matthew 16.24: 'If any man would come after me, let him deny himself and take up his cross and follow me'.[9] Possibly this gave rise to the fact that Jerusalem

[1] Theodosius 6, j.65.
[2] *Book* (or *Protevangelium*) *of James* 22.3: archaeological remains in the cave from before 1099, Ovadiah 96.
[3] Dan 61.
[4] Dan 62.
[5] Sozomen 5.21 (Bidez-Hansen 228f.).
[6] Jph 26.2.
[7] Wge 173f, 180, (194), 164.
[8] I Macc.2.15, Eusebius, *On*.132.16.
[9] Robert the Monk, *Historia Hierosolymitana* 1.2 (De Sandoli 1, 198).

pilgrims regularly wore crosses, and some of them carried wooden crosses from their own countries to Jerusalem which they would place on Mount Calvary.[1] Thus a pilgrim's attitude of mind could well be that it was a symbolic way of taking up the cross in imitation of Christ, or to use a more modern terminology, an international Way of the Cross.

To this attitude an archaeological discovery must now be added, if we are to understand the Latin Kingdom identification of holy places as archaeology. Pilgrims in this period were confused by the two trials of Jesus which were commemorated on Mount Sion, one where he appeared before Annas and Caiaphas, and the other before Pilate. But Theoderic, while he supports the site on Mount Sion as the place of the trials, rightly thinks that a rock to the north of the temple enclosure was 'one side of the palace called Antonia'.[2] It is not known how old this belief may have been. But if the palace was in fact Antonia, it was built by Herod.

The Templars seem to have held different views about the place of the two trials. The Second Guide[3] speaks about the Sheep Pool in the following way:

> This Pool is the place where those who are visiting are told that the Wood of the Cross remained for a long time. But the Templars show you another pool, and say that that is the Sheep Pool.

The existing Sheep Pool, which was merely the rectangular cistern under the small northern Church of Saint Anne,[4], was certainly unimpressive, and the larger pool immediately to the north of the Temple wall, now filled in, but called Birket Israil, would be much more impressive. But a question arises about the Wood of the Cross, for this is the first time that a pilgrim guide mentions it.

The story about the Wood of the Cross was current in Europe before the Crusades. In a twelfth-century English version,[5] Christ had taken the Wood of the Cross from the Temple, but in the French versions he took it from the Pool of Bethesda, and it is evidently on these that the Templars' new location depends. A

[1] See Thc 30.
[2] Thc 10: see Josephus, *War* 5, 238–47.
[3] 2GU 123 f.
[4] 7Gu 103 calls it 'a well'.
[5] See Oxford, Bodleian Library MS, Bodley 343, partly edited by A. S. Napier in *The History of the Holy Rood-Tree*, Early English Text Society, 103 (London, 1894) 2–35.

copy of this French story appears in Hugh of St Victor's work on the Holy Places,[1] and it is almost a word for word copy of an eleventh-century version by Master Franco of Liège, of which a translation follows.[2]

> In the time of King David a man found in a wood a tree which was of a kind which grows with three leaves. He cut it down, and took it to the King to be admired. When the King, who was versed in mysteries, saw it he reverenced it, and did so as long as he lived. Solomon also, not only out of respect for his father, reverenced it, and even plated it all with gold.
>
> When she came to hear the wisdom of Solomon the Queen of the South made a prophecy about the tree, and said 'If King Solomon knew what this wood meant he would no longer desire to reverence it.' The Chaplain to the King heard this, and went off to his master saying that he had heard it. After the Queen had departed the King sent his Chaplain after her and gave him precious gifts. He gave them to the Queen's Chaplain without her knowledge, in order that he should ask his mistress to tell him what the wood meant. He ordered him not to reveal himself to the Queen. So he came to his mistress and privately asked her about this matter. In answer she replied that on that wood would hang a man who would destroy all the kingdom.
>
> When the King heard this he took all the gold off the wood, and threw the wood down into the bottom of a pool. And so thereafter an angel used to come down every day into the pool, and when the angel descended the sick people were cured not because of the water but because of the wood.
>
> When the crucifixion of Christ took place the pool was dry, and thus the Cross was taken from there which Jesus carried on his shoulders as far as the gate.

The Templars moved the Sheep Pool. But they also made some other changes. In the north end of the Haram they rebuilt a Dome and called it 'The Throne of Jesus'. They also renamed the gate on the west of the Haram now called Bab en Nazir 'The Sorrowful

[1] This work is a paraphrase of Bede, and has no new material apart from the story added at the end. See S. De Sandoli, Vol. 1, 166. For a twelfth-century version see Honorius of Autun, *PL* 172.994.

[2] Ed. A. Wilmart, *RB* (1927) 230–231.

Gate'.[1] This is in fact the gate which leads onto the street which goes up the city to enter the Church of the Holy Sepulchre.

'The Sorrowful Gate' is mentioned only in a French Guide to Jerusalem written in about 1231, which also says that Jesus Christ was led through it on his way to Calvary. But it seems that this is a memory of what took place before 1187, since it would be hard to think that the gate obtained this name at a time when no Christians any longer passed through the Haram esh Sharif.

As a summary of what took place, Figure 19 must be analysed. We know that the Templars preferred the second Sheep Pool on the Haram wall to the one across the road to the left. But they also seem to have thought, like Theoderic, that the rock outcrop to the north was the new Praetorium. This would certainly make sense of their other holy places, especially if they were used in procession. Thus at his trial Jesus, according to the story by Master Franco, would have been sent to get his Cross from the second Sheep Pool. Then he would have come back into the Haram and had a rest at the Throne of Jesus, where he would then be helped to carry his cross by Simon of Cyrene. He would then have gone out through the Sorrowful Gate, and taken the roads marked 1 up to the Holy Sepulchre Church.

In 1187 the Haram was cleansed of Christian monuments, and Christians were excluded. But the Templars' new Praetorium was facing the road. It was therefore quite simple to change the roads for the Way of the Cross, and to make one's way up the roads marked 2. The last part of the road leading to the Holy Sepulchre church was the same. This is in fact the route of the roads of the Way of the Cross used today.

The evidence we have for any Way of the Cross before 1187 has all now been given. It certainly leads us to suppose that there was some processional Way of the Cross before that date, and that the Templars were no doubt responsible for its development. But we know nothing more.

[1] Ernoul, *L'Estat de la Cité de Jérusalem*, 21, ed. H. Michelant and G. Raymond, *Itinéraires à Jérusalem . . . rédigés en français*, Paris 1882, 48.

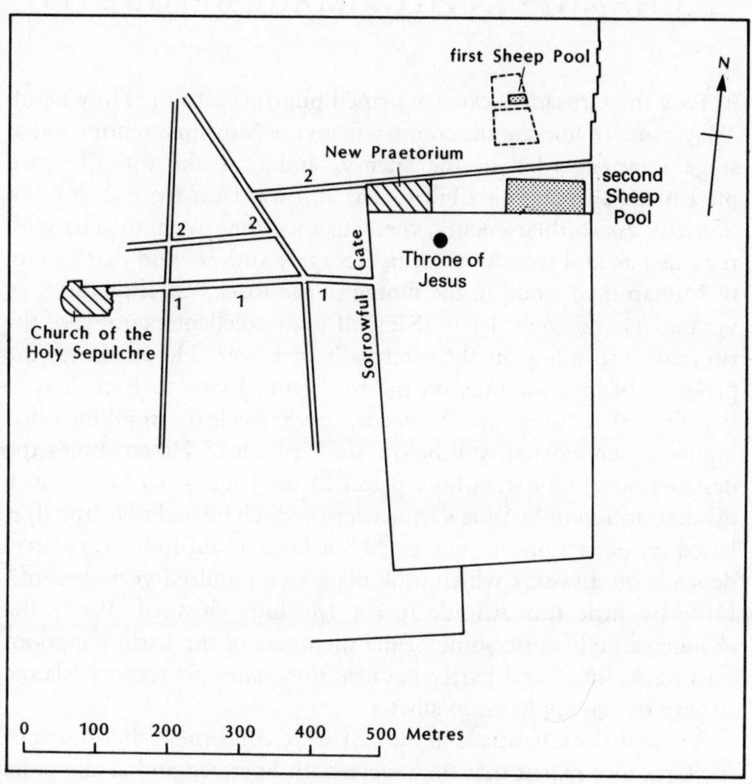

Fig. 19. The Templars' Way of the Cross

4. CHANGES IN PILGRIMAGE BEFORE 1187

In 1099 the Crusaders came as armed pilgrims into the Holy Land. They came to liberate the country from the Muslims, whom at that stage they regarded as the enemy, and to make the Christian pilgrimage a lasting possibility. The aim was clear from their point of view. As to their enemy, the Muslims, they were to start with regarded as idol worshippers, in fact early authors said that an idol of Muhammad stood in the Dome of the Rock,[1] so little did they yet understand about Islam. Saewulf is an excellent example of the rumours prevailing in the aftermath of a war. He attributes the presence of highwaymen on the road from Joppa to Jerusalem to the fact that they are Saracens, perhaps little thinking that highwaymen existed well before the Crusades.[2] He attributes the destruction of Christian holy places to the pagans, so for instance his description of St Saba's Monastery (which he had not visited) is based on plain rumour, and as Abbot Daniel said four years later, depends on disasters which took place two hundred years before.[3] Little by little this attitude to the Muslims changed. Partly the change came because some of the members of the Latin Kingdom learned Arabic,[4] and partly because they came to respect Islamic society by having Muslim allies.[5]

As far as the Christians in the east were concerned, the advent of the Crusades meant that they were both liberated and at the same time assigned to the second rank after the Latins, who were the conquerors. The relation with the Greek Church was ambivalent, and Latin clergy took the leadership away from them. The relationship with the other churches was little changed by the

[1] Fulcher of Chartres, *Hist. Hier.*, 1, 26, de Sandoli I, 112.

[2] Sae 8.

[3] Sae 21, probably referring to St Stephen the Hymnographer, *Passio sanctorum XX martyrum, AA.SS.* III, 166, compared with Dan 38. Further instances where Saewulf complains of ruin are 18 (describing a ruin in 614 by the Persians), 21, 26 and 27.

[4] Prawer 523. [5] Runciman 2, 227.

coming of the Latin Kingdom. They had always held the Greeks in honour, and now for a time they could accord the same honour to the Latins. Syria and Palestine had for long centuries been made up of little religious groups holding their own religions. Better, perhaps, that Christians should be in charge than Muslims, but the small units of society retained their allegiance to small loyalties, and patriotism was an unknown concept, apart from their loyalty to their native city or village.

One particular consequence of this local loyalty has a direct bearing on pilgrimage. From a very early date two different communities had separate holy places dedicated to the same commemoration. One early example of this phenomenon is in the position of Rachel's Tomb. Genesis 48.7 says that it is at 'Ephrath, that is Bethlehem' south of Jerusalem, and 1 Samuel 10.2 says that it is north of Jerusalem, at Zelzah on the border of Benjamin. The tomb of Rachel would certainly be a holy place both for the tribe of Judah and for the tribe of Benjamin, and in fact both the small local communities found a place for it. In the period of the Latin Kingdom the small areas of loyalty persisted, and often two or more holy places with the same commemoration. There were thus three sites pointed out in that period where Joseph was thrown in the pit.[1]

The Latin Kingdom consisted in the Latins, themselves a small group, who happened for the time being to have control of the country. But even the Latins had to defend themselves. By 1128 they had liberated all the places of pilgrimage known from Christ's life in the Gospels. But no pilgrim of the period says that he paid a visit to Caesarea Philippi or Baneas, and allowing for the fact that some later mentions of Galilee are quotations, the last pilgrim to say that he visited the holy places round the Sea of Galilee is Belard of Ascoli in 1155. Perhaps in fact he was one of the last to do so, since Galilee was soon to become a military area owing to the aggressive policy of Nur ed Din. In 1167 King Amalric made over tracts of land at Safed to the Knights Templar, and at Belvoir to the Hospitallers, and the defence of Galilee became more strict. Sites round the Sea of Galilee were henceforth shown to pilgrims only as a view from Mount Tabor.[2] Indeed by the time Theodoric made

[1] See Index, 'Joseph's Pit'.

[2] Compare the visit to Galilee in Gbe 5 with the view of Galilee in 7Gu 107 (perhaps 2Gu 118), and Jph 11.12–14.

his pilgrimage not only the area of Jericho was well defended,[1] but also the churches which were round Jerusalem, but outside the city wall, had walls built round them.[2]

The Holy Land was conquered and politically there was some stability. But the victors still had to make the holy places their own. There were three main ways of doing so. The first was their building of a great many new monasteries and churches, as we have seen for example in the churches of the Valley of Jehoshaphat. In their rebuilding they did not simply repair what the previous builders had done. In addition they imposed Latin designs, Latin decoration and Latin inscriptions on the churches. From a culture which had seemed alien to them, and designed for an alien liturgy, they produced something of their own.

Secondly they tried to discover the bodies of saints. The Holy Land would, it goes without saying, be a good place for a search. In some places they looked for and found the relics, so for instance the Patriarchs' bones were discovered at Hebron,[3] and the nails of the Cross were found.[4] Successful discoveries were treated with reverence and joy.[5] But in other cases, reported by people who were not members of the Latin community, there were failures, like that for King David and St George.[6]

Thirdly they changed the topography of Jerusalem. In one way they changed it very little, by simply taking over the Haram esh Sharif, but in another way the change was considerable. The identification of the Haram esh Sharif and the commemorations attached to the Dome of the Rock were comparatively unimportant, though the effect was to cause a change in the Holy Sepulchre. The Table of Abraham had been in the Church of the Holy Sepulchre as it had been restored by Monomachus, but in the Latin restoration it was not renewed, since Abraham's sacrifice was now remembered on Mount Moriah where, according to the Bible, it had happened. Doubtless other parallels between the Church and the Temple had less emphasis placed on them now that the Temple

[1] Thc 69f, 72.

[2] Thc 67 (Ascension), 68 (Bethany), 55 (Sion), 59 (Tomb of the Virgin), 86 (Holy Cross).

[3] See *Tractatus de Inventione Sanctorum Patriarcharum Abraham, Ysaac et Jacob, RHC* v.I. 302 and De Sandoli I, 332–6.

[4] Wge 205.

[5] *Tract, de Inv*, VII, De Sandoli I, 366, Albert of Aix, *Hist.* 6, 38, De Sandoli I, 277.

[6] Btu 24f, Jph 29.4.

was available. More important to a student of pilgrimage is the fact that it now became possible to do a religious exercise on the Passion in quite a short time, and at any time of the year.

From the start of pilgrimage and through the Abbasid period the regular pattern of pilgrimage had been geographical. Thus in the standard pilgrimage during the Latin Kingdom in Jerusalem the pilgrim went first to the Church of the Holy Sepulchre, and remembered the last moments of Jesus' life. Then he went down to the Temple of the Lord, and remembered his Presentation when he was eight days old. Indeed, if a pilgrim wished to remember them in order, the only way to remember the whole Passion was to attend the ceremonies during Holy Week.[1] The new location of Pilate's Praetorium by the Templars, if it existed, enabled people to do a short dramatic commemoration of the Passion and constituting the first stage towards the 'Way of the Cross'.

This new location seems to be an example of change which may have been a general rule in the history of pilgrimage. Where there were two places which commemorated the same event, a new emphasis on one of the two may well lead to changes in more general topography.[2]

In the course of time in the Latin Kingdom the word 'pilgrim' changed its meaning. The social order was the cause. The country was run by expatriates, but there were other Latin expatriates coming as travellers. Before the Latin Kingdom the Latin word *peregrinus* meant simply 'traveller' and there was no additional meaning of any religious nature. But the resident expatriates were not travellers, and among other things they did not have any uniform, the sign of the Cross which pilgrims put on on the Mount of Joy.[3] Before the Crusades the phrase for making a pilgrimage was 'to go to a place and pray there'.[4] The word 'traveller' was particularly applied to the armed crusaders.[5] But as 1187 came close, and the new social system was established, *peregrinus* came to mean 'pilgrim'. The earliest instances of this use are certainly in connection with Jerusalem. And in order to illustrate this point I have deliberately translated this Latin word both as 'traveller' and as 'pilgrim' in my version of Theoderic.[6]

[1] Jwü 133–157, Thc 52–64. [2] See j.39, notes 106–9.
[3] Dan 9, Thc 92. [4] For instance Sae 33.
[5] Robert the Monk, *Hist. Hier.* 7.2, *R.H.C.* occ. 3, p. 822.
[6] Certainly 'pilgrim' in Thc chapters 12, 25, 28, 30, 33, 37, 40 and 41.

The documents collected in this book display very little of what the pilgrims felt when making their journey, and this is also true of the vast majority of earlier Christian pilgrims to Jerusalem. In fact eight texts out of the nineteen which are given below are no more than guides or travel accounts for the Holy Places.[1] Four more have statements like 'This is how all the sanctuaries in Jerusalem are built',[2] but nothing more direct as a spiritual message. Even the *Work on Geography* has no emotional impact on the spirit, apart from some improving stories.[3]

The remaining five have a little more to say. Like all travellers the pilgrims are grateful to God for giving them safe journeys by sea or by land.[4] But travelling is one of the main elements in pilgrimage. Travellers were subject to dangers, and to enemies very different from those they encountered in their native country. Travel humbled them in a new way, and they use expressions like 'unworthy me' or 'the dung of all monks' to refer to themselves,[5] and of pilgrims as 'the poor'.[6]

Jerusalem is holier than other places, Theoderic tells us, in this special way:

> It is holier because it is illuminated by the presence there of our God and Lord Jesus Christ and of his good Mother, and the fact that all the Patriarchs, Prophets and Apostles have lived and taught and preached and suffered martyrdom there.[7]

This quality of holiness goes very closely with familiarity with the Bible. And some pilgrims were well acquainted with the Scriptures, for instance John of Würzburg in his discussion of St Mary Magdalene and Daniel, when he comments on the fertility of Hebron.[8] But for a pilgrim the Bible is not only well known by intellectual study and the liturgy: they also made it come alive by dramatic acts with a long tradition, like bathing in the Jordan,[9] eating the favourite fish of the Lord,[10] and, for some pilgrims, by

[1] Got, Gge, Gej, Gds, Pde, Nik, Gic, 2Gu.
[2] Gqu 10, see also 1Gu 1, Gbe 6, 7Gu 100, 107.
[3] Wge 32, 35, 37: for other examples see Thc 105 and Jph 23.4.
[4] Sae 6, 7, 28, 32, Dan 51, 56, 70, 77, 88.
[5] Dan 1A, 96, Thc 1 and see 1 Cor 4.13.
[6] Thc 22, 73, and see Ps. 41.1, 72.13, 82.3, 113.17, Matt 11.5, 2 Cor 6.10.
[7] Thc 5.
[8] Jwü 132, Dan 53.
[9] Dan 31.
[10] Dan 78.

being scourged.[1] In all these ways pilgrims experienced the Holy Land, and saw 'with their own eyes all the Holy Places where Christ our God had walked for our salvation'.[2]

Pilgrimages were partly written down because they were one of the high points of a Christian life. The experience of 'exploring and venerating'[3] the Holy Places might attract some one else to go on pilgrimage. But the works were also written down for people who could never go. John of Würzburg and Theoderic were diligent in copying down the verses which they saw in the Holy Places, partly to give an unmistakable impression of what pilgrimage was like.

For pilgrims there were wonders in the Holy Land. Saewulf marvels at the smell of balsam coming from the Patriarchs' Tombs,[4] and later pilgrims wonder at the good achievements of the Hospital.[5] But for Fretellus one of the wonders was that the Holy Land had been conquered by the Second Israel. In his prologue, addressed to Bishop Henry Sdyck, he says:

> You have sought to correct your ways, and to examine whether you have anything you know you should renounce. And you have not been ashamed to travel from, we may say, Egypt to the Promised Land, or from Babylon to Jerusalem. You have not been frightened at the length of the journey by land or by the waves of the sea, since you long for the native land of our Saviour Emmanuel, from whom the Second Israel has removed the Philistines and Canaan. So gaze on Holy Jerusalem and view this Sion. For it stands for us as an allegory of Paradise. It is the place in which now the mighty men of Israel, that is the New Maccabees, have guarded the 'litter of the True Solomon',[6] and driven out of it Idumaea and Amalek.[7]

The wonder of the Latins conquering the Holy Land could not be shared in an equal measure by, for example, the Greek Christians. But the chief wonder, common to the whole Christian

[1] Thc 63.
[2] Dan 96.
[3] Sae 31.
[4] Sae 26.
[5] Jwü 159, Thc 33.
[6] See Cant 3.7. Bernard, *de Laude Novae Militiae* 4, *PL* 182, 927 B-C compares the litter to the Holy Sepulchre.
[7] Fretellus, *Patri H.* 2, Boerens 6.

community, was theological. Saewulf says of the site of the Holy Sepulchre,

> All the prophecies and foretellings in the whole world about our Lord Jesus Christ were truly fulfilled there.[1]

Wonder and pleasure went together. Daniel praises God

> for allowing us unworthy men to see these holy places, so indescribable and unutterable[2]

and John Phocas begins his work by saying, 'It has been our joy to see holy things.'[3] Since Jesus Christ in the Holy Land 'displayed the presence of his bodily substance',[4] so Theoderic hopes to awaken in the minds of his readers a new love of Christ.

[1] Sae 9.
[2] Dan 56.
[3] Jph 1.1.
[4] Thc 112.

JERUSALEM PILGRIMAGE

Translations of the Texts

FIRST GUIDE

Any one who wishes to reach Jerusalem from places in the West should travel continually towards the Levant, and he will find the following sanctuaries in the region of Jerusalem. 1

In Jerusalem is *the chamber* covered *by a single stone, where Solomon wrote Wisdom,*[1] and in that place, between the Temple and the altar, *on the marble in front of the altar* was *shed the blood of Zachariah.*[2] *Not far* from that is the *stone to which, year after year, the Jews come. As they anoint it* they mourn, and then *depart, wailing. There too is the House of Hezekiah, King of Judah,*[3] to whose lifespan the Lord added fifteen years. 2

Then comes *the House of Caiaphas and the column* to which Christ was bound, *scourged,*[4] and beaten. *At the Gate of Neapolis* is *Pilate's Praetorium,*[5] where Christ was judged by the chief Priests.

Not far from that is *Golgotha*, the site of Calvary, *where* Christ, the Son of God, was *crucified.*[6] The first Adam also was buried there, and Abraham made his sacrifice to God. *About a* large *stone's throw* to the west of that is the place where Joseph of Arimathea buried the holy *body* of the Lord Jesus. *In that place* is a church magnificently built by Emperor *Constantine.*[7]

The Centre of the World is thirteen feet to the west of Mount Calvary. Over on the left is the Prison where Christ was imprisoned. To the right of the Sepulchre and near it is the Latin monastery in honour of St Mary the Virgin. Her house was there. In this monastery is the altar where Mary, the Lord's Mother, was standing, and with her Mary the wife of Cleophas and Mary Magdalene, weeping and mourning because they were watching the Lord on the Cross. In that place Jesus said to his Mother, 'Woman, behold thy son', and to the disciple, 'Behold thy mother!'

Two bowshots away from this place to the east is the Temple of

[1] Passages in italic type are quotations from the Bordeaux Pilgrim: Bord. 590.6.
[2] Bord. 596.1f. [3] Bord. 591.4–7. [4] Bord. 592.4.
[5] Bord. 593.1–3. [6] Bord. 593.4. [7] Bord. 594.1f.

the Lord, constructed by Solomon, in which Christ was presented by Simeon the Righteous. To the right of this Temple Solomon built his own Temple, and, between these two temples he built a beautiful portico with marble columns. On the left is the Probatica pool.

3 About a mile east of that one sees the Mount of Olives, where the Lord Jesus prayed to the Father saying, 'Father, if it be possible' and so on, and where he wrote the Our Father on a stone; and from there he ascended into heaven, saying to his disciples, 'Go, teach all nations' etc.

Between the Temple of the Lord and the Mount of Olives is the Valley of Jehoshaphat, where the Virgin Mary was buried by the apostles. In this valley the Lord will judge the world. Near that is '*the hamlet which is called Gethsemane*',[1] and near that is the garden on the far side of the Kidron Valley where Judas betrayed the Lord Jesus. Near that is the Tomb of *the Prophet Isaiah.*[2] A mile from there is *Bethany, where* Lazarus was *raised* by the *Lord*[3] on the fourth day after his death.

Thirteen or *eighteen* miles away in that direction, facing Jericho, *is the sycamore tree into which Zacchaeus climbed in order to see*[4] the Lord Jesus. *A mile away* in the opposite direction from Jericho is *Elisha's Spring*, which he blessed by throwing salt into it.

Five miles from that is the River *Jordan*, in which *the Lord was baptized by John:* the distance from this to Jerusalem is eight leagues.

Not far from that is the *mount* from which *Elijah was taken up.*[5]

4 From the Jordan it is a journey of eighteen days to Mount Sinai, where the Lord appeared to Moses in the burning bush, and gave him the Law. Moreover there is a large jar there which produces an inexhaustible supply of oil.

Mount Tabor is three days' journey from Jerusalem. The Lord was transfigured there, and it is said that Galilee and the Sea of Tiberias are said to be at the foot of this mount. It is not a sea, but the lake from which the Jordan runs.

5 South of Jerusalem, a bowshot outside the wall, is Mount Sion, and the church there was built by Solomon. There Jesus had the Supper with his disciples, and in the same place he sent the Holy Spirit upon them. There too the Virgin Mary departed this life and

[1] Matt 26.36.
[2] Bord. 595.3.
[3] Bord. 596.2.
[4] Bord. 596.4.
[5] Bord. 598.1–3.

gave up the ghost, and the apostles took her most holy body to the Valley of Jehoshaphat. At the foot of this mount is the Pool of Siloam, which springs strongly out of the ground.

Not far from that is *Shechem*, to which *Joseph*[1] came '*from the* 6
valley of Hebron'[2] to seek his brethren. In that place is the *plot of ground which Jacob gave* to Joseph his son, and his body rests there. *A mile from that is Sychar, where the Lord spoke to the woman of Samaria.*[3] Not far from that is the place where *Jacob wrestled* with the *angel.*[4]

Bethlehem is there, the City of David where Christ was born. It 7
is four miles away from Jerusalem, to the south. In that place is the church, constructed with marble columns, where Christ was born. Not far to the right of this is the Lord's Manger.

Twelve miles further on is the Village of Abraham, which is called Thocor, where Abraham himself and Isaac and Jacob are buried with their wives. On the left is the mount called 'The Lord saw', where God spoke with Abraham,[5] and where Abraham himself was ready to sacrifice his son Isaac.

[1] Bord. 587.5.
[2] Gen 37.12.
[3] Bord. 588.1–4.
[4] Bord. 588.10.
[5] Gen. 22.14.

QUALITER

[THE ARRANGEMENT OF THE CITY OF JERUSALEM: A DESCRIPTION OF THE HOLY PLACES]

1 In the Name of our Lord, Jesus Christ!

2 Any one who may wish to go to Jerusalem, the Holy City, should continue to travel eastwards, and this is how, with God's guidance, he will reach Holy Jerusalem.

3 To its west can be seen the Mount of Joy, a remarkable sight. It is one mile from this Mount to the City, and as one enters the city there is a stronghold, the Tower of David.

4 Moreover the Temple of the Holy Sepulchre is round in shape, and over the Holy Sepulchre, at the topmost point of the Temple, is a round opening. The Sepulchre of our Lord Jesus Christ is in the middle of the Temple and, while outside this too is round, the inside turns out to be rectangular. As they enter it the people go in through a door at the east, and the way to the inner part is through a second door on its own. The people come out through a door on the south. Further east is the Centre of the World. Not far from that on the east is Mount Calvary, on which the Lord was crucified, and under this Mount is Golgotha. The distance from the Mount to the Holy Sepulchre is the distance a person can throw a stone the size of his fist. On the left of Mount Calvary is the Prison and, next to the Prison on the left, the column on which he was bound. South of the Holy Sepulchre is St Mary Latin. To the east of Mount Calvary is the place where St Helena discovered the Cross of the Lord.

5 To the east of that is the Gate Beautiful, which leads to the Temple of the Lord. It is a round temple with three doors and is surrounded by a courtyard most remarkable to see. In the middle of this Temple is the 'Temple made without hands', that is, the

Tabernacle. In it are preserved, so it is believed, the rod of Aaron, the head of Zachariah the son of Barachiah, the altar which Jacob built to the Lord, the two tablets of the Testament, the Ark of the Covenant, and the manna with which the children of Israel were nourished in the desert. Moreover in the top part of the Temple there hangs a lamp of gold.

Southwards from the Temple of the Lord is the Temple of Solomon. To the east of the Temple of the Lord, outside the gate of the courtyard, is the Probatica Pool which has five porches. After leaving that through the city gate on the east comes the Valley of Jehoshaphat, containing the church and sacred tomb of the most holy and sacred Mary, and the Garden of Gethsemane, where the Lord prayed with his disciples and where he was betrayed by Judas, the traitor who was one of his disciples. 6

To the east of this place is the Mount of Olives from which the Lord ascended the heavens, and where he wrote the Our Father for the disciples. One mile from the Mount of Olives is the tomb from which the Lord raised Lazarus on the fourth day after his death. 7

Also, more than six leagues away from there, is the place where the Lord fasted for forty days, and where he was tempted by the Devil, but without giving way to him. From this mountain it is six miles to the River Jordan. 8

And south of Jerusalem, more than four miles away, is Bethlehem, the city of David in which Christ was born, and the well over which the star descended which had led the Magi to worship the Child. Close outside the gate of Jerusalem which is on the south is Mount Sion, where St Mary departed from this world. Not far from that is Aceldama, *that is, the field of blood.* A little to the south of that is the Pool of Siloam. Down the Mount and near the city walls which pass that part is the place where Peter wept after he had denied Christ. On the north, outside the city gate, is the place where St Stephen was stoned. 9

And this is how all the sanctuaries in Jerusalem have been built. I am a witness to them, for I have seen them, and have written this account, insignificant though it is. 10

OTTOBONIAN GUIDE

1 [NOW THE DESCRIPTION OF JERUSALEM IS AS FOLLOWS]

2 The entry of Jerusalem is on the west side next to the Tower of David. Beneath in the city is the Sepulchre of the Lord, and outside it is the centre of the world. From there to the north is the Prison of the Lord, and next to it is where he was bound and flogged, crowned and stripped, and where his clothes were shared out. Mount Calvary: under it is Golgotha, where the blood of the Lord fell through the rent rock. Beyond this mount is a place in which St Helena found the Cross of the Lord.

3 Beneath that to the east is the Temple of the Lord, in which there are four entries, from the east, west, north, and south. There they say was the Ark of the Lord. And there are the tables of the covenant and the seven golden lamps and the Rod of Aaron, and a room where the Archangel Gabriel appeared to the Prophet Zacharias. Near there is the Beautiful Gate which leads towards the Valley of Jehoshaphat, and on the other side of the Temple, towards the south is the Temple of Solomon, at one end of which is the cradle of Christ and the bed of his Mother, And on the other side of the Temple of the Lord is the church of Blessed Anne, the Mother of Mary the Lord's Mother. Next to it is the Sheep Pool.

4 Outside the city is the Valley of Jehoshaphat, and there is a church there in which Saint Mary was buried by the Apostles. In the same place is the place of Gethsemane where Judas betrayed Jesus to the Jews, and the place is nearby where our Lord prayed. Then there is the Mount of Olives, where the Lord ascended into heaven and wrote the 'Our Father'. Going on east from there is Bethany, where the Lord gave life to Lazarus.

5 Mount Sion is on the south of the city, where Saint Mary died, where the Lord supped with his disciples, and where he gave the

Apostles the Holy Spirit on the Day of Pentecost. Opposite this mountain is Akeldama, and on the other side to the east is the Pool of Siloam.

Bethlehem is two leagues away to the south of the city, where 6
the Lord was born, and there is the Manger where the Lord was laid when he had been born, and the Table at which Blessed Mary ate with the three kings who were seeking God. His bath is there and the bed, where also they say that 144,000 people were killed by Herod.

On the east side of the city is the River Jordan, ten leagues away. 7
Along that road is Jericho, near which is the Quarantana, where the Lord fasted forty days.

SAEWULF

A RELIABLE ACCOUNT OF THE SITUATION OF JERUSALEM

1 I am Saewulf. Though I am unworthy and sinful I was on my way to Jerusalem in order to pray at the Lord's Tomb. I could not cross the open sea with others going there by the direct route, whether because of the burden of my sins or because no ship was available. In any case I have decided to give an account of the islands through which I travelled and their names.

2 Some people board ship at Bari, others at Barletta, still others at Siponto or Trani, or perhaps make the sea crossing from Otranto, the last port in Apulia. But we boarded a ship at Monopoli, a day's journey away from Bari, one Sunday, the feast of Saint Mildred, Virgin, the thirteenth of July. It later turned out to be an inauspicious moment for us, and if God's mercy had not protected us, we should all have been drowned. That day, when we were a long way from the port out at sea, our ship suffered some damage through the force of the waves. But God was kind to us, and we got back to the shore unhurt.

3 Next we went to Brindisi. On another inauspicious day[1] we boarded the same ship again – though by now it had been mended – and put ashore at a Greek island, at the city which, like the island, is called Corphu, on the vigil of St James the Apostle.[2] From there we reached an island called Cephallonia, driven there by a great storm,

[1] 'Inauspicious day' stands for the Latin 'Egyptian Day'. Egyptian Days were considered unlucky for starting any undertaking, such as a journey. Christians observed them, despite the fact the leaders of the church disapproved. Thus Saint Augustine believed that Galatians 4.10–11 referred to these days (*PL* 35.2129) which were calculated by 'Astrologers and Chaldaeans'. Saewulf's system of computing such days may not have been the same is that used by Durandus, *Rat. Offic.* 8.4.20. See also Du Cange, *Glossarium Mediae et Infimae Latinitatis*, *s.v.* Dies, 5.

[2] i.e. 24 July.

on the first of August. Robert Guiscard died there, and there some of our men died, which caused us much grief. After that we sailed on from there and put in at Polipolis. Then we came to the important island of Patras, and went into the city there to pray to blessed Andrew the Apostle: he was martyred and buried there, and later translated to Constantinople. From Patras on the vigil of St Laurence[1] we came to Corinth. Blessed Paul the Apostle preached the word of God there and wrote a letter to its people. There we suffered many hardships. From there we made the crossing to the port of Hosta, and thus we travelled on foot (but some on donkeys) two days journey to Thebes, a city which the people call Stinas. And next day we came to Nigrepontus on the vigil of St Bartholomew the Apostle,[2] and there we bought a passage on another ship.

Moreover Athens, where the Apostle Paul preached, is two days' 4
journey distant from Corinth. Blessed Dionysus was born and educated there, and later converted to God by Blessed Paul. A church of the Blessed Virgin is there in which there is an ever-burning lamp in which there is oil but it never runs out.

Then we came to an island called Petalion, then to Andria, where they manufacture expensive satin and samite and other materials made with silk. From there we came to Tenas, then to Sura, then to Myconos, and so to Naxia, with the famous island of Crete off to one side of it. From there to Carea and Omargos and Samos and Scion and Metelina, and afterwards we came to Patmos, where Blessed John, Apostle and Evangelist, was exiled by Domitian Caesar, and wrote the Apocalypse: Ephesus is to one side (near Smyrna, a day's journey off) where later on he [the Blessed John] went living into his tomb. The Apostle Paul also wrote a letter to the Ephesians. Then we came to the islands of Leros and Kalymnos and afterwards to Anchus, the birthplace of Galen, a doctor most highly regarded among the Greeks. From there we crossed through Lido, a ruined city, where Titus preached, the disciple of Paul the Apostle. Then we came to Asum, which means 'silver'.

After this we came to famous Rhodes, which is said to have 5
contained one of the seven wonders of the world, that is to say an idol, namely the Colossus, which was 125 feet long. The Persians destroyed it, and practically the whole province of Romania when

[1] On 9 August. [2] On 23 August.

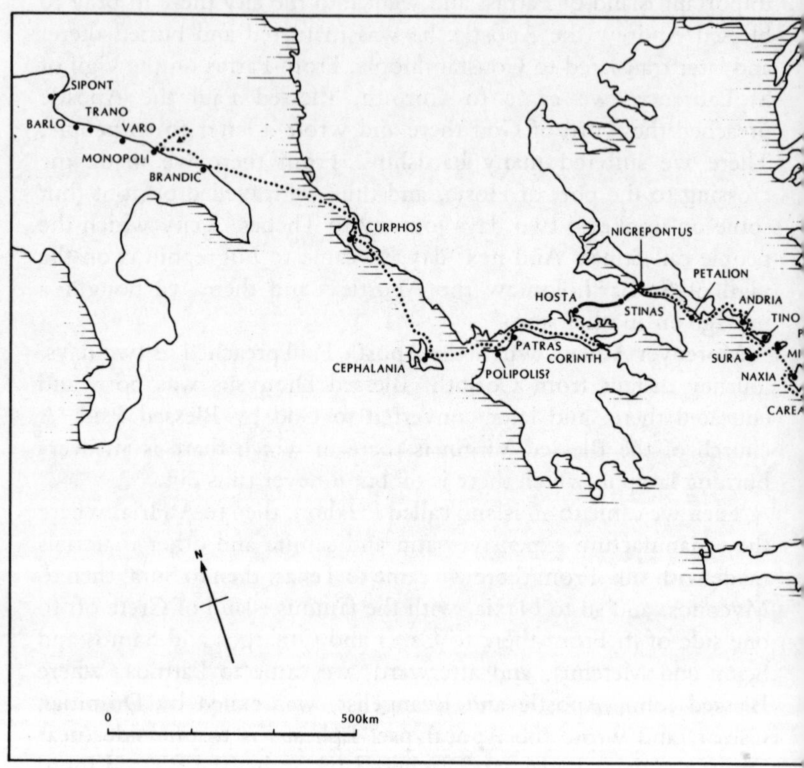

Fig. 20. Saewulf's journey from Monopoli to Jerusalem.

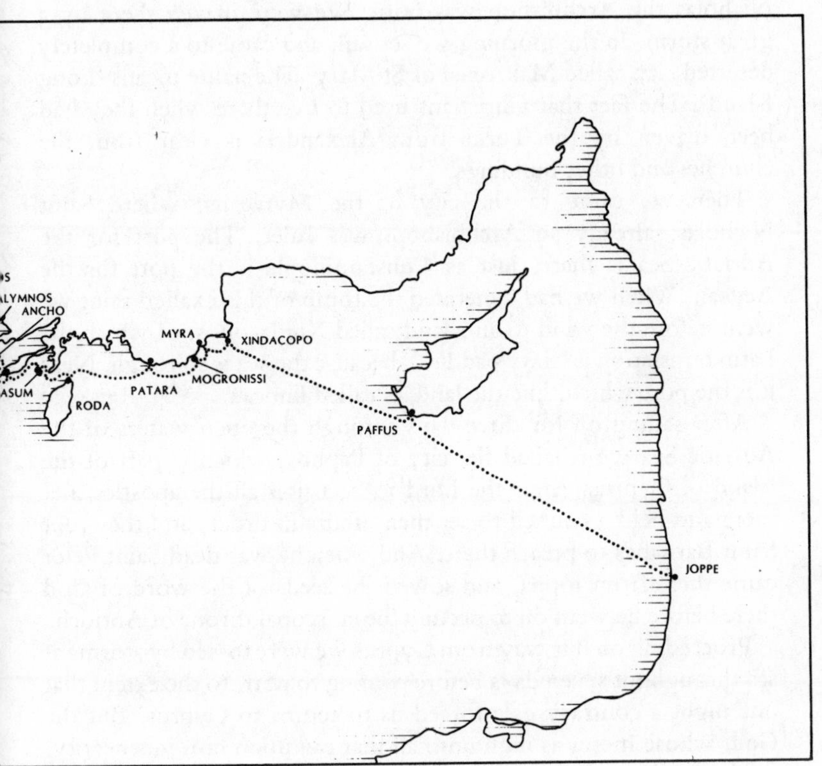
S
LYMNOS
ANCHO
MYRA
XINDACOPO
MOGRONISSI
ASUM
PATARA
RODA
PAFFUS
JOPPE

they advanced to Spain. Blessed Paul also wrote an epistle to the Colossians.

From there it was a day's journey to Patera, where Blessed Nicholas the Archbishop was born. We were driven there by a great storm. In the morning we set sail, and came to a completely deserted city called Makronisi of St Mary. The name means 'Long Island'. The fact that Christians used to live there when they had been driven by the Turks from Alexandria is clear from the churches and other buildings.

Then we came to the city of the Myraeans, where Saint Nicholas, already an Archbishop, was ruler. The port for the Adriatic Sea is there, just as Constantinople is the port for the Aegean. When we had venerated the tomb of this exalted saint we went before the wind to an island called Xindacopos, of which the Latin translation is 'sixty paddles', because the sea is so rough. Near it is the port which, like the land, is called Finica.

After sailing on for three days through the open waters of the Adriatic Sea we reached the city of Paphos, which is part of the island of Cyprus. After the Lord's Ascension all the apostles met there and held a council to set their affairs in order, and they sent Saint Barnabas to preach there. And when he was dead Saint Peter came there from Joppa, and sowed the seeds of the word of God there before he went on to occupy the episcopal throne of Antioch.

6 Proceeding on our way from Cyprus we were tossed by storms at sea throughout seven days before coming to port, to the extent that one night a contrary gale forced us to return to Cyprus. But the God, whose mercy is nigh unto all that call upon him in sincerity, we besought earnestly with all our hearts, and by his mercy we continued again with our journey to our intended destination. But for seven nights we were so discouraged by the storms and the dangers that almost all of us had lost hope of escape. Then in the morning as the sun rose, the shore of the port of Joppa[1] was visible before our eyes. And because we had been depressed by all the disturbance caused by the danger, this unexpected good fortune, beyond all our hopes, brought us a hundred times more happiness. So, after a spell of thirteen weeks – as it was a Sunday when we had gone aboard at Monopoli – during which we had lived sometimes on the waves of the sea, and sometimes in empty huts or cottages

[1] Joppa, i.e. Jaffa.

(since the Greeks do not welcome guests), with great happiness and gratitude we arrived at the port of Joppa on a Sunday.

Now I beseech you, all my most favoured friends, to rejoice with 7
hands stretched on high! Rejoice before God with me in the voice of thanksgiving, because he has dealt so graciously with me in every part of my journey, who is powerful – may his name be blessed now and for evermore! Hear then, my beloved friends, and listen to the mercy which the divine clemency showed to me – albeit the least of his servants – and to my people.

For on the very day on which we came into port a certain man said to me (as I imagine through God), 'Sir, go ashore today, in case tonight or tomorrow morning a storm comes up, and tomorrow you are not able to land!' With that I was immediately wanting to land. I hired a boat and landed with all my people.

While I was making for the land the sea was rough. The movement of the sea increased and the storm became strong, but through the divine grace which favoured me I reached the shore unharmed. That's that. We entered the city to seek shelter, and defeated and worn out by long labours we ate and drank, and retired to rest. But the next morning, when we had been at the church, we heard the sound of the sea, and people shouting, all congregating and telling of new and unheard-of horrors. We were afraid, and running along with the others came to the shore. When we were there we saw the storm, with the height of its waves equal to the hills. We noticed innumerable human bodies of both sexes who had been drowned lying miserably on the shore. We saw too the remains of ships floating nearby. No sound could be heard apart from the noise of the sea, and the sinking ships, for it drowned the shouts of the people and the sound of the crowds.

Our own ship, which was very large and strong, and up till now had contained much corn and other cargo, and bore pilgrims coming and returning, was still in the deep water, held by anchors and ropes. But how it was tossed with waves! Now was the hour of disaster, and how many of its cargoes were thrown overboard! No eye which beheld it could be so hard and strong as to refrain from tears. It was not long before the anchors gave way, through the violent waves of the current. The ropes broke, and any ships which were released to the fury of the waves were bound not to escape. For one moment they were lifted up, and the next they were down in the deep, so that gradually they drew in from the deep water to be dashed against the sand of the rocks. There they broke up, sadly going from one side to the other and being ground to bits by the storm. Because of the gale they could not reach the deep water in one piece, and because of the steep rise of the sand to reach the shore without harm.

What is the use of saying how sadly the sailors and pilgrims – some in boats, some clutching to masts or to yards or to cross-members – had all hope of escape gone. That's that. Some people were consumed with terror and drowned there and then. Some people were – as seemed unbelievable to many – clutching to the wooden parts of the ship, but as I saw they were cut to pieces or, being snatched off the timber of the ship, were taken off to deep water. Some people who knew how to swim took the chance of trusting to the waves, and many of them died, but just a few, trusting in their own strength, reached the shore safely.

So of thirty big ships, some known as Dormundi, others Gulafri and others Cats, all of them laden with palmers and merchandise, before I left the shore only a mere seven remained unharmed. Of human beings of either sex more than a thousand died that day.

No eye has seen greater misery in one day. But from all these things the Lord by his grace has saved me, to whom be honour and glory through innumerable ages. Amen.

8 So we climbed up from Joppa into the city of Jerusalem. The journey lasted two days and it was by a very hard mountain road. It was very dangerous too, because the Saracens, who are continually plotting an ambush against Christians, were hiding in the caves of the hills and among rocky caverns. They were awake day and night, always keeping a look-out for someone to attack, whether because he had not enough people with him, or because he was fatigued enough to leave a space between himself and his party. Sometimes the Saracens could be seen everywhere in the neighbourhood, and sometimes they disappeared.

Anyone who has taken that road can see how many human bodies there are in the road and next to the road, and there are countless corpses which have been torn up by wild beasts. It might be questioned why so many Christian corpses should lie there unburied, but it is in fact no surprise. There is little soil there, and the rocks are not easy to move. Even if the soil were there, who would be stupid enough to leave his brethren and be alone digging a grave! Anybody who did this would dig a grave not for his fellow

Christian but for himself! So in that road not only poor and weak people have dangers to face, but also the rich and strong. Many are killed by the Saracens and many of heat and thirst – many through lack of drink and many from drinking too much. But we with all our company arrived at our goal unharmed, *Praise be to the Lord, who has not relinquished his ear from my prayer or his mercy from me.*[1] Amen.

The entry of the city of *Jerusalem is* to the *west*, beside the Keep of 9
King *David*,[2] through the gate which is called 'David's Gate'. *First* one goes down to *the Church*[3] *of the Holy Sepulchre,*[4] *which is* called *Martyrium*, not only *because of the arrangement of the streets*,[5] but because it is more celebrated than any other church, and this is meet and right, since all the prophecies and foretellings in the whole world about our Saviour Jesus Christ were all truly fulfilled there. When the *Lord's Cross* had been found, Archbishop Maximus built the church *royally* and *magnificently*,[6] since the Emperor Constantine and his mother Helena favoured him. In the middle of the church is the Lord's Sepulchre, which is surrounded by a strong wall. The church is open above the Sepulchre, though open in such a way that when it is raining no rain falls on the Holy Sepulchre.

This church (and the city itself) is sited on the *slopes* of Mount Sion. But after the Roman princes *Titus* and Vespasian totally *destroyed*[7] the city to avenge the Lord, they fulfilled a prophecy of the Lord that goes thus: *And when the Lord drew near to Jerusalem and saw the city, weeping over it he said, 'Would that even today you yourself knew that the days were coming on you when your enemies shall surround you with a fence, and hem you in on every side, and dash you to the ground, you and your children within you, and they will not leave one stone upon another'*,[8] and so on.

We know that *the Lord* was *killed outside the gate*. But the Emperor *Hadrian*, who *was called Elijah*,[9] rebuilt the city of Jerusalem and the Temple of the Lord, and increased the area of the city to the Tower of David, which had before been far from the city. Indeed anyone can see from the Mount of Olives where the furthest city wall to the west was before and how much it has been increased. The Emperor called the city by his own name '*Aelia*',[10] which is

[1] Psalm 65.20.
[2] Got 2.
[3] Bede [Holy Places] 2.1.
[4] Got 2.
[5] Bede 2.1.
[6] Bede 2.1.
[7] Bede 1.1
[8] Based on Luke 19.41.
[9] Bede 1.1.
[10] Bede 1.1.

translated 'House of God'. Some say that the city was restored by the Emperor Justinian, and that the Temple of the Lord was like it is today. But they say that according to their own opinion and not according to the truth: for the Assyrians, whose fathers were inhabitants of this country from the first persecution, say that the city was captured and destroyed seven times after the sufferings of our Lord (and this was so for all the churches) but it was never completely destroyed.

10 Some very holy places are to be seen in the court of the Church of the Holy Sepulchre, that is to say the *Prison* where our *Lord* Jesus Christ was imprisoned after he had been betrayed, to which also the Assyrians bear witness. A little *beyond* there *is the place* where *the Holy Cross* with the other crosses was found, and where in honour of *Queen Helena* a great church was built, but it was afterwards completely destroyed by the pagans. Again in this direction, not far from the Prison, a marble column is to be seen, to which Jesus Christ our Lord was *bound* in the Praetorium, and made to suffer with cruel *stripes*. Near there is the place where our Lord was made to take his *clothes* off by the soldiers. Then there is the place where he was made to put on the purple robe by the soldiers, and *crowned* with the crown of thorns, and they *divided his raiment*, casting lots.

11 Afterwards you go up to *Mount Calvary*[1] where the Patriarch Abraham made an altar, and in obedience to God wished to sacrifice his son to him. In the same place afterwards the Son of God, whom he prefigured, was sacrificed as a victim to God the Father for the redemption of the world. The crag of the rock of this mountain is itself a witness of the sufferings of our Lord, for next to the hole in which the Lord's Cross was fixed there is a great rent, for without a rent the death of its Maker could not take place, as it says in the Passion-narrative, '*The rocks were rent*'.[2]

Below is the place called Golgotha, where it is said that by the streaming of the Lord's blood running over him Adam was raised from the dead, just as it says in the Passion of the Lord, '*And many bodies of the saints were raised*'.[3] But in the *Sentences* of Blessed Augustine we read that '*Adam was buried in Hebron, where moreover the three patriarchs were buried with their wives: Abraham with Sara, Isaac with Rebecca, and Jacob with Lia, and the bones of Joseph which the*

[1] This seems parallel to the appropriate passage in Got 2, and especially the word '*beyond*' (*superius*), which goes well with 'beyond' (*super*) in Got.
[2] Matt.27.51.
[3] Matt.27.52f.

children of Israel brought with them from Egypt'.[1] Near this place of Calvary is the Church of St Mary, in the place where the Lord's body was taken down from the Cross, and before he was buried he had spices put on him, and was wrapped in his shroud and his napkin.

Outside[2] the Church of the Holy Sepulchre but within its 12
surrounding walls, not far from the place of Calvary, is the place called 'Compas', where our Lord Jesus Christ with his own hand marked and measured the *centre of the world*,[3] as the Psalmist bears witness: '*But the Lord our King has before the ages worked salvation in the centre of the earth*'.[4] Some people say that in that place our Lord Jesus Christ first appeared to Mary Magdalen, when she was weeping and questioned him, and thought he was the gardener, as the gospel-writer says. These very holy places of prayer are contained in the court of the Lord's Sepulchre on the east. But beside the church itself, on one side and the other, there are two famous chapels, one dedicated to St Mary and the other to St John, for those two participants of the Lord's sufferings stood thus at his side, on one side and the other. In the west wall of the chapel of Saint Mary is to be seen, painted outside, the picture of the Mother of God. Mary the Egyptian was once repentant with all her heart, and praying for the help of the Mother of God, and was wonderfully consoled by the figure in the picture speaking by the power of the Holy Spirit, as is to be read in her *Life*.

On the other side of the church of Saint John is the very beautiful monastery of the Holy Trinity, in which there is the place of the baptistery. The Chapel of Saint James the Apostle is beyond this, who first obtained the bishop's throne in Jerusalem. And these buildings are arranged in such a way that a person who stands in the end one can clearly see all the five chapels from one door to the other.

Beside the door of the Church *of the Holy Sepulchre to the south* is 13
the Church of *St Mary* which is called *Latin*,[5] because the Latin language is the one in which the monks do service to the Lord. The Assyrians also say that the Blessed Mother of God stood at the crucifixion of her Son our Lord in the same spot where the altar

[1] Perhaps the reference is not to the *Sentences*, but to Jerome, *L.loc.*7.13, or *Ep.*108.11.

[2] *Outside* (*ad caput*) is comparable with Got.2 'outside it' (*in capite*).

[3] Got.2.

[4] Psalm 74.12.

[5] 1Gu.2.

now is in this church. Next to this church another one, also of Saint Mary, which is called 'Small'. Nuns are there in the service of Saint Mary and her Son. Next to this is the Hospital where there is a famous monastery dedicated in honour of St John the Baptist.

14 One goes down moreover from the Sepulchre of the Lord *for a distance of two cross-bow shots*[1] *to the Temple of the Lord, which is to the east*[2] of the Holy Sepulchre. Its court is great both in length and breadth, and it has many doors. But the principal *door* which is before *the Temple* is called '*Beautiful*',[3] on account of the sculpture and the variety of colours. This is where Peter cured the lame man when he *and John went up into the Temple at the ninth hour of prayer*, as it says in the Acts of the Apostles.[4]

The place where Solomon built the Temple of the Lord was anciently called Bethel. To this place by God's command came Jacob, and in the place where he stayed he saw a ladder whose top reached heaven, and angels going up and down on it. He said, '*This place truly is blessed*', as one reads in Genesis. '*And there he set up a stone as a pillar and built an altar, pouring oil over it.*'[5]

Afterwards in this place, by divine command, Solomon made the Temple of the Lord. He built it with magnificent workmanship without any equal, and decorated it with all the ornament about which one reads in the Book of Kings. Its height was more than the hills around it, and in its beauty and its glory it excelled all other houses and buildings. In the middle of this Temple is to be seen a rock which is high and large and hollow underneath, in which was the Holy of Holies. There Solomon put *the Ark of the Covenant*, with *the Manna* and *the Rod of Aaron*, which grew flowers and leaves, and produced an almond, and *the Two Tables of the Covenant.*[6]

15 There our Lord Jesus Christ when he was tired of the mockery of the Jews used to rest. There is the place of confession where his disciples used to confess to him. *There the* Arch*angel Gabriel appeared to Zacharias the Priest,*[7] and said '*Take a child in thy old age!*'[8] There also *Zacharias the son of Barachias was slain between the porch and the altar.*[9] There the child Jesus was circumcised on the eighth

[1] IGu.2. [2] Got.3.
[3] Got.3. [4] Acts 3.1.
[5] Gen.28.17,19. This altar appears also in Gqu.5.
[6] Gqu.5: see Fulcher of Chartres, *Hist. Hier.* 1.26, a view he retracted by 1106.
[7] Got.3. [8] Luke 1.13.
[9] Matt 23.35. See also Gqu.5.

day, and was named 'Jesus', which is translated 'Saviour'. There the Lord Jesus was offered by his parents with the Virgin Mother Mary on the day of her Purification, and received by the old man Simeon. There too, when Jesus *had reached the age of twelve years*, he was *found sitting among the doctors, listening to them and asking them questions*,[1] as is written in the Gospel. From there afterwards he drove out the oxen and sheep and doves, saying, '*My house shall be called a house of prayer*'.[2] There he said to the Jews, '*Destroy this temple, and in three days I will raise it again*'.[3] There the footprints of the Lord still appear in the rock when he *hid himself and left the Temple*, as we read in the Gospel, in order that the *Jews* should not throw *the stones*[4] they were carrying. To this place was *brought the woman taken in adultery, who was taken* to Jesus by the Jews in order that they might find out how to *accuse* him.[5]

There is the city gate on the east side of the Temple which is called 'Golden', where Joachim, father of the Blessed Mary, at the command of the angel of God, met his wife Anna. Through this gate the Lord Jesus, when he came from Bethany on the Day of Palms, entered Jerusalem sitting upon an ass, when the boys were singing, '*Hosanna to the Son of David!*'[6] Through this gate Emperor Heraclius entered when he came from Persia victorious with the Lord's Cross. Before his entry the stones fell down and closed the Gate, so that the gate was made a solid wall. That was until the angel gave him a message. Then he descended humbly from his horse and the way to enter opened up for him. In the court of the *Temple* of the Lord *to the south is the Temple of Solomon*,[7] of enormous size, and to its east is a small sanctuary which, the Assyrians say, contains *the Cradle* and the Bath *of Christ Jesus and the Bed of his* Blessed *Mother*.[8]

From the Temple of the Lord one goes north to the *Church of* Saint 16
Anne,[9] the Mother of Blessed Mary, where she and her husband lived. There also she gave birth to her daughter, the most beloved Mary, who saved all the faithful. Near there is *the Sheep Pool*,[10] *which in Hebrew is called 'Bethsaida', with five porches*,[11] about which the Gospel informs us. A little further up is the place where the woman was healed by the Lord, who touched the fringe of his

[1] Luke 2.46.
[2] Matt 21.13.
[3] John 2.19.
[4] John 8.59.
[5] John 8.36.
[6] Matt 21.15.
[7] Gqu.6, Got.3.
[8] Got.3.
[9] Got.3.
[10] Got.3.
[11] John 5.2.

garment while he was *jostled by crowds* in the street. She had *suffered a flow of blood for twelve years,*[1] and could not be cured by doctors.

17 From Saint Anne one goes through the gate leading to the *Valley of Jehoshaphat* to *the Church of Saint Mary* in this valley, where she was taken by *the apostles* after her death *to be* honourably *buried.*[2] Her tomb is revered by the faithful with the greatest honour, as is meet and right. There monks serve our Lord Jesus Christ and his Mother day and night.

There is the Brook Kidron. There too is *Gethsemane* to which the Lord came with his disciples, at the time of his *betrayal,*[3] from Mount Sion across the Brook Kidron. There is a chapel where he sent Peter and James and John, saying, '*Stay here and watch with me!*',[4] and he went forward and fell on his face and prayed. And he came to his disciples and found them sleeping. Also there are the places where the disciples slept, each by himself.

Gethsemane is at the foot of *The Mount of Olives,*[5] and the Brook Kidron beneath it is between Mount Sion and the Mount of Olives, and forms the division between the mountains. The plain between them is called Jehoshaphat.

A little further up the Mount of Olives is a chapel in the place where the Lord prayed, according to what it says in the Passion: '*And he was distant from them a stone's throw. And being in an agony he prayed more fervently, and his sweat became like drops of blood flowing to the ground*'.[6] Thereafter the price of the Lord was used to buy the Field of Akeldama, and this is also at the foot of the Mount of Olives near the valley. Its distance from Gethsemane is two or three cross-bow shots to the south, where numberless tombs are to be seen. This field is next to the tombs of the holy father *Simeon the Righteous* and *Joseph, the foster-father of the Lord.*[7] These two tombs are made in an antique manner like towers, and are cut into the rock at the bottom of the mountain. Afterwards one goes down near *Akeldama* to the fountain called *the Pool of Siloam.*[8] In this, on our Lord's command, the man born *blind washed* his eyes, and before his *eyes* had *been anointed* with *mud and saliva* by the Lord.[9]

18 One goes up from the aforesaid Church of Saint Mary *to the east.*

[1] Luke 8.44: but the biblical place is not in Jerusalem but in Capernaum.
[2] Got.4.
[3] See Gqu.6, Got.4.
[4] Matt 26.38.
[5] See Gqu.7, Got.4.
[6] Luke 22.44.
[7] Bede 5.3.
[8] See Gqu.9, Got.5.
[9] John 9.1,6.

It is a steep path which leads almost to the top of *the Mount of Olives*, to the place where our Lord *in the presence of* the disciples *ascended* into heaven.[1] That place is defended by a wall and well arranged, and there is an altar inside over the place itself, and this too is completely surrounded by a wall. In the place also where the Apostles stood, with his mother Blessed Mary, marvelling at his ascension, is the Altar of Saint Mary. There too *the two men stood near them clad in white, saying, 'Men of Galilee, why do you stand looking into heaven?'*[2] and so on. A stone's throw away from there *our Lord wrote the Lord's Prayer*[3] with his own hands upon the rock, in Hebrew, so the Assyrians state. There was a very beautiful church there, but later it had been totally destroyed by the pagans.

All these churches are outside the walls, and the Church on 19
Mount Sion is outside the wall *to the south*, a bow-shot away. There the *Apostles*[4] received *the promise of the Father*,[5] that is the Paraclete *Spirit on the day of Pentecost*.[6] There they made the Creed. In that church is a chapel *where blessed Mary died*.[7] On the other side of the church is a chapel in the place where the Lord Jesus Christ first appeared to his Apostles, and it is called 'Galilee', just as he said to his apostles, '*After I am raised I will go before you to Galilee*'.[8] This place is called 'Galilee' after the Apostles. They often used to stay there, and they were called 'Galilaeans'.

The great city of Galilee is next to *Mount Tabor*, and *a three days'* 20
journey from Jerusalem.[9] On the other side of Mount Tabor is the city called Tiberias, and then one comes to Capernaum and Nazareth. Near the Sea of Galilee or the Sea of Tiberias is the place to which Peter and the other apostles went fishing after the Lord's resurrection, and where the Lord afterwards revealed himself on the sea. Near the city of Tiberias is the field where the Lord Jesus blessed the five loaves and two fishes, and afterwards fed four thousand men with them as it says in the gospels. But I must return to the main theme.

In the Galilee of Mount Sion, where the Apostles were hidden in 21
a room *for fear of the Jews, with locked doors*, Jesus *stood in the midst* of them *saying, 'Peace to you!'*.[10] And there he again showed himself

[1] Gqu.7, Acts 1.9.
[2] Acts 1.10.
[3] See Gqu.7.
[4] See Got.5.
[5] Luke 24.29.
[6] See Got.5.
[7] See Gqu.9. and Got.5.
[8] Matt 26.32.
[9] 1Gu.4.
[10] John 20.19.

when Thomas *put his finger in his side*, and into *the place of the nails.*[1] There he *had supper with his disciples*[2] before his passion and washed their feet, and there is still a marble table there on which he had supper. In that place are the relics of Saint Stephen, Nicodemus, Gamaliel and Abibo, which were honourably laid there by Saint John the Patriarch after they had been discovered.

The stoning of Saint Stephen was outside the wall to the north, about two or three cross-bow shots away, and there is a very beautiful church built there. But this church has been totally destroyed by the pagans. Likewise the Church of the Holy Cross is about one mile from Jerusalem to the west, in the place where the Holy Cross was cut from its tree. This too had a very noble and lovely church, but it is in ruins because of the pagans. Nevertheless the church is not too much destroyed, but only the buildings and cells round it.

Further in under the wall of the city, on the slope of Mount Sion, is the church of *Saint Pèter* which is called 'Gallicantus'. There, *after* he had *denied* the Lord,[3] he hid in a very deep cave, which is still to be seen there, and wept bitterly at his guilt.

To the west of the Church of the Holy Cross is a monastery, very beautiful and large, in honour of Saint Saba, who was one of the seventy-two disciples of our Lord Jesus Christ. Over three hundred Greek monks serve God there in a community. The greater part of the monks were slain by the Saracens, but some of them devotedly served Christ inside the city walls in another monastery beside the Tower of David. The first monastery is wholly ruined.

22 *The city of Bethlehem* in Judaea is six miles away *from Jerusalem to the south.*[4] Nothing habitable is left there by the Saracens, but it is all ruined, exactly as it is in all the other places outside the walls of Jerusalem, except the monastery of the Blessed Virgin Mary, Mother of our Lord, which is large and famous. In this church there is a cave, which is below the choir and near the centre, in which is to be seen the place of the Lord's birth on the left. On the right, a little lower down, and next to the place of our Lord's birth, is the Manger where the ox and ass stood. The Lord was placed in the Manger beside them. The stone on which our Saviour's head

[1] John 20.25–27. [2] See Got.5.
[3] See Gqu.10. 'Gallicantus' means 'cock-crow'.
[4] Gqu.9.

was supported in his tomb was taken there by the priest Saint Jerome, and is frequently to be seen in the Manger. Saint Jerome himself lies buried under the north altar in this church.

The Innocents also, who were murdered as infants for Christ the infant, lie buried under the altar in the south part of the church,[1] and the two most holy women, Paula and Eustochium her daughter, the Virgin, lie in the same place. There is the marble *Table on which the Blessed Virgin Mary ate with the Three Wise Men*[2] when they had offered their gifts. And the cistern is there in the church, next to the cave of the Lord's Birth, into which *the star*[3] is said to have fallen. There is also said to be *a bath*[4] of the Blessed Virgin Mary.

Moreover Bethany, where *Lazarus was raised by the Lord*[5] from 23
the dead, is two miles away from the city to the east, on the other side of the Mount of Olives. The church of Saint Lazarus is there, in which his tomb is to be seen, and those of many Bishops of Jerusalem. Under the altar is the place where Mary Magdalene washed the feet of the Lord Jesus *with tears* and *wiped* them with her hair, *and kissed his feet and anointed them with spice.*[6] Bethphage, where the Lord sent the disciples into the city, is on the Mount of Olives, but almost nothing of it is left to be seen.

Jericho, the place of Abraham's Garden, *is ten leagues from*[7] 24
Jerusalem. It is a country very rich in trees, all kinds of palms, and all fruit-trees. There is the fountain of the Prophet Elisha. Its water was very bitter to drink and prevented people *having children.* So Elisha blessed it and *put salt* in it,[8] and it was changed into fresh water. The plain is indeed beautiful wherever you look. And from there one goes up a high mountain, three miles away, to the place *where the Lord fasted forty days, and where he was afterwards tempted by Satan.*[9]

The Jordan river is four leagues to the east of Jericho. On this 25
side of the Jordan is the region called Judaea, and it stretches as far as the Adriatic Sea, to the port called Joppa. On the other side of the Jordan is Arabia, which is very hostile to Christians and hates all worshippers of God. There is the mount from which Elijah was taken *up to heaven in a chariot.*[10]

[1] See Got.6.
[2] Got.6.
[3] See Gqu.9.
[4] See Got.6.
[5] See Gqu.7.
[6] Luke 7.38.
[7] See Got.7.
[8] Bede 9 (reading *benedicente*).
[9] Mark 1.13: see Gqu.8 and Got.7.
[10] 2 (4) Kg.2.11 (Vlg).

And *from the Jordan it is eighteen days' journey to Mount Sinai,*[1] where the Lord *appeared* to Moses in the fire of *a burning bush,*[2] and where afterwards Moses *climbed* at the Lord's command.[3] He was fasting there *forty days and forty nights,*[4] and thus he received from the Lord *two tables of stone, written with the finger of God,*[5] so that he could teach the children of Israel the Law and Commandments which were written on those tables.

26 Hebron, where the Holy Patriarchs Abraham, Isaac and Jacob lie, buried separately, and their wives with them, and similarly Adam, the first-created man, is four leagues to the south of Bethlehem. This is where King David reigned for seven years before he obtained the city of Jerusalem from the family of King Saul.[6] But today the great and very beautiful city of Hebron is ruined by the Saracens.

On the east part of Hebron are the tombs of the Holy Patriarchs. They were made in ancient times and are surrounded by a very strong castle. Every one of the three tombs is like a large church, and the sarcophaguses are reverently placed inside, that is to say for the husband and his wife. There even now to the present day, all the people who go near the tombs are greeted by the smell of balsam and the very precious spices with which the holy bodies were anointed. But the bones of Joseph, which he commanded the children of Israel to bring with them from Egypt, are collected together more humbly in another part of the castle. And the ilex, under whose shade Abraham stood and saw three young men coming towards him along the road, still lives and flourishes, according to the people who live there, and is not far distant from the castle.

27 Nazareth, the city of Galilee, where the Blessed Virgin Mary was greeted by the angel, who announced to her the birth of the Lord, is four days' journey from Jerusalem. The way there is by *Shechem, a city* of Samaria *now called Neapolis,*[7] where Saint John the Baptist received Herod's sentence that his head should be cut off. There is also the *Spring of Jacob,* where *Jesus, thirsty and weary from his*

[1] IGu.4.
[2] Exod.3.2.
[3] Exod.24.18.
[4] Exod.34.28.
[5] Exod.31.18.
[6] The foregoing description of Hebron is like the passages on the city in Jerome's works, but the verbal similarities suggest that his work may have been abbreviated and changed.
[7] Bede 14.

journey, sat on that well, and was content to ask the Samaritan woman for water, who came to draw there,[1] as it says in the Gospel.

From Shechem the way goes to Caesarea Palaestinae, from Caesarea to Caipha and from Caipha to Acre. Nazareth is about eight miles east of Acre. But the city of Nazareth is wholly ruined and all pulled down by the Saracens. Even so the place of the Lord's Annunciation is marked by a very famous monastery. The spring by the city rises very fresh, and is on every side surrounded by marble panels and columns. This is where the boy Jesus and the other boys often drew water to help their mothers.

Mount Tabor is about four miles to the east of Nazareth, and 28
there the Lord climbed and, in the presence of Peter and John and James, was transfigured. *It is full of grass and flowers,*[2] and it is so high, standing in the middle of the flat and fertile plain of Galilee, that it is taller than all the mountains for a long way round. On the top it has three monasteries, which were built in olden days, but are still there. One is in honour of our Lord Jesus Christ, the second is dedicated to Moses, and the third a little way off, is to Elijah, according to what Peter said: '*Lord, it is good for us to be here. Let us make here three tabernacles, one for you, one for Moses, and one for Elijah*'.[3]

From Mount Tabor it is about six miles north-east to the sea of 29
Galilee or of Tiberias. The sea's length is ten miles and the breadth is five. On one shore is the city of Tiberias, and on the other side Corozain and Bethsaida, the city of Andrew and Peter. The village Gennesareth is about four miles north of the city of Tiberias, where the Lord approached the disciples who were fishing, as it says in the Gospel. Two miles to the east of Gennesareth is the mountain where the Lord Jesus, with five loaves and two fishes, satisfied 5000 people. By the inhabitants this mountain is called 'The Table of the Lord', and at its foot is the very beautiful Church of Saint Peter, although it is deserted.

Six miles to the north of Nazareth is Cana of Galilee, where the Lord at the wedding changed the water into wine. It is on a mountain, but nothing is left there but a monastery, which is called 'Architriclinium'.[4] Between Nazareth and Galilee, about in the middle, is a camp called Roma, where all the people going to

[1] Bede 13, reading *sitiens*: John 4.6.
[2] Bede 16.
[3] Matt 17.4.
[4] 'Of the Master of the Feast'.

Tiberias from Acre are entertained, having Nazareth on the right side and Galilee on the left.

30 A day's journey to the north of Tiberias is *Mount Libanus*, from the *foot*[1] of which the River Jordan flows from two springs, of which one is called Jor and the other Dan. These two streams join in one and form a swift-flowing river called Jordan. It springs near the city *of Philip the Tetrarch* called *Caesarea*,[2] into whose district Jesus came and asked his disciples a question in the words, '*Whom do men say that the Son of Man is?*',[3] as the Gospel tells us. The Jordan River flows down to one side of the Sea of Galilee from its source, flowing swiftly. On the other side it makes a broad stream with its strong current, and thus, after eight days' descent, it reaches the Dead Sea. The water of the Jordan is *whiter* and more like *milk* than the other waters, *and* thus *its current* is to be seen *stretching far into the Dead Sea*.[4]

31 Now that I had explored as far as I was able each one of the Holy Places of the city of Jerusalem and the cities near it, and venerated them, I boarded a ship at Joppa on the day of Pentecost to go back to my country. But for fear of the Saracens and their fleet we did not dare to go across the deep of the Adriatic Sea. Therefore we went along the coastal cities, of which some belonged to the Franks, and others still belonged to the Saracens. Their names are these.

Next to Joppa the common name for the city is Atsuph, but in Latin Azotus. Then there is Caesarea of Palestine, then Caiphas. These cities Baldwin, the flower of Kings, possesses. Then there is Acras [Acre], a very strong city, which is called Accaron. Then Sur and Saegete, which are Tyre and Sidon. Then Gibeleth, then Beirut, and then Tartusa, which Duke Raymond possesses. Then Gibel, where are the Mountains of Gilboa. Then Tripolis and Lice. All these cities we passed.

32 But on the Wednesday after Pentecost, when we were sailing between Caiphas and Accaron, there were twenty-five Saracen ships to be seen, that is of the Prince of the cities of Tyre and Sidon, going to Babylonia with forces to help the Chaldaeans fight against the King of Jerusalem. Two ships, which were coming with us and were laden with pilgrims, abandoned our ship and, since they were

[1] Bede 10.1.
[2] See Bede 10.1.
[3] Matt 16.13.
[4] Bede 10.2.

lighter, rowed off and escaped to Caesarea. But all round our ship the Saracens sailed, staying about a bow-shot away, and rejoicing at such a prize. But our men were prepared to die for Christ. They took up arms, and when they were armed they defended the ship like a castle. There were almost two hundred men defending our dromund.

After about an hour, when he had taken counsel, the prince sent one of his sailors up the mast of the ship, which was very large, to learn what he could of our action. When he learned from him of the strength of our defence, he raised his sails and went out to sea. So on that day the Lord made us escape from our enemies. But later on three of our people's ships were arrested, and the Saracens were made rich by their spoils.

As for us, we sailed along the coast of Syria Palaestina as far as 33
we could, and after eight days we reached the port of Saint Andrew in Cyprus. On the following day we sailed towards Romania, passing the ports of Saint Simeon and Saint Mary, and after many days we came to Little Antioch. On that stretch of the journey we were often attacked by pirates, but the divine grace protected us, and nothing was lost to us either by enemy attacks or by storms. Our voyage then lay along the broad coast of Romania. We passed the city of Stamirra, and Patras of Blessed Nicholas, and came with difficulty to the island of Rhodes before the vigil of Saint John the Baptist. The current of the city of Satalus would have devoured us unless the divine clemency had defended us.

At Rhodes we took a smaller ship in order to go faster, and were once again on the way to Romania. We came to the very beautiful city of Stromlo, now completely ruined by the Turks, where we were kept waiting by a strong contrary wind. Then we came to the island of Samos, where we bought our daily food, as in all the islands, and reached the island of Scion.

There we left the ship and our companions, and started on the journey to Constantinople to pray there. After that we passed through the great city of Smyrna, we came to the island of Metelina, and then Tenit. There in the country of Romania there was the most ancient and famous city of Troy, and according to the Greeks the buildings of it still appear over an area covering many miles.

Continuing our voyage from there we came to a narrow sea 34
called the Gulf of Saint George. It looks at two shores, Romania

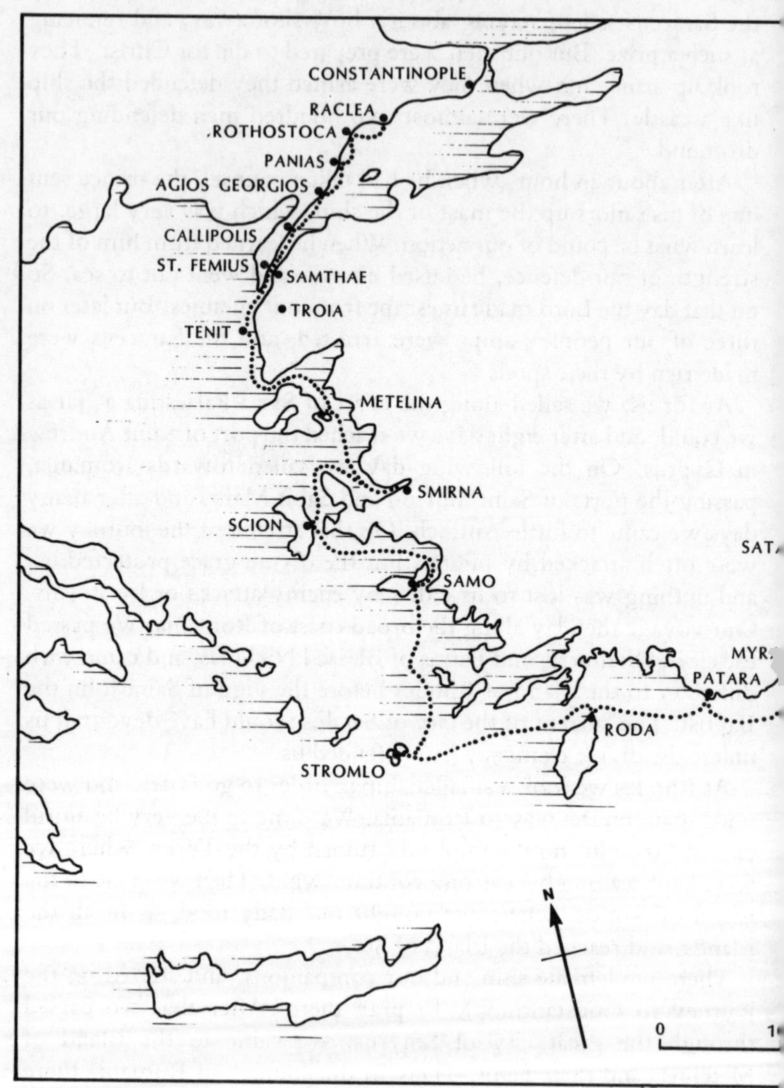

Fig. 21. Saewulf's journey from Joppa to Constantinople.

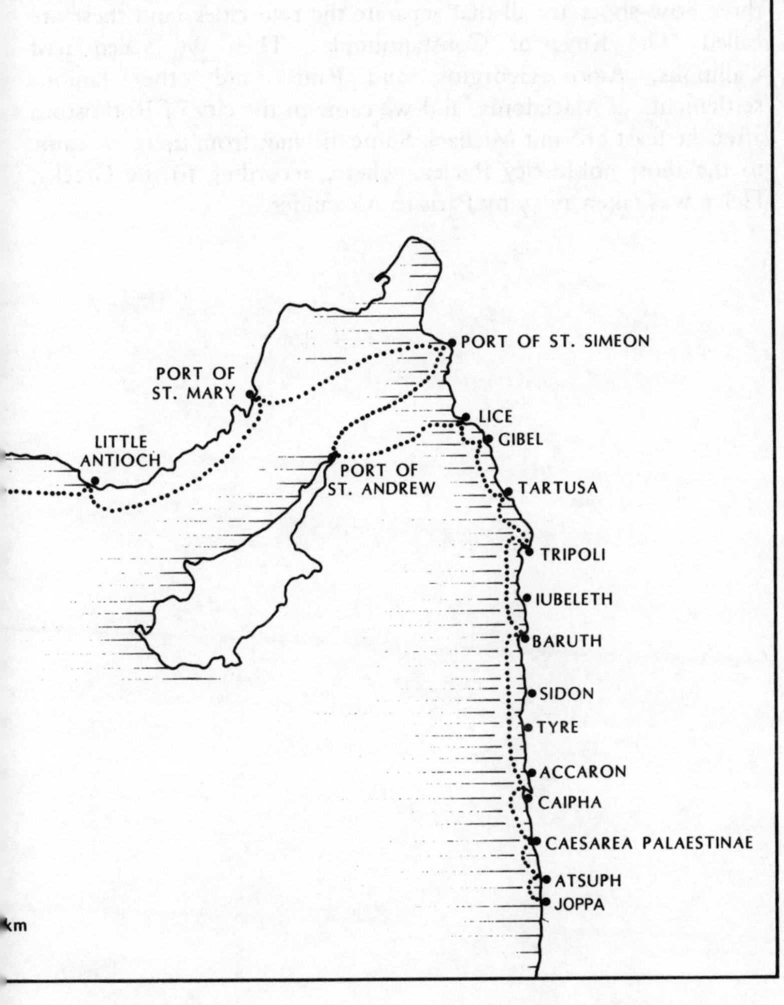
PORT OF ST. SIMEON
PORT OF
ST. MARY
LITTLE
ANTIOCH
LICE
GIBEL
PORT OF
ST. ANDREW
TARTUSA
TRIPOLI
IUBELETH
BARUTH
SIDON
TYRE
ACCARON
CAIPHA
CAESAREA PALAESTINAE
ATSUPH
JOPPA
km

and Macedonia. Through it we sailed to Saint Phemius, having Greece on the right and Macedonia on the left. The city of Saint Femius the Bishop is on one side of the gulf in Macedonia, and another city called Samthe is on the other side in Greece. Two or three bow-shots are all that separate the two cities, and these are called 'The Keys of Constantinople'. Then we sailed past Callipolis, Agios Georgios, and Panias and other famous settlements of Macedonia, and we came to the city of Rothostoca after the feast of Saint Michael. Some distance from there we came to the most noble city Raclea, where, according to the Greeks, Helen was taken away by Paris to Alexander.

GUIDE

PERHAPS BY A GERMAN AUTHOR

The Valley of Jehoshaphat. The upper part of the Valley of Jehoshaphat contains the place in which there was the farm of Gethsemane, in which Jesus at the time of his sufferings left his disciples and prayed to the Father. 1

Near this place on your way down the Valley of Jehoshaphat is the Tomb of the Blessed Virgin Mary.

A stone's throw away from this place is the place in the Valley (still of Jehoshaphat) where the Jews stoned Stephen.

Next to the place of this martyrdom the Blessed Brother of the Lord fell down headlong from the wall into the valley, and was killed by a fuller's club.

Next to this is the Pool of Siloam, by which Christ performed wonderful signs.

These places, and more too, are in the Valley of Jehoshaphat. 2
Now let us go up the Mount of Olives, at the foot of which is the Valley of Jehoshaphat. In that mountain, not right at the top but on the south side, is Bethphage, once a village of priests, where the Lord Jesus, when his sufferings were approaching, sent his disciples into the hamlet to fetch the ass and its foal.

And on top of the Mountain is the place of the venerable stone, which is marked by flagging, where the Lord Jesus, having had a beautiful conversation with his disciples, ascended to the heavens. Wise men among the Greeks who live in Jerusalem say that the earth round this stone is worthy of veneration and deserves a kiss by people who are Christians, for the reason that it was wet with the Apostles' tears on account of the absence of Christ's body, and also because they stood there looking up to heaven, when they heard a voice saying, '*Men of Galilee, why do you stand*', and so on.[1]

[1] Acts 1.11.

These holy places, and more, are on the Mount of Olives.

From here it is not more than a mile to Bethany. It is to the east, and is the village of Mary and Martha, and there is still to be seen there the Grave of Lazarus, whom the Lord raised from the dead. This place is much frequented by all the faithful, and by the Jews as well.

This too I would have you know, that the same Lazarus was wonderfully raised so that he could be a bishop in the Island of Cyprus.

3 Let us go back to the west side of the Valley of Jehoshaphat. On the western side of the Valley is Mount Sion and the city of Jerusalem.

Going up Mount Sion is a temple called the Church of Peter's Tears, because the holy women coming from the Tomb are said to have found him weeping bitterly, at the time when it was told them that they should go and tell the disciples and Peter that the Lord had been raised.

The top of the Mount is called 'Sion', and a church has been built there in honour of the Lord and of his Holy Mother, which is said to be the first Christian church.

There the Lord had supper with his disciples.

There he washed their feet.

There was the place where the Apostles took refuge for fear of the Jews.

There the Holy Spirit descended in fire of the disciples.

They they composed the Creed.

There also Blessed Mary died to this world.

This is the place which was much loved by the Lord even before his birth, by the power and the miracles of his divinity. And after his birth, by the power of his sacred body, we have the testimony of his disciples, if we wish to understand it literally. For he said, '*The Lord loveth the gates of Sion above all the tents of Jacob*'.[1]

4 Now let us go into the city itself. There is the Tomb of him who was crucified for us, over which a temple has been built. This is in the shape of the temple of Saint Mary which has been built at Aquisgranum by Charlemagne, apart from the fact that the temple at Jerusalem has only one tower, and that tower, which is over the Sepulchre, is open on top.

[1] Psalm 87.2.

Now let us go forth from the temple to the north. To the east is the Prison in which the Lord was placed, and next to the gate of the Prison towards the south is the place where the Lord was released from the Prison and sat waiting with the warders of the prison until Pilate came with the Jews and sat on the tribunal.

Next to this are steps by which people come up to the temple. Once there was a beautiful building here where the wood of the Holy Cross was found. Next to these steps a stone cross stands, of the same measurements as the cross which was born by the Lord, and which the Jews also made Simon of Cyrene carry.

Next to this cross is a small chapel where his clothes were divided, and where they cast lots over his coat.

Next to this is the place where Adam lived until his death. Near this is the place of Calvary, where the Lord was crucified and where once Abraham sacrificed Isaac. At the foot of the hill of the place of Calvary there is an altar. It is in the same place where Adam was buried.

In this city towards the Mount of Olives is the Church of the Sheep Pool. Near it is the Temple of Solomon, and to the north is the Temple of the Lord.

DANIEL THE ABBOT

1A THE LIFE AND JOURNEY OF DANIEL, ABBOT OF THE RUSSIAN LAND[1]

[2]Behold, I, the unworthy abbot[3] Daniel of the Russian land, least of all monks, humbled by many sins and lacking in any good deed, urged by my own imagination and impatience, conceived a desire to see the holy city of Jerusalem and the Promised Land.[4] And by the grace of God I came to the holy city of Jerusalem and saw the holy places and travelled round the whole of the Galilean[5] land and the holy places about the holy city of Jerusalem, where Christ our God walked with his own feet and where he performed great miracles. And all this I saw with my own sinful eyes, and merciful God let me see what I had long desired in my thoughts. My brothers and fathers, my lords, forgive me a sinner and do not despise my ignorance and crudity in what I have written about the holy city of Jerusalem, about that blessed land and the road to the holy places. For anyone who travels that road in the fear of God and in humility will never offend the mercy of God. I travelled that holy road unworthily, with every kind of sloth and weakness, in drunkenness and doing every kind of unworthy deed. Nevertheless, trusting in the mercy of God and your prayers that Christ God would forgive my countless sins, I have described this road and these holy places not vaunting myself or boasting of my journey as if I had done some good on my way. Far from it. I did nothing

[1] var: The pilgrimage of Daniel the monk (var: the Abbot). The wording of the title varies in the MSS but both this and any chapter headings are late additions.

[2] add: I desired to see the Holy City of Jerusalem and the Promised Land, for as John Chrysostom says: God will give to whomsoever he may wish wisdom, sense, wit, and cunning.

[3] 'Abbot' has been used throughout to translate the Russian *igumen*, Greek *hegoumenos*, the head of a monastery.

[4] var: the land promised by God to Abraham.

[5] vars: Promised Land; Land of Jordan.

good on my journey, but for the love of these holy places I have set down everything which I saw with my own eyes, so that what God gave me, an unworthy man, to see may not be forgotten. I feared [to be like] that lazy servant who *hid* his master's *talent* and made no profit[1] by it and so I have written this for the faithful. For if anyone hearing about these holy places should grieve in his soul and in his thoughts for these holy places, he shall receive the same reward from God as those who shall have travelled to the holy places. For many good men living at home in their own places, by their thoughts, charity to the poor, and their good deeds, attain the holy places and receive a great reward from God our Saviour Jesus Christ. And many who have travelled to the holy places and to the holy city of Jerusalem have become conceited in their own mind as if they had done something good and thus lose the reward for their labour, and of these I am the first. And many travelling to the holy city of Jerusalem go back without seeing many good things in their eagerness to return, for this journey cannot be made in haste nor can one hasten through all the holy places within and outside the city.

I, the unworthy abbot Daniel, having come to Jerusalem, spent 1B
sixteen months in that place[2] in the Laura[3] of Saint Saba and so could travel about and examine all the holy places. It is not possible without a good guide and interpreter to explore and see all the holy places. And whatever of my meagre wealth I had by me I would give to those who were well acquainted with all the holy places in the city and outside the city so that they should show me everything thoroughly, and thus it was. And by God's favour I found in the Laura a man holy and old in days and very learned. And God put it into the heart of this holy man to love me, a sinner, and he showed me in detail all the holy places in Jerusalem and conducted me all over that land as far as the Sea of Tiberias and to Mount Tabor and to Nazareth and to Hebron and to the Jordan,[4] to all these places he took me and took great pains over me out of love. And many other holy places I saw of which I shall tell later.

[1] Matt.25.25.
[2] add: in the hospice of.
[3] A laura was an early type of monastic community, part eremitic, part communal, recognizing a superior. In Russia the word came to mean a very large monastery with many buildings.
[4] add: and to Bethlehem.

2 This is the road to Jerusalem. From Constantinople[1] go 300 versts[2] along the curve of the coast[3] to the Great Sea (Mediterranean) then 100 versts to the island of Petala. This is the first island in the Narrow Sea [Sea of Marmora] and there is a large bay there and here is the town of Great Herakleia and opposite this city holy oil[4] comes out of the depths of the sea; here many martyrs were drowned by persecutors. From the island of Petala to Gallipoli it is 100 versts and from Gallipoli to the town of Abydos 80 versts.[5] Opposite this town lies St Euthymius the New.[6] Thence to Krit[7] it is 20 versts and here one enters the Great Sea, to the left to Jerusalem and to the right to the Holy Mountain (Athos) and to Salonika and Rome. And from Krit to the island of Tenedos it is 30 versts. This is the first island in the Great Sea and here lies St Abudimos the martyr.[8] And on the shore opposite this island is a great city called Troas, whither came the apostle Paul and taught the whole land[9] and baptized. And from the island of Tenedos to Mitylene island is 100 versts, and here lies the holy metropolitan[10] of Mitylene. And from Mitylene to the island of Chios is 100 versts; here lies the holy martyr Isidore,[11] and this island produces mastic and good wine and every kind of vegetable.

[1] Russian *Tsargrad*, i.e. the Imperial City. See Fig. 22.

[2] The metrology of Daniel is not always clear; one should bear in mind that there were no standards and that many of Daniel's measurements must have been rough guesses. The accepted average values of Old Russian linear measures are:

1 *versta* (or sometimes *poprishche*) = 750 *sazhens* = approx. 0·6 of a mile. (*Versta* often translates Gr. *stadion* or *milion*). Daniel also uses 'large verst', a term found elsewhere, but its value is not clear.

1 *sazhen*' (fathom) = 4 *lokots* (cubits) = 8 *pyads* (spans) = 152 cm. (But the value of a *lokot*' may vary from 38 to 46 cm, and a *pyad*' may be from 19 to 27 cm.)

All these terms are used by Daniel together with 'stone's throw' (= approx 42.5 m.) and 'bowshot' (= approx. 60–70 m.) For this information and a discussion of Russian metrology of this period see E. I. Kamentseva and N. V. Ustyugov, *Russkaya metrologiya*, Moscow, 1965, pp. 18–26, and G. Ya. Romanova, *Naimenovanie mer dliny v russkom yazyke*, Moscow, 1975, esp. pp. 16–31.

[3] var: by the narrow sea.

[4] Russ. *miro* from Gr. *miron* 'anointing oil'.

[5] var: 108;8.

[6] St Euthymius the New, 824–889, founder of a monastery near Thessalonika.

[7] W: Krithia or Karethia in the south of the Gallipoli peninsula.

[8] St Abudimos from the island of Tenedos, beheaded in the persecution of Diocletian, to whom he appeared in a dream threatening God's vengeance. See *PPBES* = *Polnyi pravoslavnyi bogoslovskii entsiklopedicheskii slovar'*, s.v. *Avudim* and *Bibliotheca Sanctorum*, Rome, 1961, s.v.*Abudemio*.

[9] add : to believe in Christ.

[10] add: George. St George of Mitylene, d. circa 810.

[11] St Isidore, martyred under Decius, 252. See Halkin, 2, p. 45.

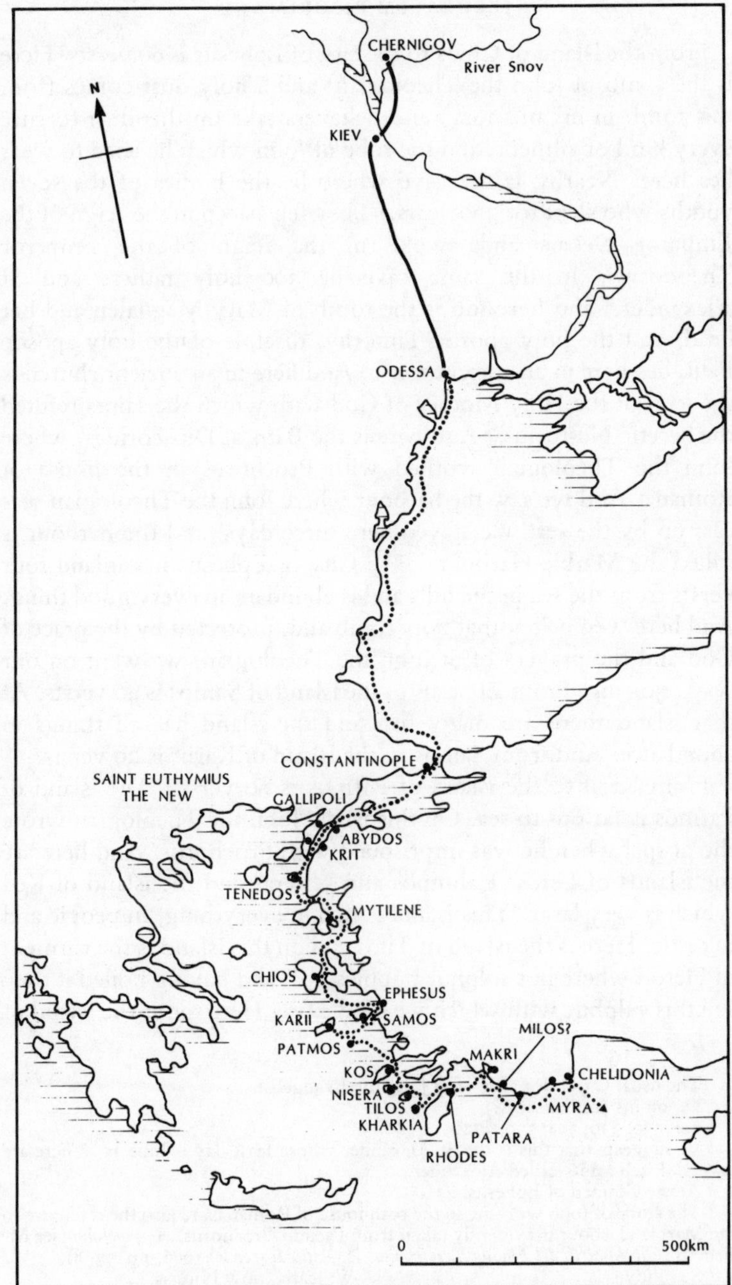

Fig. 22. Daniel's journey from Russia to Rhodes.

3 From the island of Chios to the city of Ephesus is 60 versts. Here is the tomb of John the Theologian[1] and a holy dust comes from this tomb in his memory[2] and believers take up this dust to cure every kind of ailment, and the robe of John which he used to wear lies here. Nearby is the cave where lie the bodies of the seven youths who slept for 360 years.[3] They fell asleep in the reign of the Emperor Decius and awoke in the reign of the Emperor Theodosius. In the same cave lie 300 holy fathers and St Alexander,[4] and here too is the tomb of Mary Magdalen and her head, and the holy apostle Timothy, disciple of the holy apostle Paul, lies here in an ancient tomb. And here in an ancient church is the icon of the Holy Mother of God with which the saints refuted the heretic Nestorius.[5] And here is the Bath of Dioscorides[6] where John the Theologian worked with Prochorus in the house of Romana. And we saw the harbour where John the Theologian was cast up by the sea. We stayed here three days, and the harbour is called the Marble Harbour.[7] The City of Ephesus lies inland four versts from the sea in the hills and is abundant in every good thing. And here we knelt at that holy tomb and, protected by the grace of God and the prayers of St John the Theologian, we went on our way rejoicing. From Ephesus to the island of Samos is 40 versts. At that island there are many fish and the island has all things in abundance. And from Samos to the island of Karii[8] is 20 versts.

4 From Karii to the island of Patmos is 60 versts. The island of Patmos is far out to sea. On this island John the Theologian wrote the gospel when he was imprisoned with Prochorus. And here are the islands of Leros, Kalimnos and Nisera[9] and the island of Kos which is very large. This island is rich in everything, in people and in cattle. Here is the island of Tilos and on this island is the torment of Herod where hot sulphur bubbles up[10] and having boiled it they sell this sulphur with which we kindle fire. Here too is the island of

[1] The usual Orthodox title of St John the Evangelist.

[2] i.e. on his anniversary(?)

[3] var: 330; 339; 308; 370; 372.

[4] V. suggests that this is the St Alexander whose feast day is June 10. There are several dozen saints called Alexander.

[5] At the Council of Ephesus, 431.

[6] The story of John working in the bathhouse of Romana and also the reference to the Marble Harbour is evidently taken from Pseudo-Prochorus, *Acts of John* (see M. Erbetti, *Gli Apocrifi del Nuovo Testamento. II, Atti e leggende*, 1966, pp. 73–8).

[7] See above.

[8] W: Icaria, now Nicaria.

[9] W: Lero, Kalymno, Nisyro.

[10] add: from a pit.

Kharkia.[1] All these islands hold many people and cattle and are close together, some ten versts or more between them. And here is the island of Rhodes, which is great and very rich in everything. On that island the Russian prince Oleg spent two summers and winters.[2] From Samos to Rhodes is 200 versts and from Rhodes to Makri[3] 60 versts. In that town and throughout that land as far as Miros grow black incense and gomphytis.[4] These come from out of trees like sap[?] and they gather it with a sharp iron tool. The name of this tree is zigia[5] and it is like an alder. And there is another small tree like an aspen[6] but the name of this small tree is raka[7] and there is in this tree a great worm like an earthworm but bigger under the bark of the tree and the worm burrows in the tree and wormdust comes out of the tree like wheat bran and falls from the tree like cherry-tree resin and the people gather it up and mix it with the first-mentioned wood and placing it in a pot they boil up the gomphytis incense, and casting it into skins they sell it to merchants. And from Makri to the town of Patara it is 40 versts and here is the birthplace of St Nicholas – Patara is his homeland and family.[8] And from Patara to Myra where the tomb of St Nicholas lies is 40 versts, and from Myra to Chelidonia 60 versts[9] and from Chelidonia to the great island of Cyprus is 200 versts.[10]

Cyprus is a very large island with many people and it abounds in 5
all good things. It has twenty[11] bishops and one metropolitanate and saints without number lie there. Here lie St Epiphanius,[12] the apostle Barnabas, St Zeno, St Philagrius[13] the Bishop who was baptized by the apostle Paul.

There is a very high mountain here and on that mountain St 6
Helena erected a great cross of cypress to drive away devils and cure all manner of ills and she placed in the cross one of Christ's

[1] V. says the island of Charki near Rhodes.

[2] Prince Michael Oleg Svyatoslavich, d. 1115. His imprisonment in Greece is recorded, rather vaguely, in the Laurentian Chronicle under the year 1079.

[3] W: the ancient Telmessus on the south coast of Lycia.

[4] Gr. *gomphytis storax*, a fragrant resin from trees of the genus *Styrax*.

[5] Gr. *zygia*.

[6] var: pine.

[7] var: sturika, styuryaka. Evidently from Gr. *styrax*.

[8] var: town.

[9] var: 30.

[10] var: 10; 230.

[11] var: 14; 24.

[12] Bishop of Salamis in Cyprus in the 4th century.

[13] The MSS have many variants of the name including Philagrios. Evidently this is the martyr St Philagrius, disciple of Peter and Bishop of Cyprus.

sacred nails. And in this place by that cross there occur great signs and miracles even to this day. And this cross stands up in the air, not fixed to the ground in any way but held up in the air by the Holy Spirit. And I, unworthy person, worshipped at this miraculous holy object and saw with my own sinful eyes the grace of God in that place, and I explored all round the island thoroughly.

7 And here is found the incense which falls from the sky and is gathered from shrubs. There are many of these shrubs in the mountains; they are short like grass and the good incense falls on them and is gathered up in July and August, for in other months it does not fall, but occurs only in those two. From Cyprus to the city of Jaffa is 400[1] versts by sea; from Constantinople to the island of Rhodes is 800 versts and from Rhodes to Jaffa 800 versts, so that the whole sea journey to Jaffa is 1600 versts.[2] Jaffa is a city on the coast near Jerusalem and from there one goes by land to Jerusalem. And from Jaffa to Jerusalem is 30 versts and 10 versts[3] across the plain to St George.[4] Here there was a great church[5] built in honour of St George and his tomb was in[6] the altar, for here St George was martyred. And there are many springs here; travellers rest by the water but with great fear, for it is a deserted place and nearby is the town of Ascalon from which Saracens sally forth and kill travellers on those roads. There is a great fear too going up from that place into the hills. And from St George to Jerusalem is 20[7] long versts and all in rocky hills and here the road is hard and fearsome.

8 And there is a great mountain near Jerusalem on the right hand as you go from Jaffa and its name is Armathem. And on that mountain of Armathem there is the tomb of the holy prophet Samuel and of his father Elkanah and of Mary the Egyptian, for

[1] var: (4)60; (4)90.
[2] add: from Constantinople to Jerusalem 3000 versts.
[3] var: 5;3.
[4] W: at Lydda.
[5] add: square, Russ. *kletski*. Wilson suggests 'with a wooden roof'. V. suggests that Daniel has some form of arch or foundation structure in mind. Nine churches are described as *kletski*, usually with the participle *sozdan* 'built' and twice with the participle *vsperen* (meaning not clear but connected with lifting up) and specifically relating to the roof. All are also described as 'large'. The churches are: the Church of St George (p. 126); The Church of the Mother of God, Spoudaeon (p. 130) (*kletski verkh vsperen*); the Exaltation of the Cross (p. 131); Dormition (p. 134); St Michael (p. 139); House of John the Theologian on Mt Sion (p. 141); Nativity at Bethlehem (*verkh ee kletski vsperen*) (p. 143); Holy Prophets (p. 149); St Joseph of Arimathea (p. 156). The most recent dictionary of Old Russian (*Slovar' russkogo yazyka XI–XVII vv.*, Moscow, 1980, s.v.) gives 'square' as the meaning of the word in this context. This translation has been adopted here, although some doubt remains.
[6] var: under.
[7] var: 19.

here was the dwelling and home of these saints. And the place is surrounded by a wall and so it is called Armafem.

The holy city of Jerusalem lies in valleys with high and rocky 9
mountains about it and only when you come close to the town do you see first the Tower[1] of David, and then, coming a little closer, the Mount of Olives and the Holy of Holies and the Church of the Resurrection in which is the tomb of the Lord, and then you see the whole city. And there is a flat hill about a verst from the road to Jerusalem and on this hill all dismount from their horses and place little crosses there and bow to the (Church of the) Resurrection on the road to town. And no one can hold back tears at the sight of that desired land and the holy places where Christ our God suffered his passion for the sake of us sinners. And all go on foot in great joy towards the city of Jerusalem. And there on the left hand side of the road is the Church of St Stephen the Protomartyr; in that place (Archdeacon) Stephen the Protomartyr from Judaea was stoned to death and his tomb is there. And here is a flat stony hill which split at the time of the crucifixion of Christ. It is called hell, and the city walls are only a stone's throw away. And then all the people with great joy enter the holy city of Jerusalem by the gate near the house of the son of David,[2] and this gate is on the road from Bethlehem, and here too is the Gate of Benjamin.[3] As you enter the town your path lies through the town to the Holy of Holies on the right hand and on the left hand the Holy Resurrection where lies the tomb of the Lord.

Here is the Church of the Resurrection of the Lord; it is circular, and 10
it has 12 round pillars and six[4] built. It is beautifully paved with marble slabs; it has six doors and on the galleries(?) it has 16[5] columns, and above the galleries beneath the top there are depicted the holy prophets in mosaic as if they stood there alive, and above the altar Christ is depicted in mosaic. On the great altar the Creation(?) of Adam is depicted in mosaic; above there is a mosaic of the Lord being Raised Up and on either side of the altar on two columns there is a mosaic of the Annunciation. The top of the church is not completely vaulted over in stone but is surmounted by fashioned timber planked like a floor and so there is no top and it is not covered with anything. Beneath this uncovered roof is the tomb of the Lord.[6] And the Lord's

[1] var: house.
[2] var: House of David. W: Tower of David.
[3] An apparent confusion of two gates.
[4] var: 16.
[5] var: 6; 8; 12; 40.
[6] add: an account of the Lord's Tomb.

tomb is like a little cave cut into the rock, with small doors so that men can enter stooping on their knees for it is low[1] and round, four cubits in length and breadth. And as you enter the cave by the small door, on the right hand there is a kind of shelf cut into the rock of the cave and on this shelf lay the body of our Lord Jesus Christ. This sacred shelf is now covered with slabs of marble. On the side three small windows have been cut in order to see the holy stone, and all the Christians go there to kiss it. There hang in the Lord's tomb five great lanterns with oil and these holy lanterns burn ceaselessly day and night. And the sacred shelf where the body of Christ lay is four cubits in length and two in breadth and half a cubit in height.[2] And before the cave doors there is a stone three feet [paces?] from the door[3] and on this stone sat the angel who appeared to the women and announced to them the Resurrection of Christ. This holy cave is faced with beautiful marble like a pulpit and there are 12 pillars around it also of beautiful marble. And above the cave is a beautiful chamber on pillars, round at the top and covered with gilded silver plates. And on top of this chamber stands Christ made in silver and larger than a man, and this was made by the Franks. And now it is just below the uncovered top; and there are three doors in the chamber, cunningly fashioned like a grille(?), and through these doors come the people to the tomb of the Lord. And this cave was the tomb of the Lord as I have recounted, having questioned those who have lived long there and truly know all the holy places. And the Church of the Resurrection is circular and in length and breadth it is 30 fathoms. In it there are spacious rooms in the upper part and here lives[4] the patriarch. And from the doors of the cave to the wall of the great altar it is 12 fathoms. Beyond the wall behind the altar is the navel of the earth and a vault has been built above it and high up is depicted Christ in mosaic and a scroll which reads: 'Behold I have measured heaven and earth with my hand'.[5]

11 From the navel of the earth to the Crucifixion of the Lord and to the Place of the Skull it is 12 fathoms. And the Crucifixion is to the east, on a rock the height of a lance[6] or more. This stone is round like a little hill. And in the middle of this stone on the very top there is cut a hole a cubit deep and less than a span across and here was set

[1] var: lower than a man.
[2] var: 1½.
[3] var: three pillars.
[4] var: lived.
[5] Isaiah 40.12 is the basis for this saying.
[6] Russ. *struzhie* – not clear, could be *strazhie* 'a lookout point'.

up the cross of the Lord. Beneath this stone lies the head of Adam the first-created. And at the Crucifixion of Our Lord, when Our Lord Jesus Christ gave up his spirit, then the veil of the church[sic] was rent and the rock split, and it split above the head of Adam and through the fissure flowed the blood and water from the ribs of the Lord on to the head of Adam and washed away all the sins of the human race. And the fissure in the rock is there to this day and this true sign is on the right side of the Crucifixion of the Lord.

The Crucifixion of the Lord and this holy rock are all surrounded 12
by a wall and above the Crucifixion a chamber was built, cunningly and marvellously decorated with mosaic, and on the east wall there is a mosaic of Christ crucified on the cross, skilfully and marvellously done just as if alive and even more so, just as it was then. And on the south there is the taking down from the cross, also marvellously done. It has two doors; you must go up seven steps to the door, and passing through the door, another seven steps. The floor is laid with beautiful marble slabs.

Beneath the Crucifixion where the head (of Adam) lies, there is attached as it were a little chapel, beautifully decorated with mosaic and floored with beautiful marble. And this is called the Place of the Skull, which is the place of execution, and above it, where the Crucifixion is, is called Golgotha. And from the Crucifixion of the Lord to the deposition from the cross is five fathoms. And here, close to the place of the Crucifixion, to the north, is the place where they divided up his clothing, and another place where they placed the crown of thorns on the Lord's head and dressed him in purple to insult him.

And nearby is the sacrificial altar of Abraham where Abraham 13
placed his sacrifice to the Lord and killed a ram in the place of Isaac, and in the same place where Isaac was brought Christ was offered up as a sacrifice and killed for the sake of us sinners. And nearby, about two fathoms[1] further on is the place where Christ our God was struck on the face. And a further ten fathoms[2] on is the holy prison where Christ was cast and where he remained for a while until the Jews came and set up the cross in order to crucify him. And all these holy places are under one roof in a line to the north. And from the prison of Christ to the place where St Helen found the true cross, nails and crown, and spear and sponge and reed, it is

[1] var: one fathom.

[2] var: 2; 3; 7.

25 fathoms. The tomb of the Lord and the Crucifixion and all the holy places are in a gully and there is a hill to the west above the tomb and the Crucifixion.

And here on a rise is the place to which the holy mother of God hastened as she tried to follow Christ and said in the agony of her heart as she wept: 'Where are you going my son. Why do you hasten so fast? Is there another wedding in Cana of Galilee to which you hasten, my son and my God? Do not leave me without a word, me who bore you. Speak a word to your slave!'[1] And when the holy mother of God came to this place and saw from this hill her son crucified on a cross she was horror-stricken at what she saw and sank down and was overcome with grief and sobbing. And here came to pass the prophecy of Simeon who had said earlier to the holy mother of God, '*Behold, this child is set for the fall and rising of many in Israel and a sword will pierce through your own soul also when you shall see your son put to death*'.[2] And many stood at that place, his friends and acquaintances, watching from afar: Mary Magdalene, Mary the mother of James and Salome stood there and all those who had come from Galilee with John and the mother of Jesus; all the friends and acquaintances of Jesus stood and watched from afar of which the prophet (David) said '*my friends and companions stood far off from me*'.[3] And this place is a little way from the (place of) Christ's crucifixion, about 150[4] fathoms to the west; the name of the place is Spudii (Gr. *spoudê*) which is translated as 'the hastening of the Mother of God'. And there is now a monastery on that place and a very fine tall square church built in honour of the holy Mother of God.

14 And thence to the Tower of David and his house is 200 fathoms. It is the tower of the holy prophet David and his home was also here. In this tower the prophet David composed and wrote down the psalter. This tower is marvellous, made with great stones and very high, with four corners, and all is very strong and solid and it rises from the living rock. It contains much water and it has five[5] iron doors and 200 steps to climb up and it contains a countless store of provisions. And it is very difficult to capture. And it is the chief place[6] of all that city and it is strongly guarded and no one is

[1] W: from Good Friday matins hymn.
[2] Luke 2.34–5.
[3] Ps.38 (37).11.
[4] var: 1½.
[5] var: 6.
[6] var: glory.

allowed in. But God granted wretched unworthy me to enter this holy tower and I was able to take with me only Izdeslav.[1,2]

And near the tower is the house of Uriah whom David slew 15
and whose wife he took after he had seen her washing in the bath. Here is now the guesthouse[3] of St Saba and it is a stone's throw from the tower. One may know where this bath was even in the present day; and here is the place where St Helena found the True Cross near the place of the Lord's crucifixion, 20[4] fathoms farther to the east. And on that spot a very large square church (dedicated to the Exaltation of the True Cross) was built, but now there is only a small church. Here to the East is the great door to which came St Mary the Egyptian desiring to enter and kiss [the cross], but the power of the Holy Spirit would not admit her to the church. And then she prayed to the Holy Mother of God whose ikon was in the porch near the door, and then she was able to enter the church and kiss the True Cross. By this door she went out again into desert of the Jordan.[5] And near this door is the place where St Helena discovered the true cross of the Lord, instantly restoring a dead virgin to life. And from here, going a little to the east, is the Praetorium where the soldiers brought Christ to Pilate, and where Pilate, having *washed his hands, said: 'I am innocent of this righteous man's blood'.*[6] And having scourged Jesus, he handed him over to the Jews. Here too is the Jewish prison from which the angel freed the holy apostle Peter in the night. And here once was the house[7] of Judas the betrayer of Christ. And the site of the accursed house is deserted even today, for no one will dare settle in that place on account of the curse. And a little to the east is the place where Christ cured the woman who had an issue of blood. And close by is the pit where Jeremiah the prophet was cast; here too was his house and formerly the house[8] of the Apostle Paul while he was a Jew. And going a little to the east, a short way off the road,[9] there once was the house of

[1] var: Sedeslav Ivanovich; Sdeslav. [2] add: of all my companions.
[3] Gr. *metokhion.* [4] var: 30.
[5] St Mary the Egyptian, a converted harlot from Alexandria (5th C.?). Her *vita* was very popular. See in particular *Vita Mariae Egyptiae*, 22–4, *PG*, 87, 3, col. 3714.
[6] Matt.27.24.
[7,8] Russ. *dvor* 'a courtyard, complex of buildings about a yard, a household, homestead'.
[9] add: to the left.

Saints Joachim and Anna. And here there is a cave [hewn] in the rock beneath an altar. In this cave the Holy Mother of God was born and in the same cave are the tombs of Saints Joachim and Anna.

16 Nearby is the porch of Solomon and there is the sheep pool where Christ cured the paralysed man.[1] This place is to the west of the house of Joachim and Anna, a stone's throw from it. Close by to the east is the city gate which leads to Gethsemane.

17 From the Resurrection to the Holy of Holies is about the distance of two bowshots. The church of the Holy of Holies is wonderfully and skilfully decorated with mosaics within and its beauty is indescribable; it is circular and it is artfully and indescribably painted on the outside; its walls have slabs of precious marble and it is beautifully paved with marble slabs. It has twelve round columns standing in a circle beneath the roof and eight[2] built columns and four doors; these doors are fashioned of gilded copper. And the roof is skilfully and wonderfully decorated inside with mosaic and covered on the outside with gilded copper. Beneath this roof there is a cave cut into the rock, in which the prophet Zachariah was killed;[3] formerly his tomb and his blood were here but not now. And there is a stone here outside the cave beneath the roof and on this stone Jacob had his dream; and here there was the ladder to heaven and *angels of God going up and down* and here Jacob struggled with the angel,[4] and waking from his dream said, '*This is none other than the house of God and this is the gate of heaven*'.[5] And on this stone the prophet David saw the angel standing with a naked sword and slaying the people of Israel, and he entered the cave weeping and praying to God and said '*Lo I have sinned . . . but these sheep, what have they done?*'[6] And this church is 30 fathoms in length and breadth and has four entrances. The old church of the Holy of Holies is destroyed and nothing remains of the first building of Solomon except the foundations of the church [sic] which David began. And the cave in the church and the rock beneath the roof are all that remains of the old building, and the church which is there now was built by a Saracen chieftain called Amor.

18 Here too was the house of Solomon and it was a mighty house and very great and exceedingly beautiful. It was all paved with marble slabs and supported on arches and the whole house was

[1] John 5. 2–9.
[2] var: 12.
[3] Matt.23. 35.
[4] Sense not clear.
[5] Gen 28. 12,17.
[6] 2 Sam.24. 17.

supplied with water. The rooms were made very beautiful and skilfully decorated with mosaic and columns of costly marble beautifully arranged in rows and the chambers were cleverly built on these columns and the whole house was overlaid with tin. And here is the gate of the house, very beautifully and cunningly overlaid with tin, ornamented with mosaic and gilded copper, and this gate is called the Beautiful Gate, where Peter and John healed the lame man; and that place by the gate is there to this day.[1] And there are three other gates beside this and a fifth, the Gate of the Apostles. This gate was strongly constructed by the prophet David and it is made with wonderful cunning, plated with gilded copper: inside it has skilful paintings on copper and outside it is strongly plated with iron. There are four doors to this gate, and the gate and the tower of David are all that remain of the old building, otherwise the whole building is new, for the ancient city of Jerusalem has been destroyed more than once. And by this gate Christ entered Jerusalem from Bethany with Lazarus when he had raised Lazarus from the dead. Bethany is to the east facing the Mount of Olives. And from this gate to the church of the Holy of Holies is 108 fathoms.[2]

Bethany is two versts from the city of Jerusalem, beyond the hill 19
in a valley; Bethany is a small town to the south of Jerusalem. As you enter the gates of this little town, on your right hand is a cave in which is the tomb of holy Lazarus; in this cell Lazarus fell ill and died. And in the middle of the town is a great and high church richly decorated with paintings. And from this church to the tomb of Lazarus is 12 fathoms;[3] the tomb of Lazarus is to the west of the church, and the church is to the east. In front of the town to the west is a very fine well deep in the ground and you must descend to it by steps. One verst[4] distant from Bethany in the direction of Jerusalem there is a pillar and in that place Martha met Jesus; here too Christ mounted an ass after raising Lazarus.

Gethsemane is the village where there is the tomb of the Holy 20
Mother of God; it is near Jerusalem on the Brook Kidron in the Valley of Weeping[5] and is between north-east and south-east of Jerusalem.

It is 8[6] fathoms from the city gates to the place where the Jew 21

[1] Acts 3. 3.
[2] var: 150.
[3] var: 20.
[4] var: ½.
[5] Valley of Jehosaphat.
[6] var: 20; 50 (most likely to be correct).

Ochonia[1] tried to cast down the body of the Holy Mother of God from her bier when the apostles were carrying her to be buried at Gethsemane, and the angel cut off both his hands with a[2] sword and placed them on the bier. And there used to be a convent for women on this spot but now it has been destroyed by the pagans.

22 From here to the tomb of the Holy Mother of God it is 100 fathoms. The tomb of the Holy Mother of God is in a valley in a small cave cut from the rock, with small doors so that a man may only enter by stooping, and on the floor of this cave opposite the doors there is cut a shelf into the rock and on this shelf was laid the sacred body of our most pure Lady and Mother of God and thence it was carried up uncorrupted to heaven. And this cave is about the height of a man and four cubits wide in each direction, and the chamber is beautifully faced with marble slabs; and above the tomb of the Holy Mother of God there was a great square church dedicated to the Dormition of the Holy Mother of God, but now it has been destroyed by the pagans. The tomb of the Holy Mother of God lies beneath the great altar of that church.

23 It is 10 fathoms from the tomb of the Holy Mother of God to the cave where Christ was betrayed by Judas to the Jews for 30 pieces of silver. This cave is on the other side of the Brook Kidron at the foot of the Mount of Olives.

And here, a short stone's throw to the south, is the place where Christ prayed to his Father on the night that he was delivered up to the Jews to be crucified, saying, '*Father, if it be possible, let this cup pass from me*'.[3] And there is now a small church built in that place. From here it is a bowshot farther to the tomb of Josaphat who was King of Judaea and for that reason it is called the Valley of Josaphat. And nearby in the same valley is the tomb of St James, brother of the Lord.

The Mount of Olives is a hill to the north-east of Jerusalem. From Gethsemane it is a very steep climb up the Mount of Olives, almost three bowshots, but the 'Our Father' is only one bowshot from Gethsemane.

[1] var: Othonia, Athonia, Achonia, etc. See Apocrypha on the Assumption, ed. James, pp. 200, 208, 214, 217, 221, 227. The name is usually given as Jephonias (of which the Russ. could easily be a corruption) but the Joseph of Arimathea version gives Ruben. The Greek Narration mentions the angel's 'sword of fire' – in other versions the Jew's hands wither. In Russian icons the Jew's name is Avfonii: V. I. Antonova, N. E. Mneva, *Katalog drevnerusskoi zhivopisi*, Moscow, 1963, vol. 1, pp. 74–5.

[2] add: flaming.

[3] Matt. 26, 39.

Here there is built a great church and it has a cave beneath its altar in which Christ taught his disciples to chant 'Our Father' and from here to the top of the Mount of Olives, the place of the Ascension of the Lord, is 90 fathoms.[1] 24

The place of the Ascension of the Lord is on the top of the Mount of Olives directly to the East and it is a little mound and on the little mound was a round stone above knee-height. From this stone Christ our God ascended into heaven, and this place is built about with arches, and on top of these arches has been built a circular court all paved with marble slabs. And in the middle of this court there is a small round chapel without a roof or floor and in this chapel beneath its open top lies that holy stone where stood the most pure feet of our Lord and Master. And beneath[2] this stone there is an altar made of marble slabs and on this altar they now celebrate the liturgy. Beneath this holy table is a stone faced all round with marble slabs so that you can see only a little of its top which all the Christians kiss. It has two doors and one must climb up steps to the place of the Ascension and there are 22 steps. The Mount of Olives stands high above the city of Jerusalem and from it you can see everything in Jerusalem; you can see the Holy of Holies and all the country as far as the Sea of Sodom and the Jordan and even beyond the Jordan you can see from that place, for the Mount of Olives is the highest of all the hills around Jerusalem. 25

Jerusalem is a large city with strong walls all round and it has four corners in the form of a cross. It has many valleys around it and rocky hills. It is a waterless place: there is no river, well or spring near Jerusalem except the Pool of Siloam, but all the people and beasts of that city live on rain water. And good crops grow about Jerusalem in that rocky land without rain: wheat and barley grow in abundance by God's benevolent will – if you sow one measure you reap ninety or a hundred. Is not this holy land blessed by God? And there are many vineyards around Jerusalem and fruit-trees bearing much fruit, fig-trees and mulberries and olives and carob-trees and trees of every other kind without number throughout this land. And on the Mount of Olives there is a deep cave near the place of the Ascension of the Lord and to the south, and in this cave there is the tomb of St Pelagia the 26

[1] var: 8; 50; 80.

[2] var: on; above.

Harlot,[1] and there is a stylite nearby, a very spiritual man.[2]

27 The way from Jerusalem to the Jordan runs past the Mount of Olives to the north-east, and it is a very difficult road and dangerous and waterless, for the hills are high and rocky and there are many brigands in those fearful hills and valleys. It is 26 long versts from Jerusalem to the Jordan; 15 versts to Choziba where St Joachim fasted on account of his sterility.[3] And this place is in a deep ravine nearby the road on the left. From Choziba to Jericho is 5 versts[4] and from Jericho to the Jordan 6 long versts over a plain in the sand, a very difficult road; here many choke from the heat and die of thirst; and the Sea of Sodom is near the road and it gives off a hot and stinking vapour and the heat burns up the whole of the area. ·Here, near the road, before you reach the Jordan, is the monastery of St John the Baptist, built high on a hill.[5]

28 Here about 20 fathoms from the monastery is Mount Hermon, on the left near the road. It is a sandy hill, small rather than large.

It is two good bowshots from Hermon to the old monastery of St John, where there was a great church built in honour of St John the Precursor.

29 And beyond the altar of this church on a rise close by to the east there is a little altar and a small arch and in this place John the Precursor baptized Our Lord Jesus Christ; the Jordan came to this spot and turned back and overflowed its bed, frightened when it saw its Creator coming to be baptized. And near this pool there used to be the Sea of Sodom but now it is some 4 versts further from the place of baptism, for the sea seeing God, naked, standing in the waters of the Jordan, took fright and fled; the Jordan turned back, as the prophet says: '*What ails you, O Sea, that you flee, O Jordan that you turn back?*'[6]

30 From the place where Christ was baptized to the Jordan itself is as far as a man can throw a small stone.

31 There is a pool in the Jordan and here all the Christians come to bathe; and there is a ford here across the Jordan into Arabia; here of old the Jordan parted for the sons of Israel and the people passed through on dry land. There too Elisha struck the water with the

[1] St Pelagia the Penitent, a converted dancing girl from Alexandria according to tradition.

[2] add: terrible in appearance and ancient in days.

[3] *Protevangelium of James*, 1. 3–4. James, p. 39.

[4] var: 10.

[5] var: surrounded by a wall.

[6] Ps. 114 (113), 3.

mantle of Elijah and they crossed the Jordan on dry land; and at the same pool Mary the Egyptian[1] crossed the waters to Father Zosimus to receive the body of Christ and, crossing the waters again, went back into the desert.

The river Jordan flows rapidly; its bank is steep on the far side 32
but gently sloping on the near side. Its water is very muddy but sweet to drink and one can never drink too much of this holy water and it will not make you ill or upset a man's stomach. In every way the river Jordan is like the river Snov,[2] both in width and depth, and it flows very quickly and twists in its course like the river Snov. It is 4 fathoms deep at the middle of the bathing place, as I measured and tested myself, for I have crossed to the far side of the Jordan and have travelled much along its bank. The Jordan is as wide as the Snov at its mouth. There is on this side of the Jordan at the bathing-place a sort of wood of small trees like the willow. Further up the Jordan from the pool there are many osiers but not like our osiers, but rather like *silyazhi*[3] and there are many reeds, and it has marshy areas like the river Snov. There are many wild beasts here, wild pigs without number and many panthers and lions. On the far side of the Jordan and some way off there are high rocky mountains and at the foot of these mountains there are other mountains nearer the Jordan and they are white. And there on the other side of the Jordan is the land of Zebulon and Naphtali.

And there is a place here to the east some two bowshots distant 33
from the river, where the prophet Elijah was carried up to heaven in a fiery chariot. And here also is the cave of St John the Baptist. And there is a beautiful torrent here full of water, which flows over the rocks into the Jordan; and this water is very cold and very sweet, and this was the water which John the Precursor of Christ drank when he was living in this holy cave.

There is another remarkable cave here where the holy prophet 34
Elijah lived with his disciple Elisha. And by the grace of God all this I have seen with my own sinful and unworthy eyes. And God permitted me thrice to visit the holy Jordan and I[4] was at the Jordan on the very festival of the blessing of the water and saw the grace of God come down on the waters on the Jordan and the countless

[1] See *Vita Mariae Egyptiae*, cap. 35, *PG*, 87,3,col. 3722.
[2] Probably the river Snov in the Chernigov region of southern Russia.
[3] Not identified. W: 'resembling more the willow of the desert'.
[4] add: with all my companions.

multitude of people that came at that time to the water; and all that night there is marvellous singing and countless burning candles and at midnight there is the blessing of the water; and at that time the Holy Spirit comes upon the waters of the Jordan and good men who are worthy see it; not all the people see anything, but there is joy and gladness in the heart of every Christian at that time, and when they say 'the Lord is baptized in the Jordan', then all the people enter the water and are baptized at midnight in the waters of the Jordan just as Christ was baptized at midnight. And at this place there is a mountain, very high, on the far side of the Jordan;[1] it can be seen from afar from all sides and on this mountain the prophet Moses expired, having seen the Promised Land. It is one verst from the monastery of St John to the monastery of St Gerasimus, and from the monastery of St Gerasimus to Kalamonia to the monastery of the Holy Mother of God it is one verst.

And in this place the Holy Mother of God with Jesus Christ and Joseph and James made their stop for the night while they were fleeing to Egypt; it was then that the Holy Mother of God named that place Kalamonia, which means 'good dwelling place'. Here now the Holy Spirit comes down to the icon of the Holy Mother of God. And this monastery is at the mouth of the Jordan[3] where it enters the Sea of Sodom, and the monastery is completely surrounded by a wall and there are twenty monks in it. And from here to the Monastery of St John Chrysostom it is two versts and this monastery is also surrounded by a wall and is very rich.[4]

35 And from here to Jericho it is one verst. Now this Jericho was formerly a great and very strong city and it was this Jericho which Joshua captured and destroyed utterly; now there is just a Saracen village here. And here is the house of Zacchaeus and to this day there stands the stump of that tree on which he climbed to see Jesus. In this place there was also the house of the Shunammite woman, where Elisha raised the child from the dead. Around Jericho the land is good and fertile; the land is beautiful and level and around the town there are many tall date palms and every kind of fruit tree; and there are many springs[5] and the water is distributed over the

[1] var: to the south near the Jordan; far from the Jordan to the south.
[2] add: who was served by a wild beast.
[3] add: to the south.
[4] add: and strong.
[5] add: but under the ground.

whole land. These are the waters of Elisha which Elisha the prophet sweetened.

And there is a place near Jericho, about a verst to the north-east, and in this place St Michael the Archangel appeared to Joshua son of Nun before the army of Israel, and raising up his eyes Joshua saw before him a terrible armed man, and Joshua said '*Are you one of us or one of the enemy?*'. And the Archangel said to him 'I am Michael, general of God, sent to your aid; dare and you shall conquer your enemies'.[1] And he said to him '*Put off your shoes from your feet for the place where you stand is holy*'. And Joshua fell on his face and worshipped. And there is now in that place a monastery and church dedicated to St Michael.[2] And in this church lie the twelve stones taken from the bed of the Jordan when the Jordan parted for the people of Israel; *the priests who carried the Ark of the Covenant* took *the stones according to the number of the tribes of Israel* as a memorial for their descendants.[3] The name of this place is Gilgal and it was here that the people of Israel encamped after crossing the Jordan.

And to the west of this place there is a high and very great 36
mountain called Gabaon and above this mountain *the sun stood still* for half a day until Joshua son of Nun had conquered his enemies when he was warring with Og, King of Bashan,[4] and all the kingdoms of Canaan.[5] And when Joshua was completely victorious, the sun set.

On this Mount of Gabaon is a very lofty cave and in this cave 37
Christ our God fasted for forty days, and afterwards, when he was hungry, the devil came to tempt him, saying: '*If you are the son of God, command these stones to become loaves of bread*'.[6] Nearby there was once the house of Elisha the prophet, and his cave and well are about a half a verst to the east of Gabaon. And from Jerusalem it is six versts to the monastery of Theodosius. This monastery was[7] on a hill and surrounded by a wall and could be seen from Jerusalem. There is a great cave here in the middle of the monastery and in this cave the Magi passed the night when they were avoiding Herod. Now St Theodosius lies here and many holy fathers; in the same cave lie the mother of St Saba and the mother of St Theodosius.

[1] Josh. 5. 13–16 but rather different from the RSV.
[2] add: tall and square.
[3] Josh. 4.
[4] var: of the Amorites.
[5] Josh. 10–13.
[6] Matt. 4. 3.
[7] var: is.

38 From this monastery to the Laura of St Saba is six versts. These two monasteries are to the south, and the Laura of St Saba is in the Valley of Josaphat or Valley of Weeping which valley starts in Jerusalem and passes from Gethsemane through the Laura to the Sea of Sodom. The Laura of St Saba was established by God in a marvellous and indescribable way: there was a river bed, fearful and very deep and dry and with high walls and to these walls cells are attached and held there by God in a marvellous and fearful manner. On the cliffs on both sides of this terrible ravine stand cells fixed to the rocks like stars in the sky. There are three churches here and among the cells to the west there is a wonderful cave beneath a rocky cliff, and in this cave there is the church of the Holy Mother of God, and this cave God showed to St Saba by a fiery column when he was living alone in that ravine. And the first cell of St Saba when he was living alone is here, about half a verst from the present-day Laura and from here God showed him by means of a fiery column the holy place where now stands the Laura of St Saba, and it is a wonderful place and quite indescribable. And between these three churches is the tomb of St Saba, about four fathoms from the great church, and there is a beautifully executed chapel over the tomb. And here lie many holy fathers, their bodies as if still alive; the bishop St John the Silent,[1] St John Damascene and St Theodore of Edessa and Michael[2] his nephew lie here,[3] and St Aphroditian and many other saints, their bodies as if still alive and exhaling an ineffable perfume. And I saw the well of St Saba in that ravine opposite his cell, which a wild ass showed him one night, and from this well I drank water which was sweet and very cold. In that place there is no river nor stream nor spring, but only the well of St Saba, for it is a waterless place in rocky mountains and the whole of that wilderness is dry and waterless and the fathers who dwelt in that wilderness lived by rainwater alone. And near the Laura to the south there is a place called Ruva,[5] and it is near the Sea

[1] The Russ. has 'and Sichast', evidently a corruption of Gr *hesichastos* – silent. St John (454–559) was a bishop who resigned his see to become a monk under St Saba.

[2] St Theodore of Edessa, a ninth-century bishop. See Halkin 2, p. 274.

[3] add: in the Laura of St Saba, and Cosmas of Majumas (also lies there). For Cosmas see *Cosmas episcopus Maiumae hymnographus*, Halkin, 1, p. 136.

[4] var: Aphrodit. Probably St Aphrodisius, disciple of St Saba, see *Bibliotheca sanctorum*, Rome, 1961, vol. 1, p. 130. Possibly there is an influence of the popular apocryphal *Tale of Afroditian* (about Persia and the Magi). W. suggests St Epaphroditus, disciple and helper of St Paul. Less likely in the context.

[5] var: Rova, Riva.

of Sodom. And there are high rocky mountains here with many caves in those mountains, and holy fathers lived in these mountains in this fearful waterless wilderness. Here are the lairs of the panther and there are many wild asses. The Sea of Sodom is dead and has no living thing in it, neither fish nor crayfish, nor shellfish, and if the swift current of the Jordan should carry a fish into this sea, it cannot live even an hour but quickly dies. And from the depths of this sea red[1] pitch rises to the surface and this pitch lies on the shore in great quantity and a stench comes up from this sea as if from burning sulphur, for the torment[2] lies under this sea.

And beyond the mountain three versts[3] to the east of the Laura of 39
St Saba is the monastery of St Euthemius, and here lie St Euthemius and many other holy fathers, their bodies as if still alive. The monastery is in a valley with rocky mountains all round it at some distance; the monastery was once surrounded by a wall and there was a fine tall[4] church and nearby stood the monastery of St Theoktistus at the foot of the mountain to the south of the monastery of St Euthemius; but all this is now destroyed by the pagans.

Mount Sion is high and steep on the southern side but sloping 40
and even on the Jerusalem side. And on this Mount Sion stood formerly the old city of Jerusalem which was destroyed by Nebuchadnezzar, King of Babylon, in the time of the prophet Jeremiah. But now Mount Sion is outside the city walls to the south of Jerusalem. And here on Mount Sion once stood the house of John the Theologian and in that place there was built a great square church and it is a short stone's throw from the city wall to the church of Holy Sion.

In this church on Sion there is a chamber behind the altar and in this chamber Christ washed the feet of his disciples.[5]

From this chamber, going south, you must climb a stairway to 41
the Upper Room; this is a chamber, beautifully made, standing on pillars and with a roof, decorated with mosaic and beautifully paved and with an altar as in a church at the east end. And here was the room of John the Theologian in which Christ supped with his disciples. Here John *lay on Christ's breast* and asked, '*Lord who is* the

[1] var: black and it floats.
[2] add: of Herod.
[3] var: ten.
[4] add: in a high place.
[5] add: in another room Christ ate the last supper with his disciples.

one that will betray you?'.[1] In the same place the Holy Spirit descended upon the apostles at Pentecost.

In this church on the south side there is another chamber, below on the ground floor, and it is low, and it was to this chamber that Christ *came to his disciples* when the doors were barred and *stood among them and said 'Peace be to you'*,[2] and here he made Thomas believe on the eighth day. Here too is the sacred stone brought from Mount Sinai by an angel.

And on the other side of this church, to the west, low on the ground in the same way is another room, and in this room expired the Holy Mother of God. And all this happened in the house of John the Theologian.

Here too was the house of Caiaphas. Here Peter denied Christ three times before the cock crowed. And this place is to the east of Sion.

42 And here nearby to the east on the side of the mountain is a very deep cave to enter which you must climb down 32 steps,[3] and in this cave Peter bitterly lamented his denial and above this cave has been built a church dedicated to the holy apostle Peter.

43 From here further to the south, at the foot of the mountain, is the pool of Siloam where Christ opened the eyes of the blind man.[4]

44 And here at the foot of Mount Sion is the Potter's field which they bought with the money paid for Christ as a burial place for strangers, and it is on the other side of the valley at the foot of Mount Sion to the south. And here there are many caves cut into the side of the mountain, and in these caves there are now tombs wonderfully cut in the rock; and here are interred travellers from abroad without payment, and nothing is allowed to leave this holy place because it was bought with blood of Christ.

45 Holy Bethlehem is to the south of holy Jerusalem six versts and it is two versts across the plain to the place where Abraham dismounted and where he left his young servant with the ass and took his son Isaac as a sacrifice and ordered him to carry firewood and fire, and he said '*Father, behold the fire and the wood but where is the lamb?*' And *Abraham said* to him '*God will* show us *a lamb, my child*'.[5] And[6] Isaac went rejoicing by that road from Jerusalem, and in the same place to which Isaac was brought Christ was crucified.

[1] John 13. 25 (approx.).
[2] John 20. 19.
[3] var: 20.
[4] See John 9. 7.
[5] Gen. 22. 7–8.
[6] add: he and

From there it is one verst farther to the place where the holy mother of God saw two men, one laughing and one crying.[1] And here there was once a church[2] and a monastery of the Holy Mother of God but now they are destroyed by the pagans.

From here it is two versts to the tomb of Rachel, the mother of Joseph.

From here it is one[3] verst to the place where the Holy Mother of 46
God alighted from her ass when the child in her womb obliged her, wishing to emerge.[4] And here is a great stone on which the Holy Mother of God rested after she had dismounted from the ass and from which, rising up, she went on foot to the holy cave where she gave birth to Christ.[5]

And near here is the place of the Nativity of Christ, as far from the rock as a good archer can shoot.

Here above this holy cave a great church has been built in the 47
form of a cross and its roof is raised up on arches [in a tower?] and the church is covered with tin and is decorated with mosaic. It has eight[6] round marble columns and is paved with white marble slabs. It has three[7] doors. It is fifty[8] fathoms long up to the great altar and twenty[9] fathoms wide. The cave and the manger where Christ's nativity took place are beneath the great altar like a great cavern, beautifully made, and with seven steps leading down to the doors of the holy grotto, and there are two doors, each with seven steps. And as you enter the cave by the eastern door, on the left hand there is the place down on the ground where Christ our God was born and above this place is built a holy altar on which they celebrate the liturgy.

And this place is to the east and opposite it on the right[10] hand 48
side is the manger of Christ and the holy manger of Christ is beneath a rocky mass on the west[11] side and in it Christ God was placed, wrapped in rags, and suffered all this for our salvation. These places, the Nativity and the manger, are close together, only three fathoms apart; the two places are in the same cave, and this cave is decorated with mosaic and beautifully paved. The church is

[1] *Protevangelium of James*, 17. 2. James, p. 45.
[2] add: large.
[3] var: 2.
[4] *Protevangelium of James*, 17. 3. James, p.46.
[5] ibid., 18,1. James, p.46.
[6] var: 50.
[7] var: 2.
[8] var: 8; 30.
[9] var: 8; 50.
[10] var: left.
[11] var: east.

all hollowed out below and here lie the relics of saints. And on your right hand as you come out there is a[1] deep cave beneath the church and in this cave used to lie the relics of the Holy Innocents and they[2] were taken from there to Constantinople. There is a high wall built all round this church. And this place of the Nativity was on a hill, away from men, in a wilderness; and where there now stands the place of the Nativity and the wall, is now called Bethlehem, but the ancient Bethlehem was in front of this place before you reach the place of the Nativity. Now a stylite lives there, and there is the rock of the Holy Mother of God. It was on this mountain that the first Bethlehem once was. And all the land round about Bethlehem is called Ephrata, the land of Judah, of which the prophet says '*But you, O Bethlehem Ephrathah who are little to be among the clans of Judah, from you shall come forth for me one who is to be ruler in Israel.*'[3] And this land around Bethlehem is mountainous and very beautiful and fine fruit trees stand on the lower slopes: olives and figs and carobs in countless number; and there are many vineyards about Bethlehem and many cultivated fields in the valleys.

And near the church of the Nativity of Christ outside the city wall and on a hill a bowshot to the south is the cave in which the Holy Mother of God lived with Christ and Joseph.[4]

49 And here there is a place to the east of the city, a bowshot away, called Bethel. And here was the house of Jesse, father of David, to which the prophet Samuel came and anointed David king of Israel in place of Saul.

50 Here is David's well from which David once longed to drink.

At this place the angels announced the birth of Christ to the shepherds.

And a verst[5] from the Nativity to the east in the plain at the foot of a hill is the place where the holy angels announced the birth of Christ to the shepherds. And there used to be a cave here above which a fine church was dedicated to Saint Joseph, and there was a fine monastery, but now the place is laid waste by the pagans. And the land round this place is very beautiful, with fertile fields and many olives, and this place is called Agiapimina which means 'holy

[1] var: another.
[2] var: half of them.
[3] Micah, 5. 2.
[4] add: for two years; and to this cave came the Magi with gifts and worshipped Christ and from this cave Christ fled to Egypt with his mother and Joseph.
[5] var: half a verst.

pasture'.[1] And at the foot of the mountain on the Bethlehem side is a village [belonging to the monastery] of Saint Saba.

To the south of Bethlehem is Hebron, the double cave and the 51
oak of Mamre. It is 28[2] versts from Jerusalem to Hebron and the road runs past Bethlehem to Hebron and it is 6 versts to Bethlehem and three versts from Bethlehem to the river of Etham. Of this river of Etham the prophet David says in the psalter, *You have dried up the rivers of Etham: Yours is the day and Yours is the night.*[3] This river is now dry and flows underground and appears at the Sea of Sodom into which it flows. And on the other side of this river there is a very high rocky mountain and on it a great dense forest and there is a way over that terrible mountain but it is difficult to pass along it because the Saracens have a great fortress there from which they attack. And if anyone in a small party tries to travel that road he cannot; but God granted me a good and numerous escort and thus I was able to pass that terrible place without hindrance; nearby lies the town of Ascalon from which the pagans come forth in great numbers and attack [people] on that evil road. And on that same mountain, in the forest, Absalom the son of David was killed as he fled from the violence of his father, and his mule carried him into the depths of this forest and his head was caught by the hair and he was pulled from his mule and suspended high in a tree, and he was shot through the heart by three arrows and so he died in that tree.[5]

And from here to the well of the oath of Abraham it is 10 versts, and from the well to the oak of Mamre it is six versts.

This holy oak is close by the road on your right hand as you 52
proceed, and it stands splendidly on a high hill, and around its roots God has paved the ground with white marble so that all round this fine oak is paved like a church and it is wonderful to see this sacred oak growing up from the stone in the middle of this pavement. On top of the hill near this oak is a place like the foundation of a house, level and clear without stones, and here stood the tent of Abraham near the oak and to the east of it. The oak is not very tall but very gnarled and with dense branches and there is much fruit on it. Its

[1] See W. – but his Greek etymology is questionable.
[2] var: 22.
[3] Ps.74(73),15–16. (LXX).
[4] add: and there are many lions, unicorns and panthers living there.
[5] add: and his father David grieved for him.

branches bend down near to the ground so that a man standing on the ground can reach its branches. In thickness it is two fathoms round as I measured it,[1] and the trunk is one and a half fathoms up to the first branches. It is to be marvelled and wondered at that this tree has stood for so many years on such a high mountain unharmed and undecayed but stands as firm, by the grace of God, as when it was first planted. And under this oak came the Holy Trinity[2] to the patriarch Abraham and dined with him and here the Holy Trinity blessed Abraham and Sarah his wife and granted them a son, Isaac, in their old age; here too the Holy Trinity showed Abraham a spring and there is a well there to this day at the foot of the hill near the road. And all the land round the oak is called Mamre, which is why the oak is called the oak of Mamre. From the oak to Hebron it is two versts.

53 Hebron is a great mountain and there was once a great and strong city on it and its buildings are ancient. A great number of people at one time lived on the mountain but now it is empty. The first to settle on Mount Hebron was Canaan, grandson of Noah and son of Ham, who came after the flood and the building of the tower (of Babel) and populated all this land round Hebron. And here was the land promised by God to Abraham when he was still in Mesopotamia at Haran, for there was the house of Abraham's father. And God said *to Abraham, 'Go from your country and your kindred and your father's house* and go to the *land of Canaan* and *I shall give that land to you and to your seed for ever* and I shall be with you'.[3] And now indeed is that land the land promised by God and blessed by God with every good thing: wheat and vines and olives and every kind of vegetable is there in abundance and domestic animals flourish: sheep and cattle bring forth twice a year and many bees have made their hives in the rocks of those beautiful mountains. And there are many vineyards on the lower slopes and countless fruit trees, olives, figs, and carobs, and apples and cherries and crops of every kind, better and larger than any on earth; beneath the sky there no such crops anywhere else. And the waters of this place are good and beneficial to all and this land around Hebron is indescribable in its beauty and abundance of good things. And on

[1] add: with my arms.

[2] The meal of Abraham's three visitors is the usual representation of the Trinity in Orthodox icons.

[3] Gen. 12. 1; 17. 8 (approx.).

this Mount Hebron was once the house of David and here David lived for 8 years when he was driven out by his son Absalom. And from Hebron to the double cave of Abraham it is half a verst or less. The double cave is in the rock of the mountain and in this cave is the tomb of Abraham, Isaac and Jacob. Abraham bought this double cave from Ephron the Hittite as a burial place for all his descendants when he came from Mesopotamia to the land of Canaan, and he acquired nothing before this, only the double cave for his burial and that of his posterity. And now a small but very strong enclosure has been built around this cave, and it is made of great stones, marvellously and very cunningly wrought, and the walls are very high. The cave is inside in the middle of this enclosure and the whole enclosure is paved with white marble slabs. And this cave is solidly built beneath paving[1] and in it lie Abraham, Isaac, Jacob, and all the sons of Jacob and their wives, Sarah, and Rebecca, but Rachel lies outside on the road to Bethlehem. And in the enclosure above the cave the tombs have been built separate from each other with small round chapels built on top. The tombs of Abraham and his wife Sarah are close to each other; the tombs of Isaac and his wife Rebecca are close to each other and so are tombs of Jacob and his wife Leah.

The tomb of Joseph the Beautiful is outside this enclosure, a 54
stone's throw from the double cave and this place is now (called)
Holy Abraham. And there is a high hill, one verst to the south of
the double cave, and this was the hill ascended by the Holy Trinity
and Abraham, for Abraham brought the Holy Trinity to this hill
from the oak of Mamre. And on top of this hill is a beautiful and
very high place in which Abraham, falling on his face, worshipped
the Holy Trinity and prayed and said:

'*Lord, do not destroy the righteous with the unrighteous*. But if Lord 55
you should find *fifty righteous men in* Sodom, *wilt thou not spare* O
Lord the whole of the city for the sake of the *fifty righteous?*' *And the
Lord said* to Abraham: '*If I find among the men of Sodom fifty righteous I*
shall not destroy *the whole city for the sake* of those fifty righteous
men.' Prostrating himself anew before God Abraham said, '*If there
are thirty righteous men* in Sodom wilt thou not pardon all the city?'
And the Lord *answered*, '*If I find thirty* righteous men in Sodom I
will not destroy the city'. Having prostrated himself before God,

[1] var: a bridge.

Abraham said, 'Lord, very merciful and patient to our sins, *be not angry* with thy servant *if I speak again*: if there are fifteen righteous men in Sodom, wilt thou not, O Lord, pardon the whole city for the sake of these fifteen?' And the Lord answered, 'If I find fifteen righteous men in Sodom *I will not destroy* the city, nor even if I find five'. And Abraham was silent and dared not reply.[1] From this hill the Holy Trinity sent two angels to Sodom to bring out Lot, the nephew of Abraham. And in this place Abraham then sacrificed to God, sprinkling wheat on the fire, and for this reason the place is called 'The Sacrifice of Abraham'. And this place is very high and from it can be seen the whole of the land of Canaan.

From the sacrifice of Abraham to the Valley of the Bunch of Grapes[2] it is one verst, and from the Valley of the Bunch of Grapes to the threshing floor of Atad it is one verst.[3]

56 From there to Sigor it is two[4] versts. Here there are two tombs, the tomb of Lot and the tombs of his two daughters. And on the same mountain there is a great cave and it was to this cave that Lot fled with his two daughters. Nearby are the remains of a city of the first inhabitants [of the place], high on the mountain, and this is called Sigor.

One verst[5] to the south of Sigor on a rise stands Lot's wife in the form of a stone pillar. From Lot's wife to Sodom it is two versts. All this I saw with my own eyes but I could not go on my own feet to the place[6] of Sodom for fear of the pagans, for orthodox people would not allow me to go there, saying: 'There is nothing good for you to see there, only the torment and stench which rises from that place, and you will be ill', they said to me, 'from this evil stench'. So here we turned back to Holy Abraham, and protected by the grace of God we came safely to the double cave in the enclosure and there venerated all the holy places and rested there for two days. By the grace of God we found a good large company travelling to Jerusalem and we joined them and went joyfully with them without fear and reached safely the Holy City of Jerusalem and praised God for allowing us unworthy men to see those holy places so indescribable and unutterable.

[1] Gen. 18. 23–32 (approx.).

[2] See Num. 13. 24. The Valley of Eshcol. Wilson's translation is very confused at this point.

[3] See Gen. 50. 10.

[4] var: 3.

[5] var: ½.

[6] var: sea.

[1]And to the south of Bethlehem[2] there is the monastery of Saint Chariton on the river of Etham already mentioned. It is near the Sea of Sodom in rocky mountains with a desert all around it. This place is terrible and waterless and dry and beneath it is a rocky and very awful ravine; all about the place was a wall and in the middle there are two churches in the larger of which is the tomb of Saint Chariton. Outside the wall there is a sepulchre beautifully fashioned and in this sepulchre lie holy fathers, their bodies as if still alive, and more than 700[3] lie here. Here lies Saint Cyriacus the Confessor,[4] his body completely preserved; here lie John and Arcadius the sons of Xenophon[5] and a miraculous sweet smell emanates from them. And we worshipped here in this holy place and ascended the hill to the south, a verst farther on from the monastery.

And here is a flat place in a field[6] and in this place the prophet Habakkuk was carried off by an angel when he was going to the reapers in the field with food and water, and was carried to Babylon to Daniel the prophet in the pit and, having given Daniel to eat and drink, he was seized up again by the angel and in the same hour on the same day he was back with the reapers and gave them their meal. And a kind of chapel has been built in this place on account of the miracle; Babylon is in fact forty days journey from here.

And near this place is a great square church dedicated to the holy prophets. And there is a great cave beneath the church and in this cave lie the twelve prophets in three sepulchres:[8] Habakkuk, Nahum, Micah, Ezekiah, Abdias, Zachariah, Ezekiel, Ismael, Saveil, Baruch, Amos and Hosea.[9]

And on a mountain nearby is a very large village and in this village live many Christians and Saracens. And this is the village of the holy prophets where they were born, and it was their home. And protected by the grace of God we spent one night in this

[1] add: A few days later we went to the monastery of St Chariton.
[2] add: 5 versts distant.
[3] var: 500; 800.
[4] St Cyriacus the Recluse, 449–557.
[5] See the *vita* of Xenophon and his wife Maria and their sons John and Arcadius in *PG*, 104, cols. 1011–1043.
[6] add: in a high place; to the left. See *Bel and the Dragon*, 33–9.
[7] add: travelling quickly.
[8] *Rak* = chest, coffin, tomb or sepulchre.
[9] add: Sophonius.

village and were well received by the Christians there, and rising early on the following morning we went to Bethlehem. And the chief of the Saracens, armed, escorted us as far as Bethlehem and conducted us all round those places; otherwise we should not have reached those holy places because of the pagans, for Saracens abound and carry on brigandage in those mountains. And we came safe to the holy town of Bethlehem and worshipped there at the Nativity of Christ, and after resting we went on joyfully to the holy city of Jerusalem.

57 There is a place near Jerusalem, a bowshot to the east of the Tower of David and in this place David killed Goliath. It is in a low place near a cistern and now there is a fine cornfield there.

From there it is a bowshot to a cave in which lie the remains of many holy martyrs killed in Jerusalem in the reign of Heraclius, and this place is called Agia Mamilla.

58 From this place to the True Cross it is one verst, and this place is beyond the mountain to the west of Jerusalem and in this place the footrest of Christ was cut to which they nailed the most pure feet of Our Lord Jesus Christ. And this place is encircled by a wall and in the middle is a very tall church dedicated to the True Cross and it is all beautifully decorated. And beneath the great altar, deep beneath the altar table, there is the stump of that true tree, and it is very firmly fixed and covered over with slabs of white marble, and there is a small round window cut through opposite the tree. The Iberian[1] Monastery is here.

59 From this monastery to the house of Zacharias it is four versts and the place is at the foot of a mountain to the west of Jerusalem. To this house of Zacharias came the Holy Mother of God to visit Elizabeth, and *she greeted Elizabeth, and as soon as Elizabeth heard Mary's greeting, the child in her womb leapt* for joy, and she said: Whence have *you come to me, O mother of my Lord? Blessed art thou amongst women and blessed is the fruit of thy womb.*[3] In the same house John the Precursor was born. Now in this place there has been built a tall church; on the left[4] hand as you enter this church beneath a small altar is a little cave, and in his cave John the Precursor was born. And this place was encircled by a stone wall.

60 From there it is half a verst through a ravine to the mountain to

[1] i.e. Georgian.
[2] add: the father of John the Baptist.
[3] Luke, I. 40–42.
[4] var: right.

which Elizabeth fled and said: 'Receive, O mountain, a mother and child!'[1] And immediately the mountain parted and took her in. And the servants of Herod who had pursued her, when they came to this place found nothing and returned home baffled. And this place may be recognized in the rock even to the present day. And above this place there is now built a little church, and beneath the little church is a little cave and another little church built on to the cave in front of it. From this cave flows very good water, and Elizabeth and John drank this water while they were living in the cave in the mountain guarded by an angel until the death of Herod. And this mountain is very great and has much forest on it, and around it there are many forested valleys. It is to the west of Jerusalem and the name of this place is Orini. The prophet David fled from King Saul to the same mountain from Jerusalem.

To the west of this mountain it is two versts to Rama and of this 61
Rama the prophet Jeremiah says: *A great noise was heard in Rama, lamentation and bitter weeping. Rachel is weeping for her children; she refuses to be comforted because they are not.*[2] And this Rama is a great valley and along this valley there were many villages. And the whole of the land round that valley is now called Rama, and it is the region of Bethlehem. Here into Rama King Herod sent his soldiers to kill the holy babes.

From Rama it is 4 versts to the west to Emmaus and here Christ 62
on the third day after his resurrection appeared to Luke and Cleopas when they were going from Jerusalem to this village and here Christ *made himself known to them by the breaking of bread.*[3] Once there was a large village here and a church was built here, but now all is destroyed by the pagans and the village of Emmaus is empty. It was near the road beyond the mountains on the right hand as you go from Jerusalem to Jaffa.

From Emmaus to Lydda it is four versts across the plain. Here 63
there was a very great city called Lydda, now called Rambili.[4] In this Lydda Peter cured Aeneas[5] as he lay on his bed.

From Lydda to Joppa it is 10[6] versts, continuing across the plain. 64
In this town of Joppa Saint Peter the Apostle raised Tabitha[7] from

[1] *Protevengelium of James*, 22. 2. James, p.48.
[2] Jer.31. 15.
[3] Luke, 24. 13–18. Only Cleopas is mentioned in RSV.
[4] var: Ramblia, Ramli, Raklia.
[5] Acts 10. 33.
[6] var: 5; 8.
[7] Acts 9. 36.

the dead. In the same town Peter having fasted *on the top of the house* at the ninth hour *saw a sheet coming down from heaven* fastened *at the four corners* and coming towards him; and Peter looked up and saw that the sheet was *full of four-legged beasts and every kind of creeping creature*. And *a voice* from heaven said *to him: Rise Peter, kill and eat. And Peter said: No Lord; for I have never eaten anything that is common or unclean. And the voice* from heaven said to him: *What God has cleansed you must not call common.*[1] In this place there is now a church dedicated to Saint Peter. This town of Joppa is near the sea and the sea comes right up to its walls. The town is now called Jaffa in the Frankish language. From Jaffa to Tarsuf it is 6 versts.

65 From Tarsuf[2] to Caesarea Philippi[3] it is 24 versts, travelling all the way beside the sea. In Caesarea Saint Peter the Apostle baptized Cornelius. Near here, two versts to the south of the town, is the mountain on which father Marcian (Martyn)[4] lived and to whom a harlot came to tempt him.

66 From Caesarea Philippi to Capernaum it is 8[5] versts. Capernaum was a very great city and many people lived in it but now it is deserted. It is near the Great Sea. Of this city of Capernaum the prophet says: Woe unto thee Capernaum. *Thou shalt be exalted to heaven and thou shalt be brought down to the depths of hell.*[6] It is from this city that the Antichrist will come[7] and it is for this reason that the Franks have now abandoned all the city of Capernaum.

67 And from Capernaum to Mount Carmel it is 6 versts. On this mountain the holy prophet Elijah lived in a cave and was fed by a raven.[8] On this mountain too he slew with a knife the priests of Babel (Baal)[9] and he said: *I have been very jealous for the Lord God.*[10] And this Mount Carmel is very high and about a verst from the Great Sea. From Mount Carmel to the city of Kifa it is[11] one verst.

68 From Kifa to Acre it is 15 versts. The city of Acre is very large and solidly built and there is a good harbour below the town. It is a Saracen town but it is now held by the Franks. From Acre to Tyre

[1] Acts 10. 13–16.
[2] var: Arsuf.
[3] Caesarea Maritima?
[4] Evidently St Martinianus, a Palestinian hermit. See Halkin, 2, p.88.
[5] var: 18; 50.
[6] A conflation of Matt. 11. 21 and 11. 23 or Luke 10. 13 and 10. 15.
[7] From the *Revelations* of Pseudo-Methodius of Patara.
[8] 1 Kings 17. 6.
[9] 1 Kings 18. 40.
[10] 1 Kings 19. 10. add: almighty.
[11] var: Kaifa, Kaiafa, Vifa.

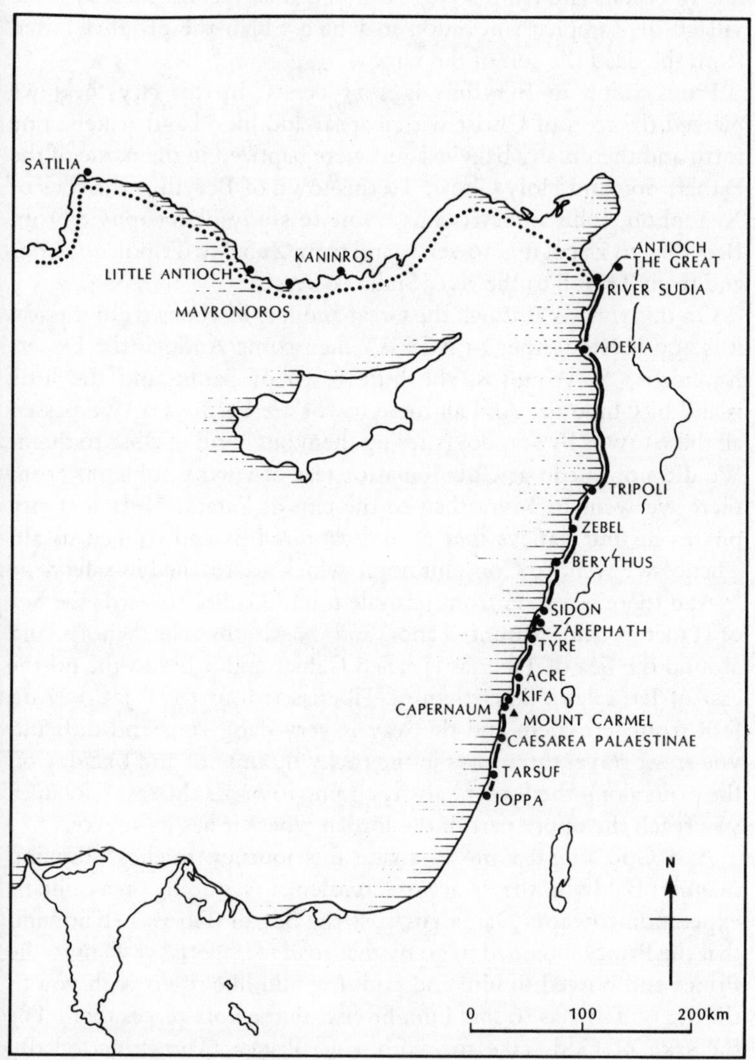

Fig. 23. Daniel's journey from Joppa to Satilia.

it is 10[1] versts and from Tyre to Sidon it is 10[2] versts. Nearby is the village of Zarephath in Sidon in which Elijah the prophet raised from the dead the son of the widow.[3]

69 From Sidon to Berythus it is 15 versts. In this city the Jews pierced the icon of Christ with a spear and blood and water came forth and then many believed and were baptized in the name of the Father, Son and Holy Ghost. To this town of Berythus the sons of Xenophon, John and Arcadius, came to study philosophy.[4] From Berythus to Zebel it is 20 versts and from Zebel to Tripoli 40 versts and from Tripoli to the river Sudia 60 versts.

70 On this river is Antioch the Great and it is 8[5] versts from the sea; it is 100 versts farther to Adekia,[6] then come Antioch the Lesser, Kaniniros, Mavronoros, the little town of Satilia and the little island of Chidonia. And all these towns are by the sea. We passed all these towns by sea, not entering them but coming close to them. We did not put in at Chilidonia for fear of enemy soldiers. From there we went to Myra then to the city of Patara. Near that city pirates in four galleys met us and captured us and robbed us all. Thence we went to Constantinople which we reached in safety.

71 And there is a road from Jerusalem into Galilee towards the Sea of Tiberias and Mount Tabor and Nazareth. The whole land around the Sea of Tiberias is called Galilee and it lies to the north-east of Jerusalem. The town of Tiberias is four days' journey on foot from Jerusalem and the way is very dangerous and difficult: you must travel three days in the rocky mountains and one day on the plain along the Jordan, always going towards the east [sic] until you reach the upper part of the Jordan where it has its source.

And God granted me to make this journey in the following manner: Baldwin, the Prince of Jerusalem,[7] was going on a military expedition towards Damascus past the Sea of Tiberias. Knowing that the Prince intended to go by that road to Tiberias, I went to the Prince and bowed to him and said: I would like to go with you to the Sea of Tiberias so that I might visit all the holy places there. For the sake of God, take me with you, Prince. The Prince gladly permitted me to go with him and attached me to his suite. Then

[1] var: 20.
[2] var: 12.
[3] 1 Kings, 17. 17–24.
[4] See p. 149, n. 5.
[5] var: 50.
[6] var: Laodicea (and others).
[7] Baldwin I, king of Jerusalem 1100–1118, called by Daniel both *knyaz'* 'prince' and *tsar'* 'king, emperor'.

with great joy I hired horses. And so we passed those dangerous places without fear or harm with the King's soldiers.[1] Without soldiers it is impossible to pass by that way; only Saint Helen has travelled that road and no one else. And this is the road to Tiberias: from Jerusalem to the well of the Holy Mother of God it is 10[2] versts, from the well to the mountains of Gilboa it is four[3] versts. In these mountains of Gilboa Saul, King of Juda, was killed, and his son Jonathan was also killed.[4] The mountains are great and rocky, dry and waterless, and there is never any dew on them. From these mountains to the well of David it is two versts, and from that well to David's cave it is 4 versts. In that cave God gave King Saul into the hands of David, who did not kill him while he slept but cut off the skirt of his cloak and took his sword and hand-covering.[5] And from these mountains to the mountains of Sichem and to Joseph's Pit it is 4 versts. On these mountains the sons of Jacob pastured their father's flock, and Joseph the Beautiful came to these mountains, sent by his father to his brothers with a peaceful greeting and blessing from Jacob their father, and they, seeing their brother Joseph, rose up and seized him and cast him into the pit which is there to this day and it is like a deep cistern[6] strongly built with great stones. At this place we chose to spend the night; it is near the main road on the right-hand side as you go.

From here it is 10 versts to Jacob's village which is called Sichar. 72
Jacob's Well is there. It is very deep and large and its water is very cold and sweet and near this well Christ conversed with the Samaritan woman. Here we spent the night.

Here, about half a verst from the well, is the town of Samaria. 73
The town of Samaria is very large and abounds in all good things. The town of Samaria stands between two high mountains. There are many fine springs of cold water within this town and innumerable fruit trees of every kind: figs, nuts, carobs and olives like woods and forests cover the whole land round Samaria and on the borders there are fertile corn fields. And all that land round Samaria is beautiful and very wonderful and the place abounds in

[1] Literally 'the Tsar's soldiers' (see preceding note). *Tsar'* would normally mean emperor, or in a biblical context king. *Korol'*, the normal word in Old Russian for a king, is not found in this text.
[2] var: 200.
[3] var: 14.
[4] 1 Sam.31. 8.
[5] 1 Sam.24 and 26. Evidently a conflation of the accounts of two separate events.
[6] var: wall.

all good things: oil, wine, grain and fruits; in a word Jerusalem obtains all its necessities from here. The town of Samaria is now called Neapolis. And there is a place here, two versts to the west of the town of Samaria, called Sebastopolis, and there is a small enclosed place here which was the prison of Saint John the Baptizer of Christ and in this prison John the Precursor of Christ was beheaded by King Herod. The tomb of John the Precursor is here and there is a fine church dedicated to him, and there is a very rich Frankish monastery.

74 From here it is 4 versts to Arimathea where there are the tombs of Saint Joseph and Saint Maleleil.[1] And it is a small town in the hills to the west above Samaria. A fine square church has been built above the tomb of Saint Joseph, and this place is called Arimathea. And from Samaria the road to the Sea of Tiberias lies to the north-east.

75 From Samaria to the town of Bashan it is 30 versts. In this town of Bashan lived Og, King of Bashan, whom Joshua, son of Nun, slew at Jericho. And this place is very dreadful and dangerous. Seven[2] rivers flow from this town of Bashan and great reeds grow along these rivers and many tall palm trees stand about the town like a dense forest. This place is terrible and difficult of access for here live fierce pagan Saracens who attack travellers at the fords on these rivers. And lions are found here in great numbers. This place is near the River Jordan and a great watermeadow[?] lies between the Jordan and the town of Bashan and the rivers flow from Bashan into the Jordan and there are many lions at that place. Nearby to the east of the town a remarkable cavern in the form of a cross has been formed. From this cave flows a spring and there is a wonderful pool there which has formed itself as if made by God. In this pool Christ himself bathed with his disciples and one may see to this day the place where Christ sat on a rock; here we unworthy sinners also bathed. In this town of Bashan also the Jews sought out[3] Christ and

[1] var: Maleil. Probably a paleographic error for Gamaliel, since the preceding word ends in *-go*. For Gamaliel, a leading Pharisee and teacher of Paul, see Acts 5. 34 and 22. 3. In the apocryphal *Gospel of Nicodemus* ch. I and XVII (A. Vaillant, *L'Evangile de Nicodème. Texte slave et texte latin*, Geneva, Paris 1968) in which Gamaliel is one of the Jewish leaders who accused Jesus and later went to inspect Christ's tomb – this visit would of course associate him with Joseph of Arimathea. By Christian tradition, probably apocryphal, he was baptized by Peter and John. He is liturgically commemorated as a saint in the Eastern and Western Churches. For the best bibliography see P. Schaff and S. Macauley Jackson, *Religious Encyclopedia*, 3rd edn, NY, 1891, s.v. Gamaliel.

[2] var: six.

[3] var: tempted.

showed him the poll-tax and said: *Is it lawful to give tribute or not?* And he said to them: *Whose likeness and inscription is this? Render therefore to Caesar the things that are Caesar's and to God the things that are God's.*[1] And Christ said, addressing to Peter: *Go to the sea and cast a hook, take the first fish that comes up and when you open its mouth you will find a shekel, take that and give it to them for me and for yourself.*[2] And by this town of Bashan Christ healed two blind men who called out to him as he passed.[3]

From Bashan to the source of the Jordan and the Custom-house 76
of Matthew it is 20 versts and the road lies all along the Jordan valley going always to the east until you reach the source of the Jordan, whose water is very sweet and pure. The Jordan flows from the Sea of Tiberias in two streams which foam wonderfully. One stream is called Jor and the other Dan and in this way the Jordan flows from the Sea of Tiberias in two streams about three bowshots apart and they continue for about a half verst separately and then the two rivers combine in one, which is called Jordan from the names of the two streams. The Jordan flows fast and pure and meanders greatly, and in every way, in breadth and depth and in its watermeadows, is like the Snov. At its source there are very many fish. And at the very beginning of the Jordan over the two streams there are two stone bridges built very solidly on arches, and beneath these bridges the Jordan flows through the arches.

Near these bridges was the Custom-house of Matthew, the 77
apostle of Christ, for here all the roads come together which lead across the Jordan towards Damascus and into Mesopotamia, and at this place Prince[4] Baldwin and his soldiers stopped to eat. We stopped also at the very source of the Jordan and we bathed in the source of the Jordan in the Sea of Tiberias. And then we went all round the Sea of Tiberias without fear or apprehension and visited on our own two feet all the holy places where Christ our God had walked. Here God permitted me too, a bad and sinful man, to go and see all the land of Galilee, which I had never expected to see: this God let me see and travel with my unworthy feet, and I saw with my sinful eyes all this holy and longed-for land. And I have written about these holy places without lying but in truth as I saw them. Many others who have reached these holy places have been

[1] Matt.22. 20–21.
[2] Matt.17. 27.
[3] Matt.20. 34.
[4] var: king.

unable to examine them properly and have been mistaken about these places, and others who have not reached them have lied much and deceived. And God found for me, wretch that I am, a holy man, ancient in days and very learned and spiritual, who had lived in Galilee for 30 years, 20 of them in the Laura of Saint Saba, and this man showed me everything faithfully, expounding from holy books. How can a sinner like me repay the sight of so many good things? We stayed by these bridges all that day and towards evening Prince Baldwin went over the Jordan with his soldiers towards Damascus, and we went to the town of Tiberias and there spent 10 days until Prince Baldwin returned with his soldiers from Damascus. We meanwhile had visited all the holy places around the Sea of Tiberias.

78 The Sea of Tiberias can be walked around like a lake, and its water is very sweet and one cannot drink too much of it. It is 50 versts long and 20 versts wide. There are very many fish in it, and one particular fish, most remarkable and wonderful, which Christ loved to eat. It is sweeter to the taste than any other fish and it is like a carp(?) and I myself ate this fish many times when I was in the town. Christ ate this fish after his resurrection when he came to his disciples who were fishing and said: '*Children, have you anything to eat?*' *And they said to him:* '*No.*' And he said: '*Cast the net on the right side.*'[1]

79 From the source of the Jordan and these bridges to the Bath of Christ and the Bath of the Holy Mother of God and the Bath of the Apostles it is 6 versts, and from the holy baths to the town of Tiberias it is one verst. This town of Tiberias was once very great, 2 versts long and one verst wide and it is near the Sea of Tiberias. In this town Christ our God performed many miracles. There is in the town the place where Christ cleansed the leper; here once stood the house of the mother-in-law of Peter the Apostle, and Christ entered this house and cured Peter's mother-in-law of the burning fever, and in this place a round church has been built dedicated to Saint Peter. Here too was the house of Simon the Leper,[2] where the harlot washed with her tears the most pure feet of Our Lord Jesus Christ and wiped them with her hair and received remission of her innumerable sins; in this town too he cured the crookbacked[3]

[1] John 21. 5–6.
[2] Actually in Bethany (Matt.26. 6, Luke 7. 38).
[3] var: deaf; blind; wicked. Evidently the woman who was made straight (Luke, 13. 13).

woman; here too took place the miracle of the centurion;[1] here they let down the bed with a sick young man through a hole in the roof, and here he took pity on the Canaanite woman. Here there is a cave with very sweet and cold water to which Christ fled when they wished to make him king in Galilee; and many other miracles Christ performed in this town. In this town is the tomb of Elisha[2] the prophet, the son of Jehosaphat[3] and here near the road[4] is the tomb of Joshua son of Nun. And here by the sea, a bowshot to the east of the town, is a great stone on which Christ stood when he taught the people who came to him from the coasts of Tyre and Sidon and from Decapolis and from all Galilee, and from here he sent the people and his disciples away, and they went to the other side of the sea in boats. Jesus himself stayed here and afterwards crossed the sea as if it were dry land, on foot, and was on the far side of the sea before the people. And when they came they found Jesus walking there, they said: '*Master, when did you come here?*' And he said to them: '*That which is possible to God is impossible to man.*'[5] It is 10[6] versts from Tiberias to that place by sea, and the place is on a rise one verst from the sea.

This place is level and grassy and here Christ fed five thousand, 80
not counting women and children, with five loaves, and twelve baskets of crumbs were left.

Nearby is the place at the foot of a hill by the Sea of Tiberias 81
where Christ appeared to his disciples for the third time after his resurrection. Christ came and *stood by the lake* and said: '*Children, have you anything to eat?*' And they said: '*No.*' And Jesus said to them: '*Cast the net on the right side as I tell you and you will find.*' *And they cast their net and this time they could not draw it in for the multitude of fish*, and when *they dragged the net on to dry land* it contained *153 great fish*[7] And they saw by the net fire and bread and baked fish, and Christ ate and gave the rest to them. There is a church built here in honour of the holy apostles. Nearby is the house of Mary Magdalene where Christ cured her of seven devils, and this place is called Magdala.

Near here on a mountain is Bethsaida, the little town of Andrew 82

[1] Actually at Capernaum. All these events happened in different places. Tiberias is not recorded as the location of any of Christ's miracles.

[2] var: Isaiah.

[3] var: Amos.

[4] add: before the town on a bay; before the town on a hill to the north.

[5] John, 6. 25 and Matt. 19. 26. A curious conflation.

[6] var: 5.

[7] John 21. 5–6.

and Peter and here is the place where he(?) brought Nathanael to Peter and Andrew.[1]

83 And here is the place by the sea where Christ came to the sons of Zebedee, and to Andrew and Peter, who were drawing in their net and tying it; and here Andrew and Peter recognized Christ and left their boat and net and went to follow Christ. And here near the sea was the village of Zebedee, the father of John, and also the house of John the Theologian. And it was here that Christ drove out the legion of devils from the two men and ordered them to enter the swine, and here the swine were drowned in the sea.[2] The village of Capernaum is near here also.

Close by is a great river and this river flows from the Lake of Gennesareth and enters the Sea of Tiberias. The lake of Gennesareth is very large, 40 versts across in all directions, and round, and it contains a multitude of fish. And near this lake is a town called Gennesareth from which the lake has its name.

84 And there is another very large town here called Decapolis, and there is a level plain near this lake on which Jesus stood teaching the people who came from Decapolis and the coast of Tyre and Sidon. Of this place the Gospel speaks.[3] And Jesus performed many other miracles by this lake.

85 And on the other side of this lake to the north-east there is a very high and very large mountain on which the snow lies throughout the summer. It is called Lebanon, and it produces the incense of Lebanon and white incense. From this Mount Lebanon flow 12 rivers, six flowing to the east and six to the south. These rivers flow into the Lake of Gennesareth and six rivers flow to Great Antioch, and this place is called Mesopotamia, which means the place between the rivers. Between these rivers is Haran from which Abraham went out. The Lake of Gennesareth is filled with much water by these rivers, and from this lake flows a great river into the Sea of Tiberias, and from that sea flows the Jordan as I have stated before when speaking of the Jordan, and it is indeed so. I could not reach Mount Lebanon on foot myself for fear of the pagans, but the Christians who lived there and were our guides told us of it in detail and would not let us go to the mountain because of the many pagans there. But I have seen this mountain with my own eyes, and

[1] var: where Philip brought Nathaniel to Jesus.

[2] Matt. 8. 28–32.

[3] Matt. 4. 25.

all the places about the Lake of Gennesareth. Lake Gennesareth is about two versts to the north east of Tiberius.

Mount Tabor and Nazareth are to the west of the Sea of 86
Tiberius. It is eight[1] long versts to Mount Tabor, and apart from a mountain and a small hill, which you must climb, the road lies on the plain. Mount Tabor is a marvel and wonder and is beyond description, made beautiful by God, and it is beautiful and very high and great. It is situated in a beautiful plain far from other mountains like a round haycock and a river flows through the plain at its foot. And Mount Tabor is covered all over with trees of every kind, figs and carobs and olives in great abundance. Mount Tabor is higher than all the other mountains about it, and stands apart from all the other mountains and it stands very grandly in the middle of the plain like a well-made haycock and it is great in circumference. And it is higher than four[2] bowshots if you shoot from the top, and 8 bowshots if you shoot from the bottom. The mountain is all rock and to climb it over the rock is very difficult and tedious; you have to climb in zigzags and the way is very hard. If you climbed briskly from the third to the ninth hour, you would scarcely be able to reach the top of this holy mountain. And on the very top of this mountain there is a place to the south-east like a small pointed rocky hillock and this is the place where Christ Our God was transfigured. And there is a fine church here dedicated to the Transfiguration, and another dedicated to the holy prophets Moses and Elias is to the north of the Transfiguration.

The place of the holy Transfiguration is surrounded by a solid 87
stone wall with iron gates; here there used to be a bishopric and now there is a Latin monastery. In front of this wall on top of the mountain there is a beautiful little glade, and it is a remarkable and marvellous work of God that there should be water at such a height on the very top of the mountain; and on this mountain there are fields and fine vineyards and many fruit trees, and from this mountain you can see very far.

And on this same Mount Tabor, in a level place, there is a very 88
marvellous cave like a small cellar cut in the rock and there was a little window at the top of this holy cave, and within the cave toward the east there has been built an altar. The cave has small doors and you descend into it by steps from the west. In front of

[1] var: 50.

[2] var: 2; 9.

the doors of this cave grow small fig trees and around it grow little trees of every kind. Formerly a great forest stood about the cave but now there are only small weak trees. In this small cave lived the holy Melchisedek,[1] and Abraham came to him here and called him thrice, saying: 'Man of God'![2] Melchisedek came out and brought bread and wine, and having made a sacrificial altar in the cave, offered up the bread and wine in sacrifice and this sacrifice was immediately carried up to God in heaven; and here Melchisedek blessed Abraham, and Abraham cut his hair and nails, for Melchisedek was hairy. This was the origin of the liturgy of bread and wine instead of unleavened bread. Of this the prophet says: '*Thou art a priest for ever after the order of Melchisedek.*'[3] This cave is a good bowshot to the west of the Transfiguration. They treated us with great honour in the monastery at the Transfiguration. We dined there and, having had a good rest, we rose and entered the church of the Holy Transfiguration and worshipped in the holy place where Christ our God was transfigured, and having kissed that holy place with love and great joy, and receiving the blessing of the abbot and all the brethren, we left that holy monastery and went round all the holy places on that holy mountain. The road to Nazareth lies past the cave of Melchisedek, and Nazareth lies to the west of Tabor. For a second time we entered with love the holy cave and bowed down before the holy altar which Melchisedek and Abraham made. This altar exists even today in the cave and holy Melchisedek comes often to celebrate the liturgy in the holy cave. And all true believers who live on this holy mountain come here and they have told me the truth of this. And we praised God who permitted us wretched and unworthy men to see these holy places and kiss them with our unworthy lips. And then we went down from Mount Tabor on to the plain and went two versts to the west towards Nazareth. From Mount Tabor to Nazareth it is 5 great versts,[4] two in the plain and three in the mountains, the way is very arduous, narrow and difficult of passage, for many pagan Saracens dwell in those mountains and there are many Saracen villages in the plain and sallying forth from these villages they kill (travellers) in

[1] add: king of Salem.

[2] add: Come out! Evidently a conflation of Elijah (2 Kings 1. 9) and Melchizedek (Gen. 14. 18).

[3] Ps. 110,4.

[4] var: 15.

those terrible mountains. It is dangerous to travel that way in a small group; only with a large escort can you pass that way without fear, and we were not vouchsafed an escort, there being only eight of us and unarmed. But trusting in God we passed through, and protected by the grace of God and the prayers of Our Lady the Mother of God, we arrived safe and without injury in the holy city of Nazareth where the holy Annunciation of the Angel Gabriel to Our Lady the Holy Mother of God took place and where Christ was brought up.

Nazareth is a small town in a valley in the mountains which can 89
only be seen when you arrive just above it. And in the middle of this town a tall church with three altars[1] has been built and as you enter this church on the left hand there is as it were a cave, small but deep, before a small altar, and this cave has two doors, one to the east and the other to the west and to both of these doors you must descend by stairs. As you enter the cave by the western door, on your right hand there is a cell with little doors and in this little cell lived the Holy Mother of God with Christ. In this holy dwelling Christ was brought up, and here is the bed on which Jesus lay, low on the ground of that little cell.

In this same cave, on the left-hand side as you go in by the 90
western door, there is the tomb of Saint Joseph, betrothed of Mary; Christ himself buried him here with his own immaculate hands. From the wall by his tomb there comes forth a holy white water like holy oil and people collect it for curing the sick.

And there is a place in this cave near the western door where the 91
Holy Mother of God sat by the door spinning crimson thread,[2] and here the Archangel Gabriel came when he was sent by God to the Virgin Mary.

And he stood before her, visible to her eyes, a little way from the 92
place where the Immaculate Virgin sat, and this place where Gabriel stood is the third column[3] from the door of the cave. And a small round marble altar has been erected here on a single small column, and at this altar the liturgy is celebrated.

Here there once stood the house of Joseph where there is now this 93

[1] var: windows.

[2] *Protevangelium of James*, 10. 1 (ed. James, p.43); *Gospel of Pseudo-Matthew*, 8,9 (James, p.74); Mary was one of the virgins chosen to weave a new temple veil: she was allotted the scarlet and purple.

[3] 3 fathoms. Cf. p.128, n.3.

holy cave, and everything took place in the house of Joseph the Betrothed of Mary, and a church has been built above this holy cave, dedicated to the Holy Annunciation. This holy place was once laid waste but now the Franks have taken it and rebuilt it thoroughly. And there is a very rich Latin bishop here who has jurisdiction over the holy place and he made us very welcome with drink and food and all (that we needed), and we spent the night in this town. Having slept well, we arose the next morning and went into the church there and worshipped at that holy place, and entering the holy cave we worshipped at all these holy places. Then we left this town and went a little way to the north east where we found a wonderful well which was deep and very cold, and to reach the water you must go deep down on a stairway. And above this well there is a church dedicated to the Archangel Gabriel, and it is round.

94 It is a good bowshot from the town of Nazareth to this holy well. At this well took place the first Annunciation of the Archangel to the Holy Mother of God. When she came for water and was just dipping her pitcher, the invisible angel called out to her saying: '*Hail, full of Grace, the Lord is with you.*'[1] Mary looked all about but seeing noone only hearing the voice, she took her pitcher and went her way, marvelling in her mind, and saying: 'What voice is this which I have heard though I saw no one?'[2] And coming in to Nazareth and entering her own house she seated herself at the place already mentioned and began to spin scarlet thread and then the Archangel Gabriel appeared to her, standing in the place already referred to, and announced the birth of Christ. It is five versts from Nazareth to the village of Esau.[3]

95 And from this village to Cana of Galilee it is one and a half versts.[4] Cana of Galilee is on a busy route and here Christ turned water into wine. And here we found a large company going to Acre, and joining it with great gladness we went with it to Acre.

Acre was once a Saracen city but now the Franks hold it. The city of Acre is on the Great Sea and has a very fine harbour below it and has everything in plenty. From Nazareth to Acre it is 28 great versts, and Acre lies to the south of Nazareth. We spent four days

[1] Luke 1. 28.

[2] Evidently the Annunciation account from the *Protevangelium of James*, 11 (ed. James, p.43). It is one of the icon formulas for the Annunciation.

[3] var: Jacob; Isaac.

[4] var: ½; 2; 4.

in Acre, and being thoroughly rested we found a large company going to the holy city of Jerusalem and joined this company and went with it rejoicing and came to Caipha, from which place we visited Mount Carmel. On that mountain there is the cave of the holy prophet Elias and here we worshipped, and went on from there to Capernaum. And from Capernaum we came to Caesarea Philippi, and the road thither goes all along the Great Sea over the plain and in some places over the sand as far as Caesarea. We spent three days in the town of Caesarea where once lived Cornelius who was baptized by the Apostle Peter.[1] And from Caesarea we went to Samaria. The road from Caesarea to Samaria is on the left into the mountains and it is 20[2] versts from Caesarea to Samaria. And we were in Samaria on the following day at midday but we went slowly on account of the heat, for those who went on foot could not travel in this heat. And that night we lay before the town of Samaria by the well of Jacob where Christ conversed with the Samaritan woman.[3]

And rising up we went by the road on which we had left 96
Jerusalem and with great joy we reached Jerusalem the Holy City in safety, and we saw nothing bad on this road, only good, and God enabled us to see with our own eyes all the holy places where Christ our God had walked for our salvation: us sinners too he permitted to visit and see the holy places, and we saw the wonderful land of Galilee with our own eyes, and God permitted me to go all over the land of Palestine. And protected by the grace of God we travelled without harm, and kept safe by the prayers of the Holy Mother of God we visited the whole land of Palestine, for all the land around Jerusalem is called Palestine. Fortified by God's help we visited these holy places and nowhere saw any pagans or wild beasts, nor did it happen to me to see any other evil nor feel even the slightest illness on my body but always like an eagle set free,[4] guarded by the grace of God and fortified by the strength of the Most High. '*If I may boast* then I shall boast of the strength of Christ, *I shall boast of my own feebleness. My power is made perfect in weakness,*' says the Apostle Paul.[5] *What shall I render to the Lord for all his bounty to me,*[6] a poor unworthy sinner, in permitting me to see such grace and walk

[1] Acts 10. 1.
[2] var: 4.
[3] John 4. 6–7.
[4] var: like a deer stepping boldly without fatigue or difficulty.
[5] 2 Cor. 12. 1,5,9.
[6] Ps. 116. 12.

those holy places and fulfill the desire of my heart and be made worthy to see what God showed his poor unworthy servant. Forgive me, my brothers, fathers and lords, and do not despise my foolishness in that I have written not cleverly but simply of these holy places and of Jerusalem and of the Promised Land, and if I have not written wisely, then at least I have not written falsely: what I saw with my own eyes I have written down.

97 And now concerning the holy light and how it descends to the tomb of the Lord: this the Lord permitted me, his poor unworthy servant, to see, and in very truth I saw with my own sinful eyes the holy light descending to the life-giving tomb of our Lord Jesus Christ. Many pilgrims tell wrongly of the descent of the holy light. One says that the Holy Spirit comes down in the form of a dove to the tomb of the Lord, and others say that lightning comes down from heaven and lights the lamps above the tomb of the Lord. This is a lie and an untruth: there is nothing to be seen at that time, neither dove nor lightning, but the grace of God comes down unseen from heaven and lights the lamps in the Sepulchre of the Lord, and of this I will speak as I truly saw it. On Good Friday after vespers they clean the Sepulchre of the Lord and wash all the lamps and fill them with pure oil without water, that is with unmixed oil, and having inserted the wicks in the holders, they do not light them but leave the lamps unlit and seal the sepulchre at the second hour of the night, and then they extinguish all the lamps and candles in all the churches of Jerusalem. On that Friday I, poor and unworthy as I am, went at the first hour of the day to Prince Baldwin and bowed down to the earth before him. And he, seeing wretched me, called me to him in a friendly manner and said to me: 'What is it that you wish, Russian abbot?' He knew me well and loved me greatly, for he is a kind and very humble man and not in the least proud. And I said to him: 'My Prince! My Lord! I pray for God's sake and the sake of the Russian Princes, permit me too to place my lamp on the holy tomb on behalf of the whole Russian land.' Then he with care and love told me to place the lamp on the tomb of the Lord, and sent with me a man, his best servant, to the custodian of the Holy Resurrection and to the keeper of the key of the tomb. And the custodian and the keeper of the key told me to bring my lamp with some oil. And bowing to them, I went with great joy and bought a very large glass lamp, and, filling it with pure oil, towards evening I carried it to the tomb of the Lord and asked for the keeper of the

key, who was alone within the sepulchre, and announced myself to him. He opened the holy doors for me, ordered me to take off my shoes and led me barefoot alone into the holy tomb of the Lord with the lamp which I had brought with me, and told me to place it on the Lord's tomb. And with my own sinful hands I placed it at the place where the most pure feet of Our Lord Jesus Christ lay; at the head stood the lamp of the Greeks and at the breast the lamp of (the monastery of) Saint Saba and all the monasteries, for they have the custom every year to place there the lamps of the Greeks and Saint Saba. And then by the grace of God these three lamps[1] were lit, but of the Frankish lamps which had been hung higher up not one was lit. And having placed my lamp on the holy tomb and bowed down before that worthy tomb and kissed with love and tears the place where the body of our Lord Jesus Christ lay, I went out from the holy tomb with great joy and went to my cell. In the morning on Holy Saturday at the sixth[2] hour all the people gather before the church of the holy Resurrection, a great multitude, both natives of that country and travellers from every land, from Babylon and Egypt[3] and from every corner of the earth they gather on that day in crowds without number, and all the places round the church and the Crucifixion of Christ are filled with people. And there is a great crush and terrible suffering for the people, and many are suffocated from the pressure of the vast number of people. All these people stand with unlit candles and wait for the church doors to be opened. At that time within the church there are only priests, and all the priests and people wait until the Prince with his retinue arrive, and then the church doors are opened and the people enter into the church and there is a great crush and pushing and the church is filled and all the galleries are full, for the church cannot contain all the people, and very many stand outside the church round Golgotha and the Place of the Skull and as far as the place where the crosses were found, everywhere is full of a countless multitude of people. And all the people both in the church and outside say nothing but: 'Lord have mercy.' They cry out ceaselessly and shout so loudly that the whole place resounds and echoes with the shouts of the people. And the faithful weep torrents of tears: if a man had a heart of stone he would weep then, for every man then

[1] add: which were below.
[2] var: seventh.
[3] add: and Antioch.

looks into himself and recalls his sins and each says within himself: 'Can it be that the holy light will not descend on account of my sins?' And thus all the faithful stand in tears and with sorrowing hearts, and Prince Baldwin himself stands in awe and great humility and tears stream wonderfully from his eyes. And his retinue stands humbly about him opposite tomb by the great altar. And on that Saturday at the seventh hour of the day Baldwin went with his retinue from his house to the tomb of the Lord, and all were on foot.[1] And he sent to the hospice of Saint Saba and summoned the abbot and his monks. And the abbot went with his brethren to the tomb of the Lord, and I, wretch that I am, went with the abbot and the brethren. And we came to the Prince and all bowed to him, and then he bowed to the abbot and the brethren and commanded the abbot and wretched me to walk by him, while the other abbots and monks he ordered to walk in front of him and his retinue he ordered to follow behind. And we came to the western[2] door of the church of the Resurrection and here a multitude of people blocked the door of the church and we could not enter. And Prince Baldwin commanded his soldiers to drive the people back by force and they made a passage as far as the tomb and so we were able to pass through the people to the tomb. And we came to the eastern door of the holy tomb of the Lord, and the Prince came after us and stood in his place at the right hand by the screen of the great altar opposite the eastern door of the tomb, for here is the raised up place of the Prince. And the Prince commanded the abbot of Saint Saba to stand above the tomb with his monks and the orthodox priests. Unworthy I was commanded to stand high above the very gates of the tomb opposite the great altar so that I might see through the doors of the tomb. All three doors of the tomb were sealed with the royal seal. The Latin priests stood on the Great Altar. And at the eighth hour of the day the orthodox priests and monks and all the clergy and hermits began to sing vespers, while the Latins on the great altar began mumbling after their own fashion. While all sang I stood there attentively watching the door of the tomb. And when they began to read the paroemias for Holy Saturday, during the reading of the first paroemia the bishop with the deacon left the Great Altar and went to the door of the tomb and looked into the

[1] var: barefoot. [2] var: eastern, rear.

tomb through a grille[?], but seeing no light in the tomb, he came back. And when they began to read the sixth paroemia, the same bishop went to the door of the tomb but saw nothing. And then all the people, weeping, cried out: 'Kyrie eleison!' which means: 'Lord have mercy.' When the ninth hour had passed they began to sing the Hymn of the Passage: '*I will sing to the Lord*.'[1] Then suddenly there came from the east a small cloud which stopped above the open top of the church and a light rain fell on the holy tomb and thoroughly soaked us who were standing above the tomb. Then suddenly the holy light shone in the holy tomb and a fearful bright flash came from the holy tomb of the Lord. The bishop with four deacons came up and opened the doors of the tomb. They took the candle from Prince Baldwin, went into the tomb and lit the candle of the prince first from the Holy Fire, then they carried the candle out from the tomb and gave it into the hand of the Prince. And the Prince took his place, holding the candle with great joy, and from this we all lit our candles, and from our candles all the people lit their candles, and all over the church people lit each others' candles. The Holy Light is not like earthly fire for it shines in a different and wonderful way and its flame is red like cinnabar and it shines in a way which is quite indescribable. And so all the people stand with lighted candles and sing in a loud voice: 'Lord have mercy,' with great joy and gladness. There can be no joy for man like the joy of the Christian who has seen the holy light of God. Anyone who has not experienced the joy of that day will scarcely credit the report of these events. However, wise and true-believing men who believe deeply will hear with delight this true account of the holy places. *He who is true to his faith in small things will be true in much*[2] but to an evil unbelieving man the truth becomes a lie. But God is my witness, and the Holy Sepulchre, and the whole company, sons of Russia, Novgorodians and Kievans who were there on that day: Izyaslav[3] Ivanovich,[4] Gorodislav[5] Michailovich,[6] and two Kashkiches[7] and many others are witness of my lowly self and of this account. But let us return to the preceding narrative. When the light shone in the holy tomb then the singing stopped and all cried out: 'Kyrie eleison,' and went from the church with their burning

[1] Exod. 15. 1.
[2] Luke 16. 10.
[3] var: Sedeslav; Seslav.
[4] var: Ivankovich.
[5] var: Goroslav; Gorodoslav.
[6] var: Michalkovich.
[7] var: Kaokich.

candles in great joy, shielding their candles so that the wind would not blow them out, and each went his own way home. From this Holy Light they light the lamps in their churches and complete the singing of vespers at home, while in the great church by the tomb of the Lord the priests alone, without the people, finish vespers. Then I and the abbot and the brothers went to the monastery carrying the lighted candles, and there we finished singing vespers and went to our cells praising God who had shown us unworthy ones his grace. In the morning of Easter Sunday, having sung matins and greeted with a kiss the abbot and the brothers, and having received absolution, at the first hour of the day, the abbot, having taken up the cross, went with all the brothers and me to the tomb of the Lord singing the hymn [kontakion]: 'Immortal one thou hast deigned to go down into the tomb.' And having entered the holy life-giving tomb, we kissed the holy tomb of the Lord with love and warm tears, and delighted in the sweet perfume left by the coming of the Holy Spirit and the lamp still burning brightly and wonderfully. For the three lamps which stood on the tomb had been lit at that time, as the custodian and keeper of the key of the Lord's tomb informed us, but the other five lamps which were hanging above the tomb were burning but their light was different, not like the three lamps which were burning particularly wonderfully. And then we came out of the tomb by the eastern door and going on to the Great Altar we exchanged kisses with the orthodox and being absolved, the abbot and the brothers and I went out of the church of the holy Raising of Christ and went to our monastery where we rested until it was time for the liturgy. And on the third day after the Raising of the Lord, after the liturgy, I went to the keeper of the key of the Lord's tomb and said to him: 'I would like to take my lamp.' He received me kindly and let me enter the tomb alone. I entered the tomb and saw my lamp standing on the holy tomb and still burning with that holy light and bowing down before the holy tomb and kissing with love and tears the holy place where the most pure body of Our Lord Jesus Christ lay, I then measured the tomb in length and breadth and height, for when people are present it is quite impossible to measure it. And having honoured the tomb of the Lord as best I could, I gave the keeper of the key a small present and my poor blessing. And he, seeing my love for the Lord's tomb, pushed back for me the slab which is at the head of the holy tomb of the Lord and broke off a small piece of the blessed rock as a relic and forbade me under oath to say anything of this in Jerusalem. And I, having bowed to the tomb of the Lord and to the keeper of the key, took my lamp with the holy oil and left the holy tomb with great joy, enriched by the grace of God and bearing in my hand the gift of the holy place and the token from the holy tomb of the Lord[1] and I went rejoicing as if I was carrying some rich treasure, and I returned to my cell full of joy. And God and the holy tomb are my witnesses that in all the holy places I did not forget the names of the Princes of Rus' and the princesses and their children, and the bishops, abbots and great lords and my spiritual children and all Christian people, these I did not forget but in all the holy places I remembered them, first praying for all the princes then for my own sins. And I thank the good God that he permitted me, unworthy as I am, to inscribe the name of the Russian princes in the Laura of Saint Saba, and now their names are now remembered in the prayers [ektenia] together with their wives and children. And their names are Mikhail Svyatopolk, Vasilie Vladimer, David Svyatoslavich, Mikhail Oleg Pankratie Svyatoslavich, Gleb of Minsk.[2] I have only recalled the names which I inscribed at the holy tomb of the lord and in all the holy places, leaving aside all the other Russian princes and nobles. I celebrated fifty masses for the Russian princes and all Christians, and forty masses for the dead. May all who read this work in faith and love receive the blessing of God and the holy tomb of the Lord and all the holy places and may they receive a reward from God no less than that of those who have visited these holy places. Blessed are those who, having seen, have believed; thrice blessed are those who have not seen but have believed. For it was by faith that Abraham came to the Promised Land, and indeed faith is the equal of good works. For the sake of God my brothers and lords do not despise my ignorance and crudity and let not this writing be a reproach to me or the tomb of the Lord or the holy places. Whoever reads this with love may he receive his reward from God our Saviour Jesus Christ and may the God of peace be with you for ever. Amen.

[1] add: and I went thither in the reign of the Grand Prince of Rus' Svyatopolk Izyaslavich (1093–1113), grandson of Yaroslav Volodimirovich of Kiev.

[2] Other MSS include other names of Russian princes, presumably reflecting the local loyalty of the scribe. See V, pp.210–213.

GUIDE IN *GESTA FRANCORUM EXPUGNANTIUM IHERUSALEM*

CHAPTER XXXI

1 The present location of the city and the position of the walls which enclose it are far different from those of its famous original plan and condition in the period of Jesus Christ. Even so it still contains reminders of that time which give just cause for its renown, honour and dignity above every other city in the world.

2 Moreover like many other cities it has four entrances, on the east, west, north and south. The one on the east is known by the inhabitants as the Gate of the Valley of Jehoshaphat, because it is the way out into that valley, which is nearby. The one on the west is David's Gate, so named because it stands next to the Tower of David. The northern is Saint Stephen's Gate because it is said that the martyr was stoned outside that gate, and a church has been founded there in his memory. The southern is the Sion Gate, because Mount Sion is on that side: it is steep, and makes this approach to the city difficult and exhausting.

3 To this day there is a fifth gate as well. It is called the Golden Gate, and is situated between the east and south gates below the Temple of the Lord. Through it the King of Heaven entered his city before his Passion, sitting upon an ass, and was received joyfully by the children of the Hebrews. This gate is never opened except on Palm Sunday. If one enters the city by this gate the Sepulchre of the Lord is to the left.

4 At the time of Christ's Passion we read that the Sepulchre was situated outside the city and was cut in the living rock. Near to it, and off slightly to one side, is a beetling rock which is cracked, for, as we read, it was 'rent' at Christ's death, and beneath is Golgotha, a place most richly deserving respect, adoration and reverence. From ancient times the tradition has been passed on that in that place Abraham was about to offer his son as a sacrifice, but offered

instead of him a ram, which stood for the Lamb and Son of God who was later to be sacrificed in that very place. A little further on is the spot called 'Calvary' by the same writer: there the Wood of the Lord, after a Jew had shown where it would be, was discovered by Blessed Helena, in the three-hundred and eighty-sixth year after Christ's Passion. In the same place the Empress founded a church, notable for its size and workmanship. It was later destroyed by the treacherous Gentiles, but its surviving ruins demonstrate what a remarkable monument it once was. Part of the Precious Wood has been preserved by Christians in those places, and it is venerated and exalted with loving reverence.

CHAPTER XXXII

Next to the place where the Cross was discovered and to its south is the 5
Church of the Mother of God known as 'Latin', since it has always been in the care of the Latins. The Virgin is said to have wept there, and torn her hair when she saw her only Son being nailed to the gibbet. Close by is the place where Mary Magdalene and the other women mourned the Saviour's death.

Directly east of this, and inside the walls of the city, is the renowned 6
Temple of the Lord, built with marvellous skill. Even though this is not Solomon's original magnificent building, nor the one which, when it had been rebuilt for a second time after Ezra, outshone every other building in the world, it does none the less have four entrances, in the same way as the first temple.

In this *place the angel*, the one who was killing the people while 7
David prayed and said, '*I am the one who sinned,*[1] I am the one who has done wickedly', is said to have stayed his hand. And the stone over which he stayed his hand is still there standing in the centre of the Temple, and even until now it has not been artificially smoothed.

In this place in the time of Solomon there used to be the Golden Lid and the *Ark* of the Covenant in which were the Tables of Moses, the *Rod* of Aaron which sprouted leaves, the Manna, and the other objects which are called the Holy Things of the Holiest. They were there up to the time of *Josiah, King of Judah,*[2] as one can read in the Book of Maccabees. But later on Jeremiah is said to have hid the Ark in Arabia near Mount Sinai. There even today, with the Mountain smoking and covered with clouds, those wishing to go

[1] 1 Sam. 24. 16–17.

[2] 2 Macc. 2.

there are turned back by the darkness and fierce heat. It is still forbidden to go into the Mount, and it can be found written in the same prophecy of Jeremiah that the ark *is not to be found* until *many nations are gathered together.* So now *the Ark is not in the Temple*, even though some believe it to be so.[1]

8 That place [sc. the Temple] is held sacred for many reasons. The child Jesus was presented there, and received by the aged Simeon. He was later discovered there when he was twelve years old, sitting among the doctors. From there he drove out the money-changers and said: 'It shall be called a House of Prayer'. And the place is to be venerated and regarded as holy on account of many miracles, signs and wonders which God has performed there.

9 Saint Anne's church is to the north of the Temple, and on the way to it is a pool. She was the mother of Blessed Mary, and this is the place where she is said to have borne the Mother of God. A water reservoir has been discovered by the Franks in front of this church, and in it can be seen the remains of the ancient pool with its five porches, preserved to this day. In the time of Christ we read that an angel came down there, and when he touched the water he healed the sick. There too Christ healed the sick man who had been thirty-eight years in his infirmity. One goes down to the pool through one of the porches, and the water there tastes bitter, and cures a good many sick people.

10 Inside the city Christians also venerate the scourging of Jesus Christ, his crowning and mocking, and other things he suffered for our sake. But nowadays it is not an easy matter to discover where they took place, particularly because since those days the city itself has so often been overthrown and destroyed.

CHAPTER XXXIII

11 Now outside the city one leaves past the upper city through David's Gate for the road leading to Bethlehem. In ancient times it was called Ephrata, and it lies two leagues south-west of Jerusalem on the way to Hebron. As we have already mentioned, the place of Christ's Birth and the Manger are there. Moreover the church there, which is very beautiful, large and finely made, enjoys the

[1] This whole chapter is based on Fulcher, *Historia Hierosolymitana*, 1,26. The version is dependent on manuscripts A,B,F,H, which is the revision of 1106 A.D.

dignity of a bishopric. The Innocents slaughtered by Herod were martyred in Bethlehem and its neighbourhood.

Returning from there towards the city one sees on the way the 12
Tomb of Rachel, Jacob's wife. Then one climbs to Mount Sion, which in Christ's day was the highest point in the city and in its centre, but is now outside. In that place is the room where the disciples had their feet washed by their Lord and Master, and he held the Supper with them, and imparted to them the sacrament of the Lord's Body and Blood. He also foretold all that was to happen at his death: and this is furthermore the place where, after the Resurrection, he sent them the Holy Spirit. There it is said that the Mother of God passed away, which accounts for the name of the church. As one can see from the inside, it was splendidly built in ancient times, but it was destroyed by the treacherous Saracens.

At the foot of Mount Sion rises a spring which looks completely 13
clear but tastes bitter. People call it the Spring of Siloam, and it sends a stream down into the torrent-bed down which the Brook Kidron comes pouring in winter. In that place the man born blind received his sight, of whom we read in the Gospel. Further south is Aceldama which was bought as a burial place for strangers.

The Brook Kidron starts to the north, and runs south through 14
the Valley of Jehoshaphat. It has no water in it unless there have been rains. In this valley,[1] between the city and the Mount of Olives, is the church of Mary the Mother of God, where she was buried by the apostles. Her tomb is still revered and honoured there, but from the earliest period of Christianity, as Blessed Jerome testifies in his writings, a remarkable building was erected in that place. It was once an unusually large, beautiful and well-planned church, but later on it was destroyed by the treacherous Gentiles, and its ruins can still be clearly seen. That is also the place where, long ago in the time of Christ, there was a small hamlet called Gethsemane, where the Son of God was put to the test and taken prisoner. There also he left behind his disciples when they were heavy with sleep, and departed from them as it were a stone's cast, across in the direction of the Mount of Olives, to pray there, and at that spot there is now a chapel dedicated in honour of the Saviour.

From that one climbs to the Mount of Olives, which is so high 15

[1] Read *valle* for *villa*.

that it dominates the whole area. That is the place where the Lord used to teach both the disciples and all those from the city who thronged to hear him. There also it is said that he taught the Lord's Prayer to the disciples and, when he was overwhelmed by the crisis of his Passion, uttered his prayers to the Father. Later on at the summit of the mountain he was taken up into heaven, as the apostles looked on. A church is there, which was founded in ancient times, and contains the tombs of many saints. From this mountain Arabia and the Jordan Valley are clearly visible, and the salty stinking sea which covers Sodom and Gomorrha, the cities which were once utterly destroyed by the wrath of God.

16 Not far down the slopes of this mountain to the south east one reaches Bethany, where the Lord raised Lazarus, and where he forgave the sins of Mary Magdalene, and where he was entertained in the house of Simon the Leper. To this day the Tomb of Lazarus is venerated there, and because the Saviour often spent time there the place is sacred and held in veneration.

17 These places are on the outskirts of the city.

18 But the River Jordan, where Christ was baptized, is ten leagues due east of the city. This river divides Judaea and Arabia. One reaches it through Jericho, which was once a great city, to the left of which is the desert in which the Lord fasted for forty days. There one sees also the high mountain where he was tempted by the Devil.

19 But Nazareth where he was conceived, and Galilee where, after the Resurrection, he appeared to the disciples, and the Sea of Tiberias, and Mount Tabor, and the first desert place where with the five loaves and two fishes he satisfied five thousand people, and the second where with seven loaves he fed the four thousand, and all the places which the King of Glory frequented as a child – all these are far from Jerusalem.

. . . .

20 Moreover the Emperor Hadrian made the city wonderfully beautiful and gave it a splendid adornment, paving its streets and squares. He is the one from whose name Jerusalem later came to be called Aelia. And he provided all the streets with drains, so that when the rains come, all the dirt in the city is washed away down them. Nor does this city lack cisterns, which always contain an abundance of water. The city occupies a walled area of a reasonable size, so that it never seems tiresomely small or tiresomely large.

ON THE SITE OF JERUSALEM, AND OF THE HOLY PLACES INSIDE THE CITY OR ROUND IT

The city of Jerusalem is situated in the mountain part of Judaea in 01
the province of Palestine, and has four gates: on the east, the west, the south and the north. To the east is the gate by which one goes down into the Valley of Jehoshaphat, and through which one goes out of the city to the Mount of Olives and the River Jordan. To the west is the Gate of David, in the direction of the sea and of Ascalon. To the south is the gate which is called after Mount Sion, through which one goes to Saint Mary's on Mount Sion. To the north is the gate which is called the Gate of Saint Stephen, because outside it he was stoned. This gate is rarely opened.

Through the Gate of David we entered the Holy City, and had on the right the Tower of David, very near to us as we entered. The Tower of David is situated on the west of the city, and it is higher than all the rest of it.

The Temple of the Lord is to the east in the lower part of the city, 02
above the Valley of Jehoshaphat. It has four entries: to the east, the west, the south and the north. There is a very large rock in the centre, where there is an altar, and there the Lord was presented by his parents and received by Saint Simeon. There also he entered when he preached to the people.

The Sepulchre of the Lord is within the city, a little to the left of 03
us as we went to the Temple. The Church of the Sepulchre is round, and very beautifully built, and has four gates which open towards the east. The Tomb of the Lord is in the middle of this church, and it is well decorated and beautifully arranged. Outside on the east is the place of Calvary, where the Lord was crucified. One climbs up it by sixteen steps, and there is a great rock where the Cross of Christ was set up. Underneath is Golgotha, the place to which the blood of Christ dripped down through the centre of the rock. There too is an altar in honour of the Holy Mother of

God. Outside to the east is the place where Blessed Helena found the Cross, and a great church is built there. In the other direction, towards the sixth hour,[1] is the hospital for poor and sick people, and the church of Saint John the Baptist. Near there is Saint Mary the Latin. In this church of Saint John the Baptist is the stone water-pot in which the Lord made the water into wine.

04 The Temple of the Lord, mentioned above, excels in beauty all the churches. There is another stone water-pot there where, as at Cana of Galilee, he made water into wine. And below the rock which is in the middle of the Temple one goes down by steps to the place which once was the Holy of Holies. There Zacharias prayed when the Angel Gabriel announced to him the birth of Blessed John the Baptist, and there is the place where the Lord sat when the Pharisees brought him the woman taken in adultery.

To the south of this is the Palace of Solomon. To the east of the Palace is the church of Saint Mary, to which one descends by many steps. There is the cradle of the Saviour and his bed and his mother's bed. To the left side of the Temple and outside its walls is the Church of Saint Anne, who was the mother of Christ's mother. Outside it there is said to be the Sheep Pool.

05 Not far outside the walls of the city to the south is the church which is called Saint Mary of Mount Sion, where the Most Blessed Lady physically died. And in this church is the place called 'Galilee', where after his resurrection Christ appeared to his disciples, and at that stage Thomas was not present with them. And in this church towards the east is the place where after eight days, when the doors were closed, he again appeared to his disciples and Thomas was present. He said: 'Peace be with you!', and showed them his hands and his side, and offered them to be touched, according to the words of the Gospel. Above one climbs up the steps to the place where he held the supper with his apostles. There is the same table on which he supped, and there he gave his body to eat, and his blood for the remission of sins. And there the Holy Spirit gave light to the Apostles on the Day of Pentecost.

To the left is the church of Saint Stephen where, when he had been brought from Caphargamala, he was buried by the Patriarch John. Below the mountain is Akeldama, that is 'The Field of Blood', which is the burial place of travellers. On the other side of the mountain is the

[1] i.e. towards the south.

church of Saint Peter, where at cockcrow he wept bitterly on account of the sin of denying. Lower down than this is the spring called 'The Pool of Siloam', where at the Lord's command the man born blind regained his sight. The city of Jerusalem has no living water apart from this.

Bethlehem, the city of David, is two great leagues away towards 06
the ninth hour,[1] and there is the Church of Saint Mary, very beautifully made. Inside is a cave where the Very Blessed Virgin Mary gave birth to the Saviour of the World, and there is the manger in which Christ was laid. In front of the cave is a marble table on which the Mother of God ate with the three Kings, and in front of the cave is a well with clear cold water, into which the star is said to have fallen, which led the three Magi to the entrance of this cave. Going out from the church there are two caves beside the door, an upper and a lower one. In the upper lies the Most Blessed Paula, and at her feet her daughter, the Most Holy Virgin Eustochium. One goes down into the lower cave by a long flight of steps, and there is the tomb in which lies the most holy body of the most Blessed Jerome, the excellent Teacher. This is Bethlehem where, and in all the district round, Herod cruelly commanded that the children should be killed.

The Church of Saint Mary in what is called the Valley of 07
Jehoshaphat is between Jerusalem and the Mount of Olives in the middle of the Valley. There is the tomb of the Mother of God, where Blessed John the Apostle buried her most holy body. Outside that church is the place called Gethsemane. The cave is there where Judas betrayed the Lord to the Jews. And a stone's throw to the right is the place of the prayer which he prayed to the Father in the hour of his passion. His sweat was like drops of blood running to the ground, and an angel appeared to him to encourage him. At the top of this mountain is a place of prayer where the Lord ascended into heaven. Nearby is another church, where the Lord composed the 'Our Father'.

Nearby is Bethphage, once a village of priests. About one mile in the direction of the third hour[2] is Bethany, where the Saviour raised Lazarus, and his tomb is there. There also is the Church of Saint Mary Magdalene, once the house of Simon the Leper, where the Lord forgave her her sins.

Moreover the River Jordan is quite a distance from Jerusalem, 08

[1] i.e. towards the south-west.

[2] i.e. towards the south-east.

about twenty miles away, and the road is rough. Jericho is two leagues from the Jordan. The Jordan runs from north to south. Near Jordan is the Church of Saint John the Baptist, where about twenty Greek monks serve the Lord. Beyond the river is Arabia.

09 Not far from this place where the Lord was baptized is the Dead Sea, where the River Jordan ends. There there used to be four cities, Sodom and Gomorrah and Admah and Zeboim, which long ago were destroyed by a just judgement of God. The Dead Sea is so called because nothing can live in it. Not even a fish swims or lives there, no creature can drink from it, and if any bird were to fly over this sea it would straight away fall in and die. That Sea is called the River of the Devil. And the mountain where the Lord fasted for forty days and forty nights is about three miles distant from Jericho.

AN ACCOUNT OF THE LOCATION OF THE PLACES 1

Hebron was *once*, from the time after the flood until the coming of the 2
children of Israel, *the capital of the Philistines and* a place where *Giants*
lived. *It was in the tribe of Judah, a priestly city and a city for fugitives.*[1]

It is six miles[2] south of Jerusalem, and is on the border between 3
the desert and Judaea,

in the country where the Most High Creator formed our first father 4
Adam.

|It is partly cultivated and partly wild.[3] 5

Hebron was founded by the giants seven years before they 6
founded Tanis, a city of Egypt.[4] Hebron was named Mamre 7
after a friend of Abraham.[5]

This is the name for the city by which a high mountain is called, at the 8
foot of which Abraham remained for a long while, and the place is
marked by an oak,[6] under which three angels appeared to him and
among them he adored one,

the 'Agias Trias',[7] that is he informs us that the Trinity is to be 9
adored by us in Unity.

He called to them to be his guests, 10

and when they were at table he brought to them sheep, milk also 11
and butter. In Hebron, moved by this vision from God he
constructed the first altar and humbly sacrificed to him over it.

[1] Jerome, *Liber locorum* 7.15ff.

[2] Jerome, *Liber locorum* 7.17 gives twenty-two miles. This paragraph and others are indented because *Descr* used them and not Fretellus.

[3] This and other paragraphs following with a vertical line in the left-hand margin have been taken from MSS D, D[1], and Vat (see pp. 12–13) of the *Descriptio* and are not normally found in Fretellus, usually because he deliberately omitted them.

[4] See Num 13.22.

[5] See Gen 14.13 and Jerome, *L.loc.* 125.4. Fretellus gives the same information in a different order.

[6] Fretellus gives the Greek name for oak ('Dyrps'), which is based on Jerome, *L.loc.* 77.1.

[7] Greek for 'Holy Trinity'.

12 Near the site of this oak the feast of the Holy Trinity is magnificently celebrated every year to the joy of the Christian congregations.

13 This oak from that time until the reign of Theodosius the Emperor remained and flourished, according to Jerome, and it is said that the trunk and the roots were there. Dry though it was, it proved to be a medicine, because whatever rider carries a piece of it with him, his animal does not vomit.

14 Hebron is called 'Arbe', which is Saracen for 'Four', and before this name 'Kariath' is added which means in the same language 'City', that is 'Cariatharbe', the 'city of four'. This is because there lie at rest in a common grave the first-created Adam, and the three great patriarchs Abraham, Isaac and Jacob, in a double cave in the field of Ephron, and their four wives with them, Eve our Mother, Sara, Rebecca and Leah.

15 Hebron is next to the Valley of Tears, and it is called by this name because in that Valley for a hundred years Adam mourned his son Abel, and in Hebron[1] he begat Seth, from whom Christ was to be born, and other sons and daughters.[2]

In Hebron is to be seen the field from the soil of which Adam was created.

16 From there[3] he was carried southwards by the Lord to have dominion in the Paradise of Eden, which in Greek and Hebrew means 'The Garden of Delights'. But according to the history of antiquity, after his fall he was exiled by God in disgrace here to Hebron, to be a poor farmer on his native soil.

17 This is the field from which the inhabitants of that region dig up and take away soil. They sell it through various parts of Egypt and Arabia as necessary for medical purposes, and it is used as a cosmetic in certain places. This field, however widely and deeply it is dug, is found to lack no soil at the end of the year, by divine grace. Since the soil of this field is red,

18 it is in harmony with the Hebrew tradition that Adam was of a red colour.

[1] Fretellus adds, 'at the command of an angel he knew Eve his wife'.
[2] Fretellus here gives section 22 below.
[3] Ms. *Vat.* of Fretellus, but not D[2], includes this section.

In Hebron the spies of the promised land, Caleb and Joshua, made their first exploration.[1] 19

In Hebron David was chosen to be King by the Lord, and anointed by Samuel. He reigned seven years, about which the Lord said: 'I have found David, a man after my own heart'.[2] 20

In Hebron were born the six sons of David, Ammon by Ahinoam, Chileab by Abigail, Absalom by Maachah, Adonijah by Haggith Shephatiah by Abital, and Ithream by Eglah.[3] 21

Caleb the son of Jephunneh possessed Hebron, defeating the three sons of Anak there, that is Sheshai, Achiman and Tolmai.

In the hillcountry of Hebron over against the Philistines is Dabir, which before *was called* Kiriath-Sepher, that is, '*The City of Letters*', which was taken by *Othoniel*.[4]

Three miles to the south of Hebron is the burial place of Lot, the nephew of Abraham.[5] 22

At the tenth mile beyond Hebron towards the Philistines is *Beersheba*, a beautiful and noble city in Israel and long before. It means '*The Well of the Oath*', *because Abraham and Isaac there* entered *into a treaty with Abimelech*.[6] In Beersheba Abraham planted a grove, where he called on the name of the Eternal God. For a long time he was settled there, and after him Isaac, to whom the Lord appeared there, blessing him and his seed. 23

Six miles from Hebron to the south is Beth-tappuah, which marks the border between Judaea and Egypt, the Philistines and Arabia.[7] It was once a rich and populous city. There the Mother of the Saviour, when the angel had warned her to flee with her son Jesus, and guided by her espoused husband Joseph, was first received outside Judaea as a guest. 24

Ten miles from Hebron to the east is the Lake of Asphalt. The lake is also called the Dead Sea and for a similar reason the Sea of 25

[1] Fretellus has this after section 13 above, and follows it with a note about the sons of Anak and the reign of David in Hebron (a shortened version of section 20).

[2] Psalm 89.20.

[3] 2 Sam 3.3.

[4] Jerome, *L.loc.* 79.12.

[5] Fretellus gives us this information after the sentence about Seth, in section 15.

[6] Jerome, *L.loc.* 51.1.

[7] See 'Bethaffu', *L.loc.*. 51.18.

the Devil, since by his cruelty and anger the four cities, Sodom, Gomorrah, Zeboim and Admah, were miserably destroyed with brimstone, and were destroyed in that lake because of their luxury, for they persevered in their wickedness. The translation of Sodom is 'silent flock' or 'blindness', of Gomorrah 'the people's fear' or 'treason', of Zeboim 'sea' or 'port of the sea', and of Admah 'delightful'.[1]

26 On the way down from Judaea a mile above the Lake is Zoar. The translation of Zoar is 'small' or 'little'. Zoar is also called Balah, which means 'submerged', and Zoara, which is a Syrian name, and it is called Balezoara when the names are joined.

This is Zoar to which Lot fled under the guidance of angels from Sodom, and by his prayers it was saved from fire and destruction. Going out of Zoar there are still signs of Lot's wife, turned into a pillar of salt.

27 Above Zoar in the mountains opposite Judaea Lot was drunk and slept with his daughters, and begat from them Moab and Ammon.

28 Zoar is called by our compatriots 'The Town of Palms'.

29 The region of these five cities is called Pentapolis, since there are five cities. Before the cities and their district were destroyed the Pentapolis was a wooded valley, and the kings of the five cities went to war. Against Chedorlaomer (or Chodolagomer) king of the Elamites, Amraphel king of Shinar, Arioch king of Pontus and Tidal king of the Gentiles there did battle Bera king of Sodom, Birsha king of Gomorrah, Shinab king of Admah, Shemeber king of Zeboim and the king of Bela. The five were overthrown, and the enemy took away the possessions and food of Sodom and Gomorrah, and took captive Lot, the nephew of Abraham.

30 Between Zoar and Jericho the district is called En-gedi,[2] the origin
of the wines of En-gedi, and the place where balsam used to grow
31 in great abundance. Above the Asphalt Lake one gathers much
alum and much tar.[3]

[1] Jerome *Heb.n.* 10.18–19, *Q.Gen.* 22.11, *L.Loc.* 43.9,15.
[2] Fretellus gives the information about En-gedi later, after section 32.
[3] Fretellus gives this information after section 21.

Alum is one of the earth's salts. In winter it is mixed with lime and water, and it is brought to maturity by the summer sun. Alumen [Latin for 'alum'] is named from lumen [Latin for 'light'], since colours with which it is mixed become lighter. 32

Tar is like a black smelly liquid, and is useful for anointing camels and removing their scabs, and for rubbing vines to rid them of the worms which eat them up.

A mountain next to the Asphalt Lake is almost wholly made of crystal salt. From the lake itself lumps of it are taken, since it is a necessary thing in those parts.

Bitumen is taken from the Lake, which is useful to doctors.

The lake is so clear that through it can be seen ancient buildings and ruins. But it is so bitter that it cannot be endured for long by any living being, and no birds fly across it. Islands are in the Lake, on which green apples grow, which would be good to eat. But if you pick them they open and are reduced to cinders. They smoke as if they were burning. The wood on the islands seems to be covered over with cinders and ashes, as if to represent the fiery end of the cities. Timber is taken by boat from the islands in the Lake, which is useful for the mainland.

If it happens to any one that he spends the night by the Lake, and he puts his bag full of wine or water on the ground, next day he will find it bitter and undrinkable, however sweet it was.

On the other side of the Lake is Zodran, an island where blessed Sabas went to keep Lent alone. But by the devil's wrath a sudden fireburst left him completely burnt. For seven days he was as good as dead, but by the mercy of God he was cured and regained his health. Nevertheless he remained beardless after that, and when he went home to his brethren they hardly knew he was Sabas.

Above the district of the Asphalt Lake on the Arabian slopes is 33
Shaveh, the ancient city which Chedorlaomer defeated.[1]

The Pentapolis mentioned above is on the border between Judaea 34
and Arabia.[2]

[The text now contains a version of Jerome, *Letter* 78, about the camps in the desert at which Moses and the children of Israel went at the Exodus from Egypt to Mount Sinai and

[1] Jerome, *L.loc.* 151.20. Fretellus puts this information below after section 40.
[2] Fretellus has 'The Lake of Asphalt' instead of 'The Pentapolis'.

Canaan. This has no relevance to pilgrimage, apart from the following passages.]

35 Sinai is a mountain in Arabia which is very high and hard to climb. The way up it is by three thousand five hundred steps. The very holy hermits and monks who live there say that the place has been, from the time of Moses, a site where heavenly angels walk. Mount Sinai is often covered with smoke and flashing with lightning. Of Sinai it is stated (and it is true) that each Sabbath a heavenly fire surrounds it but does not burn it, and whoever touches it is not harmed. It appears many times like white blankets going round the mountain with an easy motion, and sometimes it descends with a terrible sound which can hardly be tolerated, and the most holy servants of Christ hide themselves there in caves and cells of the monastery.

On top of Sinai is a revered and beautiful church, and its site is where God gave Moses the Law, written in his own hand on tables of stone. This church is so venerable that no one dares to enter it nor to climb the mountain unless they have been accepted by God in confession, and unless first they have undergone fasts and prayers. The monks and hermits are so devoted to religion that they are free from passions of the body or the spirit, and only fight for God. They are so famous that from the borders of Ethiopia up to the furthest bounds of Persia they are spoken of with respect in every oriental tongue which they have among themselves. They freely and quietly possess monasteries in Egypt and Persia, around the Red Sea and in Arabia, from which their livelihood is abundant.

36 And they are so venerable that no one presumes to offend them in anything, and if some offence occurs it is gravely punished by God. Everyone lives in separate cells round the Mount, and they live not in common, but out of a common stock. In Sinai the traces of the bush appear in which the Lord appeared to Moses in a flame of fire.

37 In the district of Hor is Mount Eden. It is called the 'Mount of Sands', since it is located in a sandy region. It is hard to climb and amazingly high, and in natural form it is like a high tower, with the steep part as if it had been cut by hand. The way round it takes more than one day. On the sides of the mountain trees are scarce. Many birds of various kinds fly round the mountain in flocks, but

the mountain itself would seem to be without plants or moisture, and is far from any living growth in the desert.

From the people who live near it I have heard it stated that, by God's design, a way of ascending the mountain was revealed to two men. One of them was nimble and energetic and easily climbed the hidden parts of the Mountain, but the other hardly managed to come half way, and there, tired and breathless, sat down. The first man got up the rest of the mountain and admired the nature of the mountain, how the place was peaceful, the air was serene, the smell of the flowers, the sweetness of the plants, the variety of the stones seen through the books, the splendour of the fountains, the abundance of fruit trees and the beauty of their fruit, the twittering and song of birds, the spaces of shade and the spaces of green grass. There he decided, and promised for himself, should God see fit, the joy of living and dying.

Looking around him he was surprised at the absence of his companion, and straight away, light-hearted, happy, smiling to himself and clapping his hands, he hurried to the brink of the mountain. He called to his friend and companion, wishing that he too would want to live on that mountain, in which he said that there was an eternal spring, and promised him it was like paradise. But he, though he was told everything by his companion, we do not know whether he was frightened by the difficulty of the mountain or deterred by God's prohibition, refused to go up and enter it and stayed in his place. But he attended to the things which he had seen and heard. He said goodbye to his companion and laboriously climbed down. He went back to the place from which he had come, and made public what he had seen and heard.

Around Mount Eden there are many other mountains, hills, rocks and mounds, which from top to bottom are carved with arches, caves, caverns and cells of various kinds, in which they say that holy hermits and monks used to live in the old days.

At the foot of Mount Eden there rises a spring from which no brook runs. If you saw it you would think that it would water perhaps two or three horses. But it waters more, and it has been proved that it never seems to get more or less.

[The extracts from Jerome, *Letter* 78 continue, and then the geographical text begins again.]

Between the *Jordan* and *Jericho is Beth-hoglah*; the name means '*the* 38 *place of a ring', for the reason that it was in the shape of a ring that* the sons of *Jacob proceeded round when they mourned him,*[1] when they brought him back from Egypt to Hebron.

39 Between Jericho and *Gilgal is Emek-achor, which* means '*the Valley of Achor', that is 'The Tumult* of the people' or '*of the crowds*'. There *Achan was stoned because he took some of the devoted thing.*[2]

40 | Jericho was captured and named by the Jebusites.

41 In *Gilgal Joshua circumcised the people for the second time, and set up the stones which they had taken from the Jordan*, since *there the Tabernacle of the Covenant remained for a long time.*[3]

42 Arabia joins Idumaea in the territory of Bostra, which is *Bozrah*, from which came Barach the Buzite. But there is *another Bozrah in the mountains of Idumaea*, about which Isaiah said, '*Who is this who comes with* dyed *garments from Bozrah?*'[4]

Trachonitis and *Ituraea* are the parts of Idumaea that *look towards Damascus*. Of these districts, *according to the Gospel of Luke, Philip*
43 | *held the tetrarchy.*[5] | Uz, the first-born of Aram and the nephew of Shem founded Trachonitis, from whom that country is called Uz, from which came blessed Job.[6]

44 Bostra was once the capital of Idumaea. Idumaea is under Syria, and in Syria is Damascus.

45 Eliezer the son of the steward of Abraham founded Damascus in that district where Cain killed his brother: for this reason *Damascus* means '*drink of blood*', *or* '*kiss of blood*'.[7]

46 | Damascus was once the capital city of Syria, but the status of

[1] Jerome, *L.loc.* 9.18. Fretellus quotes more accurately the texts from Jerome at this point.

[2] Jerome, *L.loc.* 85.17.

[3] Jerome, *L.loc.* 65.25. Fretellus continues at this point as follows:

In Arabia, between Abarim and Sinai is Montréal, which Baldwin of Boulogne, the courageous lion and First Count of Edessa, and afterwards the first Frankish King in Jerusalem, made into a fort, to keep control in Arabia for Christians, and to protect the reign of King David.

To the south of Arabia is Mount Pharan, of which the Psalm says: 'God shall come from the south, and the Holy One from Mount Pharan' [Hab.3.3].

[4] Jerome, *L.loc.* 47.9.

[5] Jerome, *L.loc.* 166.1.

[6] Fretellus places this after section 65. Between sections 42 and 45 he has a different order from the geographical work. He begins with a brief description of Damascus and its district (which we shall call in the notes following section Aa), then gives a description of Phoenicia (Bb), and then returns to a parallel passage with section 45 (Cc).

[7] Jerome, *Heb.n.* 5.6,(Cc).

capital was transferred by Antiochus to Antioch. It is called 'Syria' from Shuah,[1] the nephew of Abraham and son of Keturah.[2]

Damascus is called by a second name, 'Aram', and by a third, 47
'Arphad'. Damascus was once[3] the ecclesiastical metropolis in Syria.[4]

A district *of Damascus* according to *Zechariah* is called *Sedrath*.[5] 48

Parts of it were inhabited by Esau, who is also called Seir and 49
Edom, and from Edom part of Syria is called Idumaea.[6]

In Seir is the city Idumaea.[7] 50

In Idumaea not far from Damascus is Mount Seir. *The Horite* 51
lived in Seir whom Chedorlaomer killed.[8]

In the district of Idumaea at the third mile from the Jordan *is the river Jabbok*,[9] *which Jacob crossed* when he returned from Mesopotamia, *and wrestled with* the angel.[10]

At the fourth mile from Damascus is the place where Christ appeared to Saul and said: 'Saul, Saul, why do you persecute me?' In honour of this event there is a much-revered church in Damascus under a Greek archbishop.[11]

> Twenty four miles from Damascus to the south, and at the 52
> foot of Libanus, is Paneas, a noble city, which

is called Belynas Abilina, from the 'ableness' of the places there to 53
be inhabited, and Caesarea Philippi which comes from the name of Caesar.

Malbech is a mile to the east of the opening of the Bechar Valley 54
and very well located. It was founded by Solomon because of an abundance of good things and the luxury of having forests, and he called it Saltus Libani. When he built an ivory house, this too he called Saltus Libani.[12]

[1] *Suri* in Latin.
[2] Fretellus (Cc) gives another interpretation based on Jerome, *Heb.n.* 11.12, but the later manuscripts go back to the one in the geographical description.
[3] Instead of 'once' Fretellus has 'venerable'.
[4] Fretellus Aa.
[5] Jerome, *L.loc.* 163.11. The biblical name for *Sedrath* is 'Hadrach', Fretellus Aa.
[6] Fretellus Cc, who adds a quotation from Jerome, *Heb.n.* 10.27 and 6.3.
[7] This entry is most likely a mistake.
[8] Jerome, *L.loc.* 153.1.
[9] Reading *Iaboch*, like Fretellus.
[10] Jerome, *L.loc.* 103.19.
[11] Now Fretellus has sections on Phoenicia, and thus the opening of the next section is slightly different.
[12] Fretellus Bb.

55 At the foot of Libanus the Pharpar and Abana rise, the rivers of Damascus. The Abana runs past the mountains of Libanus, and across the plain of Arqa, and then joins the great sea in the district in which Blessed Eustachius retired when he had been bereaved of his wife and children.[1]

56 This Arqa, a virtually unbesiegable city, was founded by the Arkite, the seventh son of Canaan. It is at the foot of Libanus, eight miles east of Tripoli. Arqa is the beginning of Phoenicia, and the other end is Mount Carmel, from which Palestine begins.[2]

57 Libanus divides Syria and Phoenicia.[3]

58 Pharpar goes through Syria to Riblah, that is Antioch. It goes past its walls and, ten miles on from the city, it runs into the Mediterranean Sea into the port at Solim, namely the port of Saint Simeon, ten miles from the city.[4]

59 At the foot of Libanus not far from Paneas, are the Jor and the Dan. These are the two sources from which, under Mount Gilboa, the Jordan is formed, in which Christ was baptized by John. The valley through which the Jordan runs, from the Mountains of Gilboa to the Asphalt Lake, is called the Ghor.

The Aulon, which is *a Hebrew word*, is the name *also of the large and rural plain which runs down from the mountains*, which continues *from Libanus to the desert of Pharan*.[5] The Aulon includes the valley of
60 Scythopolis, that

is the valley which goes down from Beth-she'an to the Jordan.

61 Across the Jordan to the north are *Baal* and *Baal-meon*,[6] noble cities which were built by the *children of Reuben*. To the north is *Beth-haram*,[7] built by the tribe of Gad.

62 In the Aulon above the Jordan is *Aenon*, that is the Bethany *in* which *John was baptizing*.[8]

[1] Fretellus Bb.
[2] Fretellus Cc in later manuscripts.
[3] Fretellus has *Sedrath* instead of *Syria*.
[4] Fretellus here gives descriptions of Antioch (to which no parallel exists in the geographical work) and of Paneas (section 53).
[5] Jerome, *L.Loc.* 15.22.
[6] Jerome, *L.loc.* 47.3.
[7] See Jerome, *L.loc.* 49.12.
[8] Jerome, *L.loc.* 40.1 Fretellus gives this after section 94.

In this *corner of Bethany is Astaroth Karnaim*, where *they say Job* lived.[1] 63

Jordan divides Galilee and the land of Bostra. Jordan is translated 'descent', because it flows in a descent.[2] 64

Almost from its source the Dan runs underground to Meddan, 65
which is not far from Teman, the capital of the province of Sueta. Meddan is a fertile and broad plain, in which the stream of Dan is once more open and visible, and for this reason it is called Meddan, because Dan rises in the middle of it. In the Saracen language Medan means 'a square place', and in Latin this square place is called a 'forum'. But Meddan is so called because every year a countless crowd of people gathers in the plain, bringing anything it wants to sell, and stays there. A great army of Parthians and Arabs looks after the people as they feed their flocks in those lavish pastures. The word 'Meddan' is made up of 'med' and 'dan'. 'Med' is the Saracen word for 'water', and 'dan' means 'river'. From the plain which we have mentioned the Dan becomes a river and flows through Sueta.

Part of Sueta also is the land of Uz, and in Sueta there is the tomb of Job which even now is honoured by Greeks and Syrians and the Gentiles. In Sueta[3] is Naaman, from which came Zophar the Naamanite.

Dan goes beneath the city of Kedar, and flows along beside medical baths and the plains of Thorns till it is joined to the river Jor under Gilboa.

In the Plains of Thorns the third prince of Galilee from Tancred, 66
Gervase of Basoches, by birth of a noble Frankish family, took part in the triumph of Toldequin,[4] a King of Syria. He was carried as a prisoner to Damascus. And when Toldequin, not long after he had been drinking, was beside himself, he had his head cut off, and rendered to God this famous martyr. The next morning he was himself again and, full of sadness and anger, since in a fit of lunacy he had killed so noble a man, he buried him, but without his head.

[1] Jerome, *L.loc* 113.2, which has *Batanaea* instead of 'Bethany': Fretellus gives a more correct quotation from Jerome after section 94.

[2] Fretellus cuts out the last phrase, perhaps because it is meaningless. It may originally have come from Jerome, *Heb.n.* 70.1, where the words *descensio eorum* may have been misread as *descendendo*.

[3] Fretellus here mentions Job's other two comforters.

[4] Toghtekin.

He made it into a cup, which was richly adorned with gold and gems, as a memorial to him, and used to drink out of it.

67 Not far from Paneas the Jor makes itself into a lake. Then there is the Sea of Galilee, which starts between Capernaum and Bethsaida. From Bethsaida were Peter and Andrew, John and James, and James the son of Alphaeus.

68 At the fourth mile from Bethsaida is Chorazin, in which the Antichrist was brought up.

At the fifth mile is Kedar, a very excellent city about which it is said, '*He dwells among the dwellers in Kedar*'.[1] Kedar means 'in the dark'.

At the extreme head of the sea is Capernaum, whose faith was a subject of Christ's preaching.

69 At the second mile from Capernaum there is the slope of the mountain where he preached to the crowds and where he cured the leper. A mile from this slope is the place where the Lord fed five thousand men, from which the place is called 'The Table'. Just below is the place where Christ ate after his resurrection.

Above the shore of the Sea of Galilee is Gergesa, the place where he cured those afflicted by demons.

70 At the head of the Sea on the left, in a mountain valley is Gennesaret, a place where gold[2] is found, from which comes the name of the Lake of Gennesaret.

Two miles from Gennesaret is Magdala, from which Mary Magdalene came.

This [district is called Galilee of the Gentiles, and is in the tribes] of Zebulun and Naphtali, from which came Tobias. In the upper parts of this Galilee there were *twenty cities* which King *Solomon* gave to *Hiram, King of Tyre.*[3]

Two miles from Magdala is the city of *Kinnereth* which now is Tiberias.

71 *Herod* the Younger founded *Tiberias*, naming it *in honour of Tiberius Caesar.*[4] From Tiberias

72 the Lake is called 'of Tiberias'.

73 The circuit round this lake takes about a day. The sea has

[1] Psalm 120.5.
[2] Fretellus here has *auram*, 'breeze', instead of *aurum*, 'gold'.
[3] See Jerome, *L.loc.* 73.19. The *Work on Geography* seems to have dropped the bracketed words, which are in Fretellus.
[4] Jerome, *L.loc.* 173.18.

this natural quality that it would be undrinkable and stinking unless the rubbish of the city and the neighbouring farms are put in it.

At the fourth mile from Tiberias is the city of Bethulia, from 74
which came Judith, who killed Holofernes.

Dothaim is four miles to the south of Tiberias, *where Joseph found his brethren,*[1] and they sold him there.

Twelve miles from Tiberias is Nazareth, the city of Galilee, in 75
which Jesus was brought up. Nazareth is translated 'flower'.[2]

In the synagogue at Nazareth Jesus opened the book of 76
Isaiah, and explained its meaning to the Jews. Towards the
east part of Nazareth

a small spring rises, from which in his boyhood Jesus used to draw 77
water, as a supply for his mother and himself.[3]

Two miles from Nazareth is the city of Sepphoris, on the road which leads to Acre.

The city takes its name from Shaphat its founder. 78

Blessed Anna, the mother of the mother of Christ came from 79
Sepphoris.

Five miles from Nazareth is *Cana* of Galilee, an ancient city *in the* 80
tribe of Asher. There the young man Jesus *transformed water into wine.*
From Cana came Simon the Canaanite, Philip, and *Nathanael.*[4] 81,82

A mile south of Nazareth is the place called 'The Fall'. It is the 83
summit of a mountain,[5] from which the relatives of Jesus wished to
throw him, but he disappeared from them.

Four miles south of Nazareth is *Mount Tabor. It is in the middle of* 84
Galilee, remarkably round and high.[6] This is where Jesus was 85
transfigured, and revealed his glory to his own. On the way down 86
Mount Tabor Melchisedech met Abraham when he returned from
the defeat of Amalek, and he presented to him bread and wine.[7]

Two miles east of Tabor is Mount Hermon, and of the two 87

[1] Jerome, *L.loc.* 77–18.

[2] See Jerome, *Heb.n.* 62.24.

[3] Fretellus mentions this spring after Cana.

[4] Jerome, *L.loc.* 117.4. Fretellus gives 'Four miles', and omits 'in the tribe of Assur' and 'Simon the Canaanite' and 'Philip'.

[5] Fretellus omits this phrase and includes it later after 94.

[6] Jerome, *L.loc.* 99.22. Fretellus omits this sentence.

[7] Fretellus transposes this passage and the next.

mountains the Psalmist said: 'Tabor and Hermon shall glorify thy name'.[1] There is another Hermon in Idumaea, a neighbour to Antilibanus.

88 Melchisedek and Abraham negotiated about tithes below Tabor.

89 Two miles from Tabor is Nain, once a city in Israel, in the gate of which Jesus restored to life the son of the widow.

Above Nain is Mount Endor. Between Endor and Tabor in the plain of Nain is Qedumim, the torrent Kishon, on the bank of which Barach, by the inspiration of Deborah, defeated the Idumaeans and Sisera was killed by Jael.

90 Three miles to the east of Tabor is Sharon.[2]

91 Five miles from Tabor is Jezreel, that is Zarain, an ancient city. In
92 Jezreel Ahab and Jezebel reigned.[3] Naboth came from Jezreel, who was stoned at the plot of Jezebel, and for this reason she died, when Jehu caused her to fall. Her tomb is still there.

93 Next to Jezreel is the Plain of Megiddo, where Josiah, when he had been deceived by the King of Samaria, died. From there his body was taken away and buried in Sion.

94 A mile from Jezreel are the mountains of Gilboa, in which fell Saul and Jonathan. In the mountains of Gilboa is a village with the name Gilboa.[4]

Two miles from Gilboa is Scythopolis, the capital city of Galilee, which is also Bethshean. On the walls of this city the head of Saul was hung.

95 In Galilee is the village of Elkosh, from which the prophet Nahum came.

96 Five miles from Jezreel is the town of Jenin, from which Samaria begins.

Between Jenin and Megiddo is Gur, the place *in which Jehu, King of Israel*, slew *Ahaziah, King of Judah*.[5]

[1] Ps. 88.13.
[2] See Jerome, *L.loc.* 163.3, which Fretellus quotes after the entries on Scythopolis and Aenon.
[3] Fretellus omits this sentence.
[4] In Fretellus the name of the village is 'Zelbus'.
[5] Jerome, *L.loc.* 73.23.

Ten miles from Jenin is Samaria, and the name was also given *to* 97
the district round it.[1]

Sennacharib founded the district and from Samaria come the 98
Samaritans. When the city had been razed to the ground by Antiochus it was rebuilt by Herod the son of Antipater in honour of

Augustus Ceasar and it was called Augusta, which in Greek is 99
Sebaste. In this city John the Baptist is said to be buried, between Elisha and Obadiah. He was beheaded by Herod across the Jordan in the castle of Macheron. His body is said to have been burned by Julian the Apostate and the ashes thrown to the winds. His head was long before transferred to Alexandria by the priest Marcellus,[2] and after that it was transferred[3]

by Felicius the Monk to Aquitaine with the Three Innocents 100
in the reign of Pepin, for whom, when he was returning from the slaughter of the Vandals, twenty soldiers who had fallen in the war were restored to life by the merits of Blessed John.

But the index finger, with which he pointed to Jesus coming for his 101
baptism, the Blessed Virgin Tigris[4] took with her across the Alps, and it is now kept with the greatest honour in the church at Maurienne.

That woman was in Sebaste who devoured her child, borne 102
on by hunger, which also happened to Mariam in Jerusalem. Elisha prophesied in Samaria, who fed the hundred prophets in the caves.

In Samaria is the city of Shunem *from which the Shunammite* 103
woman came.[5] From Samaria came Simon Magus.[6] 104
Four miles from Sebaste is *Shechem*,[7] which *Hamor* built and 105
named it *Shechem* after one of his *sons*. The city was afterwards

[1] Jerome, *L.loc.* 163.15. Fretellus gives this information about the district after he has mentioned the city.

[2] Fretellus adds that it was then transferred to Constantinople.

[3] Fretellus ends this sentence 'to the country of Poitiers'.

[4] Fretellus gives the name as 'Thecla'.

[5] Jerome, *L.loc.* 161.13.

[6] Fretellus adds, 'In Samaria [*sic*] is *Tersila* from which *came Manaen*', which inaccurately reproduces Jerome, *L.loc.* 103.5.

[7] Fretellus gives roughly the same information about Shechem, which is based on Jerome, *L.loc.* 151.1–8 in a slightly different order.

called Neapolis, that is, 'New City'. The sons of Jacob destroyed Shechem and slew Hamor, grieving for the adultery with their sister. To Shechem the bones of Joseph were brought back from Egypt and buried. In Sichem at the spring near the foot of Gerizim Jeroboam made the golden calves, one of which he placed in Dan and the other in Bethel.

106 The Samaritans and Syrians also state that four mountains overshadowed Shechem, Ebal and Dan to the east and Bethel and Gerizim to the south, But

107 Jerome considers that two of them are *in the Promised Land* above *Jericho*. These are *Ebal*, where Joseph *built an altar* to the Lord of natural stone *at the command of Moses*, and Gerizim, near to it, from *both of which the voices of the persons blessing and cursing could be heard.*[2]

108 The Jebusites founded[3] Luz, a mile above Shechem, and it is called in Hebrew 'Ulammaus'.[4] This is where, at the message of an angel, Abraham wished to sacrifice his son Isaac, and sent to the foot of it the young men with the ass. In fact a ram was sacrificed
109 instead of him, | and every year the Gentiles do this in imitation of Abraham. The Sultan of Persia[5] is the most powerful among them, and the Prince of Memphis, and they sacrifice camels with their own hands.

110 After Jacob had slept there and had the vision of the ladder, it was
111 called by him 'Bethel', that is 'House of God'. But

after *Jeroboam* had placed there *the golden calf* it was called '*Bethaven*', *that is the* '*house of the idol*'.[6] Abraham called the place 'The Lord sees'.

112 Jacob erected a stone pillar there.

113 A mile from Shechem is the town *Sychar, near* the field which *Jacob gave to his son Joseph*. There is also the spring or well of Jacob, over which the Gospels tell us that Jesus conversed *with the Samaritan woman, and where a church now stands.*[7] Not far from

[1] Fretellus gives the entry on Timnath-heres here. See section 114.
[2] Jerome, *L.loc.* 65.9, but see Jerome's correction, *Ep.*108. 13, 3.
[3] Fretellus omits these words.
[4] See Jerome, *L.loc.* 43.2.
[5] The Abbasides first used the title 'Sultan' in 1063.
[6] Jerome, *L.loc.* 43.6.
[7] Jerome, *L.loc.* 165.1. Fretellus gives a version of this sentence and the one which follows earlier on, after 72, paragraph 2. Since the passage about the church is a quotation, the church may not have been there since the time of Jerome.

Shechem is the place of *the terebinth, under* which *Jacob hid the idols.*[1]

Six miles south of Shechem is Timnath Heres, *the city of Joshua,* 114
in which he remained and died, *and his sepulchre*[2] still survives there.

Ten miles from Shechem is the village of Saint-Gilles, named 115
after the Count of Saint-Gilles, who was in the Frankish army, and camped there on the day before they saw Jerusalem.[3]

Fourteen miles beyond this village is Jerusalem, the most holy 116
metropolis of Judaea.

Four miles from Jerusalem is Ephrata

> which the Jebusites founded and which afterwards Jacob called 117

Bethlehem, that is 'house of bread', in which Christ was born. 118

From Bethlehem were Boaz and Obed, the father of Isai or Jesse, 119
the father of King David, of whose line Christ descended.

Next to the place of the birth in Bethlehem there was the manger 120
in which the baby Jesus lay, but it was taken to Rome by Queen Helena, and it is honourably kept in the basilica of Saint Mary Major.

A mile from Bethlehem to the north the star was shining to the 121
shepherds at the birth of Christ, and this hymn was also sung by the angels there, 'Glory to God in the highest'. Into Bethlehem the Magi came to worship the Lord, and there by Herod the children were slain. The greatest number of the Innocents lies buried three miles from Bethlehem to the south.

Two miles to the west of *Bethlehem is Rama, of* which *it is said*, '*A voice was heard in Rama.*[4] In Bethlehem the body of Blessed Jerome and the bodies of Paula and Eustochium lie buried.

At the fourth mile from Bethlehem is Tekoa, from which came 122
Amos the prophet, whose body is entombed there.

> From this district Habakkuk was taken by an angel to 123
> Babylon. In Tekoa many prophets used to gather to discuss theology.

Four miles from Bethlehem on the way to Hebron is the church 124
of Saint Chariton where, as he was passing from this world, the whole company that was with him all passed too in the same way.

[1] Jerome, *L.loc.* 165.10.
[2] Jerome, *L.loc.* 101.1: see 203, referring to the same place.
[3] Fretellus here has a passage on Mount Shiloh and Ramah (see Jerome, *L.loc.* 157.28).
[4] Jerome, *L.loc.* 149.1.

125 A mile from *Bethlehem on the road which leads* to Jerusalem is *Chabratha*, the place in which, *when Benjamin had died, Rachel* died for sorrow.[1] There she was buried by Jacob, and over the tomb the twelve stones placed by Jacob still exist today.

126 A mile from Chabratha, to the right of the road half way between Bethlehem and Jerusalem, is Beth-Haccherem, the place where the angel struck down in one night 175,000 of the army of Sennacherib. Sennacherib escaped and returned to Nineveh, and was slain by his sons.

127 Hebrew tradition states that the first-born son of Noah was Shem, who, they say, is Melchisedek, the first after the flood to found Salem, over which he reigned as king and priest. The Jebusites possessed it afterwards, and they named it Jebus after an ancestor called Jebus, the third son of Canaan. The names were combined, and it is called 'Jebus-Salem'. Later by Solomon it was called Jerosolyma (almost 'Jebus-Salomonia'). By the poets it is called Solyma, and by Aelius Hadrian who rebuilt it, it is called Aelia. This is Sion, which means in Hebrew 'View' and Jerusalem, 'Vision of Peace'.

128 Jerusalem is the metropolis of Judaea and is situated at the navel of the earth, in the middle of the world.

129 Therefore David says 'You have worked salvation in the midst of the earth'.

130 Jerusalem excels all the cities of the world in prayer and charitable works.

131 In Jerusalem David reigned thirty-three years, when Saul had ceased to be king. Isaiah the prophet was from Jerusalem, who was cut up by King Manasseh with a wooden saw.

132 In Jerusalem is Mount Moriah, the place over which David saw the angel striking, the threshing-floor of Ornan the Jebusite, over which afterwards Solomon built the Temple.

133 He began to build the Temple of the Lord 3102 years from Adam, 1400 years from the Flood, 1200 years from the departure of Abraham from Mesopotamia, 502 from the departure of Israel from Egypt and 240 from the foundation of Tyre.

[1] Jerome, *L.loc.* 173.5.

King Solomon built the Temple (that is, Bethel) and the altar, 134
which at great expense he solemnly dedicated with devotion. But 135
in the time of King Zedekiah Nebuchadnezzar completely profaned
and spoiled them, and destroyed the city.

> Zedekiah and his sons he made to appear before him in 136
> Reblath (that is, *Antioch*, which is called by two other names,
> *Emath and Epiphania*)[1] where he killed the sons of Zedekiah in
> the presence of their father, and put his own eyes out.

Then Nebuzaradan destroyed the whole of Sion and the Temple, 137
which afterwards was rebuilt under Cyrus, King of the Persians, by Ezra the Scribe and Nehemiah. This Temple was again destroyed by Antiochus and under the Maccabees was rebuilt. This Temple was profaned by Pompey, who stayed there when he fled before Julius Caesar, and finally this third Temple was destroyed to its foundations under Titus and Vespasian.

About this Temple, some say that it was rebuilt under Emperor 138
Constantine by Helena, others by the Emperor Heraclius, and others by Justinian Augustus. But others say that it was built by a prince of Memphis in Egypt in honour of 'Alachiber', that is of God most high: and this is declared in a Saracen inscription.
Furthermore, on the arrival of the Franks nothing appeared in its 139
decoration of the Law, and nothing in Greek.

The present Temple is said to be the fourth. In the previous one 140
the child Jesus was circumcised. His foreskin was presented by an angel in the Temple to Charles the Great, and by him transferred to Gaul, to Aix. Later it was transferred by Charles the Bald to the district of Poitiers in Aquitaine, to Charroux.

In the Temple Jesus was presented by his Mother and received by 141
Simeon. From the Temple Jesus drove out the people selling and buying, and set free the woman who had committed adultery from
those who accused her. From the Temple Blessed James was 142
thrown down headlong. In the Temple there was the announcement made by the angel to Zacharias about the birth of his son. Between the Temple and the altar Zechariah the son of Barachiah died, and this altar later on was turned into a sundial by the Saracens and may still be seen in the court.

In Jerusalem,

[1] Jerome, *L.loc.* 147.27 and 23.30.

143 beside Saint Anne's and not far from the gate which goes out to Jehoshaphat,

144 is the Sheep Pool.

In the middle of Jerusalem Jesus raised a girl from the dead.

145 By Herod in Jerusalem the second James was killed by a sword: then he was transferred to Joppa and afterwards to Spain.

Inside the Temple area is the dwelling of the new Knights who guard Jerusalem.

In Jerusalem is the *Xenodochium* or the *Nosokomion*. The Greek word *xenodochium* translated into Latin is a refuge for travellers and poor people. *Nosokomion* is the hospice which cares for the sick people taken into it from the squares and alleys.

146 Beyond the walls of Jerusalem, between the Tower of Tancred and the Gate of Saint Stephen, is a dwelling for lepers.

147 It is said that a Jewish prince, Hyrcanus, was the first to institute *xenodochia* with the money which he had taken from the Tomb of David.

148 *In the area outside the city of Jerusalem* towards the east of *the Valley of the Sons of Hinnom is Topheth*, in which *the people of Israel* were not ashamed to *worship the idols of the Gentiles*.[1]

149 The Valley of Hinnom is called the Valley of Gehinnom, for the reason that there the Hebrews slaughtered their sons to demons. It is also called the Valley of the Idols, since they worshipped idols there. The Valley of Gethsemane is the Valley of Jehoshaphat, and the Valley of Gehinnom joins Gethsemane.[2]

150 In Solomon's reign the pool of Siloam was built, which is on the slope of Sion and almost in the Valley of Jehoshaphat.

151 According to the tradition of the Hebrews, Siloam rises at Shiloh.

152 Siloam's stream runs '*in silence*',[4] because it is underground.

Beneath Siloam is the spring Rogel, next to which Blessed Isaiah is said[5] to be buried. *Next to the spring Rogel is Zoheleth*, the rock to which *Adonijah brought victims to sacrifice*.[6]

153 Above Siloam to the south is the Pool of the Fuller and the field, joined to the field of the fig-tree, in which is Akeldama,

[1] Jerome, *L.loc.* 165.20.

[2] A version of this passage which is more correct appears in Fretellus in section 124 after Modein and before Adummim.

[3] Jerome, *L.loc.* 165.20.

[4] Isaiah 8.6.

[5] Fretellus omits 'is said'.

[6] Jerome, *L.loc.* 95.5.

in which travellers are buried. Above Akeldama is Gihon, in which King *Solomon was anointed*[1] to be king by Zadok the Priest.

In the Valley of Jehoshaphat they say[2] that Blessed James was buried, and from there transferred to Constantinople. In the Valley of Jehoshaphat King Jehoshaphat is buried under a steep-roofed monument. 154

A mile from Jerusalem towards the Dead Sea is Bethany, where Simon entertained Jesus as guest, and where Mary deserved pardon for her sins; there he raised Lazarus. 155, 156

Between Bethany and the Mount of Olives is Bethphage. 157

On Mount Sion Jesus washed the feet of his disciples and had supper with them. 158
In Jerusalem Judas sold Jesus to the Jews. In a fold of the Mount of Olives is the place where Jesus prayed to the Father and where he said to Peter, 'Thou couldest not watch one hour with me'. There, when Judas had come back to Gethsemane, he was betrayed to the Jews.[3] They bound Jesus, and Judas presented him by the Colonnade of Solomon to Annas and Caiaphas. Then they led him to Sion to the place called Lithostrotos, a place which is at present so named outside the door of the church. 159

Then he was led to Calvary, and after much mocking was crucified between thieves. 160

In the merchants' forum is the Church called 'Latin', for the reason that since the Apostles' times the Latins have possessed it. This also is the place where after Christ's sufferings his Mother mourned her Son and the disciple his Master. 161

Below the place of Calvary to the right, as you enter the church, is the chapel where they say that the three Maries wept for him while he was suffering on the Cross. Not far from that Joseph buried Jesus. 162

On Easter Eve each year, and with many people getting ready for it, the Sepulchre of the Lord is honoured by fire which is divinely lit. In that place which is between the Sepulchre and the Place of the Passion, Mary Magdalene appeared to Jesus.

[1] See Jerome, *L.loc.* 73.22.
[2] Fretellus omits 'they say'.
[3] Fretellus omits this sentence.

163 In the place which is called the Prison Jesus waited while the cross was being prepared for him.

164 Eight miles from Jerusalem is Eutheropolis, that is Emmaus, and
165 he appeared to two disciples going along this road. In Mount Sion
he appeared to his disciples when Thomas

166 was absent, and afterwards when he was present.

167, 168 On the Mount of Olives he ascended to the Father, | and there the
| body of Blessed Pelagia rests.

169 In Mount Sion Blessed Mary died, and from there was carried to
170 Jehoshaphat by the Apostles. In Mount Sion the Holy Spirit
171 descended on the disciples. In Mount Sion David and Solomon and
other kings of Jerusalem are said[1] to be buried. Before the Western
Gate of Jerusalem Blessed Stephen was stoned, and from there he
172 was taken to Sion and was buried with Nicodemus. | Between
| Jerusalem and Jehoshaphat is a church where they say that Saul had
| sat when they stoned Stephen.

173 Not far from Jerusalem is a cave, where at God's command a lion in one night took twelve thousand martyrs who had been killed under Chosroes.

174 At the second mile is the place where the wood of the Lord's Cross grew.[2]

175 Not far from the place of Calvary is the place in which the Holy Cross was found.

176 Having carefully searched the place of Calvary, Helena caused it to be cleansed, and broke the idol of Venus, which to shame the Christians, Hadrian had placed there.

177 The Mount of Olives adjoins the Mount of Offence, where King Solomon was seduced by women into making an idol of Chemosh and Moloch.[3]

[1] Fretellus omits 'are said'.
[2] Fretellus puts this and the next section earlier, in the middle of section 162.
[3] Fretellus places this section earlier, after section 154.

Three miles from Jerusalem is *Anathoth, from which came Jeremiah* 178
the Anathothite.[1]

A mile from Jerusalem on the way towards Gaga is a place 179
called Scopulus, where the tribe of Levites went to meet
Alexander.[2]

Five miles south of Jerusalem is the town where Mary visited 180
Elizabeth and greeted her, and where it is said that John was born.

Two miles away from Jerusalem on the road which leads to 181
Neapolis is Mount *Gibeah*,

and *the city of Phineas* where he is buried.[3] 182

A mile to the south of Emmaus is *Gabatha* where *Habakkuk* 183
rests.[4]

From Gibeah Saul became king in Gilgal.[5] In Gibeah the wife 184
of the Levite was raped.[6]

Between Jerusalem *and Ascalon near Beth-shemesh is Eben-ezer, the* 185
place in which *the Philistines seized the Ark* of the Lord.[7]

Beth-Horon is in the tribe *of the sons of Joseph. It is the city to which* 186
Joshua routed the tribes. There are two Beth-Horons, *the Upper and the Lower.* The Upper *was built by Solomon*, and the Lower *was given* to be a possession *of the Levites.*[8]

[1] Jerome, *L.loc.* 27.28. The order in Fretellus is not the same as in the *Work on Geography*, as shown in the following Table.

Work on Geography		*Fretellus*	
		Cave of the Lion	(*WG*:173)
		Beth-haccherem	(126)
		Visitation	(180)
Anathoth	(*WG*: 178)		
Scopulus	(179)		
Visitation	(180)		
		Anathoth	(178)
		Modein	(194)
		Lydda	(202)
Gibeah	(181,182)		
Gabatha	(183)	Gabatha	(183)
Gibeah	(184)		
		Ramathaim-Zophim	(204)
Eben-ezer, etc.	(185)	Eben-ezer, etc.	(185)

[2] See Josephus, *Antiquities* 11.329.

[3] Jerome, *L.loc.* 71.23.

[4] Jerome, *L.loc.* 71.24.

[5] I Sam 11.4,14.

[6] Judges 19.15,25.

[7] Jerome, *L.loc.* 33.24, who gives the readings *Bethsamys*, which is translated above, rather than the *Bethanis* of the text.

[8] Jerome, *L.loc.* 47.18.

187 In the district of Beth-Horon the prophet Joel was born and was buried.

188 At the seventh mile from Jerusalem on the road leading to Neapolis is *Gibeon*, from which came the *Gibeonites*. There is another Gibeon *near Ramah and Rimmon. This is where Solomon was given the divine prophecy* and when Joshua the son of Nun was fighting, the sun is said to have stood still.[1]

189 In the hill-country of Hebron is *Ziph*, which is also called *Carmel*. There was the village of *Nabal the Carmelite*[2]

190 This is the Carmel in which David sought victuals for his men from Nabal, when he fled from the face of Saul. Abigail met David as he was leaving Carmel and with generous presents appeased him. After the death of Nabal, David took her as his wife.

191 There is another *Ziph*,

192 from which are the Ziphites. In the desert belonging to this village, *David hid* from the face of Saul and Jonathan visited him. This was also where David stole Saul's cup and javelin.[3]

193 *At the eighth mile from* Emmaus on the road which leads to *Hebron* is the city of *Keilah, where once David hid*.[4]

194 At the ninth mile from Jerusalem on the way which leads to Ramatha is Mount *Modein*, from which was Mattathias, the father
195 of the *Maccabees*. | Once this was a city which was almost impregnable, and two seas could be seen from there, the Great Sea
196 and the Dead Sea. In Modein Mattathias and his four sons and two nephews rest under seven pyramids which are still *present*.[5]

197 On *the way down* from Jerusalem to *Jericho is Adummim*, which is now called the Red Cistern. *The Lord mentions* this when he describes the man who fell among thieves.[6]

198 Thirteen miles from Jerusalem is Jericho. | The River Jordan was divided at the arrival of Elijah and Elisha, when Elijah was taken up. He threw down his cloak to Elisha, which now is held precious in Constantinople.

[1] Jerome, *L.loc.* 67.10. Fretellus omits 'There is another Gibeon'.
[2] Jerome, *L.loc.* 93.20.
[3] Jerome, *L.loc.* 93.16.
[4] Jerome, *L.loc.* 115.16.
[5] See Jerome, *L.loc.* 133.17.
[6] Jerome, *L.loc.* 25.9.

When Jesus was walking through Jericho, Zacchaeus there climbed a sycamore tree.

199 In Jericho in the time of Saint Saba there was a hostel where much love was shown. He was the head of it, and it happened that he had as a guest a friend called Thomas from the city of Madaba. The two of them ate together, and with them were also the most holy men Paul and Theodore. It was announced to Blessed Saba that they had no wine, and no liquid at all, apart from a little gourd-juice, in which to cook the vegetables for the meal. This liquid was brought before Saba, and when he blessed it, it was changed into wine which was so plentiful that it was enough for all in the hospice for the next three days. When they returned home, he gave the wine to Thomas and his companions, and it restored those who were sick to health when they were anointed with it.

200 The blind man sat in the road by Jericho who deserved to be cured by the Lord.

201 At the second milestone from Jericho is the place where Jesus fasted forty days and forty nights, a place now called Quarantena, where the Devil tempted him and said: 'Say to the stones that they become loaves!'

Two miles from Quarantena towards Galilee is a high mountain from which the Devil showed Jesus all the kingdoms of the world.

Underneath Quarantena is the stream of the spring which was bitter, but Elisha made it fresh by pouring salt in it.

202 Twenty miles from Jerusalem is Lydda, which is Diospolis, meaning 'double city'.

203 *In the district of Diospolis is Timnath*, once *a big village, where Judah sheared his sheep*,[1] when he lay with Tamar at the crossroads (a mile from Timnath) and begot from her Perez and Zerah.

204 Four miles from Diospolis is *Arimathea*, that is *Ramathaim-Zophim, the city of Elkanah and Samuel*, and that is the place the *Gospels* mention as *Joseph's*.[2] He is buried there.

205 The pincers with which this very Joseph took down Jesus from the cross have recently been taken by the Bishop of Bethlehem to Bethlehem, and also one of the Lord's nails. Two of these are kept in the Chapel of the King of Jerusalem.

206 Two miles from Diospolis towards the sea is the Village of

[1] Jerome, *L.loc.* 97.20; see 114, which refers to the same place.
[2] Jerome, *L.loc.* 33.21.

Baths, where Nicodemus carved a wooden portrait of the Lord's face, which is now honoured in Lucca in Italy.[1]

207 Two miles from Diospolis towards the sea is Joppa, in which Peter restored Tabitha to life and where the sheet appeared to Peter. A rock is pointed out there on which appear the traces of the bonds of Andromeda.

208 Six miles from Joppa is *Assur, which Solomon built.*[2]

209 Twenty miles to the east of Assur is Dor . . .

210 . . . this is the city which, in honour of Augustus Caesar, Herod named Caesarea, and where he built a port out of white marble. There Peter baptized Cornelius and changed his house into a church and ordained him bishop, and there rest the four virgins who were prophets. They say that in this Caesarea Eusebius the Teacher was the bishop. In Caesarea was once the Tower of Strato. This is where Herod sat down in purple robes and was smitten by divine vengeance and died.

211 In the time of the Saracens Caesarea was so thriving that it became a paradise between Babylon and Babylonia (that is, Bagdad in Persia and Memphis in Egypt). There noble men and powerful

[1] The endings of the three pilgrimage accounts, the *Work on Geography*, the original work of Fretellus and the later manuscripts of D and Vat, are different. The *Work on Geography* takes the reader north from Joppa to Acre and Tripoli, and to the river Albana, then comes back to Jerusalem. Fretellus goes in the opposite direction from Mount Cain (Caymont) to Caesarea and ends with Jerusalem. D and Vat combine the two, as the following Table shows

Work on Geography	*Fretellus*	*D and Vat*
	Mount Cain	Mount Cain
	Carmel	Carmel
	Porphyrium	
	Dor	
Village of Baths		Village of Baths
Joppa		Joppa
Assur		Assur
Caesarea Pal.	Caesarea Pal.	Caesarea Pal.
[Dor]		
Scariathas		
Porphyrium		
Carmel		Carmel
Mount Cain		
Acre		
Tyre and Sidon	(after 44)	Tyre and Sidon
Sarepta	(after 44)	
Berytus	(after 44)	Berytus
Byblius		
Tripolis		Tripolis
Albana River		Albana River
Jerusalem	Jerusalem	Jerusalem

[2] *Assur* is the Arab name, but this sentence is from Jerome, *L.loc.* 35.16, which described *Assur* (Hazor) in Judah.

were buried. All round the city in the gardens were small stones with hollows for the mixed fuel of fire and spices, and when this was carried by breezes the whole city smelt sweet, evil odours were driven away, and the citizens were in good heart. But now all these things have been thoroughly destroyed.

In the rivers round Caesarea there are crocodiles, terrifying 212
reptiles. The mouth of the crocodile is unlike any mouth since its upper lip is movable but the lower part remains fixed. The crocodile has no lower exit. When the crocodile is filled with food he sleeps above the bank of the river. He seeks his accustomed trail, and then, resting on his legs with neck outstretched, he sleeps with his mouth open to let the breeze in. When the crocodile is asleep worms creep onto him, who enter his belly and feed on the food of the crocodile. But one of them acts as the doorkeeper of the rest, and as a sentry, for he fears that if the crocodile wakes up he may shut them in. This he stings and stings again the lower vein on the upper lip. Thus the crocodile is deceived by the animals.

Above all living things the crocodile hates mankind. But there is another reptile called the water-snake which loves mankind above all creatures. But he hates the crocodile and the crocodile hates him, so they constantly prey upon each other. The water-snake hides himself in the mud, and then he enters the crocodile, for as the crocodile is fishing he swallows down two or three without noticing. But the water-snake eats through the prison in which he is enclosed, creates confusion within the inner parts of the crocodile, destroys the liver and wounds the heart. Then he cuts through its side and goes out of there with his enemy dead.

I shall say briefly how crocodiles came to be found at Caesarea. In olden days there were two brothers who reigned with equal power. Because he did not have sole power the elder of them prepared a trap for his brother, who was known to be a leper. He planned that if he could have two pairs of crocodiles from the Nile in these rivers, and if his brother (who used in summer time to take his bath in the river) were perhaps to die, he would reign alone. In fact this happened, and the elder brother alone was king.

Ten miles to the east of Caesarea is Scariathas, from which Judas 213
the Traitor was called Iscariot.

Six miles from Scariathas is Porphyrium, at the foot of Carmel, 214
once an honourable city.

Mount Carmel is where Elijah conversed with Elisha over a long 215 period and where, in the presence of four hundred and forty priests of Baal, he sacrificed to God and fire from heaven was given to him. The priests were taken away captive from there across the Kishon and killed with the sword. Elijah fled from Jezebel from there and came to Horeb, but Horeb is the mountain next to Sinai.

216 Three miles from Carmel is Mount Cain, and at the spring near the foot of it Lamech killed his brother Cain with an arrow, and with his bow his leader.[1]

217 At the tenth mile from Mount Cain is Acre, which is called Ptolemais after King Ptolemy who founded it. To this port a greater number of Christian ships arrive than anywhere else on the coast between Ascalon and Mount Taurus, and to this port there come together the essentials of life from Africa, Europe and Asia. This is where annually in August springs appear on the sea shore at a point not far from the east of the walls, and streams go down to the sea. The person who drinks from these is freed from constipation if he so desires, and for this reason people gather at this spot on the way between the Euphrates and the Nile.

218 At the sixteenth mile from Acre is Tyre, which in old time was called Sarra from a certain fish which is plenteous there. This fish in their own language the Syrians call 'sar', and from this derives the name of this fish 'sarrae' or 'sardines'. The Hebrews call Tyre 'Sor', and now in the common tongue it is 'Sur'. The Phoenicians founded Tyre when they had come from the Red Sea.

219 Fourteen miles from Tyre is Sidon. Sidon was founded by Sidon, the first-born son of Canaan the son of Ham, from which come Sidones or Sidonii. In Tyre and Sidon Phoenix reigned, the brother of Cathmus of Egyptian Thebes, when he came to Syria. And from his name he called the people Phoenicians, and the whole province
220 Phoenicia. Tyre had the chief place in it. Hiram reigned in Tyre when Solomon was king in Jerusalem, and Apollonius reigned when Antiochus was king in Antioch. Tyre did not wish to receive Christ when he went along the coast, as the Syrians declare, but when Jesus had risen from the dead it received Paul, preaching the Law and the Gospel in his name. Paul afterwards knelt on the sand and prayed that Christ's mercy should strengthen it in the faith.

Not far from Tyre is the stone on which they say Jesus sat, which

[1] See Gen.4.23.

remained unharmed from his time until the Gentiles were expelled from the city, but afterwards was stolen by the Franks and also the Venetians. In its place and over the remains of it a Church has been begun, dedicated to the Saviour.

Tyre, so the Venerable Bede tells us, provided so many martyrs for God that only his knowledge could compass the number. Tyre hides Origen who is buried there.

Tyre was attacked by Alexander the Great, and he joined the wall 221
to the land, which in those days enclosed it against the sea.

The Patriarch Warmund of blessed memory, by the ongoing grace of the Lord, in our day bravely beseiged and captured Tyre, with the help of the Venetians on land and sea.

In the district of Tyre and Sidon the Canaanite woman came out and said to Jesus, 'Have mercy on me, Son of David!' And, going out of that district and through the middle boundary of the Decapolis to Galilee, Jesus restored hearing to the blind and to the dumb speech.

Six miles from Sidon on the sea side in the direction of Tyre is 222
Zaraphath of the Sidonians, in which Elisha was sent by the Lord to the widow of Zarephath in order to give him food. When they stayed together they were satisfied with a little olive oil and a little flour. The widow's son Amathus, that is to say Jonah, Elisha raised to life there. The woman collected two pieces of wood in Zarephath.

In the mountains of Sidon and Zarephath is Gath-Hepher, the 223
town from which this Jonah came.

From Sidon came Dido, who built Carthage in Africa. 224

The Phoenicians gained Sidon and possessed it, and continued to call it Sidon, since in their language 'Sidon' means 'fish'.

Eighteen miles from Sidon is Berytus, a very rich city. In 225
Berytus was a certain portrait of our Saviour which was made with his own hands by Nicodemus. Not long after the Passion of Christ and to ridicule him, the portrait was crucified in jest by certain Jews, and it produced blood and water. Hence many people believed in Christ, and as many as were anointed with a drop from the portrait were made whole again.

Twenty miles to the east of Berytus is Byblium, which is 226
Gibelet, and in Hebrew Gobel. It is the port from which wood was taken from Libanus to build the House of the Lord in Jerusalem. From Byblius it went by way of Joppa.

Twenty miles from Gibelet to the east is Tripolis, a city of people of the province. It is defended by superb walls and by the sea.

Twelve miles east of Tripoli is Albana, the river of Arqa, and from this begins the Kingdom of Jerusalem.

227 Jerusalem is the place where three things had their origin: through Judas Maccabeus public prayer for the dead, public benefits, and, through Hyrcanus, public hospitality.

228 The tower now called 'David's' was built by Herod. When Titus and Vespasian had destroyed the city they left this tower standing as a sign of victory.

229 The Citadel which David constructed for himself, and in which he composed the Psalter is between the church which is now built on (and adorns) Sion and Bethlehem, on a very high hillock, and it was present on this site till the days of the younger son of Mattathias, who destroyed both the Citadel and hillock. Titus and Vespasian, when they had destroyed the city, deprived it not only of its inhabitants but also of the Ark of the Covenant and the things inside it. They took them with them to Rome, as appears in the sculpture on the triumphal arch which is between the Palladium and the Palatine Hill, next to the church of Saint Maria Nova.

230 The keys of this Tower were first given to Duke Godfrey by the Patriarch Daybert so that he could well dispose of the patriarchate, and the titles in the church, and he was pleased to have the first rank not under the title of King, but of the Servant of God.

He vowed in addition that if the Divine Piety allowed him to capture Ascalon, he would give the whole revenue of Jerusalem into the hands of the Soldiers of God in the Holy Sepulchre and to the authority of the Patriarch. But after almost the completion of a year he met his end. It was impossible to surpass him. With indescribable mourning, he was buried in front of Golgotha, where
231 our Lord was crucified, | and on his tomb these verses were written.

Here rests a Frankish pilgrim, who the place[1]
Of holy Sion sought, a wondrous star,
Duke Godfrey. He became the Egyptian's cause
Of fear, the Arab's rout, the Persian's trap.
Elected king he would not choose the name

[1] The manuscript of the *Work on Geography* omits this line, but it is present in the late manuscripts of Fretellus.

Nor yet the crown of King, but under Christ
He chose to serve. His care was to restore
Once more the laws of Sion to herself.
In catholic faith to follow teaching true
And see that it was followed. All dissent
Around him was destroyed, and right prevailed.
He thus was crowned with all the saints above,
The soldier's pride, the people's strength, the clergy's hope.

Baldwin his brother succeeded him . . . 232
Baldwin of Le Bourg succeeded him . . .
After this the venerable Fulk was the third, the Count of Anjou and of the Cenomani.

EXTRACTS FROM A BOOK ON THE HOLY PLACES

BY PETER THE DEACON

C1 JERUSALEM AND ITS HOLY PLACES

The Sepulchre of the Lord, of which we have spoken above, has been constructed in the middle of a temple, and the temple is in the city centre towards the north, not far from David's Gate. Behind the Resurrection is a garden in which holy Mary spoke with the Lord. Behind the church and outside it is the Centre of the World, the place of which David said, 'Thou hast worked salvation in the midst of the earth.' Also another prophet says, 'This is Jerusalem: I have set her in the midst of the nations'.

2 . . . Not far from the Centre of the World is the Prison; and there is his binding and scourging, and near there is his robbing and the division of his garments.

On Calvary, where the Lord was crucified, the mountain is cleft, and one goes up on to this Mount Calvary by seventeen steps, and nine lamps hang there, each with a silver cloth. Below is Golgotha, where Christ's blood fell on the cleft stone.

3 To the east, below Mount Calvary, is the Temple of the Lord, in another part of the city, which was built by Solomon. It has four doors, the first on the east, the second on the west, the third on the south, and the fourth on the north, which signify the four quarters of the world, and outside it has eight corners, each one turning a corner of twelve paces. In the middle of the Temple is a great mount surrounded by walls, in which is the Tabernacle; there also was the Ark of the Covenant which, after the destruction of the Temple, was taken away to Rome by the Emperor Vespasian.

On the left side of the Tabernacle the Lord Jesus Christ placed his foot, on the occasion when Symeon took him in his arms, and his footprint remains there exactly as if it had been made in wax. And on the other side of the rock is the opening of the Tabernacle, into which people go down by twenty-two steps. There the Lord prayed, and there also Zacharias offered sacrifice. Outside the Temple is the place where Zacharias, the son of Barachias, was killed. Above the rock in the middle of the Temple is a golden lamp containing the blood of Christ which fell down through the cleft rock.

And not far away to the south has been built the Temple of C4
Solomon, in which he lived, which has twenty-five doors. There are 362 columns inside it, and not far away the Cradle of Christ and his Bath, and the bed of the Holy Mother of God. Below the Temple of the Lord to the east is the Gate Beautiful, by which the Lord came in, sitting on the foal of an ass. It was there also that Peter healed the lame man. To the north is the Church of Saint Anne, where Blessed Mary was nurtured for three years. And near it is the Sheep Pool, which has five porches.

THE HEADCLOTH OF CHRIST G

And the Headcloth with which Christ wiped his face, otherwise known as the Veronica, was taken away to Rome in the time of Tiberius Caesar. And the Reed with which his head was struck, his Sandals and the Bonds with which he was bound, his Circumcision and his Blood are reverently honoured in Rome.

VALLEY OF JEHOSHAPHAT, MOUNT OF OLIVES AND BETHANY I

Across the Brook Kidron is a cave, and above it a church, where on the Thursday after supper, the Jews arrested the Saviour. This place is at the head of the Valley of Jehoshaphat. . . .

Not far away is the martyrium of holy Stephen, and not far from that is the place where the Lord prayed, when his sweat became like drops of blood. And on the road to Bethany is the village from which the ass was brought.

HEBRON M2

In Hebron itself stands the House of David. Part of it remains, and to this day people still go to pray in the chamber where he lived. Not far out of Hebron – three hundred yards off, at the place called Abramiri – is the House of Jacob, where a church without a roof has been built.

. . . Abramiri is a vineyard, and in it is the cave where rest the bodies of the eleven Sons of Jacob (but the bones of Joseph are buried separately in their own church). And not far from Hebron is the tomb of Abner the son of Ner.

P1 JERICHO, THE JORDAN, THE DEAD SEA

If a man wishes to go from Jerusalem to the Jordan he goes down by way of the Mount of Olives. From the Mount of Olives Christ ascended to heaven, and it was there that he made the Pater Noster.

Mount Sion is to the south; there holy Mary died, and there the Lord had the Supper with the disciples. There too he sent the Holy Spirit on the disciples.

And in the church which is in Bethlehem is the table at which Holy Mary ate with the three kings who came seeking Christ the Son of God. Inside this church are sixty-four columns. There rest the children killed for Christ by Herod.

P3 GALILEE

. . . Mount Hermon is very lofty, and from it there is a view over the whole of Galilee, unequalled for beauty, since the whole vast plain is vineyards and olive-groves. The field is there in which the Lord ate with his disciples, and you can still see the stone on which he rested his arm. Not far from this mountain is a spring which the Saviour blessed, and it does good to sick people of all kinds.

4 In the village of Nain is the house of the widow whose son was brought back to life, which is now a church, and the burial-place where they were going to lay him is stil there to this day.

In Nazareth is a garden in which the Lord used to be after his return from Egypt.

EXTRACT FROM NIKULÁS OF ÞVERÁ

From there [Rome] there are ten miles to Ti[...]am. Then it is a day's journey to Florenciusborg, another's to Separan. The river Garileam flows there; it divides the kingdom of Rome and Sicily, and there Campania or Púll lies to the southeast, but Italia to the north. Then [...]naborg is twelve miles from Separan, then it is six miles to the mountain Montakassin, where there is a great monastery and a surrounding fortified wall enclosing ten churches. Foremost among them is Benedict's church, which women may not enter; there also is Martin's church, which Benedict had built and and in which are the finger of the Apostle Matthew and the arm of Bishop Martin; the church of Andrew is there and so are those of Mary, Stephen and Nicholas. Then it is a two days' journey to Kápa. Germanus borg is next to Montakassin. Then it is a two days' journey to Benevent, which is the largest city in Púll. South-west from there is Salerniborg, where there are the best physicians. Sepont stands at the foot of Michialsfiall which is three miles in breadth but ten in length, and it is part way up the mountain; there is Michael's cave and the silken cloth that he gave to the place. Then it is a day's journey to Barl, then six miles to Traon, then four to Bissenoborg, four to Malfetaborg, four to Ivent, then six to Nicholas in Bár, where he lies.

This is another more westerly route to Kápa: from Rómaborg to Albanusborg, from where one journeys along Flaian's [*recte* Traian's] causeway which, from one end to to the other, is a three-week journey through fens and forests; it is the most outstanding human construction. For a whole day's journey one travels through forests and each foot('s pace) is impassable, except by Flaian's causeway. Then comes Terentiana; the Romans destroyed it and it is now small. Then comes Fundiana. Then comes Gaida. Then it is a two days' journey to Kápa. Then one travels to Benevent. On from there is Manupl, then Brandeis. In that gulf are Feneyiar, where there is the patriarchal throne and where there are the holy relics of Mark and Luke.

A short distance from Duracur is Mariohǫfn. Then comes Visgardzhǫfn. Then comes Engilsnes. Then it is a short distance to the island Paciencia or Sikiley, where there is volcanic fire and boiling water as in Iceland. Then comes the town that is called 'of Martin,' which is in Bolgaraland. Then one has to sail to the island that is called Kú, where the routes from Púll and Mikligardr meet, it being northwest to Púll, but on by sea to Krít. On from Kú is the island that is called Roda. Then one has to sail across to Gríkland and to Raudakastali. Then comes Patera. Bishop Nicholas was born there and his school still stands there. Then comes Mireaborg where he was a bishop. Then it is a short distance to Jalandanes in Tyrkland. Then it is two days by sea to Kípr. There lies a gulf that Norsemen call Atalsfiord, but the Greeks call Gullus [*recte* Gulfus] Satalie. On Kípr is the town that is called Baffa, where there is the garrison of the Varangians, and where Eiríkr King of the Danes died, the son of Sveinn and brother of Knútr the holy. He donated money in Lúka so that every Danish-speaking man would drink free wine in sufficient quantity, and he had a hospital built eight miles from Plazinzoborg where everyone is given food. Pope Paschalis allowed him to transfer the archiepiscopal see from Saxland to Danmǫrk.

From Kípr it is two days by sea to Acrsborg which is in Jórsalaland. Then comes Chafarnaum, which in ancient times was called Þolomaida. Then Cesarea. Then comes Jaffa, which Baldwin, King of Jerusalem, made Christian, along with the king of Norway, King Sigurðr Magnússon. Then comes Askalon, which stands in Serkland and is still heathen. But east from Acrsborg is Syr, then Seth, then Tripulis, then Lic. A gulf, which we call Anþekio-fiord, extends inland there. There, in the gulf, is Antiochia where the Apostle Peter established his patriarchal see. All these towns are in Sýrland. The district of Galilea is inland from Akrsborg. There there is a large mountain which is called Tabor, where Moses and Elijah appeared to the Apostles. Then comes Nazaret, where the angel Gabriel came to meet with Mary, and where Christ was nurtured for twenty-three years. Then comes the village that is called Gilin. Then comes Iohannis-kastali, which was formerly called Samaria, where the holy relic of John the Baptist was found, and where there is Jacob's Well, from which Christ asked the woman to give him whereof to drink. Then comes Napl, a large town. Then comes the town that is called Casal. Then comes Maka Maria.

Then it is up to Jórsalaborg; it is the most splendid of all the cities of the world and is celebrated in song everywhere throughout all Christendom because wondrous signs of Christ's passion are still seen there. There there is the church in which there is the Lord's sepulchre and the place where the Lord's cross stood, where one can clearly see Christ's blood on the stone as if it were newly bled, and so it will always be until Doomsday. Men receive light down from heaven there on Easter Eve. It is called the Church of the Holy Sepulchre and it is open above over the sepulchre. The center of the earth is there, where the sun shines directly down from the sky on the feast of John. There there is the hospital of John the Baptist, which is the most magnificent in the whole world. Then there is the Tower of David. In Hierusalem is the Temple of the Lord and Solomon's Temple.

South-west from Jórsalaborg is the mountain that is called Synai [*recte* Sion] where the Holy Ghost came upon the apostles and where Christ ate on the evening of Maundy Thursday, and the table at which he ate still stands there. Four miles further south is Bethleem, a small and beautiful town, where Christ was born. From there it is a short distance to Bethania kastali where Christ raised Lazarus from the dead. South-east of Jórsalaborg is the lake that is called the Dead Sea, where God sank two cities, Sodoma on the far side and Gomorra on this side. The Jordan flows through there and does not mix with the waters of the lake because it is very holy water. East of the city is the mountain that is called Mons Oliveti, where Christ ascended into heaven. Between the mountain Oliveti and Jórsalaborg is the valley that is called Josaphat where there is the tomb of Queen Mary. Then it is a long way to the mountain Querencium, where God fasted and where the devil tempted him. There is Abrahams kastali. There stood Hiericho. There are Abrahams-veller. Then it is a short distance to the Jordan, where Christ was baptized; it flows from the north-east to the south-west. There beyond the river is Rábítaland but Jórsalaland, which they call Sýrland, on this side. On the bank of the river stands a certain small chapel where Christ took off his clothes and so the chapel remains in after times as a witness to the spot. Out by the Jordan, if a man lies on his back on level ground and lifts up his knee with his clenched fist on top and raises his thumb from his fist, then the pole-star is to be seen above it there, that high but no higher.

Homewards from the Jordan it is five days' traveling to Akrsborg, a further fourteen days by sea from there to Púll, which is 1800 miles, a further fourteen days on foot from Bár to Rómaborg, a short six weeks' traveling from the south to Mundia, and a further three north to Heidabœr. But the more easterly [*recte* westerly] Ilians-vegr is nine weeks' traveling. Seven days' traveling from Heidabœr to Vebiorg. Then the Scǫduborg river is mid-way between them. From Vebiorg it is two days' traveling to Álaborg.

This guide and list of cities and all this information is written at the dictation of Abbot Nicholas, who was both wise and famous, blessed with a good memory, learned in many things, sage and truthful, and there ends this narration.

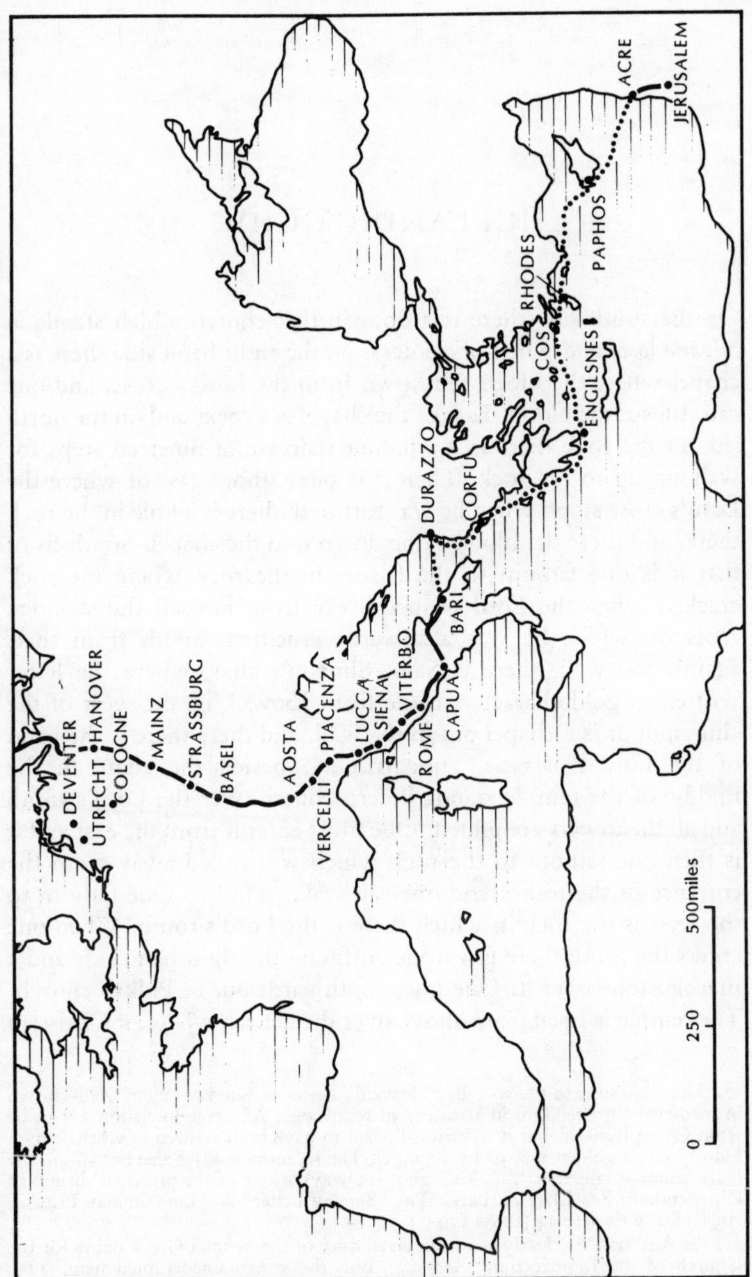

Fig. 24. Nikulás' journey from Denmark to Jerusalem.

ICELANDIC GUIDE

On the south side there is a door in that church which stands *in calvarie loco*, and when one enters, on the right hand side there is a chapel where the blood fell down from the Lord's cross, and one can still see the blood. East of the chapel is a rock, and on the north side of the rock there is a winding staircase of nineteen steps for walking up to the rock. Then it is one fathom east of where the Lord's cross stood when he was tortured; there is a hole in the rock there, and there the blood came down into the chapel. South from that it is one fathom to the fissure in the rock where the rock cracked when the Lord pushed away from himself the wooden cross on which he was afterwards crucified. South from that, against the wall, there is Saint Simeon's altar, where the letter written in gold characters came from above.[1] To the west of the church door is a chapel out in the wall, and there there is the hand of the holy Anastasia,[2] uncorrupted, beside the altar. In the middle of the temple stands Pulcro church over the Lord's tomb and all the towers are gilded. One must enter it from the east and it is then one fathom to the rock which was rolled away from the entrance of the tomb, and one can walk round it. One fathom to the west is the rock in which there is the Lord's tomb. When one enters the tomb there is a stone coffin on the right hand side and a marble stone over it. One goes southwards out of Pulkro church. The temple is open from above over the church where, if Christian

[1] The allusion is to the so-called Heavenly Letter or Sunday Letter, well-known in medieval Christendom in a variety of recensions. All agree in claiming it to be from Christ himself, but it is variously said to have been written in Christ's own blood, with a golden rod, or by an angel. The recensions differ also in naming the place where it falls to earth, although it is always at one of the principal shrines of Christendom. See Clare A. Lees, 'The "Sunday Letter" and the "Sunday Lists" ', *Anglo-Saxon England* 14 (1985) 129–51.

[2] 'St Anastasia' is clearly a misunderstanding of the normal Greek name for the Church of the Resurrection, *Anastasis*. But 'the saint's uncorrupted hand' may perhaps be a memory of the relics which in fact were preserved in the Church of St Mary of the Latins: see Thc 13.

men hold the city, light comes down from above on Easter Eve onto the candles that stand there before it. There, at the start of every other day, those who observe the Hebrew[1] service and all its rites, sing the Lord's praises. To the north of Pulkro church there is a chapel in the wall of the temple where there are still the iron chains with which our Lord was bound. To the east of Pulkro church it is four fathoms to an outer choir; it is built of stone. There in the choir is a high altar and a door on the west side and one can walk all the way round. From that corner of the choir which faces south east there are eleven steps plus twenty[2] to the south for walking down into the earth, where there is a chapel where the Lord's cross was found, and the crosses are marked there on the floor on a marble slab just as the crosses lay. To the south of the choir is a chapel set in the south wall to the east of the rock on which he was tortured; in that stands the pillar to which he was tied and where he was beaten before he was tortured and crucified. In the choir behind the high altar is the seat on which men say the Lord sat when the crown of thorns was pressed on his head before he was crucified. There are doors to the temple both on the east side and on the west. To the west of the temple is a chapel where Saint Karitas[3] lies uncorrupted. *Templum Domini* stands in a high position more to the east than in the centre of Jórsalaborg. In the middle of the Temple stands a rock one fathom high and many fathoms broad, where men say that Abraham brought his son Ysaak as an offering to God; there is an iron grille placed right around the rock. Inside the temple there are pillars of stone, both white and black, red and blue and green. To the east of Jórsalaborg is *Mons Oliveti*. On the mountain, where it is highest, stands Michael's church.[4] In it stands a high rock in which lies the stone which the Lord stepped on when he ascended to the heavens, and one can see the imprint of his left foot, fourteen inches long, as if he

[1] By 'Hebrew' presumably Syriac, Arabic, or possibly Greek is meant.

[2] 'Eleven plus twenty': B. Z. Kedar and Chr. Westergård-Nielsen, *Mediæval Scandinavia*, 11 (1978–9) 208, say that this phrase probably refers to the way down to the Chapel of St Helena, and the separate steps down from this chapel to the chapel of the Invention of the Cross.

[3] 'Saint Karitas': Kålund's edition (p. 29) says this is a mistake for 'Saint Chariton'. Jwu 165 says that this church lies to the north of the Holy Sepulchre, here referred to by the general word 'temple'.

[4] 'Michael's church': Clearly the Church of the Ascension. Perhaps this church is associated with Michael because of the church at Monte Gargano, where there is a footprint of Michael.

has stepped barefoot into clay. Between the mountain and Hierusalem is Iosafad[s]dalr. There there is Maria's church. On the south side of it there is a door and four plus forty steps for walking down into the earth to the floor of the church. In the other part of the church stands an altar and a short distance away is Maria's sarcophagus and a lid of stone covering it. There there is Maria's abbey. To the north of the church is the house where the Jews arrested the Lord, and one can still see the imprint of his fingers in the rock which he struck with his hands when the wicked men sprang at him. On the south side at the foot of Oliveti is Bethania castle where there is a convent of nuns. Near that church is the tomb of Lazarus. From Hierusalem there are two miles to Bethania, from there twelve miles to Rauda-kastali,[1] from there two to Iordan.

[1] 'Rauda-kastali': the miles indicated place this (the correct Icelandic name for the castle half way down to Jericho) at Jericho itself. The castle at Jericho was called Quarentena.

MUHAMMAD AL IDRISI

The Holy City,[1] a beautiful city of ancient foundation, lasting for 31
ever. It was anciently called Ælia.[2] It stands on a mountain, and you ascend to it from all sides. In plan it is long, and its length stretches from west to east.

The Gate of the Oratory[3] is on its western side; and this is the gate over which is the Cupola of David[4] – peace be upon him.

The Gate of Mercy[5] is on the eastern side of the city. It is closed, and is only opened at the Feast of Olive-branches.

Sion Gate[6] is on the south of the city.

The Gate of the Crow's Pillars[7] lies to the north of the city.

When you enter by the Gate of the Oratory which as aforesaid is the western gate, you go eastwards through a street that leads to the great church known as the Church of the Resurrection, which the Muslims call the Dunghill.[8] This is a church to which pilgrimage is made from all parts of the Greek empire, both from the eastern lands and the western. You may enter by a gate at the west end,[9] and the interior thereof occupies the centre space under a dome which covers the whole of the church. This is one of the wonders of the world.

The church itself lies lower than this gate, but you cannot descend thereto from this side.

Another gate opens on the north side,[10] and through this you

[1] Al Idrisi uses the classical Arab name of Jerusalem, *Bait el Muqaddas*, which means 'The Holy Building' or 'The Holy City'.

[2] The name *Iliya* was still applied to Jerusalem, and an example is Muqaddesi's description of the city written in 985 A.D.

[3] *Bab al Mihrab:* its full name was 'The Gate of the Oratory of David'.

[4] *Qubbat Da'ud.*

[5] *Bab er Rahma*, here the only name applied to the Golden Gate.

[6] *Bab Sihyun.*

[7] *Bab Amud al Ghurab.*

[8] *Qiyama*, 'resurrection', was changed by word-play into *Kumama*, 'dunghill'.

[9] The gate was perhaps reserved for the clergy, since it led to the Patriarchate. This may explain the apparent contradiction in the next paragraph.

[10] South of the Khankah Mosque.

may descend to the lower part of the church by thirty steps. This gate is called the Gate of Saint Mary.[1]

32 When you have descended into the interior of the church you come on the most venerated Holy Sepulchre. It has two gates, and above it is a vaulted dome of very solid construction, beautifully built, and splendidly ornamented. Of these two gates, one is toward the north, facing the Gate of Saint Mary, and the other is toward the south, facing which is the Gate of the Crucifixion.[2] Above this gate is the bell-tower[3] of the church.

Over against this, on the east, is a great and venerable church, where the Franks of the Greek Empire[4] have their worship and services. To the east of this blessed church, but bearing somewhat to the south, is the prison in which the Lord Messiah was incarcerated; also the place of the Crucifixion.

Now as to the great dome, it is of a vast size, and open to the sky. Inside the dome, and all round it, are painted pictures of the Prophets, and of the Lord Messiah, and of the Lady Maryam, his mother, and of John the Baptist. Over the Holy Sepulchre lamps are suspended, and above the Place [of the Grave] in particular are three lamps of gold.

On leaving the great Church and going eastwards, you come to the holy house built by Solomon, the son of David. This, in the time of the Jews, was a mosque to which pilgrimage was made, but it was taken out of their hands and they were driven from thence; but when the days of Islam came, under the Kings of the Muslims, the spot came once more to be venerated, as the Masjid al Aksa.

The Masjid al Aksa is the Great Mosque, and in the whole earth there is no mosque of greater dimensions than this; unless it be the Friday Mosque at Cordova, in Andalusia, which they say has a greater extent of roof than has the Aksa, but the court of the Aksa Mosque is certainly larger than is that of the mosque at Cordova.

[The court of] the Masjid al Aksa is four-sided, its length measures 200 fathoms,[5] and its breadth is 180 fathoms.

33 In that half [of the court] which lies towards the prayer-niche | is roofed with domes of stone set on many rows of columns. The other half is a court, and is not roofed over.

[1] *Bab Santa Maria.*
[2] *Bab es Salūbiya*, the present entrance.
[3] *Qanbinar*, 'campanarium'.
[4] *Ar Rum.*
[5] *Bā'*, 'fathom'.

In the centre of the court rises the mighty dome known as the Dome of the Rock.[1]

This dome is overlaid with gold mosaic, and is of most beautiful workmanship, erected by the Muslim Khalifs. In its midst is the Rock, which is said to have fallen down [from heaven]. It is a mass of stone of the height of a platform, and occupies the centre under the dome.

The extremity of one of its sides rises above the floor to half a man's height or more, while the other side lies even with the ground. The length of the rock is near to equal with its breadth, and is some ten ells[2] and odd by the like. You may descend into the interior thereof, and go down into a dark chamber, like a cellar, the length of which is ten ells, by five in the width, and the ceiling is above a man's height up. No one can enter this chamber except with a lamp to light him.

The Dome has four gates. The western gate has opposite to it an altar whereon the Children of Israel offer up their sacrifices. Near the eastern gate of the dome is the church which is called the Holy of Holies; it is of an admirable construction.

[The gate] to the south faces the roofed-in portion [of the Masjid al Aksa], which same was in former times the place of prayer of the Muslims. Since it was conquered by the Greeks, and it has remained in their hands even down to the time of the writing of this book, they have converted this roofed-in portion of the Mosque into chambers wherein are lodged those companies of men known as Ad Dâwiyyah, whose name signifies 'Servants of God's House.'[3] Opposite to the northern gate [of the Dome of the Rock] is a beautiful garden, planted with all sorts of trees, and round this garden is set a colonnade of marble, of most wondrous workmanship. In the further part of this garden is a place of assembly, where the priests and deacons take their repasts.

Leaving the mosque you come, on the eastern side, to the Gate of Mercy, which is now closed, as we have said before; but near to this gate is another, which is open. It is called the Gate of the Tribes,[4] and through it there is much coming and going. When you have passed out by the Gate of the Tribes you reach the limits of the archery-ground, and find there a large church, and very beautiful,

[1] *Qubbat as Sakra.*
[2] *Dhira'*, 'ell'.
[3] That is the Templars.
[4] *Bab al Asbat.*

dedicated to the Lady Mary, and the place is known as Gethsemane.[1]

At this place also is her tomb, on the skirt of the Mount of Olives. Between it and the Gate of the Tribes is the space of about a mile.

34 On the road ascending the Mount of Olives is a magnificent church, beautifully and solidly built, which is called the Church of Pater Noster; and on the summit of the mount is another church, beautiful and grand likewise, in which men and women enclose themselves, seeking thereby to obtain favour with Allah – be He exalted! In this aforementioned mount, on the eastern part, and bearing rather to the south, is the tomb of Lazarus,[3] whom the Lord Messiah raised again to life. Two miles distant from the Mount of Olives stands the village from which they brought the she ass on which the Lord Messiah rode on his entry into Jerusalem. The place is now in ruins, and no one lives there.

From the Tomb of Lazarus you take the road down to the Valley of the Jordan,[4] and between the valley and the Holy City is the distance of a day's journey. Before reaching the River Jordan is the City of Jericho,[5] lying three miles distant from the bed of the river.

On the banks of the Jordan stands a magnificent church, called after Saint John,[6] where the Greek monks dwell.

The River Jordan flows out from the Lake of Tiberias, and falls into the Lake of Sodom and Gomorrah, and these were two cities of the people of Lot which God overwhelmed because of the sins of their inhabitants. The land lying to the south of the River Jordan is one continuous desert.

Now as to what lies adjacent to the Holy City on the southern quarter: – When you go out by the Gate of Sion you pass a distance of a stone's throw and come to the Church of Sion, which is a beautiful church, and fortified. In it is the guest-chamber wherein the Lord Messiah ate with the Disciples, and the table is there remaining even unto the present day. The people assemble here on [Maundy] Thursday.

From the Gate of Sion you descend into a ravine called the Valley of Gehenna.[7] On the edge of this ravine is a church called after the

[1] *Al Jismaniya.*
[2] *Jabal az Zeitun.*
[3] *Al 'Azar.*
[4] *Wadi al Urdunn.*
[5] *Ariha.*
[6] *Sant Yuhanna.*
[7] *Wadi Jahannum.*

name of Peter, and down in the ravine is the Spring of Siloam[1] which is the spring where the Lord Messiah cured the infirmity of the blind man, who before that had no eyes. Going south from this said spring is the field[2] wherein strangers are buried, and it is a piece of ground which the Lord bought for this purpose; and near by to it are many habitations cut out in the rock wherein men enclose themselves for the purposes of devotion.

Bethlehem[3] is the place where the Lord Messiah was born, and it lies six miles distant from Jerusalem. Half-way down the road is the tomb of Rachel,[4] the mother of Joseph and of Benjamin, the two sons of Jacob – peace be upon them all. The tomb is covered by twelve stones, and above it is a dome vaulted over with stone. At Bethlehem is a church that is beautifully built, of solid foundations, spacious and finely ornamented even to the uttermost, so that not among all other churches can be seen its equal. It is situated in a low-lying ground. The gate thereof is towards the west, and there
are | marble columns of perfect beauty. In one angle of the choir, 35
towards the north, is a cave wherein the Lord Messiah was born. It lies below the church, and in the cave is the manger wherein the Messiah was found. As you go out from Bethlehem you see towards the east the Church of the Angels who told the good news of the birth of the Lord Messiah to the shepherds.

[1] *'Ain Sulwan.*
[2] *Al Hakl* the same as Akeldama.
[3] *Bait Lahm.*
[4] *Rāhīl.*

BELARD OF ASCOLI

1 Jerusalem is one day away from the western sea, twenty-five miles or thirty perna, and is on a mountain. The Citadel of Sion excels all the high cities, and is opposite the Mount of Olives to the west. The Upper Room is at the top of the Citadel, next to the wall, and this Upper Room was a large paved place, in which the supper was held and in which Christ appeared to the disciples when the doors had been shut. There the Holy Spirit came down over the apostles and disciples. There also the Blessed Virgin Mary died.

The Temple is on a level space in the city, under the Citadel to the east.

Christ was scourged in the Praetorium, that is . . . and near this place is the prison from which blessed Peter was led by the angel.

The Sheep Pool is in the same level space as the Temple, and is about a quarter of a mile distant from the Temple.

The Valley of Jehoshaphat is one stade wide, and its position is between the Mount of Olives and Jerusalem.

The top of the Mount of Olives is distant from . . .

Bethphage is between the Mount of Olives and Bethany to the east.

The Pool of Siloam is in the Valley of Jehoshaphat between Sion and the Mount of Olives.

Back . . . the Brook Kidron is in the same valley, which runs[1] when there is plenty of rain.

The farm of Gethsemane is at the foot of the Mount of Olives to the west. The garden into which Christ entered with his disciples is in the same farm, at the head of it, and in this garden is a crypt dug into the rock of the Mount of Olives: this would take nearly three hundred people. And at the end of this crypt is another smaller crypt, like the cell of one brother. In this smaller crypt Christ stood very often in prayer, and there he was captured. At its entrance

[1] Latin *deturrit*.

there appears the shape of three fingers of his sacred hand, imprinted in the rock of the crypt, which, so it is said, he made when he was captured. This crypt is now a church.

A little way off in front of this crypt is the Tomb of the Blessed Virgin, to which thirty steps go down under the earth. And in that garden is the place of prayer, where the sweat of Christ was made like drops of blood.

The place of Calvary is next to Jerusalem. About thirty paces in 2
that place lie between the place of the crucifixion and Golgotha, where the Cross was found, and the Sepulchre of Christ. They are in one church.

The place which is called Mount Calvary is large, and it is like a large sheaf of chaff. It is made of stone, not brought from elsewhere, but rising naturally out of the earth. On the top of it appears a hole sunk in the actual rock, where the cross was fixed. The hole is large and round. It is as large as the head of one man, and about three half [-spans] deep or four.

Near this place on the ground, and not up on the rock, the robbers were crucified.

In the rock of the crucifixion on the south appears the crack, which had the honour of receiving Christ's blood which flowed down his side.

The Sepulchre of Christ is a whole stone, square in its upper part, and inside similarly square, and it has a door like the door of an oven. Inside it is ten feet long or more, and about four feet broad.

The stone, which was rolled to the door of the sepulchre, is very large, and round on one side and on the other flat, and this is by the tomb.

Golgotha, where the cross was found, is a pit, distant from the place of crucifixion above five paces, and about the same distance from the sepulchre.

Nazareth is in the province of Galilee the Great, and is about 3
sixty miles or more away from Jerusalem. It is not a large city, but it has an Archbishop.

The Room of our Lady, into which the angel came to her, was a cave. It is situated at the side of the city, inside it to the east. It is not made of stones but is as it were dug out of the rock. Its length is four paces, and it is of similar breadth.

A straight road between Jerusalem and Nazareth leads to Nain, and close by is the hamlet called Endor. Between Nazareth and Nain is a plain called Pharam.

After Nain is Samaria, the city and province. After this is the city Sychar.

The Mountains of Gilboa are between Nain and Samaria.

Mount Tabor is holy, on which Jesus was transfigured,[1] and is near Nazareth, about a mile away to the east.

4 After Sychar the province of Judaea begins, in the middle of which is situated Jerusalem.

The House of Zacharias, in which the Blessed Virgin greeted Elisabeth, is seven miles distant from Jerusalem and to the west, where now there is a church in honour of Blessed John the Baptist. The village of Emmaus is near this house, and it is one great mile and a little more from Jerusalem, since these two places are about equidistant. In this hamlet, in the place where Christ appeared to the two disciples, there is now a church.

The city of Bethlehem[2] is small. It is five miles to the south of Jerusalem. In it is the Cradle of God, at the eastern end of the city. It was a spacious cave, with a broad entry, and such that if it were to rain a person could take shelter there unless the wind came in. Its size is two paces by one-and-a-half, and it is dug out in the corner[3] of the rock.

The Valley or the place of the Shepherds is one mile east of the Cradle and there is now a church there.

. . . is a day's journey away [and they sought him] among the acquaintances of the Blessed Virgin and her kinsfolk. Perhaps these acquaintances and kinsfolk were Zacharias and Elisabeth.

On the bank of the Jordan is the place of Christ's Baptism, which is twenty-five miles or more from Jerusalem, and there is a church there dedicated to Blessed John.

Around the place of Baptism is the plain of Galgala,[4] and facing us is the city of Jericho.[5]

The high mountain, Christ's desert, is one mile from Jericho, going back to the west, the way you came from Jerusalem. Half way up this mountain, but not at the top, is a cave dug out in the rock, in which Christ fasted. It is reached by a narrow path which hangs in mid-air. From the top of this mountain the Devil showed

[1] Latin *transsitus*.
[2] See section 6 below.
[3] Latin *coie*, perhaps *conie*.
[4] See section 6.
[5] See section 6.

Christ all the kingdoms of the world. The cave is about four paces long and the same width, since its shape is square.

At the foot of this mountain is the stream whose water Elisha cleansed with salt, and it is large enough to run water-mills.

Capernaum is a sea-side town beside the Sea of Galilee, and is 5
about fifteen miles from Nazareth.

The Sea of Galilee, the Sea of Tiberias, and the Lake of Gennesareth are one and the same. Next to that sea is Capernaum. And by this Capernaum on the south is the mountain where Christ often preached, and in particular gave the Sermon on the Mount.

Also by this mountain the Lord fed 5000 people with five loaves, but that city is at the foot of the mountain. In that place there are many . . . well-cut stones lying about.

On the other side of this mountain, on the south side by the sea shore, is the place where Christ ate with his disciples after the resurrection. In this place there is a church. The waves of the sea are about eight or ten paces away from this place.

It is two miles to the next place, which is Magdala, next to the sea, where Mary Magdalene came from. Two miles further on, next to the sea, is the city of Tiberias.

Near Tiberias and beside the Sea is Bethsaida, and Chorazin[1] is also next to Tiberias and beside the sea. All these cities are about seventy miles distant from Jerusalem.

The hamlet of Cana is situated between Nazareth and Tiberias. The place of the wedding is a cave dug out in rock, which would take about fifty men.

Bethany village is situated on the way down the Mount of Olives 6
towards the east, and is about three miles from Jerusalem. In this village is the Tomb of Lazarus.

The place where Mary Magdalene met Jesus on his way to the Raising [of Lazarus] is outside the village a quarter[2] of a mile, where there is clearly a road junction.

In the place of the Mount of Olives from which God ascended there appears the shape of the left foot of God imprinted in the rock. It is not possible to see clearly the length and breadth of the foot, since there only appear the prints of the ends of the toes and of part of the sole.

[1] Latin, *corocai*.
[2] Latin, *quadraginta parte miliaris*.

The city of Acraton or Acre is in the province of Galilee by the Western Sea.

Mount Libanus is in the province of Galilee, at whose foot there rise two springs, Jor and Dan, which join and form the River Jordan. This is the river which winds through the province of Samaria, and ends in the province of Judaea not far from Jerusalem, in the Lake of Sodom and Gomorrha, and thence enters the sea by a secret route.

The city of Azotus is in the province of Samaria next to the Western Sea.

The city of Jericho[1] is in this province on this side of the River Jordan. Between Jericho and the River Jordan is Galgala.[2]

The city of Gaza and Joppa are in the province of Judaea, next to the Western Sea.

In the middle of the province of Judaea is situated the city of Jerusalem.

Bethlehem[3] is a city to the south of Jerusalem, in the direction of Sion, between this city and the city of Hebron.

Mamre is a hamlet where on a hill is the House of Abraham.[4] This house is a cave dug out of the rock and it is in a corner[5] with the tree standing before its entrance.

And I, Brother Belardus of Esculum, have seen all these things, sought them out, and made notes on them, so that I may be of use to others.

[1] See section 4.
[2] See section 4.
[3] See section 4.
[4] Latin, *hobde*.
[5] Latin, *conius*.

SEVENTH GUIDE

If any one wishes[1] to enter *Jerusalem*, let him go *to the east continuously* 100
and then let him enter by the Gate of Saint Stephen. There outside the gate he was stoned. And let him seek the places of Jerusalem in order.

In Jerusalem is the Sepulchre of the Lord. At the entry gates of the Sepulchre, outside the door, is the church of Calvary, where Saint Mary was, and Saint John stood when the Lord *said, 'Woman, behold thy son; . . . son, behold thy mother'*. Outside the gate on the left side is the altar of Saint John the Baptist.

Inside the gate, again to the right, is Mount Calvary, where the Lord was crucified. Underneath is Golgotha, where the Lord's blood fell on the rock. And there was the head of *Adam, and Abraham made his sacrifice.* On the other side at the foot of Mount Calvary is a place with a column, where the Lord was scourged,
and nearby to the east, down a flight of forty-four steps, is the place 101
where the Holy Cross was found by Saint Helena.

In the Church is the Sepulchre of the Lord, and near that to the east in a place near the middle of the choir, is the Centre of the World where the Lord was laid when Nicodemus took him down from the Cross. *To the left* of that is *the Prison of the Lord*, and the next place to that is where the Holy Cross is venerated.

Next to the Church of the Sepulchre is the Church of Saint Mary which is called 'The Latin'. There it is said that *Saint Mary Magdalene and Saint Mary, wife of Cleophas* tore their hair when the Lord was placed on the Cross. There also is the hospital of Saint John the Baptist.

From that *place, two bowshots away, is the Temple of the Lord made by King Solomon*, in which are four gates and twelve doors. In the middle of the Temple is placed a great stone on which the Ark of

[1] Phrases in Italic are quotations from the *First Guide*.

Covenant was placed, and in which now is also the Rod of Aaron, the Tables of the Law, the golden candlestick and the Urn which contains the manna which fell from heaven: there too is the fire of sacrifice, and the oil is still running with which the Kings and the
102 Prophets | were anointed. Next to this place the Son of God was presented, and Jacob saw the ladder coming down from heaven,

On the left of the Choir:

> Jesus, the King of Kings has been
> Once offered, Son of Virgin Queen:
> This memory makes more precious yet
> The Holy Place in which it's set.[1]

Jacob saw the ladder, and in memory of it he also erected an altar. The right side is where the angel appeared to Zacharias. Below there is a sanctuary, in old time the Holy of Holies, where the Lord sent away the sinner taken in adultery.

> All nations that their sins confess,
> I now absolve from wickedness.

There the birth of Saint John the Baptist was announced, and there is the column, which the Saracens adored, in which is said to be the altar on which Abraham wished to sacrifice his son. There is also a church where Saint James was thrown down headlong from the Temple. And there, outside the wall of the Temple, is a certain altar beside which Saint Zacharias was killed. At the Gate of the Temple court is the Gate Beautiful.

On the other side of the Temple of Solomon, between the
103 Temple and the Golden Gate are trees. | There the children cut off branches when the Lord sat upon the ass. And there, next to the Temple of Solomon, in the corner of the city, is the Cradle of Christ, the bed of his mother, and a bath. There too is the Tomb of Saint Simeon.

To the east next to the Temple is the Gate. To the north is the Sheep Pool, and near that is the church of Saint Anne, and the well down which pilgrims go. Near Saint Anne is the Church of

[1] For a fuller version of this verse see Jwu 122.

Saint Mary Magdalene. To the north, next to the Church of the Sepulchre, is the Church of Saint Karitotius.[1]

To the south is *Mount Sion*, where a beautiful church in honour of Saint Mary has been founded, in which she was *taken to* heaven, and her *very holy body was* taken down *into the Valley of Jehoshaphat*. To the left of that is the chapel in the place where the Praetorium had been, and Christ was judged. And on the left side is Galilee, where the Lord appeared to Simon and the women. Above, next to the choir, is where the Holy Spirit descended on the apostles, and in the same church of the table *on which Christ supped*, when he said, 'Take, eat, this is my body'. And lower
down is the place where | he washed the disciples' feet, and the 104
basin is there which contained the water. In that place stood Jesus when he said, 'Peace be with you!' and there Thomas touched the Lord's side. On the left side is the altar of Saint Stephen, where he was buried.

Outside the church is a certain small church where the Praetorium used to be in which the Lord was scourged, crowned with thorns, and mocked, and this was the House of Caiaphas. Beyond Mount Sion is a church where Saint Peter fled when he had denied the Lord at the cock-crow. In the direction of the Valley is *the Pool of Siloam, and there is buried Isaiah the Prophet*.

Between Jerusalem *and the Mount of Olives is the Valley of Jehoshaphat, where* Saint *Mary was buried by the Apostles*, and there is the Brook Kidron. Also there was a *farm which* was *called Gethsemane*. There the Lord sent away Peter and the other disciples, when he *prayed, 'Father, if it be possible' and so on*. And there is the garden where he was captured by the Jews, and a stone's throw away from there is the place where he prayed, and his sweat ran down to the ground like drops of blood. Near this place is the Tomb of King Jehoshaphat, after whose name the Valley is called 'Of Jehoshaphat'. And there is a Church where |
James and Saint Simeon the Elder and Zacharias were buried, and 105
not far from that to the south is Akeldamach, or the burial place of travellers.

From the Mount of Olives the Lord ascended to the Father, and he commanded the disciples to preach to all creation. And nearby is a small church where the Lord's Prayer was made. A little way

[1] That is, Saint Chariton.

down from that is the Tomb of Saint Pelagius. Between the Mount of Olives and Bethany is Bethphage, where the Lord sent Peter and John for the ass. Not far away is Bethany, where the Lord raised Lazarus, and forgave the woman who was a sinner. And here was the House of Simon the Leper. Near here is where Saint Martha met the Lord.

The road which leads to Bethlehem from Jerusalem starts from the Gate of David, and goes down to the Church of Saint Elias, where he stood. On the road is the Tomb of Rachel. *In Bethlehem Christ was born*, and there is the Tomb of Saint Jerome, and the Well in which the star fell, and there is a painting of the Table on which Mary [ate with] the Three Kings. In this area are the Tombs of the Innocents. In the crypt of the Blessed | Virgin is the
106 altar where she gave birth. And not far from Bethlehem is the Church where the angel appeared to the Shepherds. And there is the church where Saint Mary rested when she carried the Lord. And at the far end is the road which leads to Hebron, which is five leagues away from Jerusalem.

And in that place the Lord created Adam. Not far from there is the House of Cain and Abel. And not far from there is where the Lord appeared in Trinity to Abraham. To the east is the place where Saint Mary saluted Elisabeth, and there Saint John Baptist was born and Zacharias [lived there]. Two leagues away from there is the village of Emmaus.

Outside the gate is the Church of the Holy Cross where [the Wood] was cut. In Jerusalem is the place where Saint Peter was put in prison. In the Temple is a spring of living water, and this is the reason why the Prophet says, 'I saw water issuing'.[1]

From Jerusalem to the Mount of Quarantenus is seven leagues, and at the foot of this mountain is the Garden of Abraham. Near there is Jericho, *and* two leagues *away from there is the River Jordan.*
107 *From the river to Mount Sinai* is *eighteen days' journey*. | From Jerusalem to Samaria, which is now called Neapolis, is twelve leagues, and there is the Well where *the Lord talked with the Samaritan woman*. And there is the mountain where Abraham wished to sacrifice his son. From that place to Sebaste is two leagues, where Saint John Baptist was beheaded. Some of his dust is still preserved there.

[1] Ezek 47.1.

Ten leagues on from there is Mount Tabor, where the Lord was transfigured. And close to that is Mount Hermon. In that place is the city Nain, where the Lord raised the only son of his mother before the gate. To the left is the Sea of Galilee, where the Lord satisfied five thousand men with five loaves and two fishes. To the west is the noble city Nazareth, and there the Blessed Virgin had the Annunciation by the Angel, and there was her house.

These places and others are to be venerated by the faithful. +

SECOND GUIDE

118/1 By the upper way from Accaron on your way to the Holy City there is the town of Nazareth. Two leagues on from there is Mount Tabor, in which Christ was transfigured. Near there is the city of Tiberias, and near it is the Sea of Galilee where the Lord wrought many miracles. At the end of the Sea is the table, where the Lord gave a meal to five thousand people from five loaves and two fishes.

Then comes the city of Sebaste, which is venerable for its relics of Saint John the Baptist. Then you go by Neapolis, where the well is on which the Lord sat when he was in conversation with the woman from Samaria.

119/2 From there the journey takes us to the Holy City, and first to the church of Saint Stephen, where he was stoned. From there we go on to the Church of the Holy Sepulchre, and first of all to the place of the Skull, where he suffered. There the three crosses set their seal that our prayers have been heard and that the Crucified one has been adored.

There also one goes to Golgotha, where the blood of the Lord flowed down the split rock. Then one goes to the altar, which is believed to be held up by a part of the column to which Christ was tied when he was scourged. There is a way down there to the place where the Holy Cross was discovered. This was in a cave, and the rock is still visible above it. The middle altar is in honour of Queen Helena, and the left one is in honour of Saint Quiriacus. He was a Jew, and he showed where the cross was. Having seen the miracle of the dead being raised, he was converted to the faith, and became Bishop of Jerusalem.

In the middle of the Choir of the Canons stands a very venerable place. This is because Christ was laid there when he had been taken down from the Cross and before he was taken to the Tomb: there is a light there that never goes out. The great altar is in honour of Saint Mary. Then one visits the Holy Sepulchre.

This has a southern altar in a church which is suitably 120
decorated, where the Holy Cross is kept. Next to it is another Syrian Church, in which they also keep the Holy Cross. Almost at the end of the church in the south side is the place called the Prison, where Christ was guarded while the Cross was being prepared on the mountain.

Under five columns of the church the Forty Martyrs are buried, and their identity is known by the fact that their feast is celebrated on the ninth of March. Next to the place of the Skull is the place of the blocked-up door, in which Jerome says that Adam is buried. Certain people also say that drops of the Blood filled his mouth, and that for that reason he was raised from the dead.

Next to the chief church there are three chapels on the south,
of which the first is in honour of . . . the Holy Trinity and the
last, on the side of the forum, in honour of Saint James the
Great. It is said that the Lord sat in the seat at the middle altar,
and blessed John at the right and James at the left, when | their 121
mother asked that they should 'Sit in his kingdom, one on his
right and the other on his left'. It is said that Saint John stood on
the site of his altar when Christ commended his mother to him.

Also the Most Holy Virgin stood in the place where now the great altar of the main church stands, and looked at her Son's sufferings. Outside the main church on the side of Calvary is a small chapel in honour of Mary Magdalene, where the Three Maries stood at the time of the Passion.

There is a church of Saint John Baptist, on the opposite side to 3
the main church, which is to be honoured not only because of its very holy relics, but also because of the most famous alms it gives. There it is certainly evident that there are six works of mercy to fulfil. Near there is the Church of Saint Mary the Latin, famous for a long time, and also for the famous relics it contains: the Head of Saint Philip the Apostle is there, and some of Saint Mary's hair.

On Mount Sion is the place where the Holy Spirit appeared 4
upon the Apostles in tongues of flame, and enlightened their
hearts. There | the Washing of the Feet of the Disciples took 122
place, and the same table is there on which the Supper was held.
This place is in front of the doors of that which is called 'The
Holy Spirit'. To the south is the place called 'Galilee', of which

it was said, '*He shall go before you to Galilee*'.[1] On the opposite side, to the north, is the place where Saint Mary died to this world.

On the end of this side, to the east, is an altar under which Saint Stephen, Gamaliel, Abibas and Nicodemus are buried.

Outside the court to the north is a church in honour of Saint Peter at the Cock-crow, where he hid himself after he had denied three times and the cock had crowed, and wept bitterly.

There is also inside the walls a Church of Saint Peter at the Prison, where Herod held him prisoner with two chains.

5 When we go back to the Temple of the Lord the first place one
comes to is that of the Holy Presentation. Next to that is the place
123 where Jacob slept, saw the ladder and wrestled with the angel, and
where in memory he raised a stone. Under the choir to the south is
a cave dug in the rock, which is called 'The Place of Confession'.
This is the reason. Christ was there presented with the woman, and
said to her, '*No one has condemned thee*' and so on.[2]

At the head of the Temple is the Chapel of Saint James, where he was cast down headlong, and killed with a fuller's club. But James the son of Alphaeus was the first Bishop of Jerusalem.

Not far off are pointed out the Golden Gates, by which the Lord, when he had come from the Mount of Olives, entered Jerusalem on an ass, with the children crying, '*Hosanna to the Son of David!*'.[3] These gates are only opened on the Day of Palms and at the Exaltation of the Holy Cross.

From there can be seen the place where the Manger and the Bath and the Sepulchre of Simeon are, and where Christ is said to have stayed with Simon for a year and a half.

6 Near the gate of the city which looks towards the Valley of Jehoshaphat is the Church of Saint Anne, the Mother of Saint Mary, where she was dwelling when she bore and nursed him.

Near there is the Sheep Pool which had five porches. This Pool is
124 the place where those who visit are told that the Wood of the Cross
remained for a long time, but the Templars show you another Pool
and say that that is the Sheep Pool.

From there one goes to the Valley of Jehoshaphat where the Tomb of Saint Mary is. There, before the gates of the monastery is the place called Gethsemane, where Judas betrayed him. There is

[1] Mark 16.7.
[2] John 8.10.
[3] Matt. 21.9, 15.

the hard stone which, they say, gave way to his fingers, and in that Chapel are four separate places where he found the disciples sleeping three by three.

Outside the court, a stone's throw away, is a church in honour of the Saviour, where he prayed three times, and a sweat like blood flowed from him.

Next to the walled area of Jehoshaphat runs the Brook Kidron. Within the Valley of Jehoshaphat are the Waters of Siloam, and there too, where the hermits live, is a Chapel in honour of Saint James. Akeldama is almost within the boundaries of the Valley of Jehoshaphat, the field which was bought with the thirty pieces of silver to bury strangers in. There no burial is refused.

Going up the Mount of Olives the first Church which meets one 7
is called 'The Pater Noster', for the reason that there Christ taught 125
the 'Our Father'. A stone is there, placed under the altar where he wrote with his own hand 'Our Father' in Greek letters. After that is the Church of the Holy Virgin Pelagia. In the church which is built on top of the mountain is to be seen the place of the Ascension.

Next to that, not far away, is Bethphage. Then the journey takes us to Bethany. Then to the Jordan. First one comes to Jericho, and there is the Garden of Abraham. The stream flows there from the Spring of Elisha . . . where there are twelve fountains and seventy palm trees. When one is a visitor to the left is a place which is defended by religious people, and it is called 'Quadrantena' for the reason that Christ fasted there for forty days. At the top of the mountain is where Satan tempted him. From there one goes to the Jordan.

There is also a place which is called the Charnel of the Lion 8
outside the City of Jerusalem, where the bodies of many saints lie buried. After that is the Monastery of the Georgians that is called 'At the Stump', or 'The Trunk', because there it is said that the tree for the Holy Cross was cut down. Over the place of the stump an altar has been set up.

In the road leading to Bethlehem is the Mound of Rachel, and
there is the place where Elijah is venerated, and a church has been 126
constructed for him. In the place where the Lord was born is the hammer and the nail of his crucifixion.[1] There Jerome is buried, and there are many relics of the Holy Innocents.

[1] The nail of Christ's crucifixion and the pincers were brought to Bethlehem by its Bishop according to the *Work on Geography* 205.

Not far from there is a place called 'Glory to God in the highest', because there at the moment the Lord was born the angels were heard singing together 'Glory to God in the highest'.

Between the Mount of Olives and Mount Gihon[1] is a place which is called 'At the Shepherds', because when the shepherds were watching there a light shone and the angels' singing announced Christ had been born.

Going to Saint Abraham in Hebron you first find the Root of Mamre. There is now a church there in honour of the Holy Trinity.

Beside Hebron is the place where Cain killed his brother Abel, and there too is the mountain on which each of them offered God their firstfruits. There also the earth is pointed out from which Adam was created.

127 Returning you travel by the Church of Saint John the Baptist, where he preached the baptism of penitence in the desert. There there is a spring of water which does not fail, which at the time when he preached sprung forth when he prayed.

From there the journey takes us to Saint Zacharias, where he lived with Saint Elisabeth and exercised his priesthood. There Holy Mary saluted Elisabeth, whose infant exulted in her womb.

There the journey goes through the castle whose name is Emmaus to the Holy City.

9 Next to the city is the place Gion, where there is now a monastery of the Greeks. Next to the Mount of Olives on the left is a monastery of the Syrians. In the valley between the Mount of Olives and Mount Gihon[2] . . .

From the Mount of Olives can be seen the lake which is called 'The Dead Sea', where the four cities were submerged, Sodom, Gomorrah and the rest. Into that lake the Jordan flows and is swallowed up.

10 In the city is a monastery of Jacobites, where there is the head of
Saint James and an arm of Saint Stephen the Protomartyr. The
128 Jacobites also have the church of Saint Mary Magdalene, where
they show her hair.

[1] The words opening this paragraph seem to be a mistake, but the memory of the Shepherds makes this a commemoration which goes with Bethlehem.

[2] The words referred to in the previous note here seem to be in place, but the site to which they refer seems to have got lost.

In the church of the Holy Sepulchre there are doors facing the chapel of the Syrians in which they keep the Holy Cross.

There is the gate at which Saint Mary the Egyptian stood, and could not enter without true penitence.

108 # JOHN OF WÜRZBURG

LETTER

John, by the grace of God a member of the Church at Würzburg, to my dear (and 'dear' is how I view you) colleague and member of my household, Dietrich, I bring greeting, and a vision of the heavenly Jerusalem, for you have a share in it.

I have alluded to your way of life, and find it in harmony with a disposition always to do good, and your energetic devotion to your office and duties. This is more than would even be required of a colleague who is a member of my household. Indeed I am so obliged by your good will towards me, which I always assume will be fair and kindly in any crises which affect us both, that no requests of yours will be allowed to fail to reach their appointed end, in so far as they may require my co-operation, and so far as I am able. |

109 This is why, when I stayed in Jerusalem on pilgrimage, for the love of our Lord Jesus Christ, but also remembering that you were absent, I have written this book, for the love I bear towards you, about the Holy Places. These are sanctified by the bodily presence of our Lord, the Saviour of the world, and with him his glorious mother, Mary, Eternal Virgin, and the blessed company of his Disciples. I have paid particular attention to the Holy City Jerusalem, in order to describe all the facts about it in detail and with care, and I have worked hard to collect all the inscriptions, whether in prose or verse. I believe that this description will be valuable to you if, by the Divine Will, you come to everything which I have described and see them physically. It will be easy for you to find them, and you will see the things which I have described to you easily, and without the delay and difficulty of searching for them. But if you happen not to go there and you are not going physically to see them, you will still have a greater love of them and their holiness by reading this book and thinking about it. I am well aware that, long ago, long before the present time,

these very places, and not only those in the city itself but also far away from it, have been described by a certain revered man. But,
because it is a long time since they were written | down, and since 110
this city has often been captured and destroyed, the holy places within and a short way outside the walls, with which we are chiefly concerned, were either pulled down or afterwards happened to become changed. Hence the attention which we have paid to their location, which we have seen and noted down, is not to be dismissed as exaggerated or superfluous. Of the places far away in other provinces we do not intend to speak, knowing that enough has already been recorded by other writers.[1] . . . |

. . . The Presentation of the Blessed Virgin Mary. In the Temple 4 120
of the Lord on the twenty-first of November, it is said that the
Blessed Virgin Mary, then | three years old, was presented, and 121
these are the verses there written:

[1] Now a summary of Fretellus, *Fratri R. (A Description of the Holy Places to Count Raymond)* begins. We shall refer to this as 'R', and the passages on which R. is based from the *Work on Geography* (referred to as 'G') are noted as well.

Chapter 1 is based on R.31–3, derived from G. 75 (and following matter in R.), 76, 77a, 83, 77b, 79, 80, 82, 84, 85 (and following matter in R.), 87, 86, 89, 91–4, 96a. The following points of interest occur.

110 Nazareth is described as 'the head city of Galilee'.

111 'The Fall' is 'called today "The Leap of the Lord"'.

111 'In Sepphoris it is said that the Blessed Virgin Mary was born, but, according to Jerome, as he says in the prologue to the piece of writing he gave to Heliodorus on the Birth of Saint Mary [see *PL* 30.308A], she was said to have been born in
112 Nazareth, and indeed in the very room where afterwards she was | made pregnant by the message of an angel. This is today shown in a different place, as I have seen and noted.'

112 Feast of the Transfiguration. 'In Jerusalem this feast is celebrated annually on the Day of Saint Sixtus [i.e. Aug.6] and it is a great feast among the Syrians.'

113 Nain. The son of the widow 'is said by the inhabitants to be Bartholomew, who was afterwards made an Apostle'.

113 Jezreel 'is now commonly called Minor Gallina'.

114 Jenin 'is now commonly called Crassa or Major Gallina'.

Chapter 2 is a summary of R.3.7–4.2, 5.1, deriving from G. 97, 99, 101 with following material in R, 105, 113, 108; for Shiloh and Rama see Jerome, *L.loc.* 157.28. Points of interest are the following:

114 Between Jenin and Samaria 'a plain is pointed out called Dothan, where there still appears beside the road an old cistern, into which Joseph was put by his brothers'.

Chapter 3, on Jerusalem and the Temple, is a summary of R.5.3–5.2a, deriving from (after the distance to Jerusalem) 128, 131–2, 134–5, 138, 140. Chapter 4, on the Temple, is a summary of R.5.2b, derived from G.141, till there is an original text (see p. 1). Points of interest are the following:

120 Jesus disputed with the doctors 'when he was an adult . . . twelve years old'.

120 The Pinnacle of the Temple 'is said to be on the court wall, having beneath it windows, like feathers or teeth'.

The Virgin in her sevenfold company
Of virgins, who, when future times unfold,
Shall be a Handmaid of our God, was here,
Presented to the Lord when three years old.

There she often used to receive angelic comfort, and hence the verse:

With angels' ministry the Virgin feeds.

November the twenty-first is the Presentation of the Blessed Virgin Mary in the Temple, and this prayer is said in the Temple itself:

> O God, who didst ordain that there should be presented, when she was three years old, the Holy Mother of God, herself a Temple of the Holy Spirit: Look on your loving people: And grant that we who celebrate the Feast of her Presentation, may also be made a Temple in which you will deign to dwell: Through our Lord . . .

From the Temple Jesus Christ *drove out the people selling and buying.*[1] And as a testimony to this fact there is a stone shown on the right side of the Temple. It is reverently decorated and well lit, and the Lord's footprint is still visible there, when he alone by divine power resisted a great number of men who were trying violently to cast him forth. There is another stone next to it on which our Lord
122 is painted, being | offered on an altar. This is both illustrated in the picture and explained in an inscription, which reads as follows:

The Virgin's Son, presented here,
The King of Kings, the boy most dear,
He makes this spot a holy place,
And this most rightly is the case.
The ladder Jacob saw was near
The altar he erected here –
This memory makes more precious yet
The holy place in which it's set.

Because there, on this very stone, Jacob is painted with his head lying on it, when he slept and saw a ladder pointing to the sky, by

[1] A quotation from R.5.3, derived from G.141.

which angels climbed up and down (but, although we revere the Temple, this is not true!). There this verse is written:

Thine, Jacob, is this land and place,
And shall be of thy future race!

Nevertheless this did not happen here. It happened a long way away, as Jacob was going to Mesopotamia, that is to say beside the Greater Mahomeria.

In the Temple our Lord *set the adulterous woman free from those who accused her, saying,* '*Whoever is without sin*' and so on, and then, when her accusers were silent and went away, said, '*Woman, go in peace,*
and | *sin no more again*'.[1] The place of that event is represented in the 123
small crypt of the Temple, the entry to which is on the left side of the Temple, and it is called 'The Confession'. *Into* the same place *Zacharias* is said to have entered when *the angel* made the promise to him about the conception of *John.*[2] A picture and inscription illustrate this whole event. The inscription reads as follows:

> The Angel to Zacharias, '*Fear not, Zacharias, thy prayer is heard*' and so on,[3]

and on the place where the lintel is, a portrait of Christ:

All nations that their sins confess
I now absolve from wickedness.

In *the Temple* at the *altar* which was outside in the open air, and a little more than twenty-two paces away from the Temple, *Zacharias the son of Barachias died as a martyr. On this altar in the old covenant* the Jews *used to sacrifice pigeons and doves. It was later turned by the Saracens into a sundial, but it is still to be seen.*[4] Notice too that very many Saracens even today come to this altar to pray. It is directed to the south, and this is their normal direction of prayer.

The Temple of the Lord was built by some person with marvellous panelling of marble, inside and out. Its shape is round and beautiful, and it goes round in an octagon, that is, round it it has eight corners. Its outer wall is decorated with excellent mosaics
| down to the half-way point, and the lower half is covered with 124

[1] John 8.1–7: a quotation from R.5.3, derived from G.142.
[2] Quotation from R.5.3, derived from G.142.
[3] Quotation from R.5.3, derived from G.142.
[4] Quotation from R.5.3, derived from G.142.

marble slabs. Inside the wall goes completely round, except that it is interrupted by four doors. A door on the east outside leads to a chapel dedicated in honour of Saint James, for from this side he was *thrown headlong* from *the temple*[1] roof, and killed with a fuller's club. He was the first chief priest in Jerusalem under the gracious new law. Hence the following verses are written in the same chapel on the side of the wall:

Of James, Alphaeus' son, record
  That in his face he's like the Lord:
And, like the Lord, his life will end
  For from the Temple he'll descend.
Where people listen James will teach
  Of Christ. In public he will preach.
The crowd will plot when they're annoyed.
  By fuller's club he'll be destroyed.

And these verses appear round the ciborium of the chapel, inside and above:

Of James, Alphaeus son, record
  He was the brother of the Nazarene Lord.
He was a fisherman by trade,
  And he an Israelite most true was made.
By cunning him the crowds compel
  To reach the Temple's pinnacle. Then he fell.
By clubbing he his life forsook,
  But happy then to Christ his journey took. |

125 The Temple has one door to the north towards the Cloister of the Canons,[2] and above its lintel many Saracen letters are marked. Next to that gate is the place of the water of salvation, about which the Prophet said, '*I saw water coming out of the side*'.[3] In the entry of the Temple towards the west over the porch is an image of Christ, on which this epigram is written:

This house of mine shall be called a house of prayer.[4]

To the south it has a door towards the building of Solomon and on the west it has a gate towards the Sepulchre of the Lord, and there is

[1] Quotation from R.5.3, derived from G.142.
[2] Literally 'Cloister of the Lords'.
[3] Eze 47.1.
[4] Isa 56.7, Matt 21.13.

the Beautiful Gate through which *Peter, going through it with John, answered* the poor man who was *asking them* for alms, because he was lame, and said, '*I have no silver and gold*' and so on.[1] Two of the doorways, the ones to the north and west, have six doorways joined together, that to the south has four, and that to the east two. Indeed all the doors have beautiful porches.

What we have mentioned so far is round the lower wall, but in the upper part (where, that is, the excellent mosaic work is placed) there are windows. They are so arranged that in every one of the
eight sides there are | five, except where there are doors to the 126
Temple, and those walls contain only four windows. This makes a total of thirty-six. Within this round outer wall outside the building is an inner row of great marble columns, which number twelve, and hold up the inner section, which is narrower, higher, and almost circular, and these are divided by four square piers. Between the outside and inside of the building are sixteen columns and eight piers decorated with marble veneer, and the space between is eight paces. These hold up the roof which runs between on the one hand the outside wider wall, and on the other the inner narrower one. They have most beautiful ceilings above them, and a place to walk round beside the roof, which has lead gutters to take the rain water away.

On the narrower part there is set a high round dome, painted inside and covered outside with lead. The sign of the Holy Cross has been fixed to the top by Christians, which is annoying to the Saracens. They would be very glad to see it taken down, and have offered much of their own money. For even though they do not hold the faith in the passion of Christ they still revere this Temple,
and wish to worship their Creator | there. But this is to be taken as 127
idolatry according to Augustine, who asserts that anything is idolatry which is done against the faith of Christ.

All round the Temple just below the roof there is writing. At the top towards the west it reads:

Eternal peace on this house be
From God the Lord eternally!

Blessed be the glory of God from his holy place.[2]

Towards the south:

[1] Quotation from R.5.3 and Acts 3.6.

[2] Ezek 3.2.

Well founded is the House of the Lord on a firm rock.[1]
Blessed are they who dwell in the House of the Lord.
From generation to generation they shall praise thee.[2]

Towards the east:

Truly the Lord is in this place, and I did not know it.[3]
Lord, in thy House all praise thy glory![4]

Towards the north:

The Temple of the Lord is holy, God's labour and building.[5]

Inside in the Temple in the upper cornice round the circle is set in large letters this responsory: 'Hear, Lord, the hymn', with its answer, 'Look down Lord'.[6] And on the lower cornice an inscription in letters of gold, containing some lines from the hymn 'Jerusalem the blessed'.[7]

Thus the Temple is beautifully constructed and decorated.
128 Round it there is a wide | flat court paved all over with stone, and of a square shape outside. From three sides one ascends to it with many steps. This court is built up above the level of the land round it. And on the east wall it has a broad entry through five arches joined by four columns. This wall is in the direction of the Golden Gate, through which the Lord went in procession on the fifth day before his suffering, seated upon an ass. He was welcomed with the branches of palm trees, and they praised him saying, '*Hosanna to the Son of David*' and so on.[8]

This gate, through divine providence, even though many times later on Jerusalem was captured and destroyed by enemies, has always remained intact. Moreover this gate, out of reverence for the divine and mystic coming of the Lord from Bethany through the Mount of Olives and his entry into Jerusalem, is closed inside, and the outside is blocked with stones. At no time is it open to any one except annually on the Day of Palms, to mark the memory of the historical event. Then it is solemnly opened for a procession in

[1] Breviary for Dedication, I Vespers, Ant. to Ps. 111 and Responsory after hymn.
[2] Ps 84.5. Antiphon for first psalm in II Nocturns.
[3] Gen 28.16. Responsory after Fourth Lesson in I Nocturns.
[4] Ps 29.9. Antiphon for sixth psalm in II Nocturns.
[5] Ps 65.6. Antiphon for third psalm in II Nocturns.
[6] 1 Kg 8.28f. First Lesson for Dedication Mass.
[7] Urbs beata Jerusalem, Hymn for Mattins on Octave of Dedication.
[8] Matt 21.9.

which all the people take part, pilgrims and citizens. When the Patriarch has spoken to the people at the foot of the Mount of Olives, and when the services have been finished for that day, it is again closed for the whole year as before, except that it is again
opened | on the Exaltation of the Holy Cross. Under that gate is a 129
famous burial place for the dead below the walls.

The court has on the south an open entry through three great arches, which are joined by two marble columns, and also on this side it has another entry wider than the first. On the west, in the direction of the city, it has a beautiful entry which opens through four arches held up by three marble columns. To the north the court is somewhat narrower through the fact that the Cloister of the Canons[1] has been added, but for the rest of that side it has just as beautiful a width and access. There is also a beautiful and very wide space to the south and to the west. But a little towards the north of this court the ground comes up to its level.

Such is enough for the description of the Temple and the surrounding area, but we do not refuse to give more!

On the way down from that upper court is a great gate, through which there is an entry to that side of the court of the Temple. To the right side towards the south is the Palace which is said to have
been built by Solomon, | where there is a stable. This is a 130
marvellous stable, and has so much space that it could take more than two thousand horses, or one thousand five hundred camels. Next to this Palace the Templar soldiers have many large and spacious buildings, and a site for building a large new church, which is not however yet finished. This institution has many properties and an enormous income both from this country and from other parts of the world. Its work consists in generous charity to the poor in Christ, but not a tenth as much as is done by the Hospitallers. The institution has many soldiers to defend the Christians' land. But these, I have no idea by what misfortune, and whether what is told is lies or truth, are rumoured to be tainted with the guilt of perfidy. This was conclusively proved by their behaviour at Damascus with King Conrad.[2]

Next to the buildings of the Templars, towards the east and

[1] Latin, 'Cloister of the Lords'.

[2] Conrad II, King of Germany, and Louis VII, King of France, retreated from an attack on Damascus in 1148. The Templars formed part of the army: William of Tyre, *History* XVII.1.

above the wall of the city, is the House of Simeon the Righteous.
The Blessed Virgin Mary is said often to have stayed in it because
of hospitality towards her and friendship, and to have been
entertained and fed. This was so particularly on the night preceding
131 the fortieth day from the birth | of the Lord. On that day Simeon
was going to offer the child in the Temple, and took him in his
arms and offered him at the altar. He knew by a spirit of prophecy
that it was he who for many periods of history had been awaited by
the fathers of old times with an unutterable desire, and he said
prophetically, '*Lord, now lettest thou thy servant depart in peace*', and
so on.[1] In that building, now transformed into a church, Blessed
Simeon lies buried, and his place is marked by a verse written there.
Below that church, in the crypt, there has been kept till now, and
displayed with great reverence, the wooden cradle of Christ.

6 When the time of the Lord's suffering was close Our Lord Jesus
came to Bethany just before the Day of Palms, and on the
following day, that is Sunday, he entered the holy city in the
morning with all the circumstances we have described. *Bethany* is
two miles *from* Jerusalem and *is the city in which* Simon (or Lazarus,
which is to be preferred) *often entertained Jesus, and Martha and Mary
were anxious to serve him.*[2] In Bethany Mary Magdalene, when she
had broken the alabaster bottle, in her love poured out the precious
132 | salve on the Saviour's head while he reclined at a meal. The whole
house was full of the scent with which he had been anointed. This
same Mary Magdalene, perhaps in the same place or perhaps in
another, the House of Simon the Leper, some time before when she
was a sinner, was moved to penitence. In the same manner she
came to the feet of the Lord when he was reclining at supper. She
wet Jesus' feet with her *tears, and wiped them with her hair*, and in some
other place, remorsefully *anointed them with salve*, and thus *deserved
pardon* from the Lord *for her sins.*[3] Hence when in different places in
Holy Scripture it is said that one Mary came to the Lord's feet and
another anointed his head, our teachers explain that it was 'another'
Mary because she herself had changed. Once she had come as a
sinner in bitter penitence, but now she has been forgiven, and
comes with overflowing joy.

Furthermore there is a church inside the walls of the Holy City,

[1] Luke 2.29.
[2] Quotation from R.6.2, derived from G.155.
[3] Quotation from R.6.2, derived from G.156.

near Saint Anne and a little north near the city wall, which is
dedicated in honour of Mary Magdalene. Jacobite monks live there,
and they state that in that place was the House of Simon the Leper.
He invited our Lord to supper, and Mary Magdalene was also
there, who fell down at the feet of Jesus. She wet them with her
tears, and | when she kissed them she wiped them with her hair and 133
anointed them with salve. This too they assert, that the very place
in the pavement of theirs which is marked with the sign of the
Cross is where Mary came to the feet of Jesus. They illustrate that
the fact was so by reference to a picture, and also by showing the
hair of this Mary, which until the present time has been kept in a
transparent glass vessel. They state also that it was another Mary,
the sister of Lazarus and Martha, who once in Bethany (which was
the village of those three) had broken the alabaster bottle and
poured precious salve on the head of our Lord. Her tomb, they say,
is still shown in Tiberias, since her body is buried there. But they
say that the body of Mary Magdalene lies in our part of the world,
buried at Vézelay.

Yet, as we have mentioned above, our teachers say that it was
one and the same Mary who anointed the feet and head of Jesus,
who was the sister of Lazarus, and had once been a sinner. In any
case the Gospel reading about these things is clear, but even to a
careful listener it brings doubt over the other fact, namely whether
Simon the Pharisee had an entertainment in Bethany, and whether
he invited the Lord. This would not seem suitable, because the
whole | of that village belonged to Lazarus and his sisters. And if 134
that same Simon had another entertainment (and perhaps in the
place we have mentioned), still two things are necessary: in the first
place that Mary should be said to have anointed both the feet and
also the head of Jesus, as we learn from the words in the Gospel
which say '*Simon, I have entered thy house*' and so on:[1] and in the
second place that in Bethany, that is to say in her house, the same
Mary anointed only his head, breaking an alabaster bottle over
him, and this is why it says in the Gospel, '*When Jesus was at
Bethany*'.[2] If any one wishes to know more about these things, let
him come himself, and ask the most intelligent subjects of this land
the sequence and truth of this history. As for me, I have not found
quite enough in any of the Scriptures.

[1] Luke 7.40. But Jesus only mentions Mary anointing his feet (7.44, 46).
[2] Matt 26.6.

Between this Bethany and the top of the Mount of Olives, and about half way, is *Bethphage*, once a village *of priests*,[1] and to mark where this was there are now two stone buildings like towers, from which a church has been made.

7 When the time of the Lord's suffering, as we have mentioned, came close, after the raising of Lazarus to life, Jesus came on the
135 Day of Palms | to Jerusalem. On the same day, when he had made the procession which I have mentioned before, he came back to the mountain slopes of Olivet. He was to stay there until Thursday, when he and his disciples attended the Supper of the Lord, in which he marked the end of the Old Covenant and the beginning of the New.

When the disciples inquired of him where he wished to hold the Passover, he sent some of them into the city, so that they could reach the place and prepare a room of some place to carry out this meal in the likeness of a sacrament: there is more about this in the Gospel: '*Go into the city, and you will find a man carrying a jar of water. Follow him*' and so on.[2] This Upper Room was found on *Mount Sion*,[3] in the same place where Solomon is said once to have built a marvellous house, which is mentioned in the Song of Songs: '*The tent King Solomon made for himself*' and so on.[4] This Upper Room on the upper floor is large and spacious, spacious enough to contain the mysterious Supper of the Lord with his disciples. There he identified his betrayer with guarded words, and the remainder of the disciples he strengthened with the message of his imminent suffering, and by *giving them* under the appearance of *bread his body to eat, and* under the appearance of *wine his blood to drink*,[5] saying, '*Whenever*' and so on.[6] |

136 When the supper had take place on the upper floor of this house, it is suitable that for the same mystical reason Our Lord should use the lower floor of the house to give an example of humility, in washing the disciples' feet. Whether you prefer this to have happened before or after the supper, according to the different interpretations of this passage relying on the verse in Saint John's Gospel, '*After supper he arose*' and so on,[7] is of little consequence.

[1] Quotation from R.6.2, derived from G.157.
[2] Mark 14.13.
[3] Quotation from R.6.4, derived from G.158.
[4] Song of Songs 3.7: Latin for tent is *ferculum*.
[5] Quotation from R.6.4, derived from G.158.
[6] 1 Cor 11.26.
[7] John 13.4.

But it is worth noting that the description of the event in the Church of Mount Sion also hints at different places. For in the left part of this church on the upper floor is a painting of the supper, and in the lower part, that is to say in the crypt, is shown a picture of the washing of the feet of the disciples.

When these two mysteries came to an end, Jesus went back again 8
to the *Mount of Olives* to pray. At the foot of this mountain *on the slopes*, he left his disciples behind, and went by himself from them, *a stone's throw* away, to *Gethsemane*. *He prayed to his Father, and said, 'Father, if it be thy will'* and so on. | *There he was physically* afraid, *and* 137
sweated as it were blood.[1] Coming back to his disciples and finding them sleeping, he especially rebuked Peter, and said, '*Could you not watch one hour with me?*' and to the rest of the *disciples*, '*Sleep on now and take your rest*' and so on.[2] Thus a third time he went back to the same place, and said the same prayers to God the Father, and was at length strengthened by the Father, and by himself, inasmuch as he was God. Then a *third* time he came back to the disciples, and said '*Watch and pray*'.[3] The distinction between these places, that is to say where the disciples stayed behind, and where the Lord prayed, are clearly visible in the Valley of Jehoshaphat. For next to the large church there in which is the burial of the Blessed Virgin Mary, about which we shall speak below, there is on the right of the entry to the church a chapel and a cavern, where the sorrowful and tired disciples stayed behind, with the Lord going three times away from them, and three times coming back. There is now a picture expressing this commemoration. But the place where the Lord prayed is surrounded by a new church, called the Church of the Saviour. Out of its floor rise three uncut stones like small rocks, in which it is said that the Lord prayed, kneeling down three times. So the stones there are highly reverenced both in personal devotion and in the Sacrifice of the Lord's faithful. | To this cavern went our 138
Lord, knowing that Judas was approaching, surrounded by a crowd. For Judas, while the other disciples had been staying with the Lord after the Supper, went alone to the Jews and bargained with them to betray the Lord. He received thirty pieces of silver from them as the price of betrayal, and was then approaching with a crowd. Jesus knew all this, and said in the cave to his disciples,

[1] Luke 22.41: quotation from R.7.1, derived from G.159.
[2] Matt 26.40, Lk 4.44: quotation from R.7.1 derived from G.159.
[3] Matt 26.41: quotation from R.7.1, derived from G.159.

'*Rise, let us go. Behold at hand is*' and so on.[1] Thus he left Gethsemane. He was identified by Judas' kiss and arrested. He was bound up and led away by the cohort which came with Judas.

Moreover in this cavern there are pointed out five holes in a stone, as if marked by the five fingers of the Lord's hand. I repeat that it was the Lord, now arrested and being violently treated by his persecutors, and perhaps wanting to stay there. Whatever the truth of this, as we well know he could do more courageous and stronger things than this.

9 As we have said, our Lord was betrayed by his disciple, arrested
139 and bound by the Roman soldiers, | and then led to Mount Sion,
where at that time was *the Praetorium of Pilate, called Lithostrotos*, but *in Hebrew, Gabbatha*.[2] For at that period the best part and the major defence of the whole city was at the top of that mountain. The Tower of David was there, which was the lookout point and defence of the rest of the city, and like a mother and a steward held the lower part of the city like a daughter, saying, '*Speak, daughters of Sion*' and so on.[3] But afterwards the city in that place was destroyed, and moved by the Emperor Hadrian to another site where it is now, so this mountain is humiliated, and no equal to its former eminence, now that the Tower and the other buildings have been removed. Yet there is shown to this day the place where the Praetorium and the Tower of David used to be.

At that period next to the Praetorium and south of it was that great building where the Lord had supper with his disciples. Next to the Praetorium and to the east was a court, into which he was led as a prisoner, and the whole of that night he was kept there by the guards and the princes of the Jews, waiting with him until the hour to hold the court on the following morning. In this Praetorium *Peter thrice denied* the Lord before *the cockcrow*, and there, *when the*
140 *cocks were heard crowing*, | the Lord looked at him. Then *his conscience*
made him remember the word of Jesus, and he was truly sorry. He wept bitterly, and fled into the cave, which is now called 'Cockrow' and is commonly called 'Galilee'.[4]

On *Mount Sion* Christ *appeared* to his disciples,[5] and hence these verses are found inscribed on the west wall of the church:

[1] Matt 26.46.
[2] Quotation from R.7.1, derived from G.159.
[3] Matt 21.5.
[4] Quotation from R.7.1.
[5] Quotation from R.7.1, derived from G.155.

Christ, once he'd risen, did appear
To Galilee's disciples here.
Because of this, as you can see,
This place is called 'The Galilee'.[1]

In the road which goes down from Sion into the Valley of Jehoshaphat, below the Gate of Mount Sion, and above this cave, there is a church built whose liturgy is performed by Greek monks.

On the following morning, then, the unjust court was held, and Jesus was condemned. In some place in front of the Praetorium he was beaten, slapped, and spat on. He was dressed with a red robe, and pricked with the crown of thorns. This is described in an epigram placed there, which runs as follows:

Crowned is the man, who rules by right
This universe from depth to height.

A chapel marks that place, near the Great Church of Sion and to its north, and it contains a picture of the event, with an epigram running thus: |

The crowd a sentence doth request 141
Of guilt upon the Holiest,
And God himself can fight, and take
A scourging for his subjects' sake.
The Cross of Christ has come to aid
That Simon too, on whom it's laid.
He did not bear the Cross for naught,
Which all the saints to blessing brought.

From that place, after the sentence of the cross and of guilt was passed on him, they put the cross they had prepared on the shoulder of the Lord, in order that he should carry it away to the place of execution. This was so that the prophecy might be fulfilled: '*The government shall be upon his shoulder*'.[2] There happened to come there a man from Cyrene, whom they pressed into carrying his cross to the place of a Skull, for a mystery.

At that period next to the site of the ancient city there was the Place of a Skull outside the city, which was a place selected for
people condemned to death. Their heads were | shaved, their hair 142

[1] Quotation from R.7.1.

[2] Isa 9.6.

cut off, and the wind had made their unburied skulls rot and lose their skin. So it was that this was called '*The Place of a Skull*' or perhaps it may have been *the fact that it was for this reason that their heads were shaved, because they had been condemned.*[1] This place, called in Hebrew 'Golgotha', was in an old stretch of rock, just as everywhere today the most prominent places outside cities are given over to those condemned to punishment.

While the cross was being set up and fixed to the rock, Our Lord was bound up in a place which used to be *in the fields*,[2] and as it were in prison. The place is now marked by a kind of chapel, which is still called 'The Prison of Christ'. It is directly across from Calvary in the left apse of the Church. Other people think differently about this place, as I have heard myself when I have been present there.

Afterwards in the Place of a Skull, *by the command of Pilate and at the Jews' urging*, our Lord *took off his coat, and drank bitter vinegar* and the Roman soldiers fixed him to *the gibbet of the cross.*[3] While Jesus was suffering on it, John his friend took the responsibility advised by Jesus for Mary his Mother, in order *that a chaste man* might look after *a Virgin*, since Jesus said to his Mother, '*Mother, behold thy son!*'[4] This was a demonstration, it is stated by some people, to
143 John, | or rather to himself, as much as to say, 'I suffer in this way from being a son, a sonship I derive from your motherhood. But I have no miracles that I can work from that.' And he said a similar thing elsewhere at the wedding at Cana of Galilee: '*What have I to do with you, woman?*'[5] He said this to his mother, and *afterwards* to John, '*Behold thy mother*', in the sense of the love and service of a son.

In the Place *of a Skull, while the Victim of the world was suffering on the Cross, he promised to the robber who hung on his right, who asked pardon of him, the garment of immortality. And when he was pierced with a lance on the gibbet of the Cross he sent forth blood and water, and a drop of each of the liquids opened the eyes of Longinus, who had struck him,*[6] with a feeling of compassion and faith. He decided that Jesus should not live longer under his torture. Thus our Lord breathed his last on the gibbet of the Cross, and willingly laid aside his spirit. The veil of the Temple was rent from top to bottom, and the stone on

[1] Quotation from R.7.2
[2] Quotation from R.7.2.
[3] Quotation from R.7.2.
[4] Quotation from R.7.3. John 19.26–7.
[5] John 2.4.
[6] Quotation from R.7.3.

which the Cross had been fixed, in the very part which had been touched by his blood, was cracked in the middle. Through this crack his blood flowed down to a place below, where certain people say that Adam had been buried, and he was thus baptized in the Blood of Christ. To make this point more clear they say that | everywhere a dead skull is painted at the feet of the crucified one. 144
But Adam being 'baptized in the blood of Christ' means nothing more than that he is 'redeemed by the blood of Christ', because Scripture tells us that Adam was buried in Hebron. And the ugly face of a man which people used to paint underneath the feet of the crucified one rather means Death and the destruction of Death: this is why the Lord says, '*O Death, I will be your death*',[1] that is, your destruction.

The Place of the Skull is to the right of the entrance of the great church, and on the upper floor the famous rent in the rock is treated with great reverence, and is still today pointed out to those who come there. The upper part of this building is beautifully adorned with the finest mosaic. It contains the suffering of Christ and his burial, with suitable passages of witness from the prophets here and there.

Notice that in this place the Cross was either fixed in a round hole, which is still pointed out and open (into which people put offerings), or in that part where an upright pillar of round stone is shown. Certain people say it was the latter place. This seems right and suitable. For so far as this location is concerned it should be near the right of the chapel, and near the blood which was shed into the crack. And this location makes it necessary that the | face of the 145
Lord hanging on the Cross should have been turned towards the east.

Near that place on the upper floor at the right is placed an altar dedicated in honour to the Lord's Sufferings, and that whole area is called by the name of his Sufferings. But the lower floor of the Skull contains an altar beneath it. It is called 'The Altar of the Holy Blood', and the blood of the Lord is said to have flowed down to this point through the rift in the rock. The place behind the altar is marked today by a hollow in the rock, where a lamp hangs that is continually alight.

Outside at the entrance to the Skull:

[1] Hos. 13.4: see R.7.4.

This famous place of Calvary
Is truly sanctified:
For silver pieces given as price,
For Cross, for Dish, for Guide.
The title and the Blood of Christ,
That in his body's been,
Gives us salvation and redeems,
Protects and bathes us clean.

11 In the middle of the Priest's Choir and not far from the Place of
146 the Skull, is a marble table | on top and a network of iron chains
which is like an altar. Under it there are slabs in the pavement with circles inside them. They say that the navel of the world is marked there, according to the passage, '*Thou hast worked salvation in the centre of the earth*'.[1] In that place after the resurrection the Lord is said to have appeared to Blessed *Mary Magdalene*,[2] and the place is much venerated. A lamp also hangs inside. Also in the same place some people say that *Joseph begged the body of Jesus from Pilate*. On that day, that is Friday, *he took it down from the cross, reverently washed it, anointing it with* costly *liquids* and *spices, and wrapped it in clean linen. Nearby he buried it in a garden inside a tomb which he had newly dug out of the rock. From there Jesus descended to Hell to* set *man* free. In the same place the Lord *truly rose* from the dead, *the Lion of the tribe of Judah, having conquered Death. There the angel of the Lord appeared to the Holy Women. The stone had already been rolled back from the door of the tomb. And he announced that Jesus had truly risen from the dead,* saying, '*Go*, tell my brethren', and a second time, '*Tell his disciples and Peter*'.[3]

On the same day, when evening was approaching, Christ, *hiding under*
147 *the appearance of a traveller, appeared to two | disciples. They were on*
their way, as they complained about his death, to Nicopolis, *that is Emmaus, a town six miles* west *of Jerusalem. They entertained him as a guest, and recognized him at the breaking of bread, but immediately he disappeared.*[4] Then *he appeared to the apostles (without Thomas)* in *Mount Zion. The doors were closed and he said to them 'Peace be with you'.*[5] *Furthermore on the eighth day after that* he appeared on the same

[1] Ps. 74.12.
[2] See R.7.4, derived from G.162.
[3] Quotation from R.7.3, derived from G.161,168: Matt 28.10 and 7.
[4] Quotation from R.7.5, derived from G.164.
[5] Quotation from R.7.5, derived from G.165.

mountain to *Thomas with* the rest of the disciples, when *he offered him his wounds to touch*. Then *Thomas* said, '*My Lord and my God*'.[1] Illustrations of these appearances being made are in a place on Mount Sion, in a crypt of the main church, where our Lord has also been painted washing the feet of his disciples, and with a clear description of both events.

After his resurrection Jesus *also revealed himself by the Sea of* Tiberias, *and three times in the Sea to his disciples*,[2] and besides these appearances he was also seen elsewhere by many people, not only for proof of his resurrection which was already in the past, but our resurrection to come.

The arrangement of the monument containing the | sepulchre of 12/148
the Lord is that it is almost round in shape, and is decorated inside with mosaic. On the east there is an entry through small doors, and the square place before the tomb is a porch with two gates. Through one the people are sent in who are going into the monument and the tomb, and the other is an exit for the people to leave. In this porch are the guards of the Sepulchre. There is a third small door towards the Choir. To the west of this monument and at the beginning of the tomb is placed inside it an altar with a square covering, three of the walls of which are beautifully made with cast iron work. It is called 'The Altar at the Holy Sepulchre'. The whole monument has above it a large sort of round ciborium which is covered with silver above. It is raised up in the direction of the large hole in the larger building, which is open to the sky. This larger building is round, and goes round the Tomb in a circle some distance away. The outer wall is continuous, and is painted and decorated with many large pictures of saints, and lighted with many lamps. Closer to the tomb there are eight marble columns and the same number of square piers, adorned
with as many | marble panels inside. They stand up all round, and 149
hold up the inner wall beneath the roof, which, as we have said, is open in the middle.

There follow some verses, which are to be read in various places. On the space above the lintel of the Church of the Holy Sepulchre:

> Why, Woman, weepest thou?
>   Thou seek'st a man, yet him dost worship now!
> Thou should'st remember me.
>   But while I live, I'll not be touched by thee.

[1] Quotation from R.7.5, derived from G.166.

[2] Quotation from R.7.5.

In the space above the lintel of the inner entry to the Sepulchre of the Lord:

> This place bears witness, 'Christ is risen!'
> The guard an angel sent from heaven,
> And graveclothes – they bear witness too
> That Christ is our Redeemer true.

Inside, at the place where the Lord was taken down:

> By dearest friends it's mourned, and from the Cross
> Is lifted down this Flesh, to God most dear.
> For pitiful and poor their rightful King
> Did not refuse this suffering to bear.

Inside, near to the Sepulchre of the Lord:

> Our Christ is now with spices sweet
> Within the grave enchained. |
> 150 But righteous men will go to heaven
> By aid of merit gained.
> Let man delight, but Spirits cower,
> All Hell shall groan in fear.
> The death of Adam has been changed
> Now that our Christ is here.

And also there, but in the middle:

> While thus, within a tomb of rock
> The buried Christ doth hide,
> The burial of a man takes place
> But heaven is opened wide.

We have said that the columns of the number we have mentioned
are set in a circle. But towards the east their arrangement and
number is changed, owing to the fact that a new church has been
built there, to which this is the way through. This new church, a
new addition, contains a very wide Priest's Choir and a very long
sanctuary. In it is a main altar dedicated in honour of the Anastasis,
that is, of the Holy Resurrection. Above is a mosaic picture
declaring this, and it contains an image of Christ, with the keys of
151 hell broken, and rising, taking our old father | Adam with him.
Outside this sanctuary of the altar and inside the wall of the exterior

of the building there is a wide space, and round it there is, in this new building (just as in the monument that was there before) a wide space suitable for a procession. This happens every Saturday night from Easter to the Lord's Advent at Vespers in the Holy Sepulchre. It has the antiphon 'Christ being raised from the dead'. The text of this antiphon is inscribed outside the monument at the furthest corner in raised letters of silver. When this antiphon has been sung the Cantor begins immediately, 'But in the evening' and so on, with the Psalm 'Magnificat', and with the Collect of the Resurrection, 'Almighty and Eternal', with this versicle beforehand, 'The Lord is risen from the tomb'. In the same way throughout this period of the year the Mass is celebrated every Sunday, 'Resurrexi'.

At the east end of this new church, next to the Priest's Cloister, is | 13
a deep place like a crypt, and very peaceful, in which Queen Helena is 152
said to have found the Cross of the Lord. There is an altar dedicated to the honour of Queen Helena. This queen took away the greater part of this holy wood to Constantinople. The rest of the wood was left in Jerusalem, and is now kept safely and reverently in a place on the opposite side of the Church from Calvary.

This place, even though it was once sanctified by the pouring out of Christ's blood, in modern times, even though this was superfluous, was consecrated again by Their Reverences on the fifteenth of July. And from that ceremony these verses bear witness, inscribed by some one in gold letters on this place.

This place is holy, since Christ's Blood
Had hallowed it before:
Therefore no holiness we add
By blessing it once more.
The chapels that above the place
And all around do lie
Were consecrated at the dawn
Of fifteenth of July. |

Long ago in the past on that day too, in the same month, when 153
the Holy City was still held captive by the rule of the Saracens and other races, it was freed by the army of the Christians. The commemoration of this liberation is celebrated on the same day after the renewal of the commemoration of the Consecration. In the first Mass it is done by singing 'Be joyful, Jerusalem', and the

main mass is then celebrated of the Dedication: 'This place is terrible'. For on the same day were dedicated in this church four altars, that is the Main Altar, the one on the top floor in Calvary, and two on the opposite side of the Church, that is to say one in honour of Saint Peter, and the other in honour of the Protomartyr Saint Stephen. On the following day they have a solemn commemoration both in almsgiving and Prayer of All the Faithful Dead, and particularly for those killed on the occasion of the siege of Jerusalem, whose famous burial place is before the Golden Gate. On the third day is the Anniversary of the Noble Duke of blessed memory, Godfrey, who was the prince and master of that sacred
154 expedition, and born of the German race. | The whole city observes this in solemn fashion. There is a widespread distribution of alms in the main church, which was done at Godfrey's command whilst he was still alive.

Nevertheless, although every one is anxious for his own honour, the siege of the city is not ascribed to him with any German troops, who were not least in the labours and actions of that expedition, but only to the Franks. Hence also these detractors of our race deleted the epitaph of the famous Wicher, approved by many a famous deed, because they could not deny he was German. They replaced it with the epitaph of some French soldier, as may be seen by any one who goes there. For his coffin is still visible outside at a corner, between the main Church and the Chapel of Saint John the Baptist. But his name is missing, and is replaced by another. To approve this state of affairs, and give an indication of contempt for our men and approval for the Franks, this epigram is to be read, which is inscribed on the side of the monument:

When one more year its course would run,
Eleven centuries had gone
From Virgin's birth-pangs, and the sign
Of the Lord's day-star, soon to shine. |
155 When Phoebus' light had reached the morn
Of fifteenth of July, at dawn
Jerusalem was seized by Franks
Courageous in their powerful ranks.

Against which I say:

By Franks, not French, but Germans, all
  More powerful with the sword, I shall
Recount that after long campaign
  Jerusalem was seized again.
The Holy City was set free
  From various pagans' tyranny.
From Franconia, not from France
  Lord Wicher's and Lord Guntram's lance –
Duke Godfrey's too – by this agree
  About the truth of victory.

Although Duke Godfrey, and his brother Baldwin (who was crowned king in Jerusalem after him, a thing which beforehand out of humility the Duke had refused for himself) was on our side, few of our race remained with him. Many others went home to their native land with longing and with haste. So the whole city was to such an extent occupied by other nations, that is to say by Franks, Lotharingians, Normans, men of Provence, Alverni, Italians, Spaniards and Burgundians, who were also involved in that expedition, that no part of the city – not even the smallest open
space – was distributed to the Germans. | The Germans did not care 156
for land, and had no mind to stay there, and so the liberation of the Holy City was ascribed to the Franks, and the Germans' name passed over in silence. The Franks and the other races just mentioned rule this city and the surrounding province. But this province of Christianity would very soon have extended its frontiers southwards beyond the Nile and northwards beyond Damascus, if there had been as many Germans here as there were of them. We do not wish to stay longer in our discussion of these present-day affairs. So now let us go back to the matters we had in hand.

There is a large church on the Mount of Olives today, in the 14
middle of which is a large open space. This is the place of the Ascension of our Lord. From this place, when his disciples and the other men from Galilee, together with his mother, were looking on in wonder, he was taken up, carried by a cloud into the sky. He had beforehand given his disciples a command that they should not leave Jerusalem until they had received the Spirit, the Paraclete who had been promised by his Father, in order that they should have the fullest comfort. This happened on the tenth day after the Ascension

157 | of the Lord, and fifty days from the Lord's Resurrection, that is to say, on the Day of Pentecost. The disciples were assembled in the building we have described on Mount Sion, where our Lord is said to have had the Supper, and waiting for the promise to be fulfilled. In this place there is still a mosaic picture in the sanctuary, in the apse of the Church, which displays this fact. For there are the Apostles, who numbered twelve, and there are pictures of each of them. And the picture contains also a likeness of the Holy Spirit coming down on them in the form of tongues of fire on each of their heads. It has this epigram: '*Immediately from heaven there was the sound of the coming*' and so on.[1]

158/15 We have seen these places and briefly noted the things which happened there, and other places lying beside them. Now we wish to describe the new Holy Places newly built, and dedicated to the worship of God within the walls. I start with this neighbourhood with the fact that in this city Judas received the silver pieces for the betrayal of our Lord, with which were bought the field of *Akeldama, that is the Field of Blood*. This is still given over to the burial of *strangers*, even today, and is located *to the left of Mount Sion, beside the road which leads to Ephrata*. *Mount Gihon* is above, *joining* this field *in which King Solomon received the royal crown*,[2] and other kings used to be anointed on the same mountain.

And notice that our Lord *in the centre of Jerusalem raised a girl from the dead*[3] and did many miracles on her. Next to the Church of the
159 Holy | Sepulchre, which we have described above, on the opposite side towards the south, is a beautiful church erected in honour of Saint John Baptist. The hospital is next to it, in which in various houses a great crowd of sick people is collected, some of them women and some men. They are cared for, and every day fed at vast expense. The total of persons at the time when I was present I learned from the servitors talking about it, and it was two thousand sick persons. Between night and day there were sometimes more than fifty corpses carried out, but again and again there were new people admitted. What more can I say! This house feeds so many human beings outside and within, and it gives so huge an amount of alms to poor people, either those who come to the door, or those who remain outside, that certainly the total of expenses can in no

[1] Acts 2.2.
[2] Quotation from R.6.4, derived from G.153.
[3] Quotation from R.5.4, derived from G.143.

way be counted, even by the stewards and dispensers of this house. And apart from all these expenses to do with sick people and the other poor, the same house has many men instructed in every martial art, for the defence of the Land of the Christians against Saracen attacks, and keeps men in its castles everywhere.

Next to this | Church of John is a convent of nuns erected in 160
honour of Saint Mary. The beginning of it is very near the above-mentioned church, and it is called 'At Saint Mary Major'. Not far from there, on the same side of the square, is a convent of monks, in the sanctuary erected in honour of Saint Mary. It is called At Saint Mary Latin: and there the head of Saint Philip is held in great honour, and is shown to those who come for devotion and ask to see it.

Next to the street which runs down from the Tower of David to the Temple, and on the right near the Tower of David is a convent of Armenian monks erected in honour of Saint Saba, the Most Venerable Abbot. When he was still alive the Blessed Virgin Mary did many miracles for him. Not far from there one goes down beyond another street, and there is a great church in honour of Saint James the Great. Armenian monks live there, and they also have a large hospital to serve people of their own language. The head of the Apostle is reverently kept there. He had been beheaded
by Herod | and his body was placed in a ship in Joppa by his 161
disciples and they took it away to Galicia, but his head remained in Palestine. This head is still shown in that church to strangers who arrive there.

On the way down the same street, which goes to the gate by which one reaches the Temple, and on the right, is a cross street with a long portico. In this street is a hospital with a church, which has been newly built in honour of Saint Mary, and is called the House of the Germans. Few if any people of another tongue have anything good to say about it.

In the same street, towards the gate by which one goes to Mount 16
Sion, is a Chapel built in honour of Saint Peter. In its crypt, hidden deep down, it is said that there was the Prison in which Blessed Peter was bound with iron chains. He was guarded by soldiers outside and inside, and was carefully kept prisoner at the command of Herod. But the divine power tricked their care. For the same
night an angel | saved Blessed Peter. He went away between the 162
sentries with his iron chains broken and the doors open both of the

Prison and of the city. He was guided by an angel, and he got out unharmed saying, '*Now I know in truth that the Lord hath sent his angel*' and so on.[1] At the entrance to this little church the following verses are inscribed, which deal with the miracle performed there:

There, Peter, are your clothes! Awake!
You now are free your way to take.
Your chains that once had held you fast
Are burst asunder now at last.
'The door stands open! I'll avow
That Christ in love hath saved me now.'

In the cavern of this church are the chains, made famous by the Feast of Saint Peter which happened then. I celebrated Mass with a collect which well deserves to be uttered there:

> God, who didst cause Blessed Peter the Apostle to be freed from chains in this place, and to go away unharmed . . . and so on.

This little church is modest, and is not endowed with a large income nor adorned for worship is a way which would suit so great a miracle from God, and so great a prince of the Apostles.

163 The gate which leads | in the direction of Mount Sion is called '*The Iron Gate*', *which* opened *of itself for the angel*[2] and for Peter.

Opposite the court of the Temple, that is to the north, at the gate by which one goes to the Valley of Jehoshaphat, is a large Church built in honour of Saint Anne. In this church is shown in a picture by what divine ordinances and messages the Blessed Virgin Mary was conceived from her and Joachim, just as it is told at greater length in the Life of Blessed Anna. Her feast is on the same day as Saint James the Great, and is celebrated with great solemnity there. I was also present at it. In this church a college of nuns – holy women these – serves God. On the way out of this Church is the Sheep Pool. . . .[3] . . . |

164 From the same street along which one goes out of the Gate of Jehoshaphat and above, in a neighbouring street which runs up

[1] Acts 12.11.
[2] See Fretellus *Patri H.*58 and Acts 12.10, recording an event of the biblical period.
[3] Quotation from R.5.4, derived from G.143f.

from this one, is a church, right up near the wall of the city. This is built in honour of Saint Mary Magdalene, and there are the Jacobite monks of whom we have spoken above, and we know what is said by them. In the street just mentioned from the Valley of Jehoshaphat one goes directly towards that street which leads to the Gate of Saint Stephen. And from the north you go in the direction which eventually leads into the triple street where a great many different goods are on sale, and to the Great Church of the Holy Sepulchre. In the middle of that street is an old stone arch, under the shadow of which the Blessed Virgin Mary is said to have rested with her happy and blessed Son. He was still a small baby, and she sat down to rest and give him milk. A picture placed there shows this event. This place, which is slightly removed from the thoroughfare by the buildings round it, has no church to mark it, but it is still held as a place of reverence and prayer.

Then from the street from the Gate of Saint Stephen you go directly up along the side of the Church of the Holy Sepulchre, and
a little way from it towards the north | there is a small street, near 165
which is a little church of the Syrians. The holy body of Saint Chariton the Martyr rests there, and is held in great reverence by the Syrian monks. It is almost a whole body, and is kept in a small wooden box. The lid is lifted up and shown to the pilgrims who come. This holy father was with his monks in a monastery near the River Jordan, and for confessing the name of Christ was killed by the Saracens.

. . . [1] . . . Naaman the General of Syria was not sent to that 17
water [that is, the Pool of Siloam], but to the Jordan by Elisha the Prophet. He should wash there three times and be cured of his leprosy. When Naaman understood it he was indignant and said, '*Are not Abana and Pharpar better rivers?*'[2] that is to say of his own province. At length he agreed to the advice of his servant. | He
obeyed the advice of the Prophet and was cured. . . . [3] . . . 167

In the Valley of Jehoshaphat James the son of Alphaeus *was buried, who was thrown down headlong*, as it is said, *from the Temple.*[4] In that Valley there is a beautiful Chapel in which there are signs of his burial, and these verses are inscribed above:

[1] Quotations from R.7.6, 6.1, 6.2, 6.1, derived from G.172f, 181, 177.
[2] 2 Kings 5.12.
[3] Quotations from R.6.1, derived from G.151f.
[4] Quotation from R.6.1, derived from G.154.

Because Alphaeus' son the Jews
Despite their laws divine accuse,
His death approached when he became
Defender of God's love and Name.
Alphaeus' son, when he was thrown
From eminence of Temple down,
Was hither dragged towards this cave,
And here was buried in his grave.

Then, *afterwards*, the Apostle of God was *transferred to Constantinople.*[1]

In the Valley of Jehoshaphat King Jehoshaphat was buried under a narrow pyramid,[2] whose name is the name of the whole Valley. Translated it means 'The Valley of Judgement', according to the verse, '*I will gather all nations*' and so on.[3] On each side of this Valley there are caves, in which people in the religious life live as hermits. |

168 The whole valley belongs to the monastery at the head of it, which is above the bed of the Brook Kidron, and next to the garden in which the Lord often used to meet with his disciples. In the crypt of this monastery the burial place of the Most Blessed Virgin Mary is pointed out, about which we have a great deal to say.

18 On the day of the death of the body of the Most Blessed Virgin Mary, the body was taken away and buried with due honour. All the Twelve Apostles of the Lord were present by their own will in the Church of the Valley of Jehoshaphat, and there, in the middle of the crypt, it was buried in a tomb. This is adorned with marble tablets and excellent painting of various colours. On her burial place, even though her body is no longer there, there is excellent marble panelling and a lantern like a ciborium on top, made of silver and gold. This epigram is inscribed on it:

'Jehoshaphat' this Valley's called.
The path to heaven is here installed.
In God she trusted, Heaven's Queen,
Here Mary would have buried been. |

[1] Quotation from R.6.1, derived from G.154.
[2] Quotation from R.6.1, derived from G.154.
[3] See Joel 3.12.

But hence she was raised up on high, 169
She sought, inviolate, the sky:
The Captive's Hope, their Light to see,
Who can their Way, their Mother be.

When the blessed body had disappeared, and since as it is said that according to Hebrew custom the tomb was visited and inspected on the eighth day after death, her body was not found. And hence it is a reverent belief that not only her soul, but also her body was taken up triumphantly by her dear Son. Jerome seems to state this by hesitation rather than assertion in the letter *Cogitis me, o Paula et Eustochium*, and so on.[1] But whatever the true answer, we believe that the Blessed Virgin Mary, by this fact alone, that she was able to bear her Creator, would be worthy of all blessedness, not only in the soul but also in the body. And her Son, in his perfect goodwill and power desired it and could do it. Thus this tomb of hers is honoured and reverenced as, so to speak, a spouse, and a place worthy of like honour to that which is given to the sepulchre of her dear Son.

In the entrance to this crypt there is a painting to be seen, and this inscription:

Inheritors of life that's new
Come, praise our Lord, because to you |
He gave that life which can regain 170
Salvation for the world again.

This inscription accompanies a picture of Saint Jerome on the left.

Her Sepulchre is shown at present as we say, in the middle of the Valley of Jehoshaphat. In her honour a church with wonderful marble panelling has been built there, in which everyone declares that she had been buried. On the right of this church's entry is a picture of Saint Basil, containing these words:

Against Christ's Mother's nobleness,
Against her heavenly might
Stood Julianus, so profane,
So savage in the fight.

[1] 'Jerome', *Letter* 9 (*PL* 30.122), in fact by a ninth-century writer, Paschasius Radbertus.

When dead his body here they laid,
Obedient to her will,
To Queen of our Salvation then
Be praise and honour still!
Who chose to have
This place as grave.

This, and many other things in praise of the Virgin are placed beside the painting. And on the inner part of the walls which are on either side of the Tomb and on the ceiling, the inscriptions are these.

On the right hand wall: 'Mary the Virgin is taken up to a heavenly couch' and so on.

After that in the circle: 'I saw a beautiful woman like a dove' and so on to 'a valley of lilies'.

Below that is the inscription: 'The daughters of Sion saw her. From this place the Glorious Virgin certainly ascended to the heavens, I ask you, rejoice, because unspeakably highly exalted she reigns with Christ eternally'.

On this side: 'Mary is taken up to heaven',

and on the other: 'The Holy Mother of God is taken up on high' and so on.

And in the middle: 'There is a host of angels standing round Blessed Mary sitting on her throne, through whom is declared the way open to the heavenly kingdom'.

At the foot of the Mount of Olives and towards the city, where now is shown the Burial of the Blessed Mary, is a hamlet called Gethsemane.

172/19 . . .[1] . . . | . . . [Bethlehem]. In the place of the Nativity of the Lord, in gold mosaic letters, these two verses are inscribed:

The light which angels contemplate,
The perfectness they emulate,
This One True God is brought to birth
By Virgin Mother here on earth.

[1] Quotation from R.4.4, derived from G.116–118.

. . .[1] . . . |

Thus I have finished describing the Holy Places in the Holy City 27/189
Jerusalem. I started with the Church of the Holy Sepulchre, and then I went round to the Gate of David and returned to it again. I omitted a great many chapels and churches of minor interest, which hold people of every race and tongue. For there are Greeks, Bulgars, Latins, Germans, Hungarians, Scots, people of Navarre,
Britons, Angles, Franks, Ruthenians, | Bohemians, Georgians, 190
Armenians, Jacobites, Syrians, Nestorians, Indians, Egyptians, Copts, Capheturici, Maronites and many others, which it would be a long task to list. But in these men we make an end to our book. Amen.

[1] Other quotations in chapter 19 to 26.
19. R.4.4 derived from G.120–22, 124f.
20. R.2.1, 8.2,3. 8.2, 2.2f, 8.3, derived from G.59, 201, 200, 198, 38, 30, 59.
21. R.1.2, derived from G.2–20.
22. R.3–6a, derived from G.25–44.
23. R.8.2, 8.1, 8.5, 8.4 derived from G.180, 194, 196, 202, 210, 228, 216, 215.
24. R.1.6–8, derived from G.42, 218, 220–21, 224–5, 47.
25. R.1.8f, 2.1 derived from G.46, 45, 49, 42f, 65, 51, 55f, 58, 53, 59, 64f.
26. R.2.2f, 1.5 derived from G.67–70, 74, 69.

THEODERIC

9 PROLOGUE

To all worshippers of the Holy and Undivided Trinity and particularly the lovers of our most gracious Lord Jesus Christ I write, Theoderic, the dung of all monks, a Christian.

Now grant us in Christ's sufferings
  To share in life's fragility,
That we may, joyful evermore,
  Be fit to share his royalty.

The things which in the Holy Places, the very places in which our Saviour revealed his corporeal presence, and did the ministry and the mysteries of his excellent humanity and our own redemption, we have taken pains to reveal in every detail. Everything in this book is either what we have known by being an eyewitness or what we have learned by true account from others. This is in order to satisfy by stating as much as we can the wishes of those who cannot personally follow us there, and cannot reach the Places with their eyes or hear them with their ears. Every reader will realise how much trouble this work has been to me, in order that in reading it or having it read he may learn to have Christ always in mind. Having him in mind he must be eager to love. Loving him, who suffered for him, he must suffer with him. Suffering with him he must be filled with desires. Being filled with desires he must be absolved from his sins. Absolved from his sins he must follow his grace. And following his grace he must reach the Kingdom of Heaven, which he may be pleased to confer, who with the Father and the Holy Spirit lives and reigns throughout all ages. Amen.

THE BOOKLET NOW BEGINS ON THE HOLY PLACES AS TOLD BY THEODERIC

As appears to all people reading the pages of the Old or New Testaments the land of Canaan was given to the twelve tribes of the Israelite people in possession by divine ordinance. It was divided into three provinces of which the names were Judaea, Samaria and Galilee. And in old times it had a great number of cities, villages, and hamlets and the cities' sites and names were known to every one in ancient times, But by people of today, who have come from somewhere else, and are not native to the land in which they dwell, the names of most of them are unknown, except for a few, which we shall mention in their proper place. 1

For when our dearest Lord Jesus Christ had | paid the price of his 10
blood, which with bloody hands the godless Jews poured out on the cross, Vespasian and Titus, the Roman princes, entered Judaea with their army. They razed the Temple and the city to the ground, they destroyed all the cities and villages in Judaea, and when they had driven out those murderers from their own possessions, they forced them to go away to other nations. For this reason all the deeds and property lists were erased, so that if some vestiges remain of some of the places, nearly all the names are changed.

First we must say something about Judaea, which is recognised 2
as the head of the Kingdom of the Jews. This is what we have discovered through our own eyes and ears. In Judaea the Holy City of Jerusalem is placed like an eye in a head, and from it by the Mediator, our God and Lord Jesus Christ, has poured out to all nations grace, salvation and life. On the west Judaea touches the Great Sea, on the south it is divided by the desert from the mountains of Arabia and Egypt, on the east the boundary is the Jordan River, and on the north it ends with Samaria and Idumaea. Most of Judaea is mountainous, and all round the Holy City it has high hills. But all its boundaries are lower down, so that from any of them it would be a journey up to Jerusalem. The mountains themselves are in several places rough, with very hard blocks of stone. But in other places the stone in them is very good for cutting, and in several places they have precious stone, Parian marble both red and in other colours. Moreover, wherever among all the stony places a patch of earth can be found, it can be reckoned

that it is capable of producing any kind of fruit. Therefore we have seen mountains and hills full of vines, olive trees and figs, and have also seen valleys which are full of fields and orchards.

3 On the very top of the mountains, as Josephus and Jerome bear witness, is located the city of Jerusalem, This is held to be holier and more famous than any other city or place in the world, but not because it is holy in itself or for itself. It is holier because it is illuminated by the presence there of our God and Lord Jesus Christ and of his good Mother, and the fact that all the Patriarchs, Prophets and Apostles have lived and taught and preached and suffered martyrdom there. Though there are higher mountains round Jerusalem which look down on it, it still remains on its own mountain top, and is a hilly city. Hence it happens that it steals the
11 view, and | all the mountains which surround it look at it. Then between Mount Moriah (on which is placed the Temple of the Lord) and the Mount of Olives (which raises its summit higher than the other mountains) lies the Brook Kidron and the Valley of Jehoshaphat. The valley starts by the Mount of Joy, from which one comes into the city from the north, then goes down past the Church of Blessed Mary which is called by her name, and by the tomb of Jehoshaphat, from whose death it takes its name. Thereafter it goes down near the Pool of Siloam, and another valley meets it. This goes up past the new cisterns between Mount Sion and the field of Akeldama and goes round the right hand corner of the city, enclosing two walls. Then the first valley becomes very deep. But the Tomb of *Jehoshaphat in* the middle of *the valley* is built with masonry in the form of *a pyramid.*[1] Round it is a great number of dwellings of servants of God, that is hermits, who all belong to the Abbot of Blessed Mary. The city stretches lengthwise from north to south and in breadth from west to east, and is firmly united on its mountain top by towers, walls and bulwarks over the valleys we have mentioned. A valley or a ditch is placed outside the walls, and they are defended with a wall, bulwarks and fosses, which they call a barbican.

The city has seven gates, of which six are firmly locked every night until after dawn. But the seventh is blocked with a wall, and only on the Day of Palms and at the Exaltation of the Holy Cross is it opened. Even though the city is oblong, it has five angles, of

[1] See John of Würzburg (Jwü) 17, p. 167.

which one goes inward. Underfoot nearly all its streets are made with closely-lodged large stones, and up above there are many with stone roofs, and everywhere amongst these there are windows arranged to let in light. The houses have carefully-made walls stretching up to a considerable height, but their roofs are not raised up in our manner with beams, but are a flat shape, and of equal height. The rain which falls on them is led into cisterns, and they use no other water, because they have none.

Wood there, whether for carpentry or for firewood, is expensive, since Mount Libanus, which is the only place which has much timber, cedars, cypresses and fir trees, is not only far away from the city, but also no one can go there on account of ambushes by the Gentiles.

The Tower of David is incomparably strong, made of squared 4
blocks of enormous size. It is next to the south[1] | Gate by which the 12
road goes towards Bethlehem, and its site is next to the newly-built dwelling and palace, which is heavily defended with ditches and barbicans, and is now the property of the King of Jerusalem. It is sited on the citadel of Mount Sion, and this is why it says in the Book of Kings, *'David captured the citadel of Zion'*.[2] As far as the breadth of the city is concerned the Tower is situated at about the level of the Temple of the Lord, and it has on the south Mount Sion, and on the east the Mount of Olives.

Mount Sion extends from this Tower to the Church of Blessed Mary, situated outside the walls, and from this Church almost to the Palace of Solomon, and goes up to the road which joins the Beautiful Gate to the Tower. It is wider than the Mount of Olives but lower. Given that Mount Moriah, the location of the Temple of the Lord and the Palace of Solomon, overlooks the Valley of Jehoshaphat and is a great hill, Mount Sion stands as high again over it as Mount Moriah stands above the Valley of Jehoshaphat.

In the *Field of Aceldama*, which is separated from Mount Sion only by a valley, *is the burial place of strangers.*[3] In it is the Church of the Saint and Virgin and Mother of God Mary. It is also where on the Holy Day of Palms we buried a brother who had died. His name was Adolf and he was born in Cologne. This *Field* lies next to *Mount Gihon, in which*, as the passage in the Book of Kings puts it, *Solomon received the royal crown.*[4]

[1] The reading is 'south'. [2] 2 Sam 5.7. [3] See Jwü 15, p. 158.
[4] See Jwü 15, p. 158: 2 Sam 5.7. The earlier manuscript (*Cod Vindoboen* 3529) wrongly corrects 'gyon' to 'Syon'.

Of the other buildings, public or private, we have found little or nothing to say, except for the House of Pilate, which is next to the House of Saint Anne the Mother of our Lady, and near the Pool of the Sheep. And of all the work that Herod did, as mentioned by Josephus, and as seen by me who have observed it closely, there is nothing that remains but one side of the Palace called Antonia, and the Gate which is just outside the court.

5 It now remains for us to describe the Holy Places on account of which the city itself is called holy. We thought it best to begin at the Holy of Holies, that is at the Sepulchre of the Lord. The Church of the Holy Sepulchre, full of marvellous workmanship, is said to have been founded by Queen Helena. Its outer wall goes round in the curve of a circle and makes the church round.[1] The place of the Lord's Sepulchre occupies the centre of this church, and its general arrangement is this. There is a building erected over the Sepulchre, which is finely decorated with marble panels. It is not a completely circular building, but from the circle two little walls project
13 towards the east, | and meet a third. They contain three doors, three feet wide and seven feet high, of which the first opens to the north, the second to the east, and the third to the south. One goes in by the door on the north, and out by the south, but the eastern door is there to be used by the guards of the Sepulchre.[2] Between these three doors, and a fourth by which one goes into the Sepulchre itself, there is an altar, small but venerable, where the body of the Lord, before it was put into the Sepulchre, is said to have been placed by Joseph and Nicodemus.

Then, over the entry to the Sepulchre which is behind the altar, according to a mosaic picture, the Lord is placed in the Sepulchre which was lent by these people. Our Lady his Mother stands there, and the Three Maries, well-known from the Gospel, with their phials of ointment, and presiding over them the angel himself. He has rolled the stone from the Sepulchre and says, *'Behold the place where they laid him!'*[3] Between the roof and the Sepulchre itself there is a long semicircular line of writing which contains these verses:

This place bore witness, 'Christ is risen',
And guard, an angel sent from heaven,
And grave-clothes. We bear witness too
The Christ is our Redeemer true.[4]

[1] See Jwü 12, p. 148. [2] See Jwü 12, p. 148. [3] Matt 28.6. [4] See Jwü 12, p. 149.

All these things are depicted in very delicate mosaic work, and this whole small room is decorated with the same work. Both the doors have very enthusiastic guards, who will not allow less than six or more than twelve to go in, for the place is too cramped to receive more. Furthermore they compel the people, after they have worshipped, to go outside the door.

The mouth of the Cave cannot be entered by any one without bending his knees. But arriving there he finds the treasure for which he has longed, the Sepulchre in which our most benevolent Lord Jesus Christ rested for three days. It is wonderfully decorated with Parian marble, gold, and precious stones. In the side it has three round holes through which travellers give the kisses they have for so long desired to give to the stones on which the Lord lay. It is two and a half feet wide, and a man's cubit and a foot long. The floor which is between the sepulchre and the wall has enough space for five people with their faces towards the sepulchre to kneel down.

Outside round the Chapel ten columns are arranged which, with the arches placed on them, make a circle. On this a cornice is placed
containing the scriptural passage inscribed in gold: | *'Christ being* 14
raised from the dead will never die again. Death no longer has dominion over him. In that he lives he lives to God.'[1] But at the head of the tomb and towards the west there is an altar surrounded by iron walls, doors and bars. It has a panel of cypress decorated with coloured pictures, and a roof of the same material which is above the walls. The roof of the Chapel consists in gilded plates of copper. In the middle is a round hole around which a circle of small columns is placed, and the little arches above support a roof like a ciborium, Over the roof is a gilt Cross and above it is placed a Dove, which is also gilded. Between the two columns above the main arches, that is in every small arch, single lamps hang round in a circle. And similarly between the lower columns all round two lamps hang in each opening.

Furthermore around the lower arches there are verses inscribed in each arch, which we tried to read – in vain in some of them, because of the fading of the colours. But we were able generally speaking to understand six in three arches:

[1] Rom 6.9f. Jwü 12, p. 151 says that this is the antiphon for vespers, and states that the letters were in silver.

He came unto this place so low
That he created long ago.
And thou, who now my Tomb shall see,
Thyself shall mine own Temple be!
O how joyful that we
This the heavenly Lamb see,
As the Fathers agree.
He at Ephrata bloomed,
To his Cross he was doomed.
In the rock he's entombed.
Taking Adam to the stars,
With the Devil he spars
And from trickery debars.
Causes Satan to fear,
Makes his power disappear,
And announces, 'I'm here!'

Round the iron wall which is, as we have said, at the head of the Sepulchre, with the chancels over it, is a line going round in a circle containing these verses:

Mortality is now erased,
For us by life replaced.
Freely he offers, falls the foe,
And washed away is woe.
The heavens rejoice and hell's subdued,
The Law is now renewed.
These things can teach us, Christ our Pride,
That thus this place is sanctified.

6 Moreover the floor of this Church is beautifully adorned with Parian and coloured marble. The Church itself is in the lower part held up by eight square columns, called pillars, and sixteen round columns which are made of a single stone. And the upper part (since the Church is roofed below and above like the Church at Aix) | is held up in the same way with eight pillars and sixteen columns. The lower cornice which goes round the whole church in a circle is all inscribed with Greek letters. But the area of wall which lies between the middle and the upper cornice is glorious with mosaic work of an incomparable kind. In the front of the Choir, that is, over the arch of the sanctuary, in the same style of work but

old, one sees the boy Jesus in the middle, painted with a most boyish and graceful face. To the left is his mother and to the right the Archangel Gabriel saying the well-known greeting, *'Hail, Mary, full of grace. The Lord be with thee, Blessed art thou among women and blessed is the fruit of thy womb.'*[1] This greeting is all round Christ the Lord in Latin and in Greek. Further round to the right the Twelve Apostles have their portraits as individuals in the same worksmanship, and each of them has in his hands gifts suitable to the mysteries of Christ. Among them the Emperor Constantine stands, for the good reason that with his mother Helena he was the founder of the Church. He stands in a window which is let shallowly into the walls, and he is apparelled in royal clothes. After the Apostles Michael the Archangel shines in brilliant clothes. On the left side there is a group of twelve Prophets, who all have their faces towards the beautiful Boy, and who once spoke venerable prophecies inspired by him, which they hold in their hands. In the middle of these, in the corresponding area to her son, stands the Saint and Queen Helena, with her magnificent attire.

On this wall the lead roof rests, held up by cypress beams. At the top they have a large open space, through which the light from above illuminates the whole church. It has no other windows.

Moreover the sanctuary, or Holy of Holies, was joined to the 7
body of this church with marvellous workmanship by the Franks, They celebrate in proper fashion the divine praises by day and by night, that is, with all the canonical Hours according to the Order of the Virgin Mary. They receive payment, and half what they are paid is credited to the Offerings of the Holy Sepulchre and the other half to the account of the Patriarch.

The Principal Altar is joined to the name and honour of the Lord and Saviour. Behind it is placed the Patriarch's throne, and over it is a great and venerable icon of our Lady, that hangs with an icon of
Blessed John the Baptist, and a third | icon of his paranymph Saint 16
Gabriel from the arches of the sanctuary. On the ceiling of this sanctuary is our Lord Jesus Christ. In his left hand he carries the Cross and in his right hand Adam. He looks regally into heaven, and he is entering heaven with an enormous stride, his left foot raised and his right foot still on the ground. Surrounding him are these people: his Mother, Blessed John the Baptist, and all the

[1] Luke 1.28, 42.

Apostles. Under his feet there is a line of writing, which stretches round the apse from wall to wall. It contains this inscription:

> O praise him who was crucified in the Flesh!
> O thank him who was buried for your sake!
> O bless him who has risen from the dead!

Above this on the upright line of the apse is inscribed: *'Christ went up on high to take captivity captive, and he gave gifts to men.'*[1]

Near the middle of this Choir is a small altar which is hollow, but much revered. On its floor is a small cross engraved in a round circle, and this is what it means: Joseph and Nicodemus, when they had taken the body of Jesus down from the Cross laid it there for washing.

Before the door of the Choir there is a sizeable altar which is only used for the Syrian liturgy. Thus every day when the Latins have finished their offices, the Syrians, either there in front of the Choir or in some apse of the church, are accustomed to chant their divine hymns. The Syrians have many small altars which are only usable and permitted by people of their own usage.

These are the traditions or sects which celebrate their office in the church in Jerusalem: the Latins, the Syrians, the Armenians, the Greeks, the Jacobins and the Nubians. All these have differences both in their rule of life and also in their divine office. The Jacobins during their feasts use trumpets, according to the practice of the Hebrews.

8 It is the custom in the Holy Sepulchre on the Holy Saturday of Easter when the sun rises, both in this church and in all the others througout the city, to extinguish physical light, and to await the light which comes from heaven. To receive this light one of the silver lamps is prepared, of which seven hang there in front of the Holy Sepulchre. Then the clergy and people wait in great and anxious expectation until the Lord sends his hand from on high. They pray very frequently, and among many prayers they chant, 'May God help, and the Holy Sepulchre!', and they pray with loud voices and not without tears.

17 In the mean while the Patriarch or | some of the other Bishops who have come for the receiving of the Holy Fire are often guided by a priest with a cross, in which a large piece of the Lord's Wood is

[1] Eph 4.8.

contained, and other relics of Saints. They come to visit the Sepulchre in order to find whether God has already put his gracious light in the vessel prepared for it. For sometimes it comes about the first hour, and sometimes at the third or sixth or ninth hour or even at the time of Compline. Moreover, sometimes it comes to the Sepulchre itself, sometimes to the Temple of the Lord, and sometimes to Saint John.

On the day when we poor people and other travellers were waiting for the Holy Fire, the Holy Fire came immediately after the ninth hour. Then, to the sound of church bells, the offices of the Mass were performed throughout the city, since the Baptisms and the other offices had been finished before. And as soon as the Holy Fire has come, before any one else except the Patriarch has lit his candle, it is a custom that it should be taken down to the Temple of the Lord.

By the western end, where you go out of the Church by over 9
thirty steps into the street, but before the actual exit, there is a Chapel in honour of Blessed Mary, of which the Armenians are in charge.

Then at the left of the Church on the north side there is a chapel in honour of the Holy Cross, where a great part of the venerable Wood is kept in a gold and silver vessel, which is under the guardianship of the Syrians.

Again on the same side, near this chapel and to its east, is a most venerable chapel, in which there is a venerable altar joined in honour to the Holy Cross. It has a great part of the Blessed Wood in a vessel of gold, silver, and precious stones, so that it can suitably be seen. This is kept with the greatest reverence in a beautiful niche, and Christians have the custom of carrying it, when necessity demands, as a saving sign against the pagans in battle. This chapel also is splendidly decorated with mosaic. This is the Cross which Heraclius, Emperor of the Romans, seized from Chosdroes, King of the Persians, in a battle he fought with him, and he returned it to the Christians.

Also, near this chapel and about twenty paces to the east, there is the entry to a dark chapel where another venerable altar exists. On the floor beneath the altar is a cross engraved. And there is said to
be the Prison of our Lord Jesus Christ | when he came from the 18
judgement of Pilate. He waited there when he had been brought to the place of his suffering, while they veiled his face, and the Cross

was being set up on Calvary in order that he could hang on it.

Next after this chapel stands an altar in honour of Saint Nicolas, and that is next to the gate of the enclosure wall which goes into the Cloister of the Canons, which is built round the sanctuary.

After the way into the Cloister but before you reach the other side of the Church, there is a picture of the Crucified One which is painted over the door of the Cloister, that excites all that see it to penitence. These words are written round it:

Thou passer-by, look here at me!
The pain I have was caused by thee.
For thee I suffer and repine
Because thy life has damaged mine.

10 From there you descend to the east down thirty or more steps to the venerable Chapel of Blessed Helena the Queen. It is sited outside, and has an altar dedicated in her honour. Here once again, one descends on the right side down fifteen or more steps into an underground cave. On the right of this cave in the corner is a hollow altar, and underneath a cross can be seen engraved on the floor. This is said to be the place where this Queen found the Cross. There is an altar here in honour of Saint James, Moreover this chapel has no windows, except a large hole at the top.

11 On the other side of the church, to its right, behind the Choir, stands a beautiful altar on which is part of a great column. Clinging to this the Lord was beaten and scourged.

From there you go south and before the door of the church five sepulchres are seen, of which one is finely executed in Parian marble and is next to the Choir. This belongs to the brother of the King of Jerusalem called Baldwin, the second King Baldwin, brother of Duke Godfrey. This is the inscription written over the tomb:

An equal here, King Baldwin lies,
To Judas Maccabee. He dies
His country's hope, the Church's pride,
And still of both courageous guide.
Kedar and Egypt feared his strength,
Damascus, murderous town, at length
And Dan to him the tribute gave.
Now mourn that he's in this small grave!

The third tomb is that of his brother, Duke Godfrey, who received
this very city, Jerusalem, when it had been invaded by Saracens and
Turks, by his sword and wisdom, and restored it to the Christians.
| The Patriarch had been exiled by the pagans, but he restored him 19
to his throne, and appointed clergy to this church and ordered
payment for them as they too fought for God. The fourth grave is
of the father of the present King, or Amalric, and the fifth the father
of the Abbess of Saint Lazarus.

Furthermore on the south a door is open through which it is possible to pass into the chapel which is situated under the bell-tower. This is dedicated in honour of Blessed John Baptist. The baptistry is also there, and from it one comes into a third chapel. But from the first there is a way up into the street by forty steps or more.

It remains now to speak of Mount Calvary, which like an eye in
the head shines in this church, and from which, through the Son of 12
God's death and the shedding of his blood, will come to us eternal
light and life. Before the entry of the main Church, where the gate
stands plated with bronze (and note that it is double) there are
roughly fifteen steps up to a small landing, with rails round it and
decorated with pictures. Above, watching the doors, are guards,
who allow as many pilgrims to enter as wish to, unless there is a
very big crowd. This is often apt to happen here, and if this is the
case someone might get crushed or be in danger of death.

From this porch one goes up three steps through a door. You are in a chapel which is more venerable and to be revered than any other place on earth. It is built with four vaults of great strength, and its floor is excellently laid with marble of many kinds. The roof of the ceiling is decorated with a very fine mosaic, which shows the Prophets, that is to say David, Solomon, Isaiah and several others, holding in their hands the writings of theirs which are in harmony with Christ's sufferings. No work on earth would equal that if only it were possible to see it clearly, But because the place has walls all round, it is somewhat dark.

The place where the Cross itself stood, on which the Saviour suffered death, is towards the east. It is mounted on a big step, made of excellent Parian marble on the left, and the hole shown is deep and almost wide enough to put one's head into. It is known that this is the hole in which the Cross was fixed,[1] and in it the

[1] See Jwü 10, p. 144.

pilgrims press their head and forehead to show love and reverence for the crucified one.

But on the right Mount Calvary goes down steeply, and in the
20 floor has a long, wide, and very deep | crack. It was cracked at the death of Christ. The blood which began above this horrific rock, flowing down the side is witnessed as flowing out at ground level. On top of the Mount the travellers are accustomed to place the crosses which they have brought there from their own countries, and we saw there a great heap of them, On Saturdays all the guards of the Calvary have the custom of burning them.

There is a venerable altar there, and during the whole day on Good Friday the office is performed by the clergy at that altar. On the left side of the altar on the wall there is a wonderfully beautiful picture of the Crucified One. Longinus stands on the right, his Lance piercing Christ's side, and on the left is Stephaton offering him vinegar with a sponge. There is also on his left his Mother and on the right John, and the outline makes these two larger. There are lines of Greek writing written round the picture. On the right of this altar Nicodemus and Joseph are taking down Christ, already dead, from the Cross, and this is written there: 'The Descent of our Lord Jesus Christ from the Cross.'

From here one goes down fifteen steps into the Church and one comes to the chapel called Golgotha, venerable but dark. At the back of it there is a deep window which shows to those who desire it the end of the crack which descends to here from Calvary. This is where the Blood of Christ is said to be preserved, which flowed down through the crack.

Moreover, through the arch with which Golgotha ends, that is the west side of Calvary, there can be seen a painted plate in the wall, on which these verses appear, written in gold letters:

This place is holy, since Christ's blood
Had hallowed it before;
Therefore no holiness we add
By blessing it once more.
The chapels that above the place
And all round do lie
Were consecrated on the dawn

Of fifteenth of July.
By Patriarch Fulcher and the rest
Of holy bishops they were blessed.[1] |

Before the face of the Church and between the doors the Lord 21
Christ stands in a goodly dress, as if he had just risen from the dead. At his feet Mary Magdalene lies on her face, but not touching his feet, to whom the Lord gives a manuscript containing these verses:

Why, woman, weepest thou?
Thou seek'st a man, yet him dost worship now!
Thou shoulds't remember me.
But while I live I'll not be touched by thee.[2]

On going out of the Church towards the south there is a kind of 13
square court made of squared stones, and on the left side of it, outside and next to Golgotha, there is a chapel in honour of the Three Maries, which is occupied by the Latins. Further to the south stands another chapel of which the Armenians are in charge, and beyond that stands another little chapel. But on the way out of this court to the left is a roofed street full of things for sale. The forum where things are sold is in front of the church. Closer in front stand six columns with arches above, and on the road from the Temple[3] towards the south, the Church and Hospital of John the Baptist. I would not trust any one else to believe it if I had not seen with my own eyes how splendidly it is adorned with buildings with many rooms and bunks and other things poor people and the weak and the sick can use. What a rich place this is and how excellently it spends the money for the relief of the poor, and how diligent in its care for beggars. Going through the Palace we could in no way judge the number of people who lay there, but we saw a thousand beds. No king or tyrant would be powerful enough to feed daily the great number fed in this house. And it is not surprising, for besides the properties they have abroad, whose quantity is not possible to calculate, they possess almost all the cities and villages which once belonged to Judaea and were destroyed by Vespasian and Titus. They and the Templars have put into use all the fields

[1] See Jwü 13, p. 152. A paragraph has been misplaced here. It should be in chapter 14. See John of Würzburg chapter 4.

[2] See Jwü 12, p. 149: the words 'while I live' are an addition to *Cod. Vin.* 3529.

[3] Perhaps the reading should be *ex opposito* (see Jwü 15, p. 159, line 1) rather than *ex templo*.

and vineyards, and set up military posts and well defended camps throughout the whole region against the pagans.

Then immediately to the east stands the Church of Blessed Mary, in which in obedience to an Abbess nuns daily celebrate divine praises. This place is said to be dedicated to Blessed Mary because she was said to have been sent there at our Saviour's command, while he was being tortured on the way to his sufferings, and to have been taken to one of the rooms which were there.

Immediately to the east of this another church is located, which is also consecrated to our Lady, for the reason that when our Lord
22 underwent the suffering | on the Cross for our salvation, she fainted through her great sorrow, and was borne by people there into an underground cave. There, carried away by sorrow, she lost control of herself. She tore her hair, and some of the hair of her head is preserved today in this church in a glass bottle. In the same church there is the head of Blessed Philip the Apostle which is contained in a decorated gold vessel, the arm of Saint Simeon the Apostle, and the arm of Saint Cyprian the Bishop. Monks under a rule and in obedience to an Abbot serve God in that church.

14 From here going a little southwards down a street, one arrives at the Beautiful Gate of the Temple and to the Temple of the Lord. One goes up from the lower court to the upper by twenty-two steps, and from the lower court one goes into the Temple. In front of these steps in the lower court one goes down twenty-five steps or more into a great Pool. From this, it is said, there are underground passages to the Church of the Holy Sepulchre, and this is how it is said that the Fire which is kindled there on Holy Saturday is taken to the Temple of the Lord. To this Pool the victims for the Temple of the Lord must have been taken down, since according to a commandment in the Law they had to be washed.

The outer court is double the size or rather more than the inner one, and the floor of this and the inner court are paved with big wide stones. Two sides of this outer court still stay as they were, but the other two have passed into the private possession of the Canons and Templars, and in them they have made houses and gardens. Above the steps, in front of which as we have mentioned, the Pool is located, there stand four columns with arches, and there there is the tomb of some rich man, surrounded by iron lattice-

work and made of alabaster beautifully carved. On the right, above
the southern steps there are two arched columns and on the left
there are three. Furthermore to the east there are fifteen double
steps by which one goes up from the Golden Gate to the Temple,
and following this number the Psalmist composed | fifteen Psalms. 23
Above these too there stand columns. Moreover on the south there
are two small houses placed at the two angles of the upper court, of
which the one to the west is said to have been the School of Blessed
Mary.[1]

Also, between the Temple and the two sides of the outer court, that is the east and the south, a large stone is placed like an altar. According to what certain people say has been a tradition passed on to them, it is the mouth of a Pool which is there, and according to the opinion of others it marks the place where Zachariah the son of Barachiah was killed.[2] In the north part there is the Cloister and outbuildings of the Canons.

Around the Temple there are big pools beneath the pavement, and between the Golden Gate and the fifteen steps there is a big pool, old and ruined, and in ancient times the victims who were to be offered were washed there.

The lower part of the Temple is clearly an octagon. This lower 15
part up to the centre is decorated with marble of fine quality, and
from the centre to the top, where the roof joins, the circle is most
beautifully decorated with mosaic. The circle itself which goes
around the whole building of the Temple contains the following
inscription. It starts on the front, that is the west entry, and
according to the direction in which the sun goes round, it is read as
follows.

On the front:

Eternal peace on this House be
From God the Lord eternally.

On the second side:

The temple of the Lord is holy, God's labour and sanctification.

On the third side:

[1] A paragraph reproducing John of Würzburg, 4 ('On the twenty-first . . . three years old' and the additional verse ending 'the Virgin feeds') is misplaced in *Cod. Vin.* 3529, fol. 196r to stand here. Clearly it applies to the Temple.

[2] See Jwü 4, p. 23.

This is the house of the Lord, firmly built.

On the fourth side:

Lord, in thy house all praise thy glory.

On the fifth side:

Blessed be the glory of the Lord from this Holy Place.

On the sixth side:

Blessed are they who dwell in thy house, O Lord.

On the seventh side:

Truly the Lord is in this Place, and I did not know it.

And on the eighth:

Well founded is the House of the Lord on a firm rock.[1]

Moreover on the east, beside the Church of Blessed James, a column is shown on the wall in mosaic over which this description has been written 'Columna Romana'. The upper wall is planned as
24 a more narrow circle than the octagon, and is held up inside by arches. Its roof is lead, and at the top of it there is a large ball and a gilt cross on top.[2]

One enters and goes out by four doors, each one of which faces one of the cardinal points. The church rests on eight square piers and sixteen columns, the wall and ceiling of which are finely decorated with mosaic. Round the Choir are four arches or | piers, and eight columns, which are there to hold up the inner wall with its very high roof.

Over these arches of the Choir there is a line of writing going round in a circle, which more precisely contains this inscription: '*My House shall be called a house of prayer,*[3] *says the Lord. In it whoever asks receives, whoever seeks finds, and to the person who knocks it shall be opened. Ask and you shall receive. Seek and you shall find.*'[4] In an upper circle, which is going round like the other one, this inscription is written: '*Hear, Lord, the singing and the prayer which thy servant prays before thee, O Lord, that thine eyes may be open and thy ears bent towards*

[1] See Jwü 4, p. 127, who gives the inscriptions in a different order.
[2] See Jwü 4, p. 126.
[3] See Jwü 4, p. 125. The rest is the First Lesson for the Mass of the Dedication.
[4] Matt 21.13, 7.8, 7.7: Antiphon at Communion of the Mass of the Dedication.

this house by day and by night. Look down O Lord from thy sanctuary, and from thy lofty dwelling in heaven.'[1]

In the entry of the Choir there is an altar in honour of Blessed Nicolas, enclosed in an iron wall, and above it is a frieze containing these words:

In the thousandth year, one hundred and one,
Fourth indication, epact eleven.

and on the left side:

From the capture of Antioch the 74th year, and of Jerusalem 63rd.

and on the right side:

Tripoli 62nd, Berytus 61st, Ascalon 11th years.

But on the east at that side of the choir there is a place with an iron wall all round, and doors, and it is held to be worthy of great honour, since it is where our Lord Jesus Christ, when he was brought to the Temple with his oblation on the fortieth day after his birth, was offered by his parents. At his entry into the Temple the old man Simeon took him in his arms, and took him away to the place of offering, and on the front of this place these verses are written:

The Virgin's Son presented here,
The King of Kings, the boy most dear,
He makes this spot a holy place,
And this most rightly is the case.[2]

Next to that place, and hardly a cubit away, is placed that stone on which the Patriarch Jacob once laid his head. He was sleeping on it and he saw a ladder on which there were angels going up and down. He said, *'Truly God is in this place, and I did not know it.'*[3] The front of this place contains these verses:

Though Father Jacob's body sleeps
His inner mind awake he keeps.
He saw the ladder heavenward laid
And here from stones an altar made.

[1] 1 Kgs 8.28, Deut 26.15. [2] See Jwü 4, p. 122. [3] Gen 8.28.

16 Going on from here through the eastern door one enters the Chapel of Blessed James, the Apostle, and Brother of the Lord. It is where he fell headlong from the pinnacle of the Temple, had his
25 brains beaten out by a fuller's club, and died by the hands | of the godless Jews. First he was buried in a place near the Temple in the Valley of Jehoshaphat, and afterwards he was honourably (as befits him) transferred to this place for burial. Over his grave the following epitaph is written:

Speak, stone and tomb, and answer those
Who ask 'Whose bones do you enclose?'
'They are of James the Just. He lies beneath
This old memorial place of death.'

This is a round-shaped church, wider at the bottom and narrower at the top. It is held up by eight columns, and well decorated with pictures.

Going away from this through the same door, behind the porch and to the left, there is a square place, five foot broad and long, in which our Lord stood when he was being asked about Jerusalem, which they say is in the centre of the earth. He made this reply, 'This place is called Jerusalem!' And behind the porch not far from this place to the north, there is another place containing those waters which Ezekiel the Prophet saw coming from the Temple on the right side. As one goes back into the main church there is an open porch on the south next to the Choir, and it is below the Choir. Down almost forty-five steps one goes into the crypt, where the Scribes and Pharisees brought the woman taken in adultery to the Lord Jesus and accused her. The reverend Master forgave her sins and freed her from their condemnation. After her example, absolution is customarily given there to travellers.

This church has thirty-six windows below and fourteen above, which added together make fifty. It is consecrated in honour of our Lady Saint Mary, to whose honour the main altar is joined.

Also this Church is said to have been founded by Blessed Queen Helena and her son, Emperor Constantine. Let us see then how many times and by whom this temple was built or destroyed. As one reads in the Book of Kings, King Solomon was the first to build a Temple to the Lord, by divine command, and he built it with vast expense. It was not then round, as it appears now, but oblong. This Temple remained until the time of Zedekiah, King of

Judah, who was captured by Nebuchadnezzar, King of Babylon. He was taken captive to Babylon, and with him Judah and Benjamin were similarly taken captive and exiled to the land of the Assyrians. Soon Nebuzaradan, his chief cook,[1] came to Jerusalem with his army, and burned the Temple and the City. This was the
first | destruction of the Temple. 26

After seventy years of captivity, the children of Israel came back to the land of Judah. Under the leadership of Zerubbabel and Ezra, with the favour and permission of Cyrus, King of the Persians, they rebuilt the same temple in the same place, and, as best they could, decorated it. But in rebuilding the Temple and the City together, they held, so it is said, in one hand the stones and in the other a sword, because of the constant attacks of the Gentiles living round. This therefore was the second rebuilding of the Temple.

The same city, as one can read in the History of the Maccabees, was not entirely, but at any rate in greater part destroyed by Antiochus, King of Syria. The decoration of the Temple was pulled down, the sacrifices prohibited, the walls destroyed, and the City as well as the Temple was made like a desert. Afterwards Judas Maccabee and his brothers with God's help routed Antiochus and set his generals out of Judaea. Then the Temple was rebuilt and renewed, and when the altar had been repaired they began to offer sacrifices again, and appointed priests.

This was the third repair of the Temple, which lasted till the time of Herod. He it was, as Josephus tells, who, even though the Jews opposed him, razed this Temple to the ground, and founded another with larger and more expensive workmanship.

This is the fourth rebuilding of the Temple, which lasted until the days of Vespasian and Titus, and they defeated the whole province, and thoroughly destroyed both the City and the Temple. This was the fourth destruction of the Temple.

After this, as was said just above, the present building we now see was constructed, to the honour of our Lord Jesus Christ and of his Reverend Mother by Queen Helena and her son Emperor Constantine. This, then, was the fifth renewal of the Temple.

One follows to the south, and there is the Palace of Solomon. 17
Like a church it is oblong and supported by pillars, and also at the end of the sanctuary it rises up to a circular roof, large and round,

[1] See Jwü 3, p. 118.

and also like a church. This and all its neighbouring buildings have
come into the possession of the Templar soldiers. They are
garrisoned in these and other buildings belonging to them. And
with stores of arms, clothing and food they are always ready to
guard the province and defend it. Below them they have stables
once erected by King Solomon. They are next to the Palace, and
their structure is remarkably complex. They are erected with
27 vaults, arches, and | roofs of many varieties, and according to our
estimation we should bear witness that they will hold ten thousand
horses with their grooms. A single shot from a cross-bow would
hardly reach from one end of this building to the other, either in
length or breadth.

Above them the area is full of houses, dwellings and outbuildings for every kind of purpose, and it is full of walking-places, lawns, council-chambers, porches, consistories and supplies of water in splendid cisterns. Below it is equally full of wash-rooms, stores, grain rooms, stores for wood and other kinds of domestic stores.

On the other side of the palace, that is on the west, the Templars have built a new house, whose height, length and breadth, and all its cellars and refectories, staircase and roof, are far beyond the custom of this land. Indeed its roof is so high that, if I were to mention how high it is, those who listen would hardly believe me. There indeed they have constructed a new Palace, just as on the other side they have the old one. There too they have founded on the edge of the outer court a new church of magnificent size and workmanship.

It is not easy for anyone to know how much power and riches the Templars have. For almost all the cities and villages, which were once frequent in Judaea and had been destroyed by the Romans, they and the Hospitallers have captured, and they have built castles everywhere and garrisoned them with soldiers. This is in addition to a great many properties they are known to possess in lands abroad.

18 The city wall surrounds the dwellings of the Templars to the south and east, but to the west and north the wall built by Solomon surrunds both their buildings and the outer court and the Temple. On the north side of the court there is one wall and one door of the ruins of the Antonia built by Herod.

This hill on which the Temple is placed was called in old times 'Moriah', in which King David saw the angel of the Lord stand,

and with drawn sword he slew the people, and when he said to the Lord, *'I it is who sinned. I have done wickedly, I pray that thou mightest turn thy hands to me and to my father's house. These people are sheep, what have they done?'*[1] On this hill was the threshing-floor of Araunah the Jebusite, which David bought from him for the building of the Temple.

From there through a gate a narrow passage goes between the city wall and the garden of the Templars, and one comes to the venerable Church which is called either 'At the Bath' or 'At the
Cradle of | the Lord and Saviour'. There the cradle of the Lord 28
Christ is shown towards the east, on a high wall, reverently displayed in front of a window. To the south there is a large stone shell to be seen on the ground in which the infant bathed. At the north is part of the bed of our Lady, where it is shown how she lay down when she suckled the child. The way down to this church is by about fifty steps, and it was once the House of Simeon the Righteous, and he rests in peace there.

From this church, or from the south corner of the city, the way 19
goes down the steep side of the mountain, through the forward wall which the Templars have built to guard their homes and their Palace. It leads straight down to the site of the ancient city and to the Pool of Siloam. This, it is said, is so called because the waters of this spring are coming by a hidden channel from Mount Shiloh. This information seems doubtful to me, because the mountain on which the city is located has other mountains between it and Mount Shiloh, and no valley can run straight from one to the other. And nor can such mountains be excavated because the places are so far away, for Mount Shiloh is two miles away from the city.

This question must be left unanswered, but we shall still outline to our listeners the things we know to be true. This therefore is true, and this is what we shall say. At the spring there is a good deal of soil, but though it fills the spring it no longer appears when the water descends into the other pool nearby. One goes down into the lower spring by thirteen steps. All around there are pillars which support arches, and under them there is a causeway around paved with big stones, and people standing there can draw the water which runs below. This second pool is square, and surrounded by a single wall. Once the pools were below the city, even though they

[1] 2 Sam.24. 17

are now far from it, for on two occasions the wall was taken from this city and it was added to the part round the Sepulchre of the Lord.

20 And now we think it right to arrange our subjects in the order of Christ's sufferings, who by his grace grants us to suffer with him, that together with him we may reign.

Bethany is about a mile distant from Jerusalem,[1] where was the House of Simon the Leper, Lazarus, and of his Sisters Mary and Martha in which Jesus used to be entertained very often. Bethany is
29 situated | in the valley which ends the Mount of Olives on the east.

From Bethany therefore on the Day of Palms our most dear Lord Jesus Christ set off and came to Bethphage, which is a point midway between Bethany and the Mount of Olives,[2] where a beautiful chapel has been built in his honour. He sent two disciples to bring him the ass and the colt, and standing on a great stone, which is clearly to be seen in this Chapel, he mounted the ass, and hastened through the Mount of Olives to Jerusalem. A great crowd went before him down the Mount of Olives.

Then he went across the Valley of Jehoshaphat and the Brook Kidron to the Golden Gate, which is double. At his coming one gate had its bolt drawn back, and opened by itself, and the other, with the ring of its hinge violently torn out, was opened with a great noise.[3] This is why there is a chapel there consecrated to his honour, where a gilt circle for a hinge is held in great reverence. This door is only opened on the Day of Palms and on the Day of the Exaltation of the Cross, and this is for the reason that Heraclius the Emperor passed through it when he brought back the large piece of the Wood that he had brought back from Persia. Christ then entered the Temple, and was teaching there every day until Wednesday.

21 I wish to go with him up to Mount Sion and to see what he did afterwards. But first I wish to be imprisoned with Peter, and to learn with him from Christ not to deny, but to pray. On the road which goes from the Temple up Mount Sion there stands a beautiful Chapel. In it there is the Prison, placed at a great depth underground, so that it has to be reached by seventy or more steps. In this the younger Herod imprisoned Saint Peter, and from it the

[1] See Jwü 6, p. 132. [2] See Jwü 6f, p. 134.
[3] See Jwü 4, p. 128.

angel of the Lord led him. In the entry of this chapel the following verses are inscribed:

'There, Peter, are your clothes! Awake!
  Your way you now are free to take.
Your chains that once did hold you fast
  Are burst asunder now at last.'
'The door stands open. I'll avow
  That Christ in love hath saved me now.'

Most of Mount Sion is situated outside the walls of the city on 22
the south side of it. It contains the Church joined to our Lady Saint Mary, which is well defended by walls, towers and bulwarks against the attacks of the Gentiles. This is a church in which there are religious clergy | serving God under a Provost. 30

As soon as you enter this you find to the left of the main apse a venerable place decorated with marble outside and mosaic within, in which our Lord Jesus Christ transferred to heaven the soul of his beloved Mother, our Lady Saint Mary. The structure is square at the bottom and on top it bears a round ciborium.

On the right you go up almost thirty steps to the Upper Room, which is located beyond the apse. A table is to be seen there on which our Lord supped together with his disciples, and after the traitor had gone out, he shared with his disciples the mystery of his body and his blood.

In the Upper Room to the south, more than thirty paces away, is an altar where the Holy Spirit came upon the disciples. From here you go down by as many steps as you came up to this place, and in a chapel below the Upper Room is a stone niche in the wall, where our Saviour washed the feet of his Apostles.[1]

On the right of that an altar stands in the place where Thomas touched the side of Christ during his resurrection, and for this reason it is called 'The Finger'.

From this one goes through a passage round the sanctuary of the church, and to the left of it there is a venerable altar, under which there is no doubt that the body of Blessed Stephen the Protomartyr was buried by John, Bishop of Jerusalem. It was afterwards, so I learn from my books, transferred by the Emperor Theodosius from Constantinople to Rome, and is said first to

[1] See Jwü 7, p. 136.

have been carried from Jerusalem to Constantinople by Queen Helena.

In front of the Choir a precious marble column is placed near the wall, which simple-minded people have a custom of walking round.

23 From here after his supper the Lord went out across the Brook Kidron where there was a garden. The Brook Kidron goes down the middle of the Valley of Jehoshaphat.

In the place where that garden used to be a church has been built of Blessed Mary, with certain neighbouring buildings, where her body was buried. One goes in through a porch and down by more than forty steps into a crypt. Her holy tomb stands there, a structure decorated with very fine marble and mosaic. At the entrance to this crypt these two verses are inscribed:

Inheritors of life that's new,
Come, praise our Lady, for to you
She gave that life which can regain
Salvation for the world again.[1] |

31 In a circle round it are twenty columns supporting arches. There is a frieze around, and it has a roof above. In the frieze these four verses are inscribed:

'Jehoshaphat' this valley's called,
The path to heaven is here installed.
In God she trusted, heaven's Queen,
Here Mary's burial would have been,
But hence she was raised up on high
And sought, inviolate, the sky,
The captive's Hope, their Light to see,
Who can their Way and Mother be.[2]

On the roof of the building is a round ciborium supported by six double columns, and having a ball and a gilt cross over it. Between each of the two little columns a lamp hangs. One goes into the tomb itself from the west and goes out to it to the north.

Her Assumption is very well painted on the ceiling above, below a straight line, which contains the words, 'Mary is taken up to heaven. May the angels rejoice and together may they praise our

[1] As Jwü 18, p. 169, except for line 2 of the verse, with the word 'Lady'.
[2] As Jwü 18, p. 171.

Lord.'[1] And round the sanctuary of the church a line of writing below contains these words: 'The Holy Mother of God, thou art exalted above the choirs of angels to the heavenly kingdom.'[2] From there into the church itself is up as many steps as you have gone down to enter the crypt. This church and all its neighbouring buildings are strongly defended by high walls, strong towers and bulwarks against attacks by the Gentiles. Round them they have a great many cisterns.

Going out of this crypt there is a small chapel in the left as one goes up the steps. In this church the Syrians have their own altar. Also on the ceiling over the steps by which one goes down to the crypt the journey of our Lady is painted, in which her beloved Son, our Lord Jesus Christ, accompanied by a multitude of angels, carries her soul and transfers it to heaven. The Apostles stand by mourning, and showing devoted loyalty to her. For when a Jew wished to tear away the veil which was placed on her body, which was lying on the bier, an angel with a sword struck off both his hands, and they fell to the ground, and left his arms handless.

For it is said that when our Lady died on Mount Sion, as has been said before, the holy Apostles placed her most holy body on a bier. They took her in order to bury her in the Valley of Jehoshaphat by
a path outside the walls of the city towards the south. | Some Jews, 32
not yet cured of the envy and fiery hatred which they had long felt for her and for her Son, confronted the Apostles with the idea of causing her shame. One of the Jews, more audacious than the rest (and unluckiest) came up to the stretcher, and with wicked daring tried to snatch off the veil which covered her. But this boldness was severely punished by the merits of the Blessed Virgin and by divine vengeance. For his hands and arms dried up. Then the other Jews seized the opportunity to run away.

You go then towards the Mount of Olives, and to your south 24
you see quite a large church called 'Gethsemane'. Our Saviour came there with his disciples from the garden, and said to them, *'Sit here, while I go over there and pray.'*[3] When you go into it you will immediately find a venerable altar, and, to your left, going into an underground cave, you will find four distinct places, in each of which three Apostles lay and slept. On your left there is also a large

[1] Longer version than Jwü 18, p. 171.
[2] Longer version than Jwü 18, p. 171.
[3] Matt 26.36.

stone in the corner of the cave in which Christ himself pressed his fingers and made six holes in it.

Then he went away from them about a stone's throw, and a little higher up, towards the Mount of Olives to the south, he three times made a prayer. In this place a new church has now been built, and one place of the prayer is in the left apse, the second in the middle choir, and the third in the right apse.

In the centre of the space between Gethsemane and the places of the prayers, on the side of the Mount of Olives, where the crowds met the Lord with branches of palm, there is a platform made of rocks. There on the Day of Palms the palms are blessed by the Patriarch.

Near the place where Jesus was frightened and sweated, Judas, with lanterns and torches and arms, and the servants of the Jews, arrested him, and took him prisoner. They dragged him to the court of the chief priest, that is Caiaphas. When they had mocked him for the whole night, they presented him in the morning to Pilate for judgement.

25 When Pilate had asked him many questions, he had him
conducted to the place of justice, and sat down for a tribunal at the
place called 'Lithostrotos'. This is a place located in front of the
Church of Blessed Mary on Mount Sion, and is a raised place
towards the city wall. There there is a venerable Chapel in honour
of the Lord Jesus Christ, in which part of a great column stands.
The Lord was bound to it by Pilate after he had condemned him to
hanging on the cross, and he was ordered to be flogged there.
33 There the pilgrims also have a custom of being flogged | according
to his example. In front of this Church, on a stone shaped like a
cross, this writing is inscribed:

'Lithostrotos' is named this spot,
And here the Lord his judgement got.

From here to the east, to the right in another part of the street, one goes down fifty steps into the church called 'Galilee', where there are two sets of chains with which Blessed Peter was bound. Then to the right-hand side of the altar one goes down almost forty steps into an underground cave which is very dark. Peter fled there after his denial and hid in one corner. And there he is painted, sitting down and bowing his head in his hands. He mourns the harm he has done to his loving Master, and the fact that he has denied him. The serving maid is standing threateningly over him, and before his feet stands the cock crowing. The Armenians are in charge of this Church.

From this place the Lord was taken out through the city wall, and round to Calvary. Then there were gardens there, but now the place is built over. He was led there and crucified, for as the apostle says, *'The Lord suffered witout the gate.'*[1]

Now about Christ, and the places of his about which we have learned by visiting them, we have told as best we can. Now we shall mention some notable things about some of his friends and some of the other places. After this we shall mention some of the things which have been seen by us, and some things about which other people have informed us.

Next to the road which leads to the east gate is the next place we 26
shall mention. This gate is near the Golden Gate and also next to the House of the Palace of Pilate which we have said above was near this road. The place is the Church of Blessed Anne, the Mother of our Lady Saint Mary. Her sepulchre is in an underground cave, to which one goes down almost twenty steps. In obedience to an Abbess nuns serve God there. Any one who goes to the north of the Church will find, in a deep valley beside a stony hill on which some old building stands, the Sheep Pool. This, as it is written in the Gospel, has five porticoes, and in the last one an altar is placed.

Any one who goes round the walls, beginning at the Tower of David, will find by the west corner a church and houses for lepers, beautiful and well-arranged. Going past the great cistern of the Hospitallers, and before you come to the north gate, the Church of Blessed Stephen the Protomartyr faces you from a hill. Stephen was put out of the city by this gate and stoned by the Jews, and there he saw the heavens open. In that church there is a platform in the middle with steps up to it. It is surrounded by an iron wall, and
in its centre there is a venerable altar which | is hollow, where the 34
place of Stephen's stoning had been, and where the heavens opened for him. This Church is subject to the Abbot of Saint Mary the Latin. In the north door there is a venerable Hospital, which in Greek is called a *xenodochium*.

And if you go up this road and take a road to the left, that is to the east, you will find a church which belongs to the Armenians, in

[1] Heb.13.12.

which a saint called Cariton rests. His bones are still covered in flesh as if he were alive.

27 After this, when the time and the hour of the Lord's Ascension was approaching, the Lord climbed the Mount of Olives and stood on a great rock. When the disciples were present he in his great love blessed them, and ascended into heaven. The Mount of Olives is, as has been said above, higher than all the hills which stand round the city. At harvest time it abounds in fruit, and at its summit there is a very venerable Church consecrated to the honour of the Saviour. For it is not the custom in those parts to use any consecration for the places glorified by our Lord's presence, except for this particular mountain height.

In this Church one goes up twenty big steps, and in the middle of the Church is a round structure which is splendidly ornamented with Parian and blue marble, and stands high with a high roof. In the centre of it there is a venerable altar, under which can be seen the stone on which the Lord is said to have stood when he was going to ascend into heaven. In the Church the divine offices are carried out by Canons. And the church is well defended against Gentiles by towers, great and small, by walls and bulwarks, and by sentries at night.

Going out to the west from this Church there is a dark chapel in an underground cave. One goes down to it by twenty-five steps. There in a large sarcophagus the body of Blessed Pelagia is to be seen. She finished her life as a hermit there in the ministry of God.

Then to the west, near the road going to Bethany and on the slope of the Mount of Olives, there is a most venerable Church where the Saviour was sitting. When the disciples asked him how they should pray, he taught them to pray, saying, 'Our Father which art in Heaven'. These words he wrote with his own hand, and these are the words written out completely under the altar so that travellers can kiss it. From the middle of this church one goes down nearly thirty steps into an underground cave, where the Lord is said to have stayed very often and to have taught his disciples. |

35/28 Since Jerusalem has occupied the chief position in this account, as a head to a body, we must now add the other parts of the body, the other places. So Bethany follows, a place defended both by the nature of its site and the strength of the buildings. Here stands a venerable double church. One part is for the body of Blessed Lazarus. The Lord raised him from the dead on the fourth day after his burial, and for fifteen years he governed the Church of Jerusalem. The other part is the Church of his Sisters Mary and Martha, and is glorious with their relics. There nuns serve God under an Abbess. And there our Lord and Saviour used often to be entertained.

Beyond Bethany to the east, four miles from Jerusalem, there is a mountain, and on it the Red Cistern which has a Chapel. This is the cistern into which it was said that Joseph was cast by his brethren, and it is where the Templars have erected a strong castle.

From there, over three miles away, is the Garden of Abraham. It is in a fertile plain and is near the Jordan, which runs about a mile from it. Its width is twice as great and its terrain stretches down to this neat and well-kept river. So the breadth of the Plain stretches down to the Jordan, and its length to the Dead Sea. Its fields are very suitable to grow new kinds of fruit, and it is full of trees, but they are as full of thorns as threshing-sledges! This garden is full of an enormous number of apples, but they are not of many kinds. And there we saw a harvest on the Monday after the Day of Palms.

The Templars, as their habit is by violent attacks, and the Hospitallers, have occupied many towers and large houses there, in order to give safe conduct to the pilgrims going to the Jordan through Gentile country, and to provide them with protection against any Saracen damage that they might suffer in their way down, on their return, or by staying the night there.

A mile away from these buildings is the Jordan. Its course is full 29
of bends, and its flow is rapid as it runs down on this side of the mountains of Arabia. It runs into the Dead Sea, and does not appear beyond it.

From the Red Cistern then, down to this valley, there is a terrifying desert, into which Jesus was led in order to be tempted by the Devil. At the end of this desert stands a fearful mountain, which is very high, and the top is almost inaccessible because its sides are so steep. It rises to a vast peak above, and below gapes a valley, dark and deep. This the lay people call 'Querentina', but we can call 'Of the Forty', for the reason that the Lord when he was fasting stayed there forty days and forty nights. |

The way to that place where the Lord stayed is straight up the 36
side of the mountain, and it is not a direct path but zigzagging. It is slippery everywhere, and sometimes those going up are forced to crawl on all fours. Some way up there is a door, and when you go

through it, down a small path you will find a Chapel attached to a cave. It is made of stones and is consecrated in honour of our Lady. Then you go up on this laborious path, without any steps, and you pass the large and rugged crack in the mountain. You pass through another door. Then you go up a path which winds this way and that, until gradually you reach a third door. Through it you will see a small altar made in honour of the Holy Cross. To the right of this small building the tomb of a saint called Piligrinus is pointed out, and the flesh of his hand is still shown. From this you go upwards about sixteen steps and on the east there is a venerable altar. On the west you will find the venerable place where our Lord Jesus Christ stayed. In this, it has been said, he fasted forty days and the same number of nights, and when his fasting was finished, angels ministered to him.

This place is half way up the mountain, and this means that the summit's height above is equal to the extent of the depth below. Above this a great rock appears on which the Devil is said to have sat to entrap him. From this mountain the view stretches out a long way across the Jordan into Arabia, and across the Dead Sea the boundaries of Egypt are visible. The summit of this Quarantana and a cave underground are full of stores and arms for the Templars, and they could not have a stronger defence more hostile to the pagans. As you go up and down this mountain, at the bottom of the path there is a great spring running, which gives water to the Garden of Abraham and all the surrounding plain. There, in the plain watered by the streams from this spring, the pilgrims, as has been said, pass the night, in order both to go to the Quarantana for prayer, and to wash themselves in the waters of the Jordan. On three sides of this garden there is protection against pagan attacks, and on the fourth side it is kept safe by sentries from the Hospitallers and Templars.

30 When we, the poor, came to this place for the purpose of prayer, and wanted to wash in the Jordan and to make the remainder of the visits, we arrived after sunset, as the darkness was about to begin. Looking out over this plain we could see, according to our own |
37 estimation of the number, about sixty thousand people there, almost all holding candles in their hands. These people could also be seen by the pagans who stay in the mountains of Arabia beyond the Jordan. That is to say that a greater number of pilgrims were now staying in Jerusalem that had recently been arriving there.

In the place where our Lord was baptized by John there is placed a great rock, on which our Saviour is said to have stood during his baptism. The Jordan could flow up to it but would not go over it. On the bank of the Jordan there is a church where six monks lived, but they had their heads cut off by Zangi, the father of Nur ed Din. There is also there a powerful camp of Templars.

On the way, straight back from the Jordan to Jerusalem, on the plain before you reach the mountains, is Jericho. A continuous stream, which comes down from these mountains, runs by it, but is reduced to a small village. Nevertheless it is situated in fertile lands, and this is the place where every fruit is first to ripen. It is a place full of roses, which flower with many petals, and it makes a good comparison with our Lady: *'Like a bed of roses in Jericho.'*[1] There is a great number of early grapes. This place is under the control of the Church of Lazarus in Bethany, but because of the Saracen invasions the land is without cultivation. On this road to the north, that is to the right, the mountains of Gilboa can clearly
be seen standing next to this plain. | 38

. . .[2] . . . | 31

Anyone who starts at the west gate of the city [of Jerusalem] near 32
the Tower of David, and turns south, will cross the Valley of Hinnom. This valley goes round two sides of the city, and he will cross it by the New Cistern. Then half a mile beyond it he will come to a chapel held in great veneration and consecrated in honour of our Lady Saint Mary. It is a place where she often used to rest on her way from Bethlehem to Jerusalem. In front of its gates there is a cistern, and from this the passers-by refresh themselves. Later on there is a plain in which may heaps of stones are placed. The simple travellers like to collect them together since they say that on the day of judgement they will sit on them. . . .[3] . . .

There follows the glorious City of God, Bethlehem, in which, 33
according to the sayings of the Prophets, our Lord Jesus Christ was born as a man. In it there is a venerable church which is distinguished by having a Bishop's Throne. The Principal Altar is joined in honour to our Lady Saint Mary. At the end of the right hand apse near the Choir one goes down twenty-five steps into an

[1] Ecclesiasticus 24.14.

[2] Paraphrases from part of Jwü 22, p. 179f, derived from G.34, 35, 41 and another quoted passage interpreting the Bible.

[3] Quotations follow from Jwü 19, p. 173, deriving from G.125.

underground cave, where there is a venerable hollow altar, and inside it has only a small cross engraved below. It is made of four small columns of marble, holding up a large stone. In this place these two verses are written:

The light which angels contemplate,
The perfectness they emulate,
This one true God is brought to birth
By Virgin Mother here on earth. |

39 On the right in this cave, that is towards the west, one goes down four steps and comes to the Manger, in which lay not only the fodder of the animals, but was also found the food of angels. The Manger has a white marble structure round it, and has above three round holes, through which pilgrims can give their long-desired kisses to the Manger. The crypt is reverently decorated with mosaic work. Above this cave is a venerable Chapel with a double roof, in which there is a venerable altar on the south, and to the west there is shown the tomb of Joseph of Arimathea, which is against the wall. Not *far from the Manger of the Lord*[1] there stands the tomb of Blessed Jerome, whose body is said to have been transferred from there to Constantinople by Theodosius the Younger. Also over this church a copper star shines, well gilded and attached to a pole, which means that the Three Magi came there, as one reads in the Gospel, by the guiding of a star, and there found the boy Jesus with his Mother Mary, and worshipped them. . . . [2] . . .

40 . . . [3] . . . | . . .

35 . . . [4] . . . This lake [the Dead Sea] is terrifying. Its water is black and its stench sends any one approaching it away. At the time of the anniversary of the destruction of those cities [Sodom, Gomorrah, Zeboim and Admah], stones and wood and other kinds of material are seen floating in that lake to give a sign of their destruction. . . . [5] . . .

[The statue of salt into which Lot's wife was turned.] It remains today. As the moon wanes its size goes down, and as it waxes the

[1] See Jwü 19, p. 172.
[2] A quotation from Jwü 19, p. 173, derived from G.207.
[3] Chapter 34 is paraphrased from Jwü 21, pp. 176–8, deriving from G.2, 14, 17f, 8, 13, 19f.
[4] Chapter 35 is paraphrased from Jwü 21, 22, p. 178, derived from G.22, 25.
[5] There follow quotations from Jwü 22, p. 178, derived from G.26.

size is renewed again. It has its head turned backwards. . . . [1] . . .

Ten miles from Hebron to the north, and on the shore of the 36
Great Sea is Gaza, now called 'Gazara', in which Samson did many miracles, and one night took its doors away. Eight miles from Gaza
the well-defended city of Ascalon | is situated on the shore of the 41
Great Sea. These cities had been located in Palestine or the Land of the Philistines.

On the shore of the Great Sea Joppa is situated, in which the Apostle Peter brought Tabitha back to life. The city is by modern people called 'Jafis'. Near there is Arimathea, from which came Joseph, a noble citizen, who buried Christ. There too is the plain that is in the land of Judah where the angel snatched up the Prophet Habakkuk. He had put some loaves in his wallet, and was going into the field so that he could take it to the harvesters. But he was taken to Babylon in order that he might give a meal to Daniel when he was shut up in the lions' den.

Going out of the Holy City to the west, through the Gate next to 37
the Tower of David, to the right is a road to a Chapel. In it there is a descent by almost a hundred steps to a very deep underground cave, and there are placed innumerable corpses of travellers, which are said to have come there in this way.

> One year the pilgrims came to Jerusalem to pray there, and they found the city full of Saracens. Since they could not get in, and did not wish to go away, they besieged them in the city. Because they had neither the arms nor the stores to achieve such an arduous task they began to be hard pressed by the lack of these things they needed. And while they were thus weakened the Saracens, seeing that they could not resist them, suddenly attacked them from the city and killed them all with the sword.
>
> Since the stench was arising from the corpses of so many people they decided they should all be burned. But that night there was sent by God a lion, who took all those bodies into the cave, with its narrow mouth. If any single small particle of these bodies can be taken by sea, provided they are taken on board the ships are said to return automatically to their port.

Over a mountain [near to Jerusalem] there is a very fertile and 38

[1] Quotations from Jwü 22, pp. 178–80, derived from G.32, 31f, 63, 34.

well-tended valley, in which is located a noble church. It stands in honour of our Lord Jesus Christ and of his beloved Mother, and there, in a hollow altar, the place is reverenced in which the trunk stood from which was cut the Cross. On it the Saviour hung for our salvation. The Syrians are in charge of this church, and it is strongly defended against Gentile attacks by towers, walls and bulwarks. The place is also well provided with houses, council-chambers, rooms and other buildings for domestic use of every kind, and has a high roof, with a small wall decorated with
42 battlements. | King Solomon is said to have cut this tree down, and to have placed it in a suitable position until the coming of the Saviour. He is said to have had a cross carved in it, for he saw in spirit that the salvation of the world would be assured by the death of Christ.

Then one goes to Saint John, or to the place which is called 'The Woodland', where his father Zacharias and his mother Elisabeth dwelt, and where Saint John *was born*. This is also the place where Saint Mary came, after receiving the greeting of the Angel in Nazareth, and greeted Elisabeth.

This place is near the mountains of *Modin*,[1] in which dwelt Mattathias and his sons when Antiochus besieged the City and the children of Israel. This mountain area is now called 'Belmont'.

These mountains are beside the castle of Emmaus which people now call 'Fontenoid', where Jesus on the very day of his resurrection appeared to the two disciples.

And this is beside the Mountains of Ephraim which are called Zophim, and the large city of Ramatha, which is now called 'Rames', from which were Elkanah, the father of Samuel the Prophet, and Hannah his mother.

Next to Sophim is Beth-horon, which is now called 'Beter'.

From there on the right side or the west, and two miles from the city, one goes up Mount Shiloh, from which the sweet springs in the valley round it get water. There the Ark of the Covenant of the Lord remained from the entry of Israel into the Land of Promise until the time of the priest Eli.

At which time, because the sins of the Israelites required it, it was captured by the Philistines. It was kept by them for seven months after its capture, and during that time they were touched by

[1] See Jwü 23, p. 180f, derived from G.180, 194.

punishments from God. So they brought back the Ark on a cart to Beth-Shemesh. During that time God had had his fill of anger against either priests or people for the keeping of the Ark, and the inhabitants of Kiriath-Jearim, that is Gibeah, took it away from Beth-Shemesh and made a place for it themselves. And the Ark was afterwards taken by David and all Israel from Gibeah with hymns of praise. They placed it in the City of David, that is, on Mount Sion. After this, when King Solomon had built the Temple to the Lord, as has been said above, on Mount Moriah, where the threshing-floor of Araunah the Jebusite had been, he placed the Ark in the Temple.

In Shiloh also the Prophet Samuel was buried, and hence the earlier name was changed to 'At Saint Samuel'. There is now a congregation of monastic profession there, called 'The Grey Men'.[1] |

Six miles west of Shiloh Lydda is located on the plain, and at 39/43
Lydda has been buried, so it is said, the Holy Martyr George. Hence this place has had its name changed and is now called 'At Saint George'.

From here one goes down through a cheerful well-kept plain containing the countryside between the mountains and the sea, to a road which leads to Accho, that is, Ptolemais. On the way many cities and villages, old and new, are to be seen, among them Caphar Gamala, Caphar Semala, the village now called Cacho which is situated in a very fertile land, the fortified city now called Caesarea of Palestine (but once Strato's Tower), the mountains of Caipha, by which a village of the same name lies. This is completely ruined now. The thirty pieces of silver were made there which were given by the Jews for the price of the blood of Christ to Judas the traitor, so it is said. And on its height there is a castle of the Templars which assists people who are far out at sea to recognise the mainland.

Then on the shore of the sea in the region of Accaron there is a 40
castle in rich countryside which is called 'New'. Near it stands a large grove of palm trees, and, soon afterwards, about three miles away, stands Ptolemais, a great city, rich and full of people. But the port of Ptolemais or the anchorage of the ships is very often difficult or dangerous to enter when the south wind is blowing. In

[1] That is, Premonstratensians.

fact the edge of the shore shakes with the frequent beat of the huge waves of the sea violently breaking against each other, and since no barrier like a mountain holds back the sea when it is rough, the waves wash over the main-land for over a stone's throw.

In this city there is a house built on the sea shore by the Templars, which is very large and beautiful. Similarly the Hospitallers in the city have founded a very finely built house. And everywhere the pilgrims' ships are at anchor, since they all have to be there in the port of the city until after their passengers come back from Jerusalem and they can take them home.

Thus in the year that we were there, on the Wednesday of Easter week, we counted seventy ships in the port, not counting the ones called 'buza' which we were using to sail there and back. In this road which leads from Jerusalem, and through the places I have mentioned, there are many deserted cities and villages, which were once destroyed by Vespasian and Titus. But provisions are supplied by the well-defended castles which belong to the Templars and Hospitallers. |

44/ 41 Two miles from the Holy City on the north side stands a small church where the pilgrims have their first view of this city [of Jerusalem] and, moved with great joy, put on their crosses. They take off their shoes, humbly trying to seek the person who for them was pleased to come to this place as a poor and humble man. Three miles away there is a large village which is now called Mahomeria,[1] where there is a church consecrated in honour of Saint Mary. Next to this church is a cross carved in stone, and raised on seven steps. The travellers go up them, not unmoved, and look at the Tower of David in the Citadel of Mount Sion, which, as has been said before, is over four miles away. The old name of this place has escaped my mind.

Eight miles away again is another large village in a big range of hills. When one has come quickly down them one comes through a spacious and beautiful plain, and some mountains, to a well-defended city. In old days this was called Shechem or Sychar, but now it is called Neapolis, or 'New City'.

When we were going along this road we saw a crowd of Saracens, who were all beginning to plough with their oxen and asses a very well-kept field. And they uttered a horrid cry, which is

[1] *Malahumeria.*

not unusual for them when they start any work, but they filled us with great terror! There are a great number of pagans there, who stay everywhere in the cities and villages and farms of this province. By the generosity of the King of Jerusalem or of the Templars or Hospitallers they cultivate the land there.

The city of Neapolis which I have mentioned is situated in 42
Samaria. It is full of springs and brooks, vines and olives and all
kinds of trees, and the fertility of its fields is excellent. Coming to
this city the Lord Jesus, tired from his *journey*, sat down on the
well, where he also spoke to *the woman of Samaria*.[1] But the well on
which the Lord sat is half a mile from the city. It is in front of the
altar in the Church built over it, in which some men serve God.
. . . [2] . . . | . . . Near Shechem there are two mountains, the one 45
in which Cain is said to have offered gifts to God of the fruits of the
earth, which is now hideously dry, and the other on which Abel is
said to have offered gifts from his flock as a sacrifice to God, which
is excellently fertile in trees and all fruits. . . . [3] . . .

Six miles from this is Samaria, *also called Sebaste*[4] but now called 43
'At Saint John'. It is on a mountain which is not high, but very
strong, and from this the province gets its name *Samaria*.[5] The
ruins show that it was a great city, and it is still full of fertile fields,
vines, and all kinds of fruit. . . . [6] . . . [The head of Saint John
Baptist was transferred to Alexandria] then transferred to an island
called Rhodes [then to Constantinople]. . . . [7] . . . [John Baptist]
was buried in the crypt between Elisha and Obadiah the Prophets,
in the very cave in which the Prophet once fed the seventy prophets
who are also buried there. One enters the cave by descending
thirty-five steps.

. . . [8] . . . Jezreel, which is now called 'Ad cursum Gallinam' 44
. . . [9] . . . | . . . In a mountain beside it [i.e. Scythopolis] is an 46
extremely lofty mountain, on which the Hospitallers have built the
strongest and most spacious castle. This is for the purpose of
guarding the land this side of the Jordan from the attacks of Nur ed

[1] See Jwü 2, p. 115, derived from G.113.
[2] Quotations from Jwü 2, p. 115, derived from G.105.
[3] Quotations from Jwü 2, pp. 115–16, derived from G.105, 113, 108, 110, 107.
[4] See Jwü 2, p. 114, derived from G.99.
[5] See Jwü 2, p. 115, derived from G.97.
[6] See Jwü 2, p. 114, derived from G.99.
[7] Quotation from Jwü 2, p. 114, derived from G.101.
[8] Quotation from Jwü 1, 2, p. 114, derived from G.96.
[9] Quotations from Jwü 1, p. 113f, derived from G.92, 93, 92, 94.

Din, the Tyrant of Aleppo. Also to the west there is a castle of the Templars with the name of Sapham, which is well defended against the raids of the Turks. From this place and towards the Great Sea is Mount Hermon, at the west foot of which the Templars have set up a big castle. In the grounds of it they have made a large cistern which has a water wheel which takes the water down.

47 45 . . . | . . .[1] . . .

[Paneas] which in the year of the incarnation of our Lord Jesus Christ 1171, the pagans took from the Christians. They tore out their garrison and installed their own. . . .[2] . . .

46 . . .[3] . . .

On the left side of the Sea [of Galilee] under the lee of a mountain the Lake of Gennesaret springs out, which everywhere is sheltered by mountains. There is no trace of a general wind here, but it is said to generate its own wind by creating a breeze.[4] . . .[5] . . . |

48 In this mountain [Tabor] is a noble church that has been constructed in honour of the Saviour, in which men of the monastic profession serve God under the authority of an abbot. In this church it is said that the first Mass was celebrated. . . .[6] . . .

47 *Four miles* from Mount Tabor *towards the west* is a most glorious city *on the road which leads to Acre*,[7] Nazareth. In it stands a revered church, illustrious with the honour of a Bishop's Throne, and in name consecrated to our Lady Saint Mary. In the left apse of this church one goes down almost fifteen steps into an underground cave, and towards the east there is a small cross engraved at the foot of a hollow altar. It means that there the announcement of Christ was made to our Lady by the Archangel Gabriel. To the left of this altar, that is, to the north, Joseph her husband, the foster father of the Saviour, lies buried, and attached to his grave there is an altar. Moreover to the right, that is, to the south, there is an arched structure having only a single cross engraved beneath it, in which the Blessed Mother of God when she was born came out of her mother's womb.

Every one tells of a great and wonderful miracle about this city, |

[1] Quotations from Jwü 26 and 25, pp. 187, 185, derived from G.69, 52, 53.
[2] Quotations from Jwü 25, pp. 184–7, derived from G.59, 64, 44, 65, 67.
[3] Quotations from Jwü 26, pp. 187, 189, derived from G.67f, 74.
[4] See Jwü 26, p. 188, derived from G.70.
[5] Quotations from Jwü 26, 1, pp. 188, 113, derived from G.70, 84, 85.
[6] Quotations from Jwü 1, p. 112, derived from G.86, 89.
[7] See Jwü 1, p. 111, derived from G.84.

that whenever pagans try to attack it, they are restrained from such 49
an attempt either by being blinded or by some other divine action.

The spring in this city springs forth from a head, a lion's mouth carved in marble: *from which* the boy *Jesus* often *used to draw* and take to his *Mother*.[1] The spring is said to have had its origin in this way.

> Once upon a time, when the boy Jesus was going to draw water from the cistern, his bucket was broken by a game played by some other boys. So he took the water when it was drawn in a fold of his coat, since he had no other vessel in which to carry it. She refused to drink it, since it seemed to her that it had been brought in an unbecoming way, and he was indignant, and threw it onto the ground from his coat. And immediately this spring which is still flowing is said to have broken forth. . . . [2] . . .

. . . [3] . . . And three miles from Sepphoris there is a very strong 48
camp of the Templars on the road which leads to Acre, and very soon, just over three miles away, is Acre itself, or Ptolemaida. This road, which goes from Acre through Nazareth, Samaria and Neapolis and leads to Jerusalem is called 'The Upper', and the one which goes from Acre through Caesarea and Lydda to Jerusalem is called 'The Coast Road'.

. . . [4] . . . | . . . 49 50

. . . [5] . . . 50

These then are the cities on the coast, great cities and walled, which are located in Syria, and the provinces of Palestine and Judaea, which fall under the authority of the Christians: the other cities are in the province of Coele-Syria, namely Mamistra, Antioch and Tripolis, which is now called Tursolt, and also the city Gibeleth,
which contains a strongly-defended camp. . . . [6] . . . | . . . 51

. . . [7] . . . *Eight miles from Sarphan* [or Sarepta] is *Tyre* which is 51
now called *Surs*.[8] It stands on the sea coast, and excels all the other

[1] See Jwü 1, p. 111, derived from G.77.
[2] Quotation from Jwü 1, p. 111, derived from G.83.
[3] Quotation from Jwü 1, p. 111f, derived from G.77, 79f.
[4] Quotations from Jwü 24 and 25, pp. 182, 186, derived from G.42, (44?), 45, 49, 43, 65, 47, 51, 55, 58.
[5] Quotations from Jwü 24, 25, pp. 182, 185, derived from G.57, 219f.
[6] Quotations from Jwü 24, p. 183, derived from G.225, including the information that the ikon exists in the bishop's Church in Berytus.
[7] Quotations from Jwü 24, p. 183, derived from G.225, 224, 222.
[8] See Jwü 24, p. 182, derived from G.218.

cities by the strength of the defence of its turrets and walls. Its shape is square, and it has the appearance of an island. Round three sides it is surrounded by the sea, and the fourth is strongly reinforced by ditches, barbicans, towers, walls, bulwarks and fosses. It has only two ways out, which are guarded by quadruple doors with turrets on both sides. It is famous for its double port, like Accaron, with the civil one inside and the outer one ready to escort the ships of travellers. In the space between this double port there project two high towers built of huge blocks of stone, and they are joined by a very big iron chain which runs through their doors. When this is closed it removes the possibility of going in or out, and it only frees people to do so when it is loosened. The city is gloriously honoured by having a bishop.

Four miles from here stands a castle called Scandalium,[1] on which the waves break very high up before they go back again and are sucked into the sea.

At the third mile there stands a large village called Rubert's Castle.

There follows over four miles away Accaron or Ptolemaida, and afterwards, over three miles away Caipha, old and new.

From there, over six miles away is Caesarea of Palestine, nobly built by Herod the King with its neighbouring port.

Then, over fourteen miles away, is Joppa or Jafis. It has a port which is apt to cause shipwrecks when there is a south wind.

After this you reach first Gaza or Gazara, and the well-defended city of Ascalon, all of which have been mentioned above. These are all the cities along the coast, and[2] all of them are large and have walls.

We have set out all this information about the holy places, in which our Lord Jesus Christ, who took on the form of a servant for our sake, displayed the presence of his bodily substance. Partly they have been seen by us, and partly known to us by the true accounts of other people. We therefore hope to awaken the minds of our readers or hearers to a new love of him, by the things which we have described here.

[1] *Scendelim.*

[2] Manuscript text ends here. The rest is in the margin.

JOHN PHOCAS

A GENERAL DESCRIPTION OF THE SETTLEMENTS AND PLACES BELONGING TO SYRIA AND PHOENICIA ON THE WAY FROM ANTIOCH TO JERUSALEM, AND OF THE HOLY PLACES OF PALESTINE

It has been our joy to see holy things, the Holy Places in which of 1.1
old God was at work. First through Moses he led his people in their flight out of Egypt with signs and wonders; and with a mighty hand he struck down the Gentiles and subdued them, Sehon King of the Amorites and Og the King of Basan and all the kingdoms of Canaan. And there with outstretched arm he established them at their first arrival, and multiplied them very greatly, as we learn from the sacred Scriptures.

Then in the last days, through the sacred Incarnation of his Only-begotten he sanctified them, and accomplished the miracle of creating us anew.

Should we thus be the only ones to have a part in this blessing, as
if it were food and we were gluttons? Where then will the liberal 2
kindnesses appear by which we express the results of our love and
the particular quality of human life? We must attempt, therefore, as 3
best we can, to paint a picture, using words on our canvas, and to those who love God to give a full written account of what we saw directly with our own eyes.

To those who have already seen the places I shall appear to be 4
doing something unnecessary. For if the object of speaking is to 5
represent what was seen, and if no representation is ever equal to the original experience, I shall clearly provide less delight than is to
be gained by seeing. What then is the reason? I think it will more 6
clearly teach those who have not shared in these excellent places with their eyes, or those who from time to time have heard about

7 the places from the words of those who have not examined them. Furthermore, it will give some pleasure to those who have seen the places, for if anything was a pleasure to see, it is also a pleasure to hear it described.

2.1 There was indeed a time when Theopolis of Antiochus on the Orontes took pride in the size of its theatres, the beauty of its porticoes, the temples which had been founded there, the multitude
2 of its citizens and its rich possessions. It outdid by far almost every other city in the East. But time and a barbarous hand caused this good fortune to vanish, even though it still remained dazzling with its towers and the might of its defences, and the fertility of the running water round it. For the River provided a defence of the city, encircling it and coming up to its towers with watery caresses.

3 Theopolis was excellently supplied with waters coming from the Castalian Spring, for the stream was divided into various channels and, with brooks that ran everywhere, flowed into every part of the city. For the noble founder of the city had covered the whole city with the water and distributed them with a generous hand from the Spring, for he brought them through the hills into the city.

4 There the famous suburb of Daphne is ornamented by the growth of plants of every kind, and there too is the Marvellous
5 Mountain, whose citizen is the Marvellous Simeon. Beside that lies Mount Maurus and the Crag, in which in former times many godly men sought God and found him. Even now some of them are left there and dwell in the groves of these mountains, attracted by their beauty.

6 Moreover the Castalian Spring flows from between two hills, and flows vigorously from the foot of a mountain which projects into the sea. One sees a huge portico roofing over the water of the Spring and from this, divided into two streams, the water flows
7 abundantly. One stream is brought round the city on lofty supports, and comes round to the high ground on the right of the city like a river in the air. The other stream runs down to the plains on the left of the Spring, it waters the meadows and irrigates the plain of Daphne, and then joins the River Orontes on the left.

8 The Marvellous Mountain, on a crest between the city and the Sea, is remarkable, and is a delight to every one who arrives within sight of it. It lies next to the city and Roso, and on either side has the mountains called the Crag and the one called Caucasus.

Round the foot of the mountain, with countless bends the River 9
Orontes flows, and then goes into the Sea.

On the summit of this Mountain was that great man, now at 10
rest. In his heart he set a ladder, and his body too was set up on
high. He desired to become a heavenly person while still in the
body, and to be midway between God and man. How this miracle 11
occurred to this man so beloved of God I will now explain. The 12
masons had quarried deep into the solid rock, and he had cut away
the summit of the Marvellous Mountain with the aim of founding a
monastery in it. But he left in the centre of it a natural pillar with
steps in it, as the Word puts it, *'Setting his feet upon the rock.'*[1]
Towards the rising sun he erected a most beautiful Church to God
in which he collected his disciples. He therefore remained up in the
air, while they remained inside the Church all night, and offered to
God the worship which befits his holy ones.

After this city of Antioch comes Laodicea, a large city and well- 3.1
populated, even though the passage of time has also diminished the
grandeur of the place. After it comes Gabala or Jebel, and after that
the castle Antaradus or Tortosa. Thus as far as Tripolis there are 2
important castles along the coast, but inland there runs a large
range in which live the Assassins. They are a Saracen race, and are
neither Christians nor of the Mohammedan persuasion. Rather
they are a sect on their own. They acknowledge God and call their
leader God's Ambassador, and at his command they are sent to the
rulers of great nations and kill them with the sword. They too die
in the adventure, for they are outnumbered when they have
undertaken the deed, and this martyrdom they believe to be the
way to immortality.

After this range comes Libanus, beautiful and justly famed in the 4.1
Scriptures. It is an enormous range dressed like a cloak with
snowdrifts from top to bottom, and it is a delight to see with its
pines, cedars, cypresses and its variety of fruit trees. Christians live 2
on the side facing the sea, and the side facing Damascus and Arabia
is assigned to the Saracens. Soon after the snow has melted rivers,
beautiful and cold, flow down to the sea from its clefts and caverns,
and the streams are cold as ice.

Near the foot of the hills is Tripolis, which the founder set on a 3
peninsula.

[1] Psalm 40.2.

4 Indeed a thin ridge comes down from Libanus and projects into
the sea like a tongue. It has a hill at its east end on the top of which
5 the founder fixed the city. This city is extremely small in
circumference, but it is nevertheless most beautiful with its high
walls and beautiful buildings.

5.1 After that comes what is called Jebelet and after that Berytus, a
large city and well populated, surrounded with meadows. It is
outstanding for the excellence of its port, but in fact the harbour is
not natural but artificial. It is embraced by the city in a crescent, and
on the horns of the crescent are built two great towers. A chain is
stretched from one to the other, and confines the ships inside the
harbour. This forms the boundary between Syria and Phoenicia.

6.1 Then comes Sidon and its harbour, celebrated in song as 'The
Twin', whose situation the writer of *Leucippe*[1] has so well
2 described. If you stay there you can see how the real harbour and
3 the entry strait agree with the written description. About three
bowshots outside the city is a Church enclosed by a long roofed
colonnade, and against the apse of the Church lies a stone on
which, according to the common report, Christ the Saviour of the
World, stood and taught the multitudes.

7.1 After Sidon comes the village of Sarepta on the sea shore, and a
Church of the Prophet Elijah is being built in the middle of the
town at the house of the widow who entertained him.

8.1 From there one reaches Tyre, an outstandingly beautiful city
outdoing practically all the rest in Phoenicia. This too is built on a
2 peninsula and is arranged on the same plan as Tripolis. But Tyre
extends over a far broader site than Tripolis and exceeds it in the
3 setting and beauty of its buildings. The approach to the harbour is
precisely similar to the harbour of Berytus, even though the latter is
of far greater area and beauty and exceeds it in the height of its
towers.

4 Two bowshots outside the city is a huge stone on which it is said
Christ rested and sent Peter and John, the holy Apostles to look for
bread. When they had gone and fetched it they went with the
Saviour to a place in the neighbourhood with a spring. There the
Saviour sat down, and when he had eaten with the Apostles he was
drinking the water and blessed it. And to this day this spring truly
presents a spectacle hard to describe. It rises there in the middle of

[1] Achilles Tatius, *Loves*, p. 37.

the meadows, a miraculous object and an encouraging sight for
travellers. Indeed it is said that it is bottomless. 5

Around it is a construction which is arranged as follows. Those 6,7
who first devoted their labours to the spring built round it an
octagonal tower. They raised it to a considerable height, and
arranged outlets at each of the upper corners. At the same level they
made channels stretching on arches across the meadows, and since
they had forced the water up under pressure, it gushed out and
liberally watered the surrounding meadows. Thus if a person 8
stands on the tower and looks round him, he sees a continuous
spread of plants growing, and even in the summer season the whole
tract of meadows around him is continually watered.

Going on from there one arrives at Ptolemais or Akke. This city 9.1
is large and is more populous than any of the others. Into it came all
the passenger ships, and all those who travel abroad for the sake of
Christ visit it, whether they come by sea or land. The atmosphere 2
there is polluted because of the great crowds who arrive there.
From time to time diseases break out and they cause deaths among
them, which causes a stench and makes the air deadly. This is the
irremediable fault of this city.

On the right is Carmel and the shore containing all Palestine. To 3
the left one has Galilee and Samaria.

Thus the first place one reaches from Ptolemais is Sepphoris, a 10.1
city of Galilee which has almost no houses, and displays no trace of
its original prosperity. After that comes Cana, an extremely small 2
village, to be seen to this day, where the Lord transformed the
water into wine. Then, among some sizeable hills, and at the 3
bottom of the valley which they form, is set the city of Nazareth.
Here, by God's great and bountiful mercy, the announcement was
made by the Archangel Gabriel to the Virgin Mother of God of the
great mystery, the Incarnation of Christ our God for our salvation.

Entering this town by the main gate one reaches the Church of 4
the Archangel Gabriel. And to the left of the sanctuary in the 5
church one can see a small cave, and in it there flows a spring which
produces clear water. In this spring the Wholly-immaculate
Mother of God, when she was given in marriage to the Righteous
Joseph and was under his protection, used to go out every day and
draw water.

And in the sixth month after the conception of the Forerunner
she was about to draw water in the usual way, and received the first

greeting from Gabriel. She was troubled and afraid, and went away to the House of Joseph. There she heard the Archangel's voice again, saying, *'Hail, thou that art highly favoured!'* and she replied to him, *'Behold, the handmaid of the Lord. Be it unto me according to thy word.'*[1] In that place she received the Word of God in her utterly immaculate Womb.

6 Later on this House of Joseph was transformed into a most beautiful church, and there in a place on the left of the sanctuary is a cave, with its opening not very deep underground but visible near
7 the surface, with its mouth decorated with white marble. Above it is painted the winged angel coming down beside her who is to be a Mother yet has no husband. He greeted her with good tidings, as he diligently found her, diligently engaged in spinning. The picture suggests that he is addressing her, but she was amazed at this unexpected sight, and she quickly turns from him in confusion. Her purple thread is dropping from her hand, and she is leaving the room in fear. She meets a woman, a beloved member of her family, and embraces and kisses her.

8 Entering the opening of the cave you descend a few steps and then you see that ancient dwelling of Joseph, in which after returning from the Spring the Virgin, as I have said, received the good tidings
9 from the Archangel. So in this place the good tidings were uttered where a black stone cross is fixed on white marble beneath the altar.

On the right of this altar one sees a small cell in which the
10 Sovereign Mother of God used to sleep. On the left of the Good
11 Tidings there is another dark cell | in which our Lord Christ, after his return from Egypt, is said to have lived, until the end of the
12 Forerunner's work. Then, as the Holy Scriptures tell, *'when Jesus heard that John had been arrested, he left Nazareth and lived in Capernaum'*.[2] After that comes a range formed of a number of hills, and in it is the precipice from which the Jews were about to cast the Lord down. But he passed through the midst of them, and went his way to Capernaum.

11.1 After that range there is a great plain, and in the plain near the range of hills is Mount Tabor, 'The Heaven on Earth', the soul's
2 glory, and the one delight of the eyes of orthodox people. For a divine beauty overshadows the mountain with its presence, which
3 rejoices the spirit. The mountain is round in shape and moderately

[1] Luke 2.28, 38. [2] Matt 4.12f.

high. On its summit are two monasteries in which Christians 4
propitiate God in different languages but with a single intent. At
the place where the saving Transfiguration of Christ occurred there
is a company of Latin monks. And on the left the Nazirites 5
belonging to us are sanctified and sanctify that holy place.

And the Saving Transfiguration of Christ took place on the 6
summit of the mountain at the site of the Latins' monastery. In the
sanctuary of the church is the place where the Lord was transfigured
in the presence of Elijah and Moses, and of his three chosen disciples,
Peter, John and James. This place is enclosed with bronze railings. 7
And at the place where the Lord's feet were set one sees a white boss, 8
in the middle of which is engraved the Holy Cross. From this there
wafts an inexpressible fragrance, which delights the nostrils of any
one who approaches it. About a stone's throw outside the monastery 9
is a small cave, into which, after the awesome Transfiguration, the
Lord entered, and commanded the disciples not to tell any one what
they had seen until he had been raised from the dead.

On the north side of the mountain is the Cave of Melchizedek, 10
which well deserves a visit. In it are pierced many caves, which
have upper and lower chambers, and remarkable lodgings and cells
serving as dwellings for ascetics. In these many great saints
followed the ascetic course. Near this cave is a temple at the very 11
spot where Melchizedek met Abraham returning from the battle,
and blessed him and received him as a guest.

If you look from this holy mountain to the first east[1] you will see 12
the marshes and valley of that holiest of rivers, the Jordan. And if 13
you look further off in the direction of the sunrise you see the
district of Libanus, and the two great mountains between which
lies Damascus. If you turn to look to the left of the Jordan a little 14
further, you see very clearly and directly the Sea of Tiberias. At the
far end of it a small mound is to be seen, at which the Lord blessed
the loaves, and gave them to five thousand people to eat, and where
after his resurrection he ate with the disciples, when they caught a
hundred and fifty-three fish.

And to the north of Mount Tabor there is another mountain on 15
the edge of the plain, about twelve stades away or perhaps more.
On its slopes is the city of Nain, in which the Lord raised the 16
widow's son from the dead. Eastwards from this city is the place 17

[1] Slightly to the north of east.

Endor, and between Tabor and Nain and Endor runs the Brook Kishon, of which David says, *'Do unto them as thou didst to Midian: as to Sisera and Jabin at the River Kishon, who were destroyed at Endor.'*[1]

12.1 A day's journey away is the city Sebaste, which Herod the
2 Tetrarch restored in Caesar's honour. In it is the venerable head of
him who was the greatest of men born of woman, John the Baptist,
3 whom Herod the Less slew at his banquet. In the middle of this city
is the prison into which he was thrown because of his accusations
4 against Herodias, and there also his head was cut off. This Prison is
underground, and has twenty steps leading down to it. In the
centre of it is an altar containing the spot where he was beheaded by
5 the guard. On the right of the altar is a coffin in which is preserved
6 the body of Saint Zacharias, the father of the Forerunner. And on
the left side is a second coffin in which lies the body of Saint
7 Elisabeth his mother. And in the walls on either side of the Prison
rest the remains of several other saints and of the disciples of the
8 Forerunner. Above the Prison is a church in which lie two coffins
carved in white marble. The one on the right contains the dust of
the body of the venerable Forerunner after it was burned, and the
9 other the body of the Prophet Elisha. Above this, in the church, the
left hand of the Forerunner is displayed in a gold vessel, and this
10 itself is completely encased in gold. In the central upper part of the
city is a mound, on which Herod's palace stood in ancient times,
where the banquet took place, and the abominable girl danced, and
as the reward for her dancing took the Holy Head of the Baptist.
11 This place has now been made into a Romaic monastery, and the
12 church of this monastery is domed. On the left of the altar is a small
chamber, in the middle of which one sees a small marble circle
lying over a very deep pit, in which the venerable Head was first
discovered of the Forerunner, venerable even to angels. This is the
place where Herodias buried it.

13.1 Then, after travelling on for about fifteen stades, comes the
capital of Samaria, Sychar, which later came to be called Neapolis.
It lies between two mountains, the feet of which touch it on both
2 sides. The slopes on the right belong to the mountain on which the
Samaritans say that Abraham spoke with God, and intended to
sacrifice Isaac, and that was where the Patriarch carried out the
sacrifice, according to their version, though they do not know

[1] Psalm 83.9f.

what they are saying. For the holy mountain in question is the 3
pavement of Golgotha, at which the Saviour of the World
underwent his saving Passion. At the foot of this mountain is the 4
place which Jacob gave to his son Joseph, and it contains the Well of
this very Jacob. At it the Lord, when weary, sat down and had with
the Samaritan woman the conversation recorded in the Holy
Gospel. It was of that mountain that the woman said to the Lord, 5
'Our fathers worshipped in this mountain.'[1] And the Lord, through the 6
words he spoke to her, taught all people how they must worship in
spirit and in truth.

It is eighty-four stades from Samaria to the Holy City, and the 14.1
whole journey is on a paved road. But it is a very dry countryside,
short of rain, though it produces vines and trees.

The Holy City lies among deep valleys and hills, and it is a
surprising city to see. For at the same time the city seems to stand 2
higher than everything and to be low down, for it does indeed
stand higher than the Judaean countryside, but it is low in
comparison with the neighbouring hills.

This Holy Place is divided in two. On the lower part of the hill 3
on the right is set the Holy City, with its wall running to meet the
valley, and all the ground above it is planted with vines. That is
where the stoning of the Protomartyr Saint Stephen took place. To 4
the left of this, and beyond the valley, is the Mount of Olives,
where the Lord often liked to spend time, and sanctified the whole
of the place by his prayer, his teaching, and his Holy Ascension to
the Father.

Holy Sion is in front of the Holy City, lying on its right. The 5,6
outer boundary of the city is as follows. There is a fortified area
containing Holy Sion, the Mother of All the Churches. This church
is very large, and has a barrel-vaulted roof. Entering its beautiful 7
gates there is on the left the House of Saint John the Theologian, in
which the Most Holy Virgin stayed after the resurrection, and
where she fell asleep. And in that place there is a chamber fenced in 8
with iron rails, and at the place where the Most Holy gave up her
spirit to her Son and God there are two houses.

To the right of this church and on the right of the sanctuary is the
Upper Room, to which there is a staircase of sixty-one steps. This 9
church has four domed vaults. And in the left part of the Upper

[1] John 4.20.

10 Room one sees the place where the Lord's Supper was held. In the
apse of the bema is the Descent of the Holy Spirit on the Apostles.
11 And beneath this church the Washing took place. Opposite is the
church at which stood the House into which Christ came to the
12 Apostles when the doors had been locked. In this the Protomartyr
Stephen was buried after he had been stoned, and was transferred to
another place next to Gamaliel.

13 The Tower called David's lies by the northern part of the city,
and is an enormous tower. Even though every one in Jerusalem
states that it is David's, yet to me personally there is doubt about
14 the probable time when it was made. In fact Josephus reports that
this tower was made of polished white stone, like the Temple and
the other two towers later founded by Herod, named Phasael and
15 Mariamme. But this one is erected in ordinary stone. Perhaps the
base seen today was built on the very ancient tower.

16 Next to this is the gate leading into the city, and when you enter
it you walk along a broad street. On its right, next to the Royal
Palace, is situated the Metochion of our Holy Father Saba.

17 Proceeding along the street about a bowshot you will find the
famous Church of the Lord's Sepulchre, whose appearance is as so
18 many others have reported it. The cave which served as the
Sepulchre for the Lord's body is in two parts. In one part of it lies the
stone which was rolled against it, which is protected by a white
marble casing, and in the other part on the north the stone is hewn so
that it stands about a cubit above the floor surface. On that the Giver
of Life was laid dead and naked. One sees that the shelf was plated
with pure gold by my Lord and King Manuel Porphyrogenitus and
Comnenos.

19 And near this is the place Golgotha, containing the Place of the
Skull and the hewn base of the Cross, and the split cleft in the rock
at the time when Christ was undergoing his Crucifixion. Beneath
the cleft is a hollow in the rock, which contained Adam's skull and
20 the drops of the Lord's blood which fell onto it. The church above
21 Golgotha is in four bays and vaulted. And near this church is a large
underground church in which was discovered the venerable and
life-giving Cross of the Lord Christ.

22 And in the eastern part of the city is the Temple, the Holy of
23 Holies. This Temple is of outstanding beauty. It has a domed roof,
and one sees it on the site of the famous Temple of Solomon. It is
24 decorated inside and out with variegated marble and mosaic. On

the left of the Temple are two rooms, in one of which is painted the
Meeting of Christ the Lord, since that was the place where the
Righteous Simeon took the Lord Christ in his arms. And in the 25
other the marvellous ladder which Jacob saw set up to heaven, and
the angels of God ascending and descending. The very stone can be
seen on which the ladder which is represented in the painting stood,
and on which Jacob's head rested.

On the right side one finds an opening leading down to a cave 26
underneath the Temple. In this was buried the Prophet Zacharias, 27
whom according to the Gospel the Jews slew between the Temple
and the altar. And outside, all round the Temple, is a large paved 28
court, which, I suppose, is the ancient floor of the Great Temple.

Near the gate which leads out towards Holy Gethsemane is the 29
Church of Saints Joachim and Anna, at which the Nativity of the
Immaculate Virgin took place, and near this the waters of the Sheep
Pool.

Leaving the city at that point on its east side, in the middle of the 15.1
deep cleft in the ground which divides the Mount of Olives from
the Holy City, lies the place called Gethsemane, which contains the
tomb of our Most Holy Lady the Mother of God, and the garden to
which our Saviour often resorted with his disciples.

There are three churches there. The one furthest to the left is 2
built round the underground pit in which is the Holy Tomb of the
Mother of God. This church is completely vaulted with a long
barrel vault. And in the middle of it stands her tomb like an ambo. 3
It has been hewn out of the rock in the shape of a building with four
vaults. And in the east side from the same rock a kind of conch has
been carved, with a white stone roof, on which the immaculate
Body of the Most Holy Mother of God was laid by the Holy
Apostles when they brought it here from Sion.

The second church, higher up, is the cave in which the Lord 4
made his prayer, and the Apostles were drowsy and lay down to
sleep. And near the foot of the Mount of Olives, about a stone's 5
throw off, according to the Gospel, is the third church, in which
the Lord, when he had reproved the disciples for their sloth, went
away and prayed again, when his sweat dripped down like drops of
blood. The betrayal took place in the same garden, and Judas falsely 6
kissed the Lord and the company of Jews seized him.

On the other side from the garden, high up towards Sion, is a 7
church, and below it a cave, into which Peter went after his denial,

and sat down and wept bitterly. In it there is a painting of the
8 Apostle as he mourned. And above Gethsemane and the Church of
the Prayer one sees the Mount of Olives, which is, as I said,
separated from the Holy City by the Valley of Jehoshaphat and the
9 Brook of the Valley of Weeping. The place is a hill rather higher
10 than the city. Because of this when you view it from the direction
of the city it does not appear very large. But from the side facing
the Jordan and Bethany it is very lofty indeed, and its slopes
continue all the way down to the desert.

11 On the summit of the mountain is the place at which the Saviour
often addressed his disciples after the resurrection, and later
12 accomplished the most awesome mystery of his ascension. Near
that place and below it is the cave in which Saint Pelagia completed
her ascetic course, and there her holy body rests in a stone coffin.
13 And near this is another church where the Lord imparted to his
14 disciples the prayer 'Our Father'. On the left part of the city[1] has
been added a Romaic monastery, which, so it is said, has been built
on the foundations of the one erected by the venerable Melania.

15 On the other side, away from this mountain and beyond the city
in the direction of Samaria, there is a monastery to which the holy
and sacred body of the Protomartyr Saint Stephen, after he had
been stoned and had been buried in the place I have already
16 mentioned beneath Gamaliel, was transferred. Moreover the brook
which comes from Gethsemane passes by the Laura of Saint Saba
and the desert of Ruba, which is near the Dead Sea of Sodom.

16.1 Beside Gethsemane, about a bowshot away, stands 'The Jar', a
rock monument which is square in plan and higher, I should think,
that two spears. It is shaped like a pyramid and has a sharp top. An
Iberian monk has shut himself inside it, and takes care of his own
2 salvation. Beyond this is a great rock in which various artificial
caves have been made. They are called 'The Virgin's Caves', and in
them monks dwell, not many of them orthodox but more
3 Armenians and Jacobites. After that opens up the gorge containing
4 the Valley of Weeping. And beyond this is the Potter's Field, which
was bought for the burial of strangers with the price paid for the
5 Lord. After this comes the Pool of Siloam, the waters of which
6 irrigate that place, which is very dry. Beyond that level meadows
7 cover the floor of the valley, and one sees many trees there. But the

[1] The word 'city' must be a mistake.

Spring is surrounded by roofs and closely-set columns, and is most
beautiful.

So the valley leads away to the Laura of Saint Saba, as we have 8
already said, which is eleven miles away. At that point the Valley 9
broadens out into a dry gorge, and one sees there the Laura and the 10
Church and the Saint's Tomb. In front of the Laura on both banks of 11
the gorge are caves and little turrets, in which live those who have
hated the world and its luxury for the sake of the Kingdom of Heaven;
they undergo the unbearable heat there, putting out the flame which
can be extinguished with the flame which is unquenchable.

In the part where the Church is and the Tomb of the divinely- 12
inspired Saint, Father Saba, the valley is three times as wide and
deep as a vast chasm. The Saint built towers along the brow, and 13
set the Church in the middle of the towers. He built the new
hermits' cells round them, as described in the account of his
miraculous life. Moreover the Church is full of pleasant things, and 14
large, long and full of light. Its floor is decorated with slabs of 15
marble, which are not expensive, since they are taken from the
desert, but even so they are colourfully arranged.

In front of the Church is a paved court, and in the centre of it is 16
the Tomb of the Great Man, our Father Saba. It rises above the
ground about a span, and it is sheltered under white marble. Close 17
to it and round it in the ground one sees the monuments of the
Holy Fathers who lived their glorious lives in the desert. And 18
among them one sees also the tombs of the ancient Poets, Cosmas
and John: near them those of the Forty Inspired Men who were 19
chosen from the rest, and of whom six spoke directly with God.
Their names are Stephen, Theodore and Paul. The fourth came
from the great city, the fifth was an Iberian, and the sixth, famous
for his spiritual vision, was the Stylite John.

When you return to the Holy City, not along the valley but 17.1
along the hills beside it, you find, before you have gone six miles,
the monastery of our Holy Father Theodosius the Coenobiarch.
This monastery is surrounded by a number of towers, and about a 2
bowshot in front of it is the furnace, in which, as is shown in the
Saint's life, the coals which had stopped burning became alight in
his hand. In the middle of the monastery stands the Church, which
has on top of it a circular roof, and beneath it the cave which
contains his Tomb. Nearby are several more chambers in which
rest the remains of great saints.

3 As you go down the steps of the cave you will find on one side the opening of another cave which the disciples of Saint Basil entered, and restored his own tomb at the bidding of the Saint, as we are informed in *The Lives of the Fathers*, and afterwards for forty days at the time of the liturgy he was seen praising God with the Saint and his brothers.

18.1 Opposite this monastery on the right, near the bottom of the desert of the Jordan, is the monastery of Saint Euthymius the
2 Great, and this too is defended by walls and great bulwarks. In the middle of it stands the Church, and this too has a barrel-vaulted roof. Below this is the cave which has in the middle of it the Tomb of the great Euthymius. It is very like the Tomb of the Inspired Saba, and this too has a shelter of white marble. In it are buried with the Saint the remains of the Holy Fathers Passarion and Dometianus.

19.1 You go on for about twelve miles when you leave this
2 monastery. Then you find a large gorge, through the middle of which runs a brook. On the far side of this gorge is the Monastery of Choziba. It is a place about which no report will be believed, and only when it is seen are its wonders to be understood.

3 Indeed the recesses of caves are the monks' cells. And the Church itself and the cemetery are set in the chasm of the rock, and everything is so blasted by the burning sun that one can see the rock
4 emitting tongues of flame like pyramids. In fact the water which the monks drink is of the kind which comes from a pool, when the midsummer sun hangs above the pools and heats it to boiling-point
5 with its fiery rays. In this monastery we saw several sanctified men, one of whom was a standard-bearer who spoke directly with God,
6 and this Old Man's name is Luke. It was dangerous climbing to the monastery because the place is so steep, and because of the fierce glare of the sun.

20.1 After this there is a long, narrow and extremely rough track leading out to the edge of the desert. On the track there come into view two ridges between which the track passes on its way to Jericho. At that place not even one foundation stone is to be found, but the whole arrangement of the place is confused. The reason for this being so is because the whole district is well watered, and is
2 used for a garden for the monasteries situated in the desert. The ground is parcelled out and shared among the Holy Monasteries. It is all planted with trees and vines, and for this reason the monks

have set up towers among the monks' allotments, from which they harvest fruit in plenty.

The whole region is desert, and the Jordan and the Dead Sea of 3
Sodom appear in our estimation like that of the landscape of
Achris. The only evident difference is that Lake Achris is the source
of the water which runs from it to settle in several valleys, which
the inhabitants of that district call 'strugae'. But here the Jordan
runs towards the Lake, and the width of the desert is a great deal
more than the plain of Achris.

On the right of the double ridge I have mentioned is the shore of 21.1
the Dead Sea, and beyond it Segor. And there beyond this desert
one can see the great desert of Ruba, which is beyond the track
which leads to the two monasteries of Saint Euthymius and the
Laura.

On the left of the ridges and the track can be seen the mountain 2
on which, after the Saviour had fasted for forty days, the Tempter
brought against him two temptations, even though he was later
defeated and went away in disgrace. Facing this mountain and, as I 3
reckon, six miles away, there is a mountain, and on the mountain is
a church at which Michael, Captain of the Host, spoke with Joshua
the son of Nun.

Near the Jordan have been built three monasteries, that is the 22.1
Prodromos, Chrysostom [and that of Kalamon]. The monastery of
the Prodromos was completely demolished by an earthquake. But
it has now been newly rebuilt by the munificent hand of our
Emperor, crowned by God, Manuel Porphyrogenitus and
Comnenos, because the head of the community spoke freely to him
about it being rebuilt.

About two bowshots from it flows that holiest of rivers the 2
Jordan, in which my Jesus in his humility accomplished the great
mystery of my re-creation through his Baptism. On the bank,
about a bowshot from the river, is a square domed building. Up
to that point, before it retreated from him, the Jordan ran up, and
received naked him who is clothed in the clouds of heaven. There
the right hand of the Forerunner touched his head, and the Spirit,
in the form of a dove, came down on the co-equal Word, and the
voice of the Father witnessed to the Redeemer that he was his
Son. 23.1

Between the monastery of the Forerunner and the Jordan is the very small mountain Hermoniim, on which the Saviour stood.

There John pointed to him, and declared to the crowds that this was the one who takes away the sin of the world.

2 And between the monasteries of the Forerunner and of Kalamon
is a monastery which has been utterly destroyed by the River
Jordan, that of Saint Gerasimus. Nothing at all of it is now visible
except a few remains of the Church, two caves, and a hermit's
column. Here the hermit is a great Old Man who is an Iberian. He
is gracious and works miracles, and when we met him we were
greatly helped by our converse with him. Indeed a divine grace
possessed the Old Man.

3 Now we have decided to tell, for the sake of those who are eager
to make divine things their delight, a nice little story of a miracle he
performed a few days before our visit to him.

4 In the twists and turns of the bed of the Jordan there are
5 places where reed grow thickly. Families of lions used to live
6 in them. Two of them used to appear each week at the Old
Man's hermitage. Leaning their heads against the column
they looked at him in a way that meant they wanted food, and
when they were given it they went peacefully off to their
7 usual place by the river, quite happy. Their food was pulse
soaked in water, or perhaps pieces of bread made of rice-
wheat or barley.

8 They continued to appear and, by the way they were
looking at him, to be begging for their usual food. But the
Old Man could not see how to provide for the animals'
appetite. So it turned out that when the holy Old Man had
received nothing to eat for a space of twenty days, he said to
9 them, 'Animals! we have nothing to sustain the weakness of
our nature by eating what we need. But God is quite easily
able to fulfil our needs, and by his dispensation he will
provide for us. Thus we must go to the streams of the Jordan,
10 and bring ourselves a small piece of wood. From it we will
make crosses, and we will give them as blessings to those
11 who come to pray. And we shall receive from them in return,
as each decides, a few coppers with which we can provide
food for me and for you.'

12 When he had spoken and the animals had heard him, they
13 went down just like humans to the waters of the Jordan. And
the amazing thing is that not long afterwards they brought

back two pieces of wood under their chins. They put them down at the base of the column, and went hastily back to their marshes by the Jordan.

But enough of this! We are occupied with an account of the Places. 14

Indeed the Monastery of the Calamon is also built with towers 24.1
and walls of squared masonry, and the Church which occupies the
central place is domed and set on barrel-vaults.

A second Church, also vaulted, is attached to the right of it. It is 2
very small, and was erected, so it is said, in the days of the
Apostles. In its apse is represented the Mother of God holding the
Saviour Christ in her arms, which in its composition, its colour and
its size, resembles the icon of the Most Holy Hodegetria in the
capital. It is reported on the basis of ancient traditions that this was 3
painted by the hand of the Apostle and Evangelist Saint Luke. The 4
many miracles and the awesome fragrance which issued from the
icon argue for the truth of the report.

And after that, about five stades away, stands the Monastery of 5
Chrysostom. About a bowshot from it stood a hermit's column on 6
which the Great Man remained in quietude. He was an Iberian by
race, simple in his way of life, impressive in his words, who had
before for a long time continued in ascetic exercises on a rock
situated near the Attalian Sea. There was a time when we ourselves 7
met the man, when we were on campaign with the Honourable
Emperor and Porphyrogenitus Comnenos.

Across the Jordan, facing the Baptism, are some thickets, and 25.1
among these, about a stade away, is the Cave of John Baptist. It is
very small, and a tall man cannot stand upright in it. And there is 2
another cave like it in the depths of the desert in which the prophet
Elijah was staying when he was snatched away in the chariot of
fire. The area between these caves and the course of the Jordan is 3
said to be the desert in which the marvellous Zosimas was held
worthy to see the peer of angels, the Egyptian lady. From those 4
mountains begins the desert leading to Sinai, Raithu, and the Red
Sea. But now let my account of the desert be brought to its close. 5

On the right of the Holy City, Jerusalem, that is the side of the 26.1
Tower of the Prophet David, is a hill entirely covered with vines.
In the slopes of this stands a Monastery of the Iberians, within the
enclosure of which it is said that the wood of the Venerable Cross
was hewn.

2 Round that place is the country of Oreine, and it is well-named, because it is more mountainous than any hill-country for a distance
3 of many stades round it. And about fourteen stades from the Holy City is the House of the Prophet Zacharias, into which after the Annunciation the Wholly Immaculate Virgin arose and went in haste and greeted Elisabeth, and the child leaped in her belly for joy, leaping as if he was receiving the Lord. There the Virgin uttered the marvellous prophetic song.

4 At that place is a village in which a church is built above a cave, and in the recesses of the cave the birth of the Forerunner took place. And near this, about two bowshots away, and in a higher part of the mountain, is the cleft rock, which received the Mother of the Baptist, when she fled with the child in her arms at the time when Herod murdered the children.

27.1 Outside Jerusalem, between the two roads, one of which leads to the Hill Country and the other to the Monastery of the Coenobiarch and the Laura, is a ridge, and the road on it leads from
2 Holy Sion to Bethlehem. The city of Bethlehem is about six miles
3 from the Holy City. At the half way point from the Holy City is a Monastery of the Holy Prophet Elijah, which was erected by the ancient men who loved God, but had fallen down completely because of the earthquake. But this too the universal benefactor, my Lord and King, raised from the foundations, the work being done under the direction of a certain Syrian who was abbot.

Now the country between this monastery and Bethlehem forms a triangle with the Tomb of Rachel, which is a roofed building with a square vaulted structure.

4 On the left of Holy Bethlehem, between it and the Monastery of the Coenobiarch, one sees the Field, and in the Field a cave in which the blessed Shepherds were out of doors and heard the angels sing 'Glory in the Highest', and answering 'To God, and on earth salvation' when the bearing of my God took place by the Virgin Mother of God.

5 Holy Bethlehem is founded on a paved hill, which contains both the Holy Cave and the Manger. It contains also the Well from which David longed to drink, and a Church set at the back of the Cave, which a visitor sees to be big both in length and height, cross-shaped, and roofed with imperishable wood. The roof near the sanctuary is supported on a stone vault.

6 But this most beautiful and most spacious Church also was

erected by my most moderate Emperor's liberal hand. He
decorated the whole church with gold mosaic. And in gratitude for
this generosity the Latin pastor intruded into that place at once set
up the Emperor's portrait in several places, and even in the holy
sanctuary above the Cave.

This is the arrangement of the Cave, the Manger and the Well. 7
On the left of the bema is the entry of the Holy Cave, and next to it 8
is the Well from which, both in body and soul, David, Christ's
ancestor, longed to drink. Two men of his court cut their way
through the Gentiles' ambush, drew this water in a bucket, and
brought it to him as he burned with thirst. And he, by pouring it
on the ground to God, is acclaimed to this day for the memorable
action he performed.

From the entry of the Cave to the bottom is a descent of sixteen 9
steps. Towards the north side is the Holy Lodging in which the 10
Virgin gave birth to the Saviour Christ, and the whole creation
beheld God in Flesh, and the whole world was renewed. Mortal
man that I am, I am made rich when the divinity of my God and
Creator shares my poverty.

Then, one step down, one sees the manger of the animals, a 11
regular square in shape, which men of old cased with white marble,
making in the middle of it an aperture like a navel, through which
one can see part of it. That is the Manger which came close to the
Unapproachable, more immense than heaven, and far more
spacious than earth and sea and the subterranean regions. For he
whom they did not suffice to contain, this Manger received when
he was an infant, and had room to spare. At the picture of it I 12
delight, and with my whole awareness I am in that Holy Cave, and
I see all the circumstances of the Lord's birth. I see the repose in the
Manger of the one who has been born, and the awesome love of the
Saviour towards me, and his consummate humility by which he
has counted me worthy of the Kingdom of Heaven. Indeed I see
that Cave as a palace, and the King sitting on the Virgin's lap as if
on a throne. And I see choirs of angels surrounding the Cave, and
the Magi bringing their gifts to the King. I am thus filled with
complete gladness, and I rejoice as I understand the depth of the
grace which is bestowed on me.

The artist has painted with his artist's hand in this very Cave the 13
mysteries which were accomplished here. For round the apse is 14
depicted that great mystery of the world by which the Maiden

reclines on the couch, with her left hand placed beneath the other elbow, and with her cheek leaning on her right hand. She is looking at the Child, and her inner temperance is shown in her smiling face and the good colour of her cheeks. For her face is not strained, or pale like that of a woman who has just given birth, but as the one who was counted worthy to bear in that supernatural way she must also have been spared the pains of nature.

15 There is the ass and the ox and the manger and the Child and the
flock of the shepherds. But when a voice came from heaven to their
ears they fled away from their flocks. They leave the sheep
neglected, feeding by the grass and the spring, and they entrusted
the care of the flock to the dog. They stretch their heads towards
heaven, turning to listen in the direction of the singing, and all
standing in different attitudes so that each one can hear more easily
and stand up without difficulty. To some their crooks seem useless
now, and for others their gaze is directed to the sky. They draw
back their hands as if they were throwing something, and thus
extend their capacity for hearing from all sides. But they had no
16 need to hear twice, for eyes are more to be trusted than ears. For the
angel has met them, and is revealing to them that the Child is lying
in the manger.

17 And the animals of the flock take no notice of the sight, but go
their way in their simplicity, some bending down to the grass and
18 others making off to the spring we have mentioned. But the bitch,
the animal which is fierce to strangers, seems to notice that the
vision is unusual. The Magi, dismounting from their horses and
carrying their gifts in their hands, kneel, and in awe offer them to
the Virgin.

28.1 About two miles outside Bethlehem inside the Monastery of the
Coenobiarch, is the cave in which the Magi, having been warned
not to return to King Herod, returned to their country another
2 way. And about twelve miles from there near the desert of Ruba is
the Monastery of Saint Chariton.

3 A considerable way beyond that is the double tomb of Abraham in Hebron, and the oak Mamre, at which the Patriarch Abraham entertained the All-holy Trinity.

So much, then, for our account of the Places from Ptolemais, through Galilee, as far as the Holy City of Jerusalem, of the Jordan, and the Holy Desert.

29.1 The places along the coast are as follows. | About six miles from

the Holy City of Jerusalem is the city of Armathem, in which that
great Prophet Samuel was born. And after that, after a further 2
seven miles or more, is Emmaus, a great city situated in the middle
of a valley on a ridge which rises above it. Then there stretches out
for about twenty-four miles the Ramleh area, and in this one sees a
very large Church of the great Martyr Saint George. He was born
in these parts, and undertook great contest for the love of God, and
his holy Tomb is there. The Church is rectangular, and in the apse 3
of the bema, beneath the floor of the Holy Table, the small opening
of the Tomb is to be seen, surrounded with white marble.

Now we must speak of the many things we have heard from the 4
clergy of the Church which took place at the Tomb several years
ago. For they said that the Latin bishop, then intruded, tried to 5
open up the mouth of the Tomb. When the slab that surrounded it
was lifted a large cave was discovered, and within it the Tomb of
the Saint was found. But as they were attempting to open it, fire 6
was seen leaping from the Tomb, which cause one of them to be
half burnt, and it brought another to a sudden death.

After this comes Caesarea Philippi, a great city well populated, 30.1
which is situated on the shore of the sea, in which there is a
remarkable harbour. It is the product of human ingenuity, with the 2
hand of Herod munificently providing for its construction. In that 3
city Christ asked the apostles, *'Whom do men say that I, the Son of
Man, am?' And Peter answered, 'Thou art the Christ, the Son of God'*,[1]
thus demonstrating the fervour of his love.

After that is Mount Carmel, of which much has been said both in 31.1
the Old and the New Testaments. The Mount is a ridge which 2
begins in the direction of Ptolemais with the Bay of Haifa, and
stretches as far as the Mountains of Galilee. Near its steep end by 3
the Sea this ridge contains the Cave of the Prophet Elijah, and when
that marvellous man had finished his angelic life, he was there taken
up to heaven.

Formerly there was in that place a large monastery, which is 4
evidenced by the ruins which can now be seen. But in the course
of time, which makes everything decay, and through occasional
attacks by enemies, it had utterly vanished. Some time ago a man 5
who was a monk in Holy Orders, a Priest, grey-haired and who
came from Calabria, spent time in the place after having a vision

[1] Matt 16.13, 16.

of the Prophet. Then he made a little enclosure among the monastic dwellings, built a tower, erected a small church, and gathered about ten Brothers. In that Holy Place he now dwells.

32.1 This is the point at which the writing of this description is to end,
since at this place my return journey from the Holy Places was
2 completed. If any one who happens to read this work judges it to
be useful, that will be my reward for the work I have done, and I shall regard it as a precious prize. But if otherwise, let my offspring return to me, its begetter. With its stammers may it remind me of these Holy Places, so that I can recreate their memory in my mind. For that too will be a sweet delight.

APPENDIX

OUTLINE OF THE GEOGRAPHICAL WORK AND FRETELLUS TO BISHOP SDYCK

Note: the number on the far left of the column is the page-number in M. de Vogüé, *Les Eglises de la Terre Sainte*, Paris 1860. The subject of the chapter follows, with its reference number in this translation. If there is a parallel in Fretellus version to Bishop Henri Sdyck, the chapter heading (Boerens) is quoted. If the passage has a parallel in the late twelfth-century manuscripts of the work of Fretellus (D^2 and Vat), it is marked with a star, and references will be found in Boerens' edition.

	[HEBRON, THE DEAD SEA]		
414	Title	1	7
	Hebron	2	7
	position	3	
	Adam's creation	4	7
	nature of site	5	★
	foundation	6	
	Hebron called Mamre	7	
	Mount Mamre	8	9
	Agias Trias	9	
415	guests	10	9
	food, altar	11	
	Trinity Feast	12	★
	Tree and medicine	13	9
	name Arbe	14	8
	Valley of Tears, Field	15	8
	exile of Adam	16	★
	Adam's Field, sale	17	8
	Adam red-coloured	18	

	Spies	19	9
	David	20	9
	David's sons, Dabir	21	
	Lot's Tomb	22	8
	Beersheba	23	
	Beth Tappuah	24	
	Asphalt Lake	25	10
	Zoar	26	11
416	Lot's drunkenness	27	
	Village of Palms	28	11
	Pentapolis	29	
	En-gedi	30	23
	Asphalt Lake	31	11
	alum, petrol, bitumen	32	★
	Zodran	32	★
417	Shaveh	33	24
	border Judaea–Arabia	34	11
	[ARABIA]		
	Jerome's *Letter 78* is now quoted at length. Among the additions the following are of special interest.		
417	Sinai	35	★
418	end of section on Sinai	36	
419	Mount Eden	37	★
420	Beth-hoglah	38	23
	Emek-achor	39	23
	Jebusites capture Jericho	40	★
	Gilgal	41	23
	Bostra, Trachonitis, Ituraea	42	24
	Uz	43	★
	Bostra	44	See 217
	[DAMASCUS]		
	Founder	45	28
	Damascus once capital	46	★

	two names, metropolis	47	25
	Sedrath	48	25
421	Esau, Idumaea	49	28
	City of Idumaea	50	
	Seir, Jabbok, Christ	51	28
	distance of Paneas	52	★
	Belinas	53	31
	Malbech	54	★
	Albana	55	29
	Arqa	56	★
	division of districts	57	25
	Pharpar	58	29
	Jor and Dan	59	31
	Aulon	59	32
	details on Scythopolis	60	
	Baal, Baal Meon	61	32
	Aenon	62	40
	Asteroth Carnaim	63	
	Jordan divides districts	64	32
	Meddan	65	33
	[GALILEE]		
422	Fields of Thorns	66	★
	Jordan River, Bethsaida	67	33
	Chorazim, Kedar, Capernaum	68	34
423	5,000 fed, Gergesa	69	35
	Genezareth, Magdala, Kinnereth	70	36
	name of Tiberias	71	
	name of Lake	72	36
	nature of Lake	73	
	Bethulia, Dothan, Nazareth	74	36
	Nazareth	75	37
	synagogue	76	
	Fountain, Sepphoris	77	37ba
	Sepphoris	78	
	Saint Anne	79	37
	Cana	80	37
	Simon the Canaanean	81	
	Cana	82	37
	Fall, Mount Tabor	83	38

	roundness	84	41
	Transfiguration	85	38
	Abraham	86	39
	Hermon, another Hermon	87	39
	Tithes	88	
	Naim, Deborah	89	39
	Sharon	90	41
424	Jezreel	91	40
	Ahab and Jezebel	92	
	Jezreel, Megiddo	93	40
	Gilboa, Scythopolis	94	40
	Elkosh	95	
	[SAMARIA]		
	Jenin, Gur, Samaria	96	41
	Samaria name of district	97	42
	Sennacherib, Antiochus	98	
	name, John the Baptist	99	42
	Vandals, soldiers rise	100	
	Index finger	101	42
	mother eats son, Elisha	102	
	Shunem	103	42
	Simon Magus	104	
	Shechem	105	43
	Four mountains overhang	106	
	Jerome's opinion	107	44
	Luzan	108	45
425	Abraham sacrifices Isaac	109	*
	Jacob's dream	110	45
	Betheven	111	
	pillar	112	45
	Sychar, Terebinth	113	43
	Timnath-Heres	114	44
	Saint-Gilles	115	*
	distance to Jerusalem, Ephrata	116	45
	Jebusites founded	117	
	Bethlehem	118	46
	Boaz	119	46
	Manger	120	46
	Star, Innocents, Ramale, Jerome	121	47

	Tekoa	122	48
	Habakkuk	123	
	Chariton	124	48
	Chabratha, Tomb of Rachel	125	49
	Beth-haccherem	126	68
	[JERUSALEM – I]		
426	Names of Jerusalem	127	★
	metropolis, Centre of the Earth	128	50
	scriptures confirming	129	
	excels all cities	130	★
	David's reign, Isaiah	131	50
	Mount Moriah	132	51
	time Temple was built	133	
	Solomon's expenses	134	51
	Nebuchadnezzar	135	52
	Zedekiah's fate	136	
	rebuildings	137	52
	present Temple	138	53
	decoration	139	★
	relic of Foreskin	140	54
	Jesus' doings there	141	55
	Saint's doings there	142	56
	Near Saint Anne's church is	143	
	the Sheep Pool. Girl	144	57
	James, Templars, Hostel	145	★
427	Lepers' House	146	★
	Hyrcanus and Xenodochia	147	★
	Topheth	148	58
	Valley of Hinnom	149	71
	Siloam	150	58
	source is Mt Shiloh	151	58
	name of Siloam, En Rogel, Zoheleth	152	58
	Fuller's Field, Gihon	153	61
	Tomb of James	154	58
	[ORDER OF PASSION]		
	Bethany	155	58
	Bethany, Simon, Maries	156	59
	Bethphage	157	[59]

	Sion, Last Supper	158	61
	Jerusalem, Gethsemane, Lithostrotos	159	62
	Mocking, Crucifixion	160	[63]
	Latin church, mourners	161	★
	mourners, Holy Fire, Mary Magdalene	162	★
	Prison	163	65
428	Eleutheropolis=Emmaus	164	65
	Mount Sion	165	66
	Resurrection appearance	166	66
	Ascension	167	66
	[JERUSALEM – II]		
	Tomb of Pelagia	168	★
	Sion, Mary's death	169	66
	Sion, Pentecost	170	66
	Sion, tombs	171	67
	Stoning of Stephen	172	★
	Lion's Cave	173	68
	Tree of the Cross grew	174	64
	Helena found the Cross	175	64
	Helena's doings	176	
	Mount of Offence	177	58
	Anathoth	178	68
	Scopulus	179	
	Visitation	180	68
	Gibeah	181	58
	city of Phineas	182	
	Gabatha	183	69
	Gibeah, Saul, Levite's wife	184	
	Eben-ezer	185	69
	Beth-Horon	186	70
	Joel's village	187	
	Gibeon, another Gibeon	188	70
	Ziph	189	70
	Abigail	190	
	another Ziph	191	70
	David's doings there	192	
429	Keilah	193	71
	Modin	194	69
	impregnability	195	★

	Tombs of Maccabees	196	69
	[JERICHO]		
	Adummim, Jericho	197	71
	Jordan	198	72
	story of Saint Saba	199	★
	Jericho, blind man	200	72
	Quarantena, Spring	201	73
	[JOURNEY TO NORTH]		
	Lydda	202	★
	Timnath	203	★[71]
	Arimathea	204	★69
	Bethlehem bishop takes relics	205	★
430	Village of Baths	206	★
	Joppa	207	★
	Assur	208	★
	Dor	209	[74]
	Caesarea	210	74
	in Saracen's time	211	★
	crocodiles	212	★
	Scariathas	213	★
	Porphyrium	214	[74]
	Carmel	215	★74
	Mount Cain	216	★73
	Acre	217	★
	Tyre	218	★
	Tyre, Warmundus	221	26
432	Zarephath, Sarepta	222	26
	Gath-Hepher	223	26
	Sidon, Dido	224	26
	Berytus	225	27
	Gibelet, Tripolis, Albana	226	★
	[JERUSALEM – III]		
	Three foundations	227	★
	Tower of David	228	75
	Citadel	229	★
433	Tower, Godfrey's vow	230	76
	Godfrey's epitaph	231	★
	Succeeding kings to Fulk	232	

A LIST OF SOURCES

A. ABBREVIATIONS COMMON IN THIS LIST

AB = *Analecta Bollandiana*, Paris and Brussels, 1882 ff.
BGA = *Bibliotheca Geographorum Arabum*, Leyden 1870 ff.
CSCO = *Corpus Scriptorum Christianorum Orientalium*, Paris, etc., 1903 ff.
CSEL = *Corpus Scriptorum Ecclesiasticorum Latinorum*, Vienna 1866 f.
CSL = *Corpus Christianorum, Series Latina*, Turnhout 1953 ff.
Eg. Tr. = *Egeria's Travels*, tr. J. Wilkinson, London 1971.
FC = *Fathers of the Church*, ed. R. J. Deferrari.
GCS = *Die griechischen christlichen Schriftsteller der ersten drei Jahrhunderte*, Leipzig – Berlin 1897 ff.
Loeb = *Loeb Classical Library*, London and Cambridge, Mass. 1912 ff.
NPNF = *Nicene and Post-Nicene Christian Fathers*, New York 1887 – 92 Oxford 1890–1900.
NTA = *New Testament Apocrypha*, ed. E. Hennecke–W. Schneemelcher, tr. R. McL. Wilson, 2 vols, London 1963.
PG = *Patrologia Graeca*, ed. J. P. Migne, Paris 1857 ff.
PL = *Patrologia Latina*, ed. J. P. Migne, Paris 1844 ff.
PO = *Patrologia Orientalis*, ed. R. Graffin–F. Nau, Paris, 1907 ff.
RHC = *Receuil des Histoires des Croisades, Historiens Occidentaux*, Paris 1844–95.
SC = *Sources Chrétiennes*, Paris 1940 ff.
TGA = *Textes Géographiques Arabes*, tr. A. Marmadji, Paris 1951.
TU = *Texte und Untersuchungen*, Leipzig 1882 ff.

B. ALPHABETICAL LIST OF AUTHORS BEFORE 1099

The figures which follow the names in this list indicate years. Names in brackets are authors to whom a work has been wrongly ascribed.

Achilles Tatius 390
Adomnan 685
al Muqaddesi 985
Armenian Lectionary of Jerusalem 417–38
Breviarius sixth century
Commemoratorium 808
Georgian Kanonarion 700–750
Constantine 715–1009
Passion of the Forty Martyrs 639
Protevangelium of James 150
Short Account (Brevarius) of Jerusalem 6th c.
Bede 702–3
(Bede) 7th c.
Bernard the Monk 870
Bordeaux pilgrim 333
Christian Druthmar 870
Cyril of Jerusalem 348–51
Cyril of Scythopolis 557
Egeria or Etheria 384
Epiphanius the Monk a. 638–89: b. & c. 715–1009
Epiphanius of Salamis 374–94
Eusebius of Caesarea 303–39
Eutychius of Alexandria 939–44
Gregory of Tours 585
Hippolytus of Thebes 460–90
Hrabanus Maurus 830
Ibn Abdi Rabbih 913
Istakhri 951
Jerome 377–419
(Jerome) 850
John Euchaita 1050

Josephus 77, 94
Justin Martyr 155
Lucian the Priest 415
Nasir i Khosrau 1047
Origen 231–46
Paschasius Radbertus 850
Paulinus of Nola 403–9
Piacenza pilgrim 570
Procopius of Caesarea 550–8
Rabanus Maurus 830
Silvia or Egeria 384
Sophronius of Jerusalem c. 614
Sozomen 439–50
Strategius 760
Theodosius 518
Ya'kubi 874–91
Yahya Ibn Said 1050–63

C. CHRONOLOGICAL LIST OF SOURCES

Where possible this chronological list of works gives under each entry the date of the work, the author's name, the title of the work, the edition to which references are made elsewhere in the book, and any English translation known to the compiler.

If an author is known to have spent any significant time in the Holy Land his name appears in capitals. An author whose name appears in brackets is one to whom a work has been wrongly ascribed.

A.D.

77–78 JOSEPHUS, *The Jewish War*, ed. and tr. H. St J. Thackeray, Loeb vols 2 and 3, 1927–8.

c. 94 JOSEPHUS, *Antiquities of the Jews*, ed. and tr. H. St J. Thackeray and others, Loeb vols 4–9, 1930–63.

c. 150 *Protevangelium of James* (Eng. tr. by O. Cullmann) *NTA* I, pp. 374–388 and M.R. James, *The Apocryphal New Testament*, Oxford 1924.

c. 155 JUSTIN MARTYR *Dialogue with Trypho*, ed. P. Maran, *PG* 6; tr. T. B. Falls, *FC* 6.

after 246 ORIGEN, *Against Celsus*, ed. M. Borret, *SC* 132/136, 1967/8; tr. H. Chadwick, Cambridge, England, 1965.

315–320 EUSEBIUS, *Demonstration of the Gospel*, ed. I. A. Heikel, *GCS* (VI) 1913; tr. A. C. McGiffert and E. C. Richardson, *NPNF*, 1890.

before 331 EUSEBIUS, *Onomasticon*, ed. E. Klostermann, *GCS* (III.2), 1904.

333 BORDEAUX PILGRIM, *Travels*, ed. P. Geyer and O. Cuntz, *CSL* 175, pp. 1–26; part tr. J. Wilkinson, *Eg. Tr.* pp. 153–161.

before 348 CYRIL OF JERUSALEM, *Catechetical Lectures*, ed. A. A. Touttée and P. Maran, *PG* 33. Note that the last five (mystagogical) lectures may belong to Cyril's successor John of Jerusalem, bishop 386–417 A.D.

374–377 EPIPHANIUS OF SALAMIS, *Against the Heresies*, ed. K. Holl, *GCS* (I.1–3) 1915–33.

384 EGERIA, *Travels*, ed. A. Franceschini and R. Weber, *CSL* 175, 1965, pp. 37–90 and parts of Appendix, pp. 93–103; tr. J. Wilkinson, London 1971, pp. 91–147 and 180–210: 'e' page references are to this translation.

387–389 JEROME (b) *Questions on the Hebrew of Genesis*, ed. M. Adriaen, *CSL* 73.

JEROME (c) *Book of Places (Liber locorum)*, ed. K. Klostermann, *GCS* (Eus. III.1), 1904.

JEROME, *Commentaries on Zephaniah*, ed. M. Adriaen, *CSL* 76–76A.

390 JEROME, *Interpretation of Hebrew Names*, ed. P. Lagarde, *CSL* 72.

c. 390 Achilles Tatius, *Loves of Clitophon and Leucippe*, ed. R. Hercher, *Erotici Scriptores Graeca*, vol. 1, Leipzig 1858.

400 JEROME, *Letter* 78, ed. Hilberg, tr. Fremantle.

403 Paulinus of Nola, *Letter* 31, ed. W. Hartel, *CSEL* 29.

404 JEROME, *Letter* 108, ed. I. Hilberg, *CSEL* 55, 1912; tr. W. Fremantle, *NPNF* II.6, and in part j 47/52.

415 LUCIAN THE PRIEST, *Letter on the Discovery of Saint Stephen*, ed. J. P. Migne, *PL* 41, 807–9.

417–439 *The Armenian Lectionary of Jerusalem (Codex Arm. Jerusalem 121)*, ed. A. Renoux, PO 35; English summary, J. Wilkinson, *Eg. Tr.* pp. 262–77.

439–450 SOZOMEN, *Ecclesiastical History*, ed. J. Bidez–G. C. Hansen, *GCS*, Berlin 1960; tr. C. D. Hartranft, *NPNF* II.2.

460–490 Hippolytus of Thebes, *Texts*, ed. F. Diekamp, Münster-i-W, 1898.

early 6th c. *Short Account of Jerusalem (Brevarius)*, ed. R. Weber, *CSL* 175 and 176 pp. 852 f.; tr. J. 59/61.

before 518 THEODOSIUS, *The Topography of the Holy Land*, ed. P. Geyer, *CSL* 175; tr. J. 63/71.

c. 557 CYRIL OF SCYTHOPOLIS, *Lives*, ed. E. Schwartz, *TU* 49.2 (1939); Fr. tr. A. Festugière, *Les Moines de l'Orient*, III.1, 1–3, Paris 1961–3.

before 558 PROCOPIUS OF CAESAREA, *Justinian's Buildings*, ed. and tr. H. B. Dewing and G. Downey, Loeb 7, 1961.

c. 570 THE PIACENZA PILGRIM, *Travels*, ed. P. Geyer, *CSL* 175; tr. J. 79/89.

c. 585 Gregory of Tours, *The Book of Miracles*, ed. T. Ruinart, *PL* 71.

7th–9th c. (Bede) *Homily on Palm Sunday*, ed. J. A. Giles, *PL* 94, 507.

c. 614 SOPHRONIUS OF JERUSALEM, *Anacreontica*, ed. M. Gigante (=*Opuscula, Testi per esercitazioni accademiche*, 10/12) Rome 1957; tr. J. 91/92.

639–689 Epiphanius the Monk, *Account of the Holy City and the Holy Places*, first version, tr. J. 117/121 above excluding sections prefixed by (j) and (n); text edited by H. Donner, *ZDPV* 87 (1971), 66/82.

c. 639 *The Passion of the Forty Martyrs*, ed. H. Delehaye, *AB* 23 (1904).

c. 685 Adomnan, *On the Holy Places*, ed. L. Bieler, *CSL* 175; tr. J. 93/116.

700–750 *The Georgian Kanonarion*, ed. (with Lat. tr.) M. Tarchnischvili, *Le Grand Lectionnaire de l'Eglise de Jérusalem*, *CSCO* 188–9, 204–5 (Iber. 9–10, 13–14).

702–703 Bede, *On the Holy Places*, ed. I. Fraipont, *CSL* 175; tr. J. A. Giles, *Patres Ecclesiae Anglicanae*, 12 vols, London 1843–4.

715–1009 Epiphanius the Monk, *Account of the Holy City and the Holy Places*, second version, including sections prefixed by (j) in the translation on J. 119/121 but excluding sections prefixed by (s) and (n): text ed. Donner.

715–1009 Epiphanius the Monk, *Account of the Holy City and the Holy Places*, final version, incorporating both previous versions and section (nU), J. 120, text ed. Donner.

715–1009 *A Life of Constantine*, ed. M. Guidi, Rome 1908 (= *Rendiconti della R. Academia dei Lincei, Classe di scienze morali, storiche, e filologische*, XVI, 5ª, 16 June 1907): extract tr. J. 202/3.

c. 760 STRATEGIUS, *The Capture of Jerusalem by the Persians*, ed. with Fr. tr. G. Garitte, *CSCO* 203 (Iber. 12).

c. 808 *Memorandum on the Houses of God and Monasteries in the Holy City (Commemoratorium)*, ed. T. Tobler and A. Molinier, *Itinera Hierosolymitana et Descriptiones Terrae Sanctae*, St Gallen–Paris 1879 (reprint), Osnabruck 1966, pp. 301–5: tr. J. 137/8.

c. 830 Hrabanus Maurus, *Homilies*, ed. J. Pamelius–G. Colvenerius, *PL* 110.

c. 850 'Jerome, Letter 9' by Paschasius Radbertus: see C. Lambot, *RB* 46 (1934) 265–282.

c. 870 BERNARD THE MONK, *Travels*, ed. T. Tobler and A. Molinier, *Itinera Hierosolymitana*, pp. 309–20; tr. J. H. Bernard, *PPTS* 3, 1893, and J. 141/145.

c. 870 Christian Druthmar, *Exposition of Matthew*, ed. M. de la Bigne *et al.*, *PL* 106.

874 Ya'kubi (or Ibn Wadhih), *History*, ed. M. T. Houtsma, Leyden 1883; extracts Fr. tr. *TGA*.

913 Ibn Abdi Rabbih, *The Collar of Unique Pearls (Al Iqd al Farid)*, Cairo 1876; extracts Fr. tr. *TGA*.

before 939 Eutychius of Alexandria, Said Ibn al Batriq, *Annals*, ed. L. Cheikho (reprinted as), *CSCO* 50 (Ar. 6); Lat. tr. I. Selden *et al.*, *PG* 111.

951 ISTAKHRI, *The Roads of the Kingdoms*, ed. M. J. de Goeje, *BGA* 1870, 1873; extracts Fr. tr. *TGA*.

985 AL MUQADDESI, *Description of the Muslim Empire*, ed. M. J. de Goeje, *BGA* 1906; extracts Fr. tr. *TGA*.

1047 NASIR I KHOSRAU, *Account of a journey in Syria and Palestine*, ed. C. Schefer, Paris 1881.

c. 1050 Yahya ibn Said of Antioch, al Antaki, *Annals*, ed. I. Kratchkowsky–A. Vasiliev, *PO* 18.

c. 1050 John Euchaita, *Letters*, ed. J. Bollig–P. de Lagarde, Göttingen 1882.

1101 FIRST GUIDE (1Gu). R. Hill (ed. and tr.), *Gesta Francorum et aliorum Hierosolymitanorum, The Deeds of the Franks and the other Pilgrims to Jerusalem*, Oxford 1962, 98–101. This is based on an earlier version of the text than the edition in *RHC* III. xxxvif, 491–543, namely on Vatican manuscripts Reg. Lat 340 (f. 127) and 641, both written in the twelfth century. Translation by A. Stewart, *PPTS*, 1894. Reference by chapters.

1103 QUALITER (Gqu). Following the *History* of Baldric of Bourqueil. This translation is from Tobler–Molinier, *It. Hier*. vol. 1, 347–9. Reference by paragraphs in the translation.

1101–3 OTTOBONIAN GUIDE (Got). S. G. Mercati, 'Santuari e reliquie Constantinopolitane secondo il codice Ottoboniano Latino 169 prima della conquista Latina (1204)', in *Rendiconti della Pont. Acc. Rom. di Archaeologia*, 12 (ser. III) 1936, 153–4. Reference by paragraphs in the translation.

1101–3 SAEWULF (Sae). From the manuscript Corpus Christi College Cambridge MS 111. A. Rogers, *PPTS* 4, London 1896, 31–52. This is the next edition after the first by M. d'Avezac, *Relation des Voyages de Saewulf à Jérusalem et en Terre Sainte pendant les années 1102 et 1103*, Paris 1839. Translated by W. Brownlow, *PPTS*, 1892. Reference by chapters.

1102–6 GUIDE PERHAPS BY A GERMAN AUTHOR (Gge). Guide from the following manuscript: Bistumsarchiv, Trier, Abt. 95, Nr. 93, fli. 61, published by De Sandoli, vol. II, 153–7. Reference is by chapters.

1106 Fulcher of Chartres, *Historia Hierosolymitana*, ed. H. Hagenmeyer, *Fulcherii Carnotensis Historia Hierosolymitana (1095–1127) mit Erlaüterungen und einem Anhange*, Heidelberg 1913. The original version of 1106 by two separate scribes is described in the introduction. The edition of 1118 is based on manuscripts A and others, and his second edition is based on manuscript C and others: see Hagenmeyer, *op. cit*, pp. 92–104.

The description of the Dead Sea is in Bk 2, chapters 4 and 5 and of Jerusalem in Bk 1, chapter 26.

1106–8 ABBOT DANIEL (Dan). Translated from the reprint of M. A. Venevitinov, *Zhitie i knozhenie Danila rus'kyya zemli igumena 1106–1108* (Palestinskiy pravoslavnyy sbornik, 3 (I, 3), 9 (III, 3), St Petersburg 1883–5) by Klaus-Dieter Seeman, *Abt Daniil: Wallfahrtsbericht* (Slavische Propyläen, 36), Munich, 1970 (with detailed introduction and notes). The present English translation avoids the literary polishing of Mme B. de Khitrowo's French translation (from which Sir Charles Wilson made the first English translation) which glosses over some difficult passages, no doubt because the standard dictionary of Old Russian by I. I. Sreznevsky had not yet appeared. Instead W. F. Ryan attempts a fairly literal rendering of Daniel's relatively simple and direct Old Church Slavonic with an admixture of the spoken language.

Reference is by chapter but the chapter headings of Venevitinov's edition have been omitted because they were certainly not written by Daniel.

For further reference see the still valuable introduction and notes to C. W. Wilson, *The Pilgrimage of the Russian Abbot Daniel in the Holy Land 1106–1107 A.D.* (Palestine Pilgrims' Text Society, 4), London, 1897, and for the work of Daniel in the wider context of Russian pilgrimage literature see Klaus-Dieter Seeman, *Die altrussische Wallfahrtsliteratur. Theorie und Geschichte eines literarischen Genres*, Munich, 1976.

1109 GUIDE ATTACHED TO GESTA FRANCORUM EXPUGNANTIUM JHERUSALEM (Gfe). Chapters 31–33. *RHC* III (1866) xxxvi, and pp. 509–512, and De Sandoli, J., 147–194. Reference by paragraphs in translation.

1110 (Sigurðr) (Sig) Extract translated by Joyce Hill from Bjarni Aðalbjarnson, *Snorri Sturluson, Heimskringla III, Íslensk Fornrit 28*, Reykjavík 1951, 249–51. Reference by chapters. English translations of whole work by Erling Monsen (with A. H. Smith), *Heimskringla, or the Lives of the Norse Kings, by Snorre Sturlason*, Cambridge 1932, and by Lee M. Hollander, *Heimskringla, History of the Kings of Norway, by Snorri Sturluson*, Austin, Texas, 1964.

1114 *DE SITU URBIS JERUSALEM* (Gds). This is a guide to Jerusalem which is independent of the description of the Holy Land which follows it. It is edited by M. De Vogüé, *Les Eglises de la Terre Sainte*, Paris 1860, 412–14, with reference to the paragraphs of the Latin original. The manuscript is quoted below under the *Work on Geography*. Translated under the misleading title 'Fetellus' by J. R. S. Macpherson in *PPTS* (1892) 1–7.

1114 Acardus de Arroasia, *Tractatus super Temple Domini*, ed. P. Lehmann, *Corona Quernea. Festschrift für Karl Strecker (Schriften der MGH, 6)*, Leipzig 1941.

c. 1115 Ekkehard of Aura, *Hierosolymita, RHC* V (1) 11–40.

1120 Albert of Aix, *Historia Hierosolymitana*, *RHC* IV (1879) 265–713.

1128–37 THE WORK ON GEOGRAPHY (Wge). The main work is from a manuscript in Paris, Bibliothèque Nationale, Fonds Latin No. 5129, beginning with the heading, *Descriptio locorum circa Hierusalem adjacentium*, and edited by M. de Vogüé, *Les Eglises de la Terre Sainte*, Paris 1860, 414–33. Additions are from late manuscripts of Fretellus' work beginning *Reverentissimo patri et domino H.* in manuscripts D and Vat: Douai, Bibliothèque Municipale, ms. 882, f. 35v–48, and Vatican, Bibliotheca Apostolica

Cod. Reg. lat. 712 (olim 48 et 1181) f. 72–84). These additions are not part of the work by Fretellus. Translated under the title 'Fetellus' by J. R. S. Macpherson, *PPTS*, 1892, pp. 8–54, as far as De Vogüé's anonymous writer is concerned. Reference by paragraphs numbered in the translation.

1128–1180 A Canon of Hebron, *Tractatus de Inventione sanctorum Patriarcharum Abraham, Ysaac et Jacob. RHC* V, i, 302–314.

1137 PETER THE DEACON (Pde). From the manuscript Cod. Casinensis 361 p. 67–80 (XII c.). Extracts from *De Locis Sanctis*, edited by R. Weber, *Corpus Christianorum, Series Latina*, 175 (1965) 93–8. Translated by J. Wilkinson, *Egeria's Travels*, Jerusalem and Warminster 1981, 179–210.

1137 Rorgo Fretellus, *Descripcio cuiusdam de locis sanctis [= Patri H.]*, ed. P. C. Boeren, *Rorgo Fretellus de Nazareth*, Amsterdam 1978, 6–46.

c. 1140 NIKULÁS OF ÞVERÁ (Nik). Translation by Joyce Hill of an extract from MS AM 194, 8vo (1387 A.D.), ed. Kr. Kålund, *Alfræði íslenzk: islandsk encyklopædisk litteratur*, I (Samfund til Udgivelse af Gammel Nordisk Litteratur, 37), Copenhagen 1908. Extracted lines 20.31–23.21. Reference is by lines in this book. This translation has already appeared in the *Harvard Theological Review*, 76 (1983) 178–81, and is copyright 1983 by the President and Fellows of Harvard College. Reprinted by permission. Part of the extract in this book is translated by B. Z. Kedar and Chr. Westergård-Nielsen, *Mediæval Scandinavia*, 11 (1978–9) 203–6, and other parts of the journey in two articles by F. P. Magoun, *Harvard Theological Review*, 33 (1940) 267–89 and *Mediæval Studies*, 6 (1944) 314–54.

<1141 Hugh of St Victor, *de Locis circa Jerusalem*, from a manuscript in Paris, Bibliothèque Nationale, Fonds latin, n. 15009, ed. M. Haureau in *PL* 175, cxlii–clii, and De Sandoli, II, 159–68.

1148 Rorgo Fretellus, *Liber locorum sanctorum terrae Jerusalem*

[=Fratri R.], ed. De Sandoli, II, 119–51, and see Boeren, op. cit. 53–63.

c. 1150 AN ICELANDIC PILGRIM (Gic) Translation by Joyce Hill from the same manuscript and the same edition as Nikulás, lines of extract 26.17–31.6. Reference is by lines in this book. Another English translation is by B. Z. Kedar and Chr. Westergård-Nielson, *Mediæval Scandinavia*, 11 (1978–79) 206–9.

1154 AL IDRISI (Gid). Translation by G. Le Strange from a manuscript edited by J. Gildemeister, in *ZDPV* 2 (1885), in *PEFQS* 1888, 31–5. Reference by pages in that translation.

c. 1155 BELARD OF ASCOLI (Gbe). From a manuscript in Bibliotheca Vaticana 1110 (13 c.), fol. 141b–143a, transcribed by Lucia Buzi and edited by De Sandoli, Vol. II. 43–49. Reference is by chapters.

1157 CONSTANTINE MANASSES. A Greek iambic poem describes the marriage journey of the bride, Princess Theodora, who was to marry King Baldwin III.[1] It was written shortly after the marriage. It describes some of the main places of pilgrimage, but is not in great enough detail to be translated here. Edited by K. Horna, 'Das Hodoiporikon des Konstantin Manasses', *BZ* 4 (1904): the pilgrimage sections are on pp. 331–4.

c. 1160 SEVENTH GUIDE (7Gu). From a manuscript in Erlängen University, No. 515, f. 7–8 (XIII c.) edited by Tobler, *Descr.*, 100–107, and translated by A. Stewart, *PPTS*, 1894. Reference is by pages in Latin text.

>1160 Theotonius, *Duo itinera ad Terram Sanctam*, *AA.SS. Feb.* III, 108–22.

1166–73 BENJAMIN OF TUDELA (Btu). Ed. and tr. M. N. Adler, *The Itinerary of Benjamin of Tudela*, London 1907. Reference is to Adler's pages.

c. 1170 SECOND GUIDE (2Gu). From a manuscript at Vienna, Pergament 4 (new number 609, ff. 21 ff. (1300 A.D.), edited by Tobler, *Theod.*, 118–28 and translated by A. Stewart, *PPTS*, 1894. Reference is by pages in Latin text.

c. 1170 JOHN OF WÜRZBURG (Jwü). From a principal manuscript of Tegernsee, Munich City Library No. 19418 (XIII c.). T. Tobler (ed.), *Descriptiones Terrae Sanctae ex saeculis VIII, IX, XII et XV*, Leipzig 1974, 108–92. Reprinted in De Sandoli, vol. 2, 225–95. Translated by A. Stewart, *PPTS*, 1890. Reference is by pages in Latin text.

1168–74 THEODERIC (Thc). From the same manuscript as the *Second Guide*, fol. 9 ff. T. Tobler (ed.), *Theoderici Libellus de Locis Sanctis editus circa A.D. 1172*. St Gallen–Paris 1865, 1–112, reprinted in De Sandoli, vol. 2, 311–90. M. L. and W. Bulst, *Theodercus, Libellus de locis sanctis, (Editiones Heidelbergenses* XVIII), Heidelberg 1976, the version here translated. Translated by Aubrey Stewart, *PPTS*, 1891. Reference is by pages in the Bulstsi Latin text.

c. 1181 IBN JUBAIR, tr. R. J. C. Broadhurst, *The Travels of Ibn Jubayr*, London 1952.

1185 JOHN PHOCAS (Jph). From a manuscript at a friend's house in Chios of the editor Leo Allatius. For his edition see *PG* 133, 928–61. Another edition with some suggested corrections to Allatius' text is that of K. M. Koikylides and K. Phokylides, *Archaia Latinika, Hellenika, Rossika kai Gallika tina Odoiporika ē Proskynetaria tes Hagias Ges*, Jerusalem 1912. Translated by A. Stewart, *PPTS*, 1889. Paragraphs as in the *PG*, subdivided into sentences.

INDEX

The first number in the reference is to the text (see above) and the number following it after a dash is the page number in this book. Where no modern place-names are given the site is well-known. A query means that it was unknown, even to the crusader authors.

ABBREVIATIONS

*	See under this name	*Com.*	see *Commemoratorium* in *JPBC*
BVM	Blessed Virgin Mary	ho.	House
ch.	Church	m.	modern name

mon. monastery